The Costa Rican Women's Movement

Pitt Latin American Series

Billie R. DeWalt, General Editor
G. Reid Andrews, Associate Editor
Carmen Diana Deere, Associate Editor
Jorge I. Domínguez, Associate Editor

Ilse Abshagen Leitinger, Editor and Translator

The Costa Rican Women's Movement ✹ A Reader

UNIVERSITY OF PITTSBURGH PRESS

Published by the University of Pittsburgh Press, Pittsburgh, Pa. 15261
Copyright © 1997, University of Pittsburgh Press
Manufactured in the United States of America
Printed on acid-free paper

10   9   8   7   6   5   4   3   2   1

Library of Congress Cataloging-in-Publication Data

The Costa Rican women's movement: A Reader / Ilse Abshagen
Leitinger, editor.
       p.   cm. — (Pitt Latin American series)
Includes bibliographical references and index.
ISBN 0-8229-3862-6 (acid-free paper). —
ISBN 0-8229-5543-1 (pbk.: acid-free paper)
1. Feminism—Costa Rica.   2. Women—Costa Rica—Economic
conditions.   3. Women—Costa Rica—Social conditions.   4. Equality—
Costa Rica.   5. Sex discrimination against women—Costa Rica.
I. Leitinger, Ilse Abshagen. II. Series.
HQ1473.C67   1993
305.42'097286—dc20   94-41579

A CIP catalog record for this book is available from the British Library.

Grateful acknowledgment is made to the following photographers
who provided photographs for this book: Luis A. Howell C.,
Betsy MacMichael, and Liz Miller.

Contents

Acknowledgments

Thanks to Alda Facio and Matilde López, members of the local editorial committee, for diverse disciplinary expertise and insight into local conditions; to Montserrat Sagot and Alda Facio for comments on the introduction; to the authors and co-authors for their contributions; to the Instituto de Estudios de la Mujer (IEM) at the Universidad Nacional, Heredia, Costa Rica, Grinnell College, Grinnell, Iowa, the Institute for Central American Development Studies (ICADS), San José, Costa Rica, and the Council for International Exchange of Scholars, Washington, D.C., for institutional support. My special thanks to editor-in-chief Catherine Marshall of the University of Pittsburgh Press for support and advice, and to in-house-editor Nancy Fleming for creative editing, perceptive thinking that respects the editor's opinion, and for help in conveying Costa Rican women's insights and experiences to non-Costa Rican readers. Working with Nancy was an inspiration. Sincere thanks to Toby Ewing, Sarah Shikes, and Beth Prullege for editing assistance in Costa Rica.

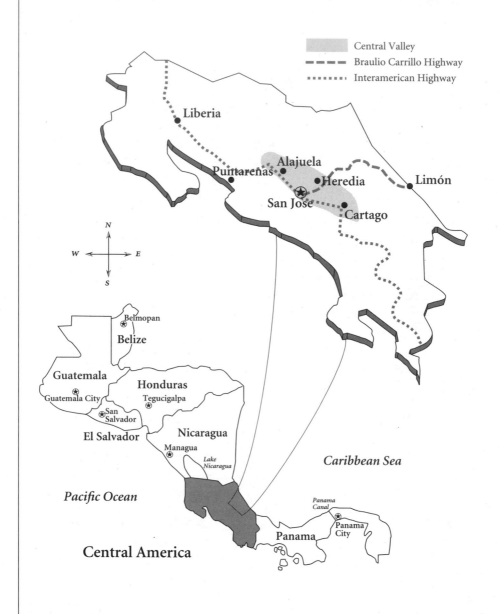

Costa Rica

Central Valley
Braulio Carrillo Highway
Interamerican Highway

Liberia

Puntarenas
Alajuela
Heredia
San José
Cartago
Limón

N
W · E
S

Belmopan
Belize

Guatemala
Guatemala City

Honduras
Tegucigalpa

San Salvador
El Salvador

Nicaragua
Managua
Lake Nicaragua

Caribbean Sea

Pacific Ocean

Panama Canal
Panama City

Panama

Central America

The Costa Rican Women's Movement and Costa Rican Feminism in the Early 1990s

Multiple, Dynamic, Action-Oriented

Ilse Abshagen Leitinger

Ilse Leitinger with former student Carol Weirs, taken at Annual Women's March Against Violence, November 24, 1995, San José. Poster reads, "No More Violence and Abuse."

THIS COLLECTION OF READINGS represents a conscious decision to offer a broad vision of the complex dimensions of the women's movement and feminism in Costa Rica during the early 1990s. The term *women's movement* is not identical with *feminism* in Costa Rica. Most contributors to *The Costa Rican Women's Movement: A Reader* would agree that, despite much overlap between the two movements, feminism is more far-reaching in advocating social change by empowering women than is the women's movement, which may strive for more limited economic, social, or political improvements.

Unlike many other readers on Latin American women which are written *about* women's movements or feminism, the selections in this reader were written by true insiders. The authors—members of the Costa Rican Women's Movement or feminists—are working toward their goals in neighborhoods, communities, or organizations. Most are native-born; others are long-term residents of the country. Given the problems their society faces, Costa Rican women cannot afford the intellectual luxury of merely thinking about or researching the women's movement and/or feminism; instead, they must turn their insights or inquiries into action—the key social-science concept is *investigación-acción*—for improving women's, and thus all Costa Ricans', lives. The belief that commitment to action at the grassroots is essential shows clearly in the authors' biographical summaries, which can be found at the end of each article.

Costa Rica: A Context of Contrasts and Contradictions

In Costa Rica even a mild expression of opinion, disagreement, or opposition—an ever-so-measured criticism—carries more weight than the same expression would in another culture. Costa Ricans—*Ticas* or *Ticos* in local parlance—are characterized by a pervasive national tendency to avoid conflict and extremes of violent confrontation, preferring instead to get along *sin hacer olas* (without making waves). Moreover, the Costa Ricans' commitment in social situations centers on their families and rarely extends to the community (Cersósimo, 1986), as that would require disciplined cooperation of a sort that clashes with Costa Rican individualism. This orientation may well be the result of the centuries of marginalization of Costa Ricans in the backwaters of political power, and of their extreme poverty during that time, which caused them to be timid in social interaction (Rodríguez, 1979).

Costa Rica is a small society of great geographic, climatic, biological, and social-historical contrasts. As far as women are concerned, the most pertinent characteristic of the social-historical context in Costa Rica during the early 1990s is the presence of strong contrasts, if not contradictions, which manifest themselves in a number of ways.

First, having experienced extreme isolation and poverty for hundreds of years and having developed a system of coping with that condition, Costa Ricans today, for better or worse, live in an open society with multiple links to the rest of the world. This openness can be seen both internally, in the country's politics, and externally, in its reactions to international influences. Yet at the same time, Costa Rica is almost petulantly self-conscious of its unique identity, "our idiosyncracy," as Costa Ricans label it (Biesanz et al., 1982).

Second, under the cultural veneer of Costa Rican Spanish-Catholic homogeneity hides a remarkable ethnic, cultural, and even religious diversity. The deceptively homogeneous culture of Costa Rica's three million people has multiple roots, and its openness and widespread international linkages are recent, dating essentially from the current century. Although on the surface, Costa Rican society seems mestizo, based on the original Indian-Spanish fusion of peoples and cultures, a closer examination reveals admixtures from around the globe. In addition to the particularly strong Spanish influence, European linkages include those to England, France, Germany, Italy, and the East European societies. Other elements in the mixture are derived from North America (mainly the United States), the Caribbean (primarily Jamaica), and Asia (mainly but not exclusively China). Also notable for their contributions in many fields are Jewish immigrants of various national origins, some of whose families have been in Costa Rica for many generations (see, e.g., Biesanz et al., 1982; Escobar, 1992). Although Costa Rican society is predominantly Spanish Catholic, religious diversity is growing (Biesanz, 1982: 154). With this mosaic of people, Costa Rica is strikingly similar to other, larger Latin American societies (Miller, 1991: xiii).

However, Costa Rican society also boasts unique features. It abolished its army more than fifty years ago (see, e.g., Biesanz et al., 1982). Costa Ricans are peace loving and democratic, and they take an immense pride in the award of the 1987 Nobel Peace Prize to Costa Rica's then-president, Oscar Arias Sánchez.

Nevertheless, in a society that is famous for its love of peace and tranquility, the perturbing record of violence against women is becoming painfully visible and has given rise to an on-going public debate. And, in contradiction to their idealistic commitment to equality, Costa Ricans face the harsh social reality of a growing inequality—largely an economic inequality—which hits women doubly hard. Women continue to be disadvantaged in terms of access to resources, jobs, and power, and they suffer the all-too-well-known feminization of poverty. As a result, Costa Rican women's self-help actions can be considered highly political, even though they do not always fit the traditional concept of politics involving government institutions or political parties. The demanding challenge that women learn to take a position and act decisively stands in opposition to the traditional tendency for them to be accommodating in relations with other people—"without making waves." On the other hand, not making waves offers one great asset on which women can build: the Costa Ricans' patience and willingness to negotiate.

Costa Rican women and their attitudes toward being women and toward the women's movement or feminism are as diverse as the country; they range from consciously conservative to forcefully liberal. Their action on local problems, if not shaped by survival needs, is influenced by feminist thinking arising from local experience or from the observations of Costa Rican students returning from many different places—the Southern Cone of the Western Hemisphere, North America, and Europe, including the former USSR. Women's action on local problems is also fostered by many international development agencies or foreign advisers, and by the funding of such institutions.

No wonder then, that Costa Rican feminists today are at the vanguard of feminism in Latin America and even worldwide, provided we assess this feminism according to the principle of investigación-acción as action-oriented, not as emphasizing abstract theorizing. Costa Rican feminists do theorize, of course, but they do so in order to understand and to propose solutions to real-life problems, as part of their effort to give women better access to equal opportunity in all realms.

Several diverse examples justify this characterization of Costa Rican feminism as vanguard feminism:

1. Seeking equality of opportunity, Costa Rican women aspire to high government and other public posts: At the time of this writing in early 1993, women hold two ministry posts (Justice and Culture); one presidential hopeful (or precandidate) in 1993 was a woman; and, even though there are only four state universities, one university president is a woman. Women also function as legislators, judges, ambassadors, and other high-level professionals.
2. The 1980s have seen an escalation in the number of women's organizations, be they dedicated to income generation, the defense of women's rights, the fight for equality, or women's well-being. One prominent example is the Fundación Ser y Crecer (FUNCRESER), which since 1990 has been working with incest victims (Leitinger, 1993).

3. Stipulating that women's rights include freedom from violence, more women file complaints about sexual harassment and rape than ever before.
4. In their search for control over all aspects of their lives, Costa Rican women have achieved recognition of new sensitive topics as the subjects of research and of bills introduced in the Costa Rican legislature as a prelude to a national debate on such issues. Foremost among these topics is abortion (Ansorena, 1993).
5. Seeking contacts with women worldwide, Programa Interdisciplinario de Estudios de Género (PRIEG) at the Universidad de Costa Rica hosted more than two thousand women academics from around the world from February 22 to 26, 1993 for the Fifth International Interdisciplinary Congress on Women. According to participants, this was one of the best-organized, most thought-provoking women's congresses ever held.

All these examples document a truly action-oriented display of commitment to women's issues in a feminist way that challenges social power structures.

The Organization of *The Costa Rican Women's Movement*

The contributions to the reader cover a range of contrasting theoretical positions, from moderately liberal to radical, representing the diverse viewpoints that characterize Costa Rican women's perception of their realities in the early 1990s. Assessing this complexity thematically, building on and at the same time expanding Jane Jaquette's model of the roots of Latin American women's movements (Jaquette, 1989: 4), we can see that the contributions grow from four different roots: the *political roots* of human rights or political movements, the *philosophical-theoretical roots* of intellectual feminism, the *grassroots* of organizations of poor, mainly urban, women struggling to solve problems of daily survival, and—adding a historical perspective to Jaquette's model—the *individual-efficacy roots* of women with a strong sense of individualism and self-worth, who with fighting spirit act as individuals with no expectation of support from a like-minded community or group. Thus, we arrive at four different types of active women's movement or feminism in Costa Rica today.

Of course, only if women develop a conscious gender perspective, through which they recognize the bias they face in patriarchal structures and claim their right to independent participation in public life, assert their capacity for decision making about their own lives, and, above all, seek their empowerment to change social structures that oppress them, will they be feminists according to the definition employed in this reader.

Interestingly enough, despite the Costa Rican focus in this collection, the basic issues that emerge from the contributions are relevant not only in Costa Rica but in all Latin American societies. They are reflected in the seven sections of the *Reader:*

I. The Varying Faces of the Women's Movement and Feminism

"Feminism means neither unanimity of approaches nor of discourses," said Carmen Naranjo, one of Costa Rica's leading women writers (1989). Such multiplicity, which at times has resulted in profound disagreements, becomes evident in the five contributions in the opening section. They introduce the reader to specific evidence on the basis of various theoretical positions, liberal to radical, and spring from the four roots of the women's movement. In so doing, they confirm the validity of the proposed conceptual framework for assessing the diversity of Costa Rican women's positions.

II. Making Women Visible in Costa Rican History

This section offers an introduction to what is yet to be discovered about women's past contributions to Costa Rican society. The authors almost unanimously agree that research on making Costa Rican women visible throughout history is only now beginning. The reason for this gap is that in many instances, documentation of women's contributions had not been identified; in others, however, existing documents have not been analyzed with an appropriately revised gendered conceptualization of history (Clotilde Obregón, pers. comm., April 27, 1992).

III. The Quest for Women's Equality

This section focuses on women's legal status, the principle of equality according to the law. All the contributors acknowledge that, despite egalitarian laws, true equality between the genders is not yet a social reality. This entire section relates primarily to human rights, or the political roots of the women's movement and feminism.

IV. Women Suffering Discrimination

Turning from legal equality, expressing theoretical-philosophical theory, the discussion swings to manifestations of inequality in social reality. The section examines different aspects of discrimination on the basis of race, class, sexual preference, and physical handicaps, and also considers violence against women in the family, including incest. In essence, these contributions relate most meaningfully to the individual-efficacy roots of feminism, and they must be weighed as an important contribution to the ongoing dialogue in a society that likes to avoid outright confrontations or espousals of strong stands.

In recent years, topics of concern to women have one after another literally burst into public consciousness. Thus, in the late 1970s and early 1980s Costa Ricans for the first time dared to discuss and research violence against women. During the mid-1980s, they found it possible to seriously consider the issue of sexual preferences, and by the late 1980s incest had become a legitimate topic. Now, in the early 1990s, the issue of abortion is in the foreground. In all instances, the process began with grassroots self-help efforts to solve a problem. Local leaders then invited professional help and that in turn led to academic discussion and research which was followed by a move into politics or legislation, which then finally encouraged a broad debate throughout the entire society, including the media (see, e.g., Minsky, 1991). Although this process does not bring instant solutions, it is a necessary approach *à la Tica* to an eventual negotiated solution.

V. Women's Organizations and Organizations Working with Women

This section is probably the most complex and diverse thematic area of the *Reader,* and its few contributions stand not only for the organizations mentioned by name but for many others that cannot be represented because of the limits of space. These include women's movement organizations, organizations working with and for women, feminist organizations, religiously based organizations, concerned government institutions, foreign development organizations, and local nongovernmental organizations with foreign funding. In some, one can witness the transition from women's movement to feminism. The variety is endless: Women as economic producers, as political actors, as community leaders, as educators, as providers of a multitude of social services, and as recipients of such services. In this context, one also must acknowledge foreign influences, through foreign organizations, advisers, training of local experts, and funding for local projects.

VI. The Women's Movement and Feminism in the Arts

Here the contributors explore contrasting dimensions, as women artists in various media question women's identity and roles. Costa Rican women painters document traditional women's roles as they depict the limits and hardships these traditions imply. A woman writer's poignant analysis of twenty-seven centuries of Western literature brings her readers face to face with the devastating myths and stereotypes of patriarchy. Yet, even now, as other contributors demonstrate, popular music extols these same myths and stereotypes.

VII. The Constantly Evolving Status of Women's Studies

The focus of the final section of the *Reader* is on Women's Studies, the academic exploration of women's vital contribution to society's survival, and the need for a social transformation that will allow women equal access to and choices of opportunities and rewards. According to the fourfold mission of Costa Rican universities, this includes teaching and research with a gender perspective, the diffusion of gender-relevant information, and extension work with women at the grassroots level. The section focuses first on programs that in the fall of 1993 inaugurated a joint master's program in Women's Studies at two Costa Rican universities and then offers various examples of specific research that represents this new field of Women's Studies.

Taken together, the readings document the multiple, dynamic, action-oriented quality of women's efforts, together with a growing theoretical understanding of women's unique experience (Miller, 1991). They describe the social-historical context within which the women's movement and feminism have emerged in Costa Rica and the growing concern with making women visible. They illustrate the great diversity among those who are attempting to move women from self-awareness to self-confidence, control, and power. They document their work toward ending the violence against women and their attempts to eliminate exploitation and to create equal opportunity. They also suggest possible future trajectories of these movements and invite further documentation, exploration, and, of course, action.

Each of the seven sections begins with an introductory overview and an abstract of each reading in that section. Each reading concludes with a brief biographical summary that not only demonstrates the commitment of the author or authors but also provides a view of the complexity of women's activities in Costa Rica. More prosaically, these summaries underscore the fact that it is often impossible in the Costa Rican setting, scholarly or otherwise, to make a living in only one job or activity, even when one works at it full time.

References

Ansorena Montero, Aixa. 1993. "Disapproval of Abortion in Costa Rica: An Anthropological Study of a Forbidden Topic." Paper presented at the Fifth International

Interdisciplinary Congress on Women, February 22 to 26. Universidad de Costa Rica. San José, Costa Rica.

Biesanz, Richard, Karen Zubris Biesanz, and Mavis Hiltunen Biesanz. 1982. *The Costa Ricans*. Englewood Cliffs, N.J.: Prentice Hall.

Cersósimo, Gaetano. 1986. *Los estereotipos del costarricense*. San José, Costa Rica: Editorial de la Universidad de Costa Rica.

Escobar, Francisco. April 19, 1992. "500 años de destierro." *La Nación. Revista Dominical*, pp. 16–17.

Jaquette, Jane S. 1989. *The Women's Movement in Latin America*. Boston: Unwin Hyman.

Leitinger, Ilse Abshagen. 1993. "Work at the Grassroots, Networking, and Multiple Efforts Towards Change in the Contemporary Costa Rican Context." Paper presented at the Fifth International Interdisciplinary Congress on Women, February 22 to 26. Universidad de Costa Rica. San José, Costa Rica.

Miller, Francesca. 1991. *Latin American Women and the Search for Social Justice*. Hanover and London: University Press of New England.

Minsky Acosta, Larissa. November 17, 1991. "¡Violación! El poder detrás del sexo." *La Nación. Revista Dominical*, pp. 6–9.

Naranjo, Carmen. 1989. *Mujer y cultura*. San José, Costa Rica: EDUCA.

Rodríguez Vega, Eugenio. 1979. *Apuntes para una sociología costarricense*, 3rd. ed. San José, Costa Rica: Editorial Universidad Estatal a Distancia (UNED).

The Costa Rican Women's Movement

I ✳ THE VARYING FACES OF THE COSTA RICAN WOMEN'S MOVEMENT AND COSTA RICAN FEMINISM

Clockwise from top left: May Brenes Marín, Montserrat Sagot with Ilse Leitinger, Paula Antezana Rimassa, Alda Facio Montejo, and Paquita Cruz

SECTION I EXPLORES the complexity of existing interpretations of the women's movement and feminism in Costa Rica. Its five selections represent a wide spectrum of women's concerns. A historical sketch portrays unusual women of the past, mid-nineteenth-century individualists of extreme individual efficacy, and early-twentieth-century civic women intent on fighting for political rights. The second selection introduces a highly intellectual enterprise of a feminist publication; the third describes a feminist organization created in part by leaders who were educated abroad and who worked with women at the grassroots level, an organization that found its courage with the political left but has since acquired independence from this origin. The fourth selection presents an organization that rose from the grassroots women's movement and is turning feminist because of its experiences. The section closes with the thoughts of a famous writer and feminist on the ancient and—feminism notwithstanding—still compelling patterns of patriarchy.

Different Times, Women, Visions: The Deep Roots of Costa Rican Feminism, by Yadira Calvo Fajardo

Yadira Calvo, an authority on intellectual and literary history and a feminist, first focuses on individual efficacy as she describes the young intellectual Manuela Escalante and the woman soldier and war hero Pancha (Francisca) Carrasco. Neither of these two mid-nineteenth-century women belonged to the women's movement or was a feminist, yet in their stubborn self-esteem each was a highly unconventional nineteenth-century precursor of feminism. Moreover, Pancha Carrasco has become a symbol of the women's movement today; the Colectivo Pancha Carrasco, a women's support organization that dates from 1986 and works to promote participation, organization, skill training, and consciousness raising of grassroots urban and rural women, bears her name.

Thereafter, when Calvo refers to suffragists and the resulting demand of women for full participation in society, she documents the political roots of both the women's movement and feminism.

Thus, in this overview covering a century and a half, the author suggests that Costa Rican feminism began with the unconventionalism of a few nineteenth-century women who defied the dictates of society. The movement then passed through a stage when women defended political institutions, even though these institutions excluded them, and continued with the struggle of mid-twentieth-century women for their own right to vote. Feminism has now, in the late twentieth century, brought to women the consciousness that, beyond the right to vote, women's rights include the right to enter any field in which they choose to make their mark.

The Group *Ventana:* An Assessment, by Rosalía Camacho, Alda Facio Montejo, and Ligia Martín

Describing the trajectory of the magazine *Ventana,* Rosalía Camacho, Alda Facio, and Ligia Martín, three outstanding intellectuals and activists, present clearly the theoretical-philosophical roots of feminism. Their aim is to raise the consciousness of their fellow intellectuals in order to change society.

The authors assess the role of a small group of university women which was among the first in Costa Rica to call itself feminist, and the group's decision in the early 1980s to publish a feminist magazine, *Ventana,* in order to interpret feminism to professional and university women. The rationale was that many educated women did not fully understand what feminism stood for, but, if offered a clear idea of its meaning, they would be able to share their insights with women of grassroots organizations with whom they were working as professionals and educators.

Although *Ventana* ran into difficulties and had to discontinue publication while editorial committee members took on various other obligations, the magazine made an essential contribution to early feminism in Costa Rica.

Improving the Quality of Women's Daily Lives: Costa Rica's Centro Feminista de Información y Acción, by Ana Carcedo, Montserrat Sagot, and Marta Trejos

The analysis of the Centro Feminista de Información y Acción (CEFEMINA) introduces the reader to an action-oriented, popular grassroots women's organization. Originally related to a political party on the left, CEFEMINA, the oldest explicitly *feminist* organization in Costa Rica, illustrates the political roots of feminism, even though it is no longer tied to a specific political ideology. Authors Ana Carcedo, Montserrat Sagot, and Marta Trejos, long-time members and officers of CEFEMINA, are representative of Costa Rican foreign-educated, consciously feminist leaders.

This study traces the history of CEFEMINA, with its peculiarly Latin American orientation toward solving all women's—but especially poor women's—problems in the quality of daily life. The authors survey the organization's major fields of activities.

The Alianza de Mujeres Costarricenses, a Popular Movement: An Impassioned Plea for Action-Oriented Feminism, by Ana Hernández

Ana Hernández, a women's leader who became a feminist through her work with the nonprofit Asociación Alianza de Mujeres Costarricenses (Alianza), describes this women's-movement type of organization. Dating from 1952, the

Alianza is the oldest women's organization in Costa Rica. It provides a variety of services. At its San José headquarters, it maintains a documentation center, conducts leadership training with audiovisual materials, offers legal assistance, and publishes a monthly newsletter and a great variety of popular educational materials.

The author, a member since 1969 and the organization's president since 1989, demonstrates that—over time—struggles to solve the problems of poor and working-class rural and urban women have turned the organization more and more consciously feminist. She discusses the Alianza's work *against* poverty, social or domestic violence, and family disintegration, and *for* children's centers, women's training, schools, community projects, legal support, and land ownership by peasant women.

Most of the women with whom the Alianza works would not understand the word *feminism*. Yet in their commitment to improving women's lives, building self-confidence, developing skills, involving women in community action, and empowering them to make decisions for themselves and their communities, they are part of the legion of Costa Rican women whose lives exemplify feminist consciousness and goals but who do not know they are feminists.

Women's Liberation from Servitude and Overprotection, by Carmen Naranjo Coto

In a different vein, Carmen Naranjo's short essay, based on her book *Mujer y Cultura,* emphasizes the time-worn, traditional techniques of patriarchy for keeping women under control. The essay highlights the two cultural patterns which, complementing each other, have been responsible throughout Costa Rican history for women's position in society: human servitude and patriarchal society's overprotection. Both have imprisoned women in the "preordained" task of housework. To liberate women is to offer them choices for making decisions for themselves about their development, self-identity, and vocation.

In true Tica fashion, the author delivers her message in a seemingly understated way. Yet Naranjo was one of the earliest participants in the debate about the role of women. As minister of culture in the early 1970s, she created the Centro Nacional para el Desarrollo de la Mujer y la Familia. In 1984 Naranjo, together with Alda Facio, Mirta González, and Laura Guzmán, three theoretical-philosophical feminists, organized the well-known lecture series Women and Society, which took place under the auspices of the Cátedra Libre Eugenio Fonseca (Eugenio Fonseca lecture series) that treats diverse topics at the Universidad de Costa Rica (UCR) (University of Costa Rica).

1 ✸ Different Times, Women, Visions

The Deep Roots of Costa Rican Feminism

Yadira Calvo Fajardo

The roots of feminism in Costa Rica can be traced back to women who claimed the right to be individuals even though their behavior failed to conform to the standards that custom considered suitable for a woman of their era. The next stage of feminism included women who defended democratic rights, although these rights applied only to men and not to the women themselves. This period was followed by one in which women consciously demanded their own rights as citizens. Today, the feminist movement encompasses women who with increasing awareness insist on freedom from domination and freedom to participate in all spheres of life.

Nineteenth-Century Unconventional Women: Precursors of Feminism?

Considering the invisibility of women in Costa Rican history, it is not surprising that we know amazingly little about some highly unconventional women who lived in the nineteenth century and who, by today's standards, would be considered feminists. Knowing so little, we wonder what caused them to disobey the rules of behavior of their time. Here are the stories of two of such women.

Manuela Escalante, considered the "first feminist" of Costa Rica, died on May 26, 1849. At her death, the lavish praise of the nation's press converted her into a new "wise woman," in the style of Molière. Her obituary in *El Costarricense* (cited in Acuña, 1969, 1: 113) lets us imagine her in the drawing room of her illustrious family's home in the city of Cartago, holding the center of attention during gatherings of high society, surrounded by political emigrés famous for their intelligence and wisdom.

At such gatherings, Manuela displayed her great learning, showing her knowledge of forms of rhetoric "from antithesis to prolepsis, from apostrophe

5

to personification" (Acuña, 1969: 1). When she was not reciting the eclogues of Garcilaso, the odes of Fray Luis, the songs of Herrera, or *The Moral Epistle* of Rioja, she was discussing metaphysics, practicing rhetoric, or challenging the latest findings in geology. In short, learned gentlemen gaped in surprise when they met Manuela. Her erudition and poise were truly exceptional during a century in which Costa Ricans believed that to safeguard their chastity, girls should never handle pencils (which were tools for intellectual pursuits), or have access to mirrors (which would reveal to them their own beauty), or approach windows (which might give access to potential lovers).

Of Manuela's learning there is no doubt, but was she a feminist? The answer to that question is more difficult to establish. Whether she was inhibited because of a respect for the restrictions placed on women's pursuits or was simply too busy because of her desire to learn, Manuela apparently did not record her beliefs and views—at least nothing written by her has yet been found. Apart from the reports of her vast erudition, we know nothing of her except that she was a kind of scandalous figure for her time because of her intellectual gifts and that she died a "spinster" at age twenty-six (Acuña, 1969: 1).

Even if Manuela was not a feminist in her thinking, she at least was a woman who lived her life in frank opposition to what was expected of women of her time. For this alone she deserves a prominent position in the history of the Costa Rican feminist movement, for she was isolated and unrivaled in her century. Manuela is also a symbol of the loneliness and near-anonymity in which the lives of women evolved in Costa Rican history.

Next to the image of Manuela in high society rises that of a weatherbeaten woman of the people—Pancha Carrasco (Acuña, 1969: 1). In 1856 Pancha enlisted as a cook in the Costa Rican army of President Juan Rafael Mora to fight against the invasion of William Walker, who attempted, with U.S. backing, to convert Central America into a territory with slavery (see Obregón, chap. 7 below). Although it was most unusual during the 1850s, this simple woman could read and write, and she served as President Mora's secretary (Calvo, 1991b). Tempted more by the smoke of combat than by the hearth's fire, she abandoned her cooking pots in Rivas, southern Nicaragua. Gathering munitions for the combatants in her apron and verbal threats for the enemy in her mouth, she went into battle.

In the Battle of Rivas on April 11, 1856—a glorious date in Costa Rican annals—Pancha and a German doctor simultaneously shot at an enemy soldier who was manning a cannon. With his battle companions, the soldier fled from the shots, leaving the cannon behind. Amid cheers, Pancha was carried in triumph on the shoulders of her companions. Though her actions were confirmed by veterans of the 1856 action, no mention of the incident appears anywhere in the documents of the time—another instance of the cloak of invisibility with which historians have shrouded women.

In February of 1857, Pancha was present when Costa Ricans destroyed four steamships of the enemy on the San Juan River. There she worked at the bedside of soldiers sick with cholera, helping to give comfort and dignity to their deaths. During this time she also compiled lists of the dead and transcribed messages, news, and orders of the president.

After the war, President Mora decorated Pancha with a medal for heroism. When she died thirty-four years later, she received the military honors of a general at her funeral, attended by high dignitaries of government and church.

Although neither ever heard of feminism, both of these intrepid women—young Manuela Escalante in her high society drawing room and forty-year-old Pancha Carrasco with her apron loaded with bullets—dared to transgress the limits imposed on women of their time. Their actions encouraged a later generation of Costa Rican women who, still without any gender conscience, joined with men in public protests in the early nineteenth century. These protests were not in pursuit of their own rights but were an effort to safeguard institutions from which only men would benefit.

Women Defending Institutions That Excluded Them

In their battles for others, women in the first decades of the nineteenth century defended the freedom of the press at a time when they themselves barely aspired to the right to read and write (Junta de Protección Social, 1989). Later in that century, in 1889, women turned out again, this time to defend men's right to vote; much time and effort would still be required before women themselves would be permitted to vote. Led by teachers, women returned to the streets in 1919, protesting a government coup even though Federico Tinoco, the deposed president, still wanted to fire married women teachers because he deemed them impure. In 1943, in response to a new threat to the legalization of men's vote, women again united with them in a public demonstration under the cry of freedom. Their action was decisive in turning the course of events, but their own right to vote continued to be denied even by those for whose rights they had demonstrated. Four years later, in 1947, thousands of women held a protest march when democratic liberties were threatened even though, once again, those liberties could be exercised by men only (see Sharratt, chap. 8 below).

Women Fight for Their Own Rights

During the nineteenth century and up until the middle of the twentieth, Costa Rican women supported male citizens' political freedom and their right to vote. The explicit fight for their own rights dates only from the twentieth century, and it moves slowly from a clamoring for general civil rights to a focus on political rights, primarily the vote. On July 19, 1914, Angela Acuña aroused a storm when, in one of her first public actions at the Sociedad Federal de Trabajadores, she referred to Costa Rican women's right to work. Acuña, then a student at the Universidad de Costa Rica, was pioneering a struggle that would be greeted with jeers and contempt in the newspapers of the country. Journalists made jokes at her expense and exuded ill will when she succeeded in having the Civil Code changed in 1916; the code was revised to permit women lawyers to carry out all functions of the legal profession except that of being notaries (which required the lawyer to be an active, i.e., voting, citizen). Nevertheless, the measure stood and she remained firm in her conviction; her next goal would be the political rights of women (Calvo, 1989: 79ff; 1991a: 21).

Several years of frustration and failed attempts convinced Angela Acuña of her need for allies. In the 1920s, support was growing throughout the Western world for women's claim to their voting rights (Portugal, 1991). On October 12, 1923, Angela founded the Costa Rican Liga Feminista (Feminist League) as a subsidiary of the Liga Internacional de Mujeres Ibéricas e Hispanoamericanas (Iberian and Hispano-American Women's International League) in Madrid (Acuña, 1969, 2: 353). With that, the first serious steps in the struggle for women's rights had been taken. As president of the Feminist League, Acuña initiated action with a care that seemed almost timid, requesting the president of the republic, Julio Acosta, to give women the right to vote in the coming elections (Calvo, 1989: 102).

In the same year, the Fifth International American Conference met in Chile. Although all the discussants were men, the members adopted a resolution that future conferences should study the means of abolishing constitutional and legal restrictions on women's political rights. Then, during the sixth conference in Havana in 1928, which is now remembered as the first International American Conference to allow women to speak, Doris Stevens, a North American, expressed her disagreement with laws written for the well-being of women without their consent. Because "no man," she said, "no group of men, no government, no nation, nor any group of nations ever had the right to rob us of what we claim today. We ask for the restoration of the rights which were taken from us, our human rights" (cited in Acuña, 1969, 2: 363). Despite pressures exerted by an international group of women to have educator Lydia Fernández represent Costa Rica at that conference, the government had followed tradition and sent a man, Alejandro Aguilar Machado, who participated in the creation of the Comisión Interamericana de Mujeres (CIM) (Inter American Commission of Women). The commission was originally composed of seven members named by the Unión Panamericana, the precursor of the Organización de Estados Americanos (OEA) (Organization of American States), and later by representatives of each country of the continent. Costa Rica has always been represented, just as she has always been represented in the Unión de Mujeres Americanas (Union of American Women), the organization that traditionally names the Woman of the Americas of the Year. (In 1957, at age 79, Angela Acuña was given this award [Calvo, 1989: 212].)

But the suffragist struggle in Costa Rica was associated fundamentally with Acuña's Feminist League. After their first timid request, the women realized what they would be facing. They were not so dismayed by President Acosta's refusal of their request. Rather, what perturbed the league members was the reaction of the media, which hurried to remind them that, according to the law, women, children, and the insane could not vote (Calvo, 1989: 103).

From then on, the league dedicated all its efforts to ensuring that women would no longer be grouped with children and the insane. In 1931 they proposed to the Costa Rican Legislative Assembly a bill granting the vote to a limited group of women who, because of intellectual capacity demonstrated by titles and professions, could prove their good sense, wisdom, and maturity. They also asked the representatives to explain what other credentials women would have to present to win the vote, stating that they would be willing to obtain them. But their voices made no more impression on the assembly than did the sounds of the falling rain (Sharratt, chap. 8 below).

Thereafter, the Feminist League sent a new petition to the Legislative Assembly every year, and each year the representatives answered with the hackneyed story that a woman in her home occupies a throne to which she, like a queen, should devote all her time and interest. The controversy was enervating and at the same time amusing. Members of the league went to the press in 1934 and said that such kingdoms of the home were "fairy tales for the golden times of yore" (Calvo, 1989: 154) and that women were queens only in ballads and verses. Men then answered more forthrightly; they admitted frankly that a woman's role as reproducer of the species tied her to the home to such an extent that this should be her permanent place. The suffragists accepted the obligation of women to be mothers, but they differed in their interpretation of the role, giving it a social and political scope "that requires a moral-ethical quality which is infinitely superior to the one needed for the exercise of the vote" (Calvo, 1989: 159). In the end, the suffragists' reasoning mattered little: lawmakers merely raised their eyebrows and continued to reject women's claim to the vote. The year was 1934.

Almost ten years later, after their participation in the public protests of May 15, 1943, in which they defended the legality of Costa Rican men's right to vote, the members of the league believed their hour had finally come. Thousands of citizens, women and men, had given public evidence of their civic conscience, showing their disagreement with the government's disrespect for the popular will. For the first time, it seemed that the women's campaign was evoking respect and sufficient recognition and that public awareness of the repeatedly refused request for the vote was on their side. Presidential candidate León Cortés declared, "The nation must give increasingly more tangible proof of its confidence in Costa Rican women, giving them legally the civil rights they so nobly have won" (Calvo, 1989: 186). As a result, a bill presented to the assembly on May 20, 1943, proposed a modification of the election law to reflect the idea that the vote must be exercised "by male and female citizens for whom it constitutes a duty and a right" (Calvo, 1989: 187).

But women were not yet to have the vote in Costa Rica. The argument was raised that the bill had been proposed in a pre-election period and had come from the Democratic party, the same party that had benefited from the women's demonstration. Thus, the bill was killed by the accusation of political opportunism and election campaign manipulation. Then, on August 2, 1947, several thousand women, organized by a large number of women teachers, took to the streets to demonstrate in favor of the right to vote in the next election. As earlier, and building on the demands Stevens had voiced at the Havana conference, in 1943, they did not ask for the right to vote but they again protested that they had been deprived of the right to vote. This time, the demonstration was a deciding factor in achieving the concession of the political rights to women in the 1949 Constitution. One of the decisive arguments was that women's participation at that moment had been sufficient proof of their patriotism (Sharratt, chap. 8 below).

Costa Rican men seem to have been unaware that women, as a group, had proved their patriotism from at least the time of their protests during the first decades of the twentieth century. And given that women expected for themselves few of the "democratic" liberties they were defending, the women's efforts were perhaps more patriotic than the similar efforts of Costa Rican men. Women were always ready to give aid in critical moments to protect rights whose enjoyment was beyond their reach.

More Than the Vote

Recognition in the 1949 Constitution of women's right to vote closed the chapter of suffragism. The loud voices raised by the feminists of the 1930s and 1940s softened in later decades because they were satisfied that their wish had been granted. The younger women, though, came to understand that they had barely won a first battle and the vote was only the beginning of new struggles about to start.

Now that the phase of suffragism has been overcome, we women have become aware that by gaining the right to vote we have attained only half of our political rights. The other half is our right to be elected, and that we have not yet achieved. Since 1949, the year in which the Constitution gave us the vote, the female representation in the Legislative Assembly has reached barely 6 percent. Only 10 percent of labor union jobs and 11 percent of municipal positions are held by women. In some presidential administrations, women have not occupied a single ministerial post; in others, such as the one of President Oscar Arias Sánchez, whose election campaign slogan spoke of a "Costa Rica with the soul of a woman," the highest post for which a woman was named was vice minister. In the following administration, that of President Rafael Angel Calderón (1990–94), the cabinet included two women ministers. When the Proyecto de Ley sobre la Igualdad Real de la Mujer (Bill for Women's True Equality) suggested that in the decade of the 1990s at least 30 percent of high political posts should be occupied by women, the argument was raised that such a measure would be discriminatory against men (see Ansorena, chap. 12 below, and Badilla, chap. 13 below). Yet, very few seem to understand that a Legislative Assembly in which 94 percent of the members are men constitutes solid proof of the discrimination against women.

The feminist movement of today must therefore set itself other goals. We want, exactly as Doris Stevens announced in 1928, the restoration of the rights that were taken from us. And we are not willing to give one inch in this long battle to recover what belongs to us. The goal is no longer one of voting or not voting. What we are insisting is that we shall make our mark, in whatever field we choose to do so.

Biodata

Yadira Calvo Fajardo is a philologist, lecturer, essayist, and writer. Until August 1993 she was a professor at the Universidad de Costa Rica and at the Universidad Autónoma de Centro América (UACA) (Autonomous University of Central America). She is now retired and devoting herself to freelance writing and to work as a contributor for the San José newspaper *La República*. Her books include *La mujer, víctima y cómplice [Women: Victims and accomplices]*, published in 1981, with a second edition scheduled; *Literatura, mujer y sexismo [Literature, women, and sexism]*, 1984, second edition, 1991; *Angela Acuña: Forjadora de estrellas [Angela Acuña, forging stars]*, 1989; *Las Líneas Torcidas del Derecho [The twisted reasoning of the law]*, 1993, and *De Diosas a Dragones (From goddesses to dragons)*. She received the 1989 prize in the essay category of the Universidad Nacional's annual UNA-Palabra (Words at UNA) literary competition; the prize was for her work on sexist language, *A la mujer por la palabra*. The title, a takeoff on the proverb, "Él que toma a la anguila por la cola y a la mujer por la palabra no toma pez ni toma nada," translates loosely as, "If you try to take an eel by the tail or women by their word, you don't get anything." In 1990, she was awarded the Aquileo J. Echeverría prize, also in the essay category, for the same work.

References

Acuña, Angela. 1969. *La mujer costarricense a través de cuatro siglos*, Vols. 1 and 2. San José: Imprenta Nacional.

Calvo, Yadira. 1989. *Angela Acuña: Forjadora de estrellas*. San José: Editorial Costa Rica.

———. 1991a. "Angela Acuña y la procesión de Sanchos." *Mujer/Fempress*. Special issue, "Precursoras del feminismo en América Latina," p. 21.

———. 1991b. "Pancha Carrasco: Del fogón al campo de batalla." *Mujer/Fempress*. Special issue, "Precursoras del feminismo en América Latina," p. 20.

Junta de Protección Social de San José. 1989. *100 años de vivir en paz y democracia*. San José.

Portugal, Ana María. 1991. "Cronología, 1651–1961." *Mujer/Fempress*. Special issue, "Precursoras del feminismo en América Latina," pp. 56–60.

2 ✸ The Group Ventana

An Assessment

Rosalía Camacho, Alda Facio Montejo,
and Ligia Martín

The contributions of the group Ventana (Window) will probably not be documented in patriarchal history, just as the contributions of many of our predecessors in the struggle to achieve a society that will offer justice for women have not been acknowledged. If our accumulated experience is to benefit younger groups in Costa Rica today, we must ensure that the significant theoretical and practical contributions Ventana has made toward strengthening the Costa Rican feminist movement are recorded. Although Ventana does not presently carry out any formal projects, Ventana played an important role in Costa Rican Feminism.

Ventana was one of the first organizations in Costa Rica to call itself feminist and to espouse self-consciousness and pursue a specific project—a magazine directed principally at professional women—with the goal of reaching other women. In 1981 we, a group of university women, began to meet to discuss the form in which we might publicize feminist theory and practice, both little known at that time. Worse than the lack of knowledge of Feminism was the fact that most of the women at the university had an erroneous understanding of the substance of the feminist movement in other countries. Myths about Feminism suggested that the movement attracted only frustrated women—those who are unattractive, hate men, or want to destroy the family through some form of licentiousness or sexual deviation.

As we met over the first several months, we weighed various strategies that might allow us to reach Costa Rican university women. We selected that group as our focus for two reasons. First, we ourselves were university women and therefore knew that group better than other segments of the female population; second, we believed that if we could motivate university women and raise their consciousness, they could integrate those new values in their work with women of other social strata.

During our early meetings we realized that we needed to clarify our ideas about the origin and nature of the oppression of women. We then naturally evolved into a support and consciousness-raising group, in which we were able to deepen our understanding of Feminism on the basis of our own experiences, not just those of women in other countries or other segments of our own country. And, because we wanted to understand intellectually what we were learning emotionally in our support sessions, we decided to study feminist theory as a group. We also decided that, as soon as possible, we would initiate a project that would allow us to reach other women.

Our discussions of the nature of this project were heated. We knew that organizing women at the grassroots level of society was necessary and that in a Third World country most women are poor and face problems of mere survival. However, we doubted that our group, which then consisted of about ten women, could have much impact in solving those problems. We decided that a better strategy would be to reach women who later would work with such grassroots organizations. By working with this intermediate group of women we could present a clearer idea about problems confronting women in particular and the community as a whole. We therefore opted for creating a feminist magazine, reasoning that a magazine would open a necessary, and so far nonexistent, forum in which women could express their concerns and publish their research and artistic or literary creations. At the same time, this magazine would furnish space for readings and discussions about women's problems. We did not want to propose solutions because we did not believe we had all the answers. We could, however, offer the ideal medium for those looking for solutions to women's problems: a publication with a theoretical gender perspective from which to interpret the situation of women.

We determined that the content of the magazine would be optimistic and that problem statements would go hand in hand with a commitment to arrive at nonpatriarchal solutions. To evoke this optimism, we called our magazine *Ventana* (Window). A window suggests permanent communication between outside and inside, a place from which one can look out over a strange world and call out to other women.

As feminists, we wanted to destroy myths and stereotypes and invite our readers to walk with us down an untraveled path in their quest for feminine identity. We invited other women to participate and soon received poetry, articles, proposals, commentaries, drawings, testimonials, and, most important, their support. Meeting regularly, we learned our new jobs as editors and felt enriched by all we as women wanted to say.

Ventana's first issue was published in 1982. It covered a wide range of topics, with articles on women's political participation, sexual pleasure, the need for critical awareness of statements or information about women, the question of androgynism (absence of gender conflict) in peace studies, problems of Costa Rican workers, the Double Day, machismo, aerobics and women's need for physical exercise, and questions of contraception, both female and male. (It is interesting to note that, of the ten authors listed in that first issue in 1982, five are also contributing to *The Costa Rican Women's Movement*.)

Over the next two years, *Ventana* published three additional issues, at considerably irregular intervals. Publishing a magazine is expensive, and we faced great economic difficulties. We received no support, since at that time financing agencies supported only income-generating, not consciousness-raising, projects. Moreover, the group suffered from attrition. In 1985 several of our members went abroad to study, and some joined other groups. Their departures added to our frustration at not bringing out the magazine more regularly, and we decided to stop publication.

We turned then to other activities, such as lectures, writing articles for other publications, and offering workshops. In 1987 we put out a call to other women to join the group Ventana. With new energy we increased our activities. We initiated a permanent colloquium in the Humanities Division of the Universidad de Costa Rica on various topics related to women. We brought out a small bulletin for International Women's Day on March 8. We conducted workshops and continued to write for other publications.

After several months, differences of opinion about teamwork—new needs as well as unfulfilled expectations—caused the group to break up. Some of us continued with Ventana, while others created new groups or joined already existing groups. We do not see these divisions as signs of failure; feminist groups in other countries have experienced similar restructuring. Groups often divide when they are going through a process of reorganizing. Individuals with similar needs and expectations break away to form new groups. Others draw upon the successes and limits of earlier organizations to broaden and enrich the feminist movement with new ones. All of this is constructive change, providing that the older groups do not attempt to "enlighten" the path of the new ones, and the newer groups refrain from believing that they are the true pioneers of the feminist movement in the country.

In retrospect, our experience with Ventana has taught us valuable lessons. Members of a support group will see the world in different ways, and personalities will conflict from time to time. But if the members want to reach consensus, they must work together with respect, confidence, solidarity, and commitment. Only then can the group resolve conflicts and reduce friction in ways that will ensure that members are not harmed and the group is strengthened. This task is not easy. Groups must be aware of changes in the interests and needs of their members if painful break-ups are to be avoided. Yet we insist that groups must accept separation if the expectations and interests of the members become too vastly different.

Currently, Ventana does not carry out any specific group projects. Nonetheless, those of us who remain in the collective still meet several times each month to enrich our lives by sharing our personal experiences and lending each other emotional support in difficult situations. We also share news about topics that interest us, personal undertakings, or the work of organizations in which we are participating. Each of us works in her own way to improve women's condition—in organizational training programs, producing teaching materials, conducting action-oriented research with poor women, extending feminist theory, or developing the theory of alternative law from a woman's perspective. As a group we have worked to promote legislation concerning women, eliminate threats to programs that serve women, and denounce specific violations of women's human rights.

Thus, Ventana continues above all to be a support group, although in character slightly different from the one in earlier years. Today's members of Ventana are still optimistic, and we can see that our early efforts have borne fruit. Other magazines that treat women's problems from a feminist perspective are now in circulation, and school teachers, university professors, and women's groups still use the old issues of *Ventana*. We see much interest among young women in learning what Feminism is, and we note with satisfaction that many women have lost their fear of identifying themselves as feminists.

In sum, we are satisfied to have been one of the first groups to contribute toward establishing a gender identity among Costa Rican women. At the time Ventana first met, conditions for feminist work were difficult, and we experienced rejection, ridicule, and even aggression from both men and women. We did not then have the support of feminist theory that we now have, nor did we enjoy solidarity with most then-existing women's organizations. Better conditions and perspectives for feminist work prevail today. Some organizations working with poor urban and rural women base their efforts on a gender perspective. Some church women are rereading church doctrines. New partners in our conversations, such as a feminist lesbian group, are enriching the women's movement. Last but not least, two state universities have established special programs for gender studies (see Ferro, chap. 28 below, and Guzmán, chap. 29 below), and in the fall of 1993, have embarked on a joint master's program in Women's Studies.

To all of this—or perhaps because of all of this—may be added the many professionals who work from a gender perspective: psychologists, lawyers, anthropologists, mathematicians, medical doctors, nurses, philosophers, and many others not named here. Evidently, conditions have improved. But that does not mean our struggle is less difficult or that our goals are within our reach. Only if women throughout the world cooperate can we ensure the end of patriarchy.

Biodata

Rosalía Camacho is a Costa Rican who graduated from the Universidad de Costa Rica (UCR) in law. She also studied theater and has entered the newly established joint master's program in Women's Studies of the UCR and the Universidad Nacional. She has participated in activities related to women's rights and until recently was deputy director of the Programa Mujer, Género y Justicia, Instituto Latinoamericano de Naciones Unidas para la Prevención del Delito y Tratamiento del Delincuente (ILANUD) (United Nations Latin American Institute for the Prevention of Crime and Treatment of Offenders). She also has collaborated in developing modules for women's self-management groups.

Alda Facio Montejo is a Costa Rican with degrees in chemistry from Roger Williams College, Rhode Island, and in law from UCR; she has a master's degree in comparative jurisprudence from New York University. She is the director of ILANUD's Women, Gender, and Justice Program, has served as a judge, and has worked at the Instituto Interamericano de Derechos Humanos (Inter-American Institute of Human Rights) in San José. With Laura Guzmán, of Programa Interdisciplinario de Estudios de Género (PRIEG) Interdisciplinary Gender Studies Program) of the UCR, and Rhonda Copelon (of the City University of New York), Facio has taught the PRIEG/UCR graduate extension seminar Sex, Gender, and Law. Her published work appears in the *Boletín del Comité Latino Americano para la defensa de los derechos de la mujer* (Lima, Peru) and in *El otro derecho* of the Latin American Legal Services Institute (Bogotá, Colombia). She serves as a correspondent for the Latin American feminist monthly magazine *Mujer/ Fempress*. Her book *Cuando el género suena cambios trae. Una metodología para el análisis de género del fenómeno legal (Gender awareness rings in change. A methodology for a general analysis of the law)*, 1992, is in its third edition and is being translated into English for use in Asia and Africa.

Ligia Martín, a Costa Rican, studied social anthropology in Mexico and has a master's degree in rural sociology from the Universidad de Costa Rica. She teaches at the Universidad National. She has variously worked as a consultant for international agencies, for example, in developing training modules for women's self-management groups for UNICEF through the Centro de Estudios para la Acción Social (CEPAS)

(Research Center for Social Action), functioning as regional coordinator of a project assessing women and community health of the Consejo Superior Universitario Centroamericano (CSUCA) (Council of Central American Universities); as consultant on an analysis of indigenous and Afro-Caribbean women's groups in the province of Limón, sponsored by the Defensoría de la Mujer, Ministerio de Justicia (Office of the Women's Defender, then in the Ministry of Justice) and the Fondo de las Naciones Unidas para Actividades de Población (United Nations Population Fund); and as coordinator of an analysis of the situation of women in agriculture sponsored by the Instituto Interamericano de Cooperación para la Agricultura (IICA) (Inter-American Institute for Cooperation in Agriculture) of the Organización de Estados Americanos (OEA) (Organization of American States). Since 1993 she has been coordinator of the new Defensoría de la Mujer, which is now part of the recently established Defensoría de los Habitantes (of Costa Rica), or the Office of the Ombudsman. To ensure its freedom of action, this office is an independent government institution and is no longer part of the Ministry of Justice.

3 ❊ Improving the Quality of Women's Daily Lives

Costa Rica's Centro Feminista de Información y Acción

Ana Carcedo, Montserrat Sagot, and Marta Trejos

The Centro Feminista de Información y Acción (CEFEMINA) (Feminist Center for Information and Action) grew out of the Movimiento para la Liberación de la Mujer (MLM) (Women's Liberation Movement). In 1974, a group of women formed MLM to begin discussions, research, and campaigns from a feminist perspective in Costa Rica. These women had just returned from studying in Europe, where they had been influenced by the rise of the feminist movement in developed countries. Following North American and European examples, MLM organized a series of activities that promoted women's reproductive rights: contraception, abortion, and the banning of forced sterilization.

In 1977, MLM extended its activities to include a new campaign against a bill intended to prohibit the use of intrauterine devices (IUDs) on the grounds that IUDs were a tool for abortion. At that time, MLM worked to organize opposition to the bill among poor women of the southern suburbs of San José and of other communities; these women, the principal users of IUDs, were profoundly disturbed by the possible consequences of the passage of such a bill.

Given the women's well-organized opposition, the bill was never passed. MLM decided to continue its work with the women of the poorest sections of San José because the campaign against outlawing IUDs had been a valuable experience for MLM members: they had learned that they needed to revise their approaches and work methods.

A Change in Name and Philosophy: MLM Becomes CEFEMINA

First and most important, MLM members decided they knew far too little about the concrete problems of Costa Rican women in particular and of Latin

American women in general. Second, they resolved that the key to understanding the specific situation of Costa Rican women lay in the daily problems these women face, their own definition of these problems, and their own solutions for them. Thus, the daily life of poor Costa Rican women and the needs those women themselves expressed became decisive determinants for the definition of subsequent feminist strategy.

So began a never-ending process of reconceptualization, a search for new theoretical and practical insights that would provide characteristic elements of a Latin American Feminism. As part of this process, MLM formally changed its name in 1981 to the Centro Feminista de Información y Acción (CEFEMINA).

CEFEMINA's Framework for Action

As a women's organization, CEFEMINA focuses particularly on improving women's living conditions. It does not strive for an abstract philosophical ideal; rather it springs from the reality it wants to transform. Current achievements are judged in terms of their value both in eliminating discrimination against women and in the immediate improvements they make in women's lives. CEFEMINA therefore follows no preestablished paths and works toward no predetermined ideal goals; each case history must be written anew, focused on a specific problem with all members of the community sharing the responsibility for constructing a solution. CEFEMINA believes that a better future for women will be built on the foundation of a fairer, more equitable present achieved through concrete actions by women and men today.

CEFEMINA's commitment arises, then, out of the necessity of working for and with a social group that has been systematically and traditionally discriminated against—a group that represents half of society. On the basis of this human solidarity, CEFEMINA formulates its objectives, incorporates new members, and seeks collaborative ties with other groups. Because CEFEMINA's allegiance is to transforming the realities women face today, principles, analyses, and theories are merely tools to shape our work; they are constantly revised and can never take the place of the concrete objectives set for each new project.

CEFEMINA has attempted to maintain a total openness toward new possibilities and a willingness to revise earlier conclusions. We therefore see no justification for imposing ideological and political prerequisites upon those who wish to join the movement to improve the living conditions of women. Imposing such requirements on women and men already involved in such actions would be even less justifiable. Similarly, CEFEMINA's criteria for judging the appropriateness of any alliance or form of cooperation with another group can never be an ideological decision. Instead, such alliances are determined by the presence of realistic options for concrete achievements for women and for humanity in general, for CEFEMINA believes that discrimination against women has a negative effect on all people.

CEFEMINA considers itself part of a phenomenon that has begun to manifest itself openly on our continent: We as women are looking for the place in society where we can exert a positive influence on our own daily lives, our own concrete realities. CEFEMINA's practices repudiate a large part of the tenets and the dogma of fundamental Feminism, but we maintain that orthodox doctrines must give way to real actions and movements that have as their goal the improvement of the daily quality of life.

CEFEMINA's Programs

The preceding framework orients CEFEMINA's actions and programs. In addition to publishing the magazine *Mujer* (Women) as an open forum for discussion and analysis, CEFEMINA is currently sponsoring many important projects, each of which does its own fund raising. Among these projects are the following:

1. Seven projects of housing self-construction, amounting to more than two thousand houses, primarily for low-income, female-head-of-household families, which have been completed, with additional projects starting up. Most of the participants (90%) in these projects have been women and children. In these new communities, CEFEMINA develops programs directed toward the improvement of the quality of life of the women and the community in general. In such programs, women have developed the first self-help groups in health services, including education about the use of pharmaceutical products, campaigns against maternal mortality, prevention programs against domestic violence, and projects to foster income generation for women.

2. A loan service to women who want to start small businesses has been instituted. This fund serves particularly the women of the housing projects and will encourage them to start small building or construction businesses of their own.

3. On the basis of the experience obtained through the work with women in the communities of those housing projects, CEFEMINA has created a program it calls Salud Vivencial (Healthful Living). This is an all-encompassing concept that views health not as an absence of disease but as the creation of conditions that permit the development of the entire human potential. In this program, CEFEMINA has opened three clinics for service to women and children of twenty-four-hundred families.

4. CEFEMINA has promoted the creation of the first women's trade union in the country, called Mujeres (Women), which is accessible to all women who want to improve their working conditions and their lives in general.

5. CEFEMINA, together with the Comité Nacional por la No Violencia Contra la Mujer (National Committee for the Prevention of Violence Against Women), has created Mujer No Estás Sola (Woman, You are Not Alone), a program of comprehensive services to battered women, with a network of support groups throughout the country and a campaign for the prevention of violence against women (see Carcedo, chap. 18 below).

6. As part of its concern with pushing for legal changes that help women, CEFEMINA has developed the project Mujer y Administración de Justicia (Women and the Administration of Justice), with the goal of identifying concrete legal problems and pushing for changes in legislation.

7. CEFEMINA promoted the creation of the Comité por la Igualdad de la Mujer en el Deporte (Committee for Women's Equality in Sports), which in 1990 organized the first National Meeting on Women, Health, and Sports. This committee pushed for the 1990 presidential decree that stipulates that women and men athletes who compete in the same sports or events should be awarded the same prizes if the prize has a monetary value.

8. As part of the task of discussing and spreading information on women's problems, CEFEMINA organized two national conferences in 1984 and 1988 on the situation of Costa Rican women, as well as the Fifth International Congress on Women and Health, which was held in Costa Rica in 1987. In 1990 and 1991, CEFEMINA again called two national conferences, focused on the topic of violence against women, and in San José at the end of 1991, the Primer Encuentro Centroamericano y del Caribe Sobre Violencia Contra la Mujer (First Central American and Caribbean Meeting on Violence Against Women).

Conclusion

Throughout many years of action, CEFEMINA has remained true to its members' conviction that Feminism in Costa Rica must lead to giving all women—and particularly the poor—a sense of confidence and power in relation to controlling the conditions of their lives. With that conviction, CEFEMINA constantly explores new avenues of work with and for women, in response to the needs that the women themselves express.

Biodata

Ana Carcedo was born in Spain and is a naturalized Costa Rican. She has been involved in the women's movement since the mid-1970s; she is one of the founders of the

Movimiento para Liberación de la Mujer, which by 1981 had been transformed into the Centro Feminista de Información y Acción. She currently serves as CEFEMINA's president and also edits the magazine *Mujer*.

Montserrat Sagot is an anthropologist with a Ph.D. in sociology from The American University, Washington, D.C. She is a long-time member of CEFEMINA, professor of sociology at the Universidad de Costa Rica, and until recently was research coordinator of CEFEMINA. Currently, she is the chair of the master's program in Women's Studies, the joint program of UCR and UNA.

Marta Trejos is a Costa Rican who has studied sociology at the Free University of Brussels. She is one of the founders of MLM and CEFEMINA and is the executive director of CEFEMINA.

4 ❋ The Alianza de Mujeres Costarricenses, a Popular Movement

An Impassioned Plea for Action-Oriented Feminism

Ana Hernández

The Alianza de Mujeres

Those of us who work daily in the defense of women's rights, social justice, and peace must preserve the history of the women's movement in Costa Rica so that it will not be excluded from a general history of our nation. We must keep alive the experience of thousands of women who struggled to create a better life. Some say the Alianza is one of the oldest women's organizations in Central America. It is, much to our own surprise! This longevity of the Alianza reflects the persistence of simple women who are working for a popular women's organization.

The word *popular*—of the people—is most important for the Alianza. It signals our dedication to many different kinds of women, without regard to their race or political or religious beliefs. The Alianza's members join in support of equality, to solve the problems we experience in this small Central American country in which, although women are half the population, the society is characterized by the word *patriarchal* and the state calls itself our "benefactor." These conditions connect us to a series of sociohistorical and structural circumstances. They also cause us to join hands with other groups that are struggling to overcome oppression because of their class, race, or political beliefs, and that suffer the consequences of poverty, unemployment, lack of services, and even repression.

For all these reasons, Feminism is for us closely linked with the common struggle of simple people. We who work daily with women believe that Feminism touches us as women and as social beings, that it promotes solidarity and identity, and that it gives us strength to go on debating and constructing. We believe fundamentally in the strength and capacity of women to open paths toward well-being and freedom for themselves and for all human beings. On this basis we speak of justice, equality, peace, and development. We believe in a popular Feminism that does not need labels or fancy names. "Popular" for us encompasses thinking and action because we believe theory and practice go hand in hand. And we do not speak of women as "poor"; if we did we would be opening doors to demagogues who exploit the word for their own gains.

The Alianza has many faces. Peasant women, housewives, working women, professionals, indigenous and black women—all these have given character and permanence to the Alianza since 1952. Many joined under watchwords such as "defense of women's rights," "children's rights," and "peace." We began in urban neighborhoods and grew in the zones of banana plantations. From every corner of Costa Rica women came to us, and we learned with them as we shared sadnesses and joys, took one another's hands, and grew strong enough to go on.

We are sure our struggles inspired many women who took action for their goals but did not want to acknowledge us. These women learned to participate and began to think of themselves as strong. They supported struggles for land for peasant women, for children's centers, for training centers, for schools, and for community works. They confirm for us the Alianza's autonomy as a popular women's organization.

Regardless of where we are, we are women and we maintain our identity as women working with women. Many who watch us from the realm of politics are afraid of us as they see us work, express opinions, and advance. We find it interesting that when it comes to straightforward battles, agreements are often reached more easily among women than among mixed-gender groups or men's organizations that represent the system of patriarchy.

Today, in order to respond to the multiple demands simple women bring to us, the Alianza has extended its activities in many directions. We work throughout Costa Rica. Many women come to us because of our new ideas for defending women's rights, not through formal legislation or proclamations— which after all have not improved our situation very much—but through offering alternative strategies, understanding that we are all human beings who are attacked and who are discriminated against by society.

The services the Alianza offers are not paternalistic. Our principle is to let the women speak and decide, for we know we are strongest when we act together. Of course, the economic crisis has hit us hard, as mothers, workers, and citizens. But we multiply our actions and our creativity to survive. We recognize the feminization of poverty in inflation, social violence, the disintegration of the family, domestic violence, and poverty itself. Against all these, we women organize ourselves. We plan our actions and our demands, and we make decisions. We do not want to be merely companions who are manipulated. We want to participate directly.

We women are conscious of the need to bring about a society in which we can grow, develop, be happy, and consider ourselves full human beings with complete equality, freedom, and responsibility. We want to be a great movement of women who, together with other organizations and groups, construct what we seek, namely: to have others treat us as human beings, to listen to us with respect, to have no person tell us to shut up. We are not all-powerful or irreverent; we are simply women who think, feel, and act. We do not suffer from the disease of lust for power; we merely express the authority of our opinion to act from our own perspectives and necessities as women.

Feminism has so many characteristics that can serve to unite us rather than divide us; problems of gender are also problems of class, not separated from politics. The world changes every day, and we cannot remain behind and permit others to speak of us as objects. We are actors in history, and we will construct our new history in a spirit of strength and love and with an eye on the future.

The Alianza in 1992

In 1992, the Alianza was operating in fourteen regions of the country, from the Pacific Southwest near Panama and the Caribbean coast in the east, to the northern lowlands near the Nicaraguan border, to the dry coastal strip of the Pacific Northwest, and to major population centers of the Central Valley. Each region contains three to five local groups of women with vastly differing needs; members may be rural or urban and may live in either long-established or recently initiated neighborhoods.

The Alianza works with limited resources: Local groups raise funds for their own needs, and each group's work is done mainly by volunteers. The central office of the Alianza counts on some financial support, especially for legal counseling and advisory work, from the Dutch, nongovernmental, internationally connected Organización Católica de Participación en la Financiación de Programas de Desarrollo (Catholic Organization for Participation in the Financing of Development Programs).

Daily activities are dictated by members' needs. The Alianza's governing body meets monthly, and, of course, for annual planning once a year. Thus, in March 1992, representatives of all groups from around the country gathered in San José to determine the plan of action for the year. (Junta Directiva Nacional, 1992). Besides proposing a strengthening of the organization itself and of its training programs for legal advisers, Alianza members requested technical training for income-generating projects and workshops and training or counseling sessions on domestic violence, human sexuality, management, and marketing. In many of these programs the Alianza cooperates with the Asociación de Trabajadoras Domésticas (Association of Domestic Workers).

The text of the following flier shows what one local women's group achieved. It is an example of our action-oriented Feminism, which gives women decision-making power through self-confidence and inspires community-focused problem solving.

Women in Action—An Open Letter to All Neighbors in Calle Cochea

The group Alianza de Mujeres of Calle Cochea wishes to inform you that:

On March 10, 1992, we had a meeting with the manager of Metrocoop, requesting the establishment of the promised bus service for this community.

On March 17, 1992, we met with the manager of Metrocoop and municipal officials to arrive at concrete agreements and draw attention to other community problems, such as public safety.

On March 31, 1992, we attended the session of the municipality to verify that the agreements were being carried out. We obtained the bus schedule to which Metrocoop has committed itself. This schedule will be put up for all to see. Let us watch for it.

Together we have achieved this.

Reminder to all women—we meet every Wednesday at 3:00 p.m. in the meeting rooms of the San Josecito Catholic Church for training sessions for women on topics such as law, health, psychology, and organization. We are expecting you.

Alianza de Mujeres de Calle Cochea

Biodata

Ana Hernández is a Costa Rican women's leader who became a feminist through her experience of working with the Asociación Alianza de Mujeres Costarricenses (AMC) (Alliance of Costa Rican Women). "I learned about women in my work and studies with women of the Alianza."

References

Junta Directiva Nacional. Programación 1992. March 14, 1992. Internal document.

Acknowledgment

I acknowledge the help of all the women from whom I learned to be a woman and to help other women.

5 ❊ Women's Liberation from Servitude and Overprotection

Carmen Naranjo Coto

Critics of feminism say it has concentrated on actions for women who are "with it" or "up to date"—those who all along have been conscious of the problems women face. They claim feminism had to become a kind of escape valve, a way of appeasing the different social strata and muffling their impatience over injustices and discrimination, even though the relief women felt by venting their frustrations offered neither a solution nor an inspiration to seek full incorporation into society.

Servitude: Women's Gravest Problem

To my way of thinking, the core problem of women lies in the human servitude to which they have been subjected throughout history. Servitude does not foster communication, respect for rights, or human consideration. Rather, it cancels creativity and blocks personal and social fulfillment.

Women have always been servants, their image cloaked in domesticity. The architecture of the home clearly fits that image. We see women busy in the bedroom, kitchen, dining room, or some other room dedicated to housework—rarely do they enter the living room, study, or library except to clean these areas and put them in order. Even in recent times, as appliances and new housekeeping techniques have made housework more versatile and creative, women's duties in the home have remained limited to the exercise of specific skills.

Women's domestic image also carries over to the workplace. In factories, they gather in large halls, working at product-assembly conveyor belts, where they perform tasks step by step, like mutilated housework.

In the office, women labor to print out the creative works of others. Similarly, in other areas of business, women always serve, translating their experience as buyers into the commercial experience of sellers. Only in exceptional cases and under extraordinary conditions do women move beyond manual labor and enter the world of intellectual contributions.

Of course, manual labor is not humiliating as such, nor does it always represent human servitude. After all, manual labor itself uses some creative talent; in the highest arts, intellectual and manual labor are combined. Servitude begins when humans are confined to only one type of work, when they are prevented at all costs from going beyond that area which is declared to be their customary tasks. Circumscribed by gender typing, work then brings about human servitude because it sacrifices—through manifold limitations—creative human potential and thus virtually imprisons the worker. Human servitude occurs also when we deny human beings the opportunity of acquiring experience on their own, reasoning that such recourse is simply not permissible for a specific gender.

The Overprotection of Women

The so-called protection of women has placed limits on them in all areas. Ideals proclaiming women's purity and weakness and their inability to suffer and survive have disqualified women at the very moment when they should have begun their apprenticeship for a life full of opportunities and enriching challenges. The extent of the disqualification into which the feminine world has been locked appears in the desolate figure of the widow who must suddenly satisfy all of the spiritual and material demands of her family.

This overprotection of women determines their "appropriate" tasks, modeled after the tasks they fulfill at home. In areas that demand cordiality—a certain touch, the lending of help, the giving of care—women must be involved.

The Tragedy of Housework

Since I am using terms that can be willfully blurred or jumbled, let me clarify myself: I do not underrate housework, which indeed allows creativity and affords enjoyment and personal fulfillment. Working in the kitchen, sewing, weaving, decorating, cleaning, generally improving the home—these activities can be constructive activities, providing a sense of satisfaction and usefully uniting the family. To share obligations, to participate in household duties, to learn to divide housework produces harmony, shared efforts, communication, and broader understanding. It is when household obligations always rest with one person, who then becomes a permanent tireless servant, that they lead to irritated exhaustion. In most cases, the weight of those obligations is misunderstood, and as a result the family is not strengthened but rather weakened or exhausted.

I have frequently pointed to the tragedy that we acknowledge housework only when efficiency is lacking—when bread burns, buttons come off, furniture grows dusty, shirts are poorly ironed, and some tasks are forgotten. We accept the unending routine, performed day after day, with gratitude and silent recognition, simply by failing to notice or honor it, as if it did not merit appreciation. We recognize or, administratively speaking, evaluate that routine only when we criticize, show defects, or complain belligerently about errors or about the partial or total neglect of tasks.

The Goals of Women's Liberation

From various points of view, when we speak about women we must speak about liberation, but not in the sense of breaking with what constitutes a woman's intimate being, individual characteristics, possibilities of fulfillment, and free choice. To liberate is not to determine behavior or establish patterns but instead to break with what up to now has been limitation, difficulty, and negation. To liberate is to open horizons for a wide array of options.

The term *liberation* has indeed been so poorly understood that many women insist they do not want to liberate themselves. Applauding the traditional role they have played and weighing its privileges and disadvantages, they state themselves to be against all that cuts them off from that role. They fail to appreciate that this role grew out of a history that viewed women as family property, little-wanted beings, precisely because they were deemed to be so limited. Those women do not understand that liberation will not affect their interests and preferences because the goal is not to liberate specific groups of women. The mission is broader: It encourages social change so that all individuals may achieve, on their own, the very best life possible, within their own set of responsibilities toward the meaning of life. To liberate means balancing equality of facilities and opportunities with equality of duties and rights.

Sometimes it seems that in our world we place more value on a perfectly cooked potato than on our chance to offer to women the environment they need to grow and become stronger, to achieve self-realization as human beings. Our current conditions seem to lack respect for interests, callings, or curiosities that differ from traditional conceptions. But all individuals have the right to develop their potential and to orient their creative energy so as to achieve the best results for themselves and society. Limitations, discrimination, and prejudice lead only to frustrations and injustice, which we must eliminate from our communities.

The voices that demand justice have a long history and have expressed their demands clearly in all ages. Women want to go beyond traditional conventions and live in freedom with equality of rights, opportunities, and responsibilities.

When we speak about liberating women from ties, bonds, limitations, and prejudices, some critics deliberately misinterpret our words to mean introducing women to licentiousness, social vices, masculine behavior, and some sort of near-barbarism. These critics also contend that female liberation goes against the principles of the family and that it threatens the fundamental bases of society. They harbor strong prejudices against women, considering them basically weak, in need of protection, without spiritual or moral strength, and incapable of judging between good and evil or of acting prudently and with equilibrium. Maybe family and social life was easier for men when they could count on servitude, obedience, and submission of women. But one day, though it may come late, the time of justice will come, and the hand of justice will knock at our door and take over. It is now knocking at the doors of many people, both women and men.

But it is also true that liberating women will mean liberating them from the foolish excuses behind which they have hidden, such as the perception that they are the queens of the home or the power behind the throne. To the contrary, a feminist reading of their situation shows clearly that women are the hidden victims, eternal servants of routine and boredom, riding in the last car of the train, doing laundry or dishes, and preparing delicious foods for others, not for themselves.

Liberating women does not mean putting them on a pedestal, proclaiming them to be divine, exceptional creatures who can be touched only in dreams or mystic visions. Such an image would rob them of soul and body—of everything they have—and would send them into nothingness. To liberate them, in reality, is to strengthen their own development, future, and destiny. It is not to make women into people who merely go along, who are only distant others, but to give them the role of independent interpreter, hand in hand with other interpreters. It is to open a space for their voices, their judgments, their points of view. It is giving them the opportunity of creating and fulfilling themselves.

To liberate women is to free them from traditional roles, double- and triple-shift workdays, exhausting routines, limited geographies, and endless waiting, prohibitions, and fears. It is to fill them with freedoms, hopes, decisions, and joys. It is to show them that their horizons are wide and that they have within them their own spaces in which to grow, to be, to share, and to aspire to carrying out a vocation, a wish, or a mission. Liberating women is to make them look into an illuminated mirror and stop seeing themselves only as a complement to someone else.

Biodata

Carmen Naranjo is a Costa Rican who holds a licenciatura degree in philology from the Universidad de Costa Rica. She has written novels and short stories and is also an essayist and poet. From 1972 to 1974, she was the Costa Rican ambassador in Israel. As minister of culture, youth, and sports (1974–76), she established in the Ministry of Culture the Oficina Nacional de la Mujer (National Women's Office), which has evolved into today's Centro Nacional para el Desarrollo de la Mujer y la Familia (CMF) (National Center for the Development of Women and Family), or more popularly, Mujer y Familia, Ministerio de Cultura, Juventud y Deportes (MCJD) (Ministry of Culture, Youth and Sports). She has also been the director of the Museo de Arte Costarricense (Museum of Costa Rican Art) (1982–84); director of the Editorial Universitaria Centroamericana (Central American University Press) (EDUCA; 1984–92), at that time the official publisher for the Consejo Superior Universitario Centroamericano (CSUCA) (Council of Central American Universities). She is a member of the Academia Costarricense de la Lengua (Costa Rican Academy of the Language). In 1984, with Alda Facio, Mirta González, and Laura Guzmán, she organized the first lecture series on Women and Society under the auspices of the Cátedra Libre Eugenio Fonseca (Eugenio Fonseca Lecture Series) at the UCR. Currently, she continues writing and is frequently invited to lecture abroad. In early 1996, on occasion of the fiftieth anniversary of the award of the Nobel Prize in Literature to Chilean poet Gabriela Mistral, Carmen Naranjo was one of fifty writers throughout the world to receive—from the Chilean government—the Medal Gabriela Mistral.

Acknowledgment

This article is based on a chapter in *Mujer y Cultura*, published by Editorial Universitaria Centroamericana, 1989.

Angela Acuña B., the first woman lawyer in Costa Rica, Costa Rican ambassador
to the OAS, founder of the Liga Feminista, fighter for the women's vote

IN COSTA RICA, women's history is beginning to attract not only professional historians but also feminists from other disciplines who are intent upon documenting women's contributions to Costa Rican life throughout history, particularly over the last five hundred years. Scholars working in the field are using two approaches: They reassess existing documentation, considering it from a gender perspective, and they explore social history as it relates to women, i.e., by focusing attention on individual women, whether by gathering oral recollections or by analyzing a variety of hitherto unknown or untouched documents. This section offers examples of both of these approaches, as well as some insight into differences of interpretation that may result from the different points of departure.

Women in Colonial Costa Rica: A Significant Presence, by Cora Ferro Calabrese and Ana María Quirós Rojas

Introducing women in the province of Costa Rica during colonial times, Cora Ferro Calabrese and Ana María Quirós Rojas speak about the same individual efficacy noted earlier in this *Reader* (see Calvo, chap. 1, and introduction). They trace this growing sense of identity as they document women's tenacity, their stubborn sense of self-worth, their often unsuccessful struggles for justice, and their economic enterprises. Some women skillfully used openings in the colonial system to make tangible contributions to survival in a society dominated by the fusion of three kinds of patriarchy—the Spanish colonial power, the Catholic Church, and Indian tribal societies.

The authors' research is based on 939 documents, covering the period 1519 to 1825, from the archives of the Curia Metropolitana (Metropolitan Curia) in San José, Costa Rica. Ferro and Quirós give an overview of colonial Costa Rica and analyze the position and activities of women in colonial society, describing women's power, position in matrimony, and social status, as well as patterns of violence against women. They show that although women were active and occasionally powerful in economic and church affairs, they were easily presumed guilty of licentious behavior and, throughout the period, had to struggle against patriarchal control and domination. The authors conclude that women in colonial Costa Rica suffered the effects of the above-mentioned triple patriarchy, that the contribution of women to the well-being and stability of colonial Costa Rica has not received the attention it deserves, and that the history of the period should be rewritten to concede to women their rightful position.

Contradictory Aspects of Costa Rican Women's History During the Nineteenth Century, by Clotilde Obregón Quesada

Clotilde Obregón looks at women in the context of independent Costa Rica in the nineteenth century. The study documents contradictory dimensions in the experiences of nineteenth-century Costa Rican women. Although their legal status, for example, deteriorated with the introduction of the "progressive" French legislation that superseded traditional Spanish law, women's opportunities for educational and economic activities were considerable and, in fact, were improving toward the end of the period. Many of these women demonstrated the same individual efficacy referred to earlier.

The Suffragist Movement in Costa Rica, 1889–1949, by Sara Sharratt

In her analysis of the sixty years of suffragist struggle between 1889 and 1949, Sara Sharratt details the political roots of the women's movement. She documents women's fate in the educational system and the Catholic Church as well as women's support of Costa Rican democracy at a time when women were subject to the legal constraints of discriminatory Costa Rican constitutions. For years women supported democratic struggles without being allowed to share in the political benefits. Teachers and other educated women were particularly active in these political struggles, although the successes did little to advance their own situation. Women finally focused on their own right to vote, achieving it, after tenacious and courageous efforts, only forty years before Costa Rica celebrated its 1989 "Centennial of Democracy." During the suffragist movement, women believed they could become equal participants in an integrated democratic system. Today's feminists have come to doubt that this is possible without profound societal transformation.

Unusual Costa Rican Women: Three Who Were Proclaimed "Distinguished Citizens of the Nation," by Ana Isabel Gamboa Hernández and Sara Gurfinkiel Hermann

In their discussion of women awarded the Costa Rican Benemeritazgo de la Patria (Award for Distinguished Citizenship), Ana Isabel Gamboa and Sara Gurfinkiel echo the same theme Yadira Calvo introduced in the first selection in this *Reader*. They describe women of strong identity, self-confidence, initiative, and commitment or, to use the earlier term, individual efficacy. At the same time, the authors reveal the machista pattern of thinking that characterizes the process of awarding the Benemeritazgo.

To be declared a distinguished citizen by the Costa Rican Legislative Assembly is the highest honor a citizen may receive, an honor that as a rule is bestowed only several years after the recipient's death. Up to September 24, 1992, when the recently deceased former president Pepe Figueres was awarded this honor, 51 men had received the award, but only three women had been award recipients. The authors offer short life stories of these three women—María Emilia Solórzano, a president's wife; Emma Gamboa, an educator; and Angela Acuña, a woman lawyer and civil rights activist. The authors propose that lack of education, the patriarchal enforcement of women's traditional roles, and an androcentric perception of appropriate criteria for selection of distinguished citizens are the most likely reasons for the limited number of women represented.

Peasant Women's Autobiographies: Women's Double Contribution to the Rural Economy, by Zaira Escamilla Gutiérrez and Lorena Vargas Mora

The final contribution in this section is one of the few in this volume—and in available sources on Costa Rican women in general—that refer to rural women. Zaira Escamilla and Lorena Vargas let five peasant women speak for themselves through selections from their autobiographies, illustrating yet another example of the individual-efficacy roots of today's women's movement. The authors' selections focus on women's twofold contribution to the Costa Rican agricultural economy through their work in the fields and their efforts toward their families' survival. In this male-dominated rural society, women, through their courage and hard work, make a vital economic contribution and traditionally have viewed their contribution as natural, offering it without seeking to share control of the product of their labor. In more recent years, however, farm women have branched out into nonfarm activities for wages and have become more involved in their communities.

6 ❊ Women in Colonial Costa Rica

A Significant Presence

Cora Ferro Calabrese and Ana María Quirós Rojas

It is difficult for women to survive in any society in which strong patriarchal systems of different cultural origins come together and reinforce each other. In colonial Costa Rica, it was particularly difficult because three patriarchal traditions—those of the Spanish colonial system, the Roman Catholic Church, and indigenous tribal societies—converged during colonization. More than a generation after major centers in Mexico, Guatemala, and South America had been settled, colonists entered Costa Rica from the Pacific coast, where they established only weak institutions and existed in complete isolation under conditions of extreme poverty (see, e.g., MacLeod, 1980; Monge Alfaro, 1976).

The contributions of women to the struggling colonial society have not been acknowledged by most experts on the colonial history of Costa Rica (see, e.g., Fernández, 1889; Monge Alfaro, 1976), but even five hundred years of patriarchal history have not entirely eliminated their traces. We hope to rescue women from this invisibility and, in doing so, to strengthen the historical record.

Light and Shadow: Colonial Women's Lives

The present study is based on an ongoing analysis of 2,609 documents from the years 1519 to 1825 which are stored in the Curia Metropolitana in San José (Ferro and Quirós, 1992). These records were transcribed from early church language into modern Spanish by two Costa Rican historians (Thiel, 1896, 1897, 1898; Blanco Segura, 1967). They have also been indexed in part (CD, 1985, 1986).[1] In terms of analysis, however, historians have hardly touched this rich resource.

Throughout Central American history, religious centers such as monasteries, convents, or ecclesiastic offices have functioned as archives for a variety of records. These stored documents contribute significantly to our ability to reconstruct the culture and history of the women of Costa Rica and their social, political, and economic roles in earlier periods. Of the 2,609 documents in the Metropolitan Curia, 939 (36%) refer to women. Of that number, 455 (48.5%) relate to women and economic power, 380 (40.5%) to women and the institution of matrimony, 87 (9.2%) to violence against women, and 17 (1.8%) to women and social status. The documents reveal glimpses of women who were active, enterprising, capable, and decisive, yet at the same time constrained by cultural circumstances, limited by religious convictions, and, over time, deprived of their power through a process of impoverishment and subordination.

In what follows, we begin with a sketch of some aspects of the historical context of the colonial period. We then present an analysis of women in various spheres of society, focusing on their economic power, their social status, their position in matrimony, and the problem of violence against women. We include some anecdotal records to show the hard historical reality these women faced daily and the frequently prejudiced assessment of those who wrote the historic documentation.

Historical Context

The development of the province of Costa Rica during the colonial period was influenced by three factors. First, the distance from Guatemala—at that time the center of the Capitanía General, the regional colonial government—placed Costa Ricans at the margin of political processes and decisions. Second, the legal obstacles against trade with Costa Rica's neighbor Panama, which then belonged to another colonial region, put Costa Ricans at an economic disadvantage. And third, the fierce resistance against colonization on the part of the Indians between the Talamanca Mountains and the Caribbean coast threatened the internal peace of the province.

Costa Rica's economic, social, and political development was slow and was concentrated almost entirely in the highlands of the Central Valley, with poor communications to both coasts. As late as 1731, one document called the province "the end of the world . . . no doctor, no surgeon, no pharmacy, no barber, no hospital, no medicines, women are healers and provide barbershop services to priests and other residents" (Blanco Segura, 1967: 258).

The situation these contemporary documents consider so deplorable demonstrates women's capacity to face the challenges to their survival. For example, during this early period, women settlers produced flour and cakes to feed their families, and they also exchanged extra flour and cakes with traders for clothing. Some of their products were eventually exported to the ports of Portobelo, Panama, and Cartagena, Colombia. This early contribution of women in the development of such small industries was undoubtedly important, although it usually is not acknowledged by the historians.

Historians have also presented the conquest and colonization of the Americas as a missionary enterprise (Dussel, 1983). Religiosity imbued all colonial institutions, and baptism served as an instrument of domination over indigenous peoples. Through baptism, they became subjects of the Spanish king, who took their riches and legitimized the abuse and sexual exploitation of their women. "Our missionaries converted them, took their gold, even their women and children and the other goods, and left them as formally baptized" (Fernández, 1889: 547).

The Indians suffered lamentable exploitation, and most of the weight of this injustice fell on women. However, all the records we analyzed were written almost as though Indian women did not exist. The documents reveal that colonists considered "male Indian workers"—whom they counted in a 1529 census—as if they were the only inhabitants of these lands (Thiel, 1896, no. 99: 28–29). In 1684 statistics, Indian women appear only with reference to their work as maids in the houses of *doctrineros* (missionaries) or in the censuses used as the basis for the collection of tributes (Thiel, 1897, no. 107: 133). There, for tax purposes, the doctrineros had to take annual counts not only of the number of married, single, and widowed Indian men but also of the number of unmarried Indian women (Thiel, 1987, no. 106: 123).

The colonists did have one further interest in Indian women: They were used to repopulate the land to compensate for the scarcity of laborers and the decrease in tributes collected by the king. Therefore, in 1796, the captain general in Guatemala revoked a rule barring Indian women from marrying Ladinos (Spanish-indigenous mixed population) (AF, n.d., no. 36). Simultaneously, religious institutions added to their goals the provision of dowries so that young Indian women could qualify for marriage.

The sparse data we collected document not only the barbaric treatment indigenous women received but also the fate of the Spanish women who participated in the conquest. Few traces now exist of the women colonists—of their thinking, their actions, or their lives. In fact, their names appear in the documents only rarely. For example, although a listing of the village of Garabito for the year 1569 carries the names of all male conquistadores, noting the number of Indians each received, only one woman conquistadora is listed. Even though she was powerful enough to be allotted 400 Indians, she has no name. She was identified only by her descent from a Spanish male: "the heiress of Miguel Sancho" (Thiel, 1896, no. 100: 44).

Women and Economic Power

Of the 455 documents that mention women and economic power, 351 (77%) reflect some dynamic participation of women in the economic life of the colony. Most of these records related to inheritances, dowries, wills, collections of money, arrangements of debts, real estate, and property in slaves. Many documents clustered around two institutions: *cofradías* (brotherhoods, religious associations) and *capellanías de misas* (chaplaincies for saying mass). The cofradías and capellanías de misas were the core of the religious life of the province, and the economic activities of women were directly related to them.

Within the rigid structure of cofradías, women were limited to either receiving benefits from, or providing money to, the organization. The first time a woman appears in such a document is in 1604, when the board of the Cofradía de la Purísima gave a dowry to a "Señorita Catalina Quesada, Spaniard, daughter of Juan Quesada, Spaniard, deceased, and the Indian woman María Ojeda. The endowed women had a special place in the procession of the day, the public demonstration of the cofradía's splendor" (Thiel, 1897, no. 102: 70). In cofradía activities, women, always in association with their husbands, supported the organization with their dowries or money. However, although they donated the capital for cofradías, women held no positions of power. Some were awarded honorable titles, such as "Patroness of the Year"; others were appointed as inspectors, responsible for supervising cleanliness and decoration of the religious functions or processions.

In contrast to their lack of power, women received the direct blame for the moral deterioration of some cofradías when licentious customs grew up. Contemporaries presumed that women took advantage of the ample physical space in the cofradías to commit adultery: reasons for choosing the location were given as lack of privacy and space in the women's own small houses, married women's fear of their husbands, and young women's fear of their mothers (Blanco Segura, 1967: 202).

A 1640 document first mentions the participation of women in capellanías: "Captain Alonso de Sojo and his wife Lucía de Alas bought the cattle ranch in the valley Mata Redonda," which was indebted to a capellanía (Thiel, 1897 no. 104: 94–95). Later, women commonly participated in capellanías by donating gifts or money for a pious cause. A 1669 document reads: "In the city of Espíritu Santo, Doña María Vásquez Vallejo, wife of the official Juan Fernández Salinas y Serdas, with her husband's authorization, donated to Nuestra Señora de los Angeles a cacao grove of 280 trees at the Madre de Dios River, Matina, its product to be invested to construct the church Nuestra Señora de los Angeles in Cartago, so that Mass would be said in that church every Sunday and on all feast days and holidays" (Thiel, 1897, no. 105: 106).

In many cases, a woman who was left in difficult circumstances after her husband's death and was unable to continue the high contributions for capellanías ceded the income from her holdings—or even their title—to the capellanías. Transactions of capellanía properties discussed in church courts provoked numerous lawsuits, sometimes involving women. Often the bishop had to intervene, "a true plague of annoyance and setbacks for authorities and people" (Blanco Segura, 1967: 196). Large debts of capellanías, lawsuits, or appeals required the participants to travel to the archdiocese in León, Nicaragua. The situation was very serious, for noncompliance for such debt obligations carried the threat of excommunication (Thiel, 1898, no. 117: 296). A document of March 3, 1729, illustrates: "Doña Feliciana Chinchilla gave up the income from her house in Cartago . . . encumbered with 800 pesos from different capellanías. The authorities examined . . . the house, [and] allowed a reduction of the sum, but she had to pay what she owed with the products of her hacienda in Matina" (Thiel, 1898, no. 119: 342).

Though the documents we studied do not specifically mention women slave owners, slaves were often included in the list of goods in deeded property given in transactions to create capellanías. Thus, one can infer that because a high number of women were involved in the creation of capellanías, the number of women owning slaves was probably also high. An 1811 document lends credence to this inference in citing a "Petition made by Tomasa Guzmán that Father Felix García be charged 140 pesos he owes her for a slave she sold him" (CD, 1985, no. 18: 44).

Thus the economic link between women and capellanías led to women's impoverishment and loss of power. In some cases, only the names of rivers—such as the María Aguilar, El Virilla, and María Torres—bear witness today to the women who once owned large holdings of land and property. Historians need to study the relationship between women's losses and the growing economic power of ecclesiastic institutions over the centuries.

Women and the Institution of Matrimony

Of the 939 documents relating to women, 439 were linked to matrimony. Matrimony and economic issues were closely interrelated because the policies that governed matrimony also directly affected benefits of crown and church.

From the beginning of the conquest, marriage between Spaniards and indigenous people had been encouraged in Costa Rica, despite the law of the Viceroyalty against such marriages. That law was revoked in 1796. While these marriages had increased the Christianization of the Indians, they had created problems for women and children, inasmuch as Indians of this area practiced their own patriarchal system of polygamy. Christian marriage obliged them to give up this practice, so many second or third wives and their children were abandoned. Yet, Christian marriages relieved problems of population dispersion as Christian-Indian marriages stabilized families and settlements. Nonetheless, despite the emphasis on institutionalizing marriage, the number of marriages was very low, and 35.9 percent of births were illegitimate in the seventeenth century (Thiel, 1897, no. 109: 116).

The documents in the archives focus primarily on special permits for marriage and sentences to obligatory marriage. The many applications for special marriage permits were handled speedily, a sign that matrimony was held in high favor. Most special requests were necessitated by close blood relationships or a woman's illegitimate-birth status.

Women had an active role in men's sentences to obligatory marriage because of nonfulfillment of a marriage promise. Most claims were brought by women, but the judge almost always decided in favor of the man. A rare decision in favor of the woman occurred if there were several children, if an announcement of the betrothal had been made as the church required, or if a man of high civil or religious rank filed a claim on behalf of the woman. For example, Cayetana de Soto declared that Bernardo de Fuentes refused to marry her after he had given his word and the bans had been announced twice in church. The case was resolved when Fuentes was jailed and was required to declare in writing that he would marry Cayetana (Thiel, 1898, no. 117: 297). In 1728, in a similar case, Captain Cayetano de Herrera, citizen of Escazú, accused Pedro Rojas of the same place of having seduced his daughter Petronilla. The judge sentenced Rojas to a fine of 100 pesos, one year of exile, and court costs of 39.25 pesos (Thiel, 1898, no. 120: 341).

These crimes were punishable by prison and exile, and a few men did in fact go to jail as a result of claims presented by women. In 1722, "María de la O Lobo, 16 years old, brought a suit for nonfulfillment of a marriage promise against Franscisco Romero, 19 years, for having misled her with a promise of marriage. María was placed under guardianship at the house of Sr. Mier Ceballos. Franscisco Romero went into hiding but was found after two days and put in jail. The judge brought the two face to face and Romero, after some evasion, promised to marry María" (Thiel, 1898, no. 117: 298).

Applications for divorce or annulment showed two different patterns for women and men. Much to our surprise, women's claims for divorce were characterized by charges of violence or abuse—namely, mistreatment, adultery, or the husband's alcoholism. Reasons that supported applications filed by men were that the woman was an illegitimate child or a domestic servant or that she refused to live where he was living.

Most church proceedings recorded offenses against matrimony and the ethics of marriage. In truth, though, the documents tell very little about the frequency with which some of the offenses against matrimony mentioned by contemporary historians were committed. The most frequent offenses were adultery with women of mixed race and servants, incest, abduction, rape, or abduction with rape. Nevertheless, the archives also document other types of crimes, such as mistreatment, concubinage, abandonment, pregnancy, or public slander by a husband.

Violence Against Women

In colonial Costa Rica, as in all patriarchal societies, a woman lived her life in an environment that sanctioned violence against her. This violence pervaded her marital life, was enacted in legislation, and was manifested in sexual or physical mistreatment.

Rape, abduction with rape, mistreatment, abandonment, pregnancy resulting from deception, and even homicide were common in colonial times. A 1724 document reports a case in which the daughter of Francisco Chaves was seduced and raped by Esteban Chaves; three of his friends also raped and beat her. In such cases, the courts usually confined the aggressor to jail until he agreed to marry the victim, thereby causing further violence by forcing the woman to marry her aggressor. In this particular case, however, guilt was not proved and, as the young woman did not want to marry Esteban, her father withdrew the accusation. Esteban was freed but was required to pay 16 pesos for trial costs (Thiel, 1898, no. 118: 313).

Incest, adultery, and concubinage were other forms of sexual abuse, in which, as a rule, the male came out ahead. In 1785, for example, a Heredia priest had María del Rosario Molina beaten in his presence, claiming she falsely accused her husband, Marcelo Herra, of incest with their daughter (Blanco Segura, 1967: 254). The case of Felipe Arburola offers another illustration: "He lived in concubinage with Dolores Campos, with whom he had had three children. He wanted to put his life in order when he was widowed from his legitimate wife. But at the time of filing for the matrimonial papers, Campos confessed she had had relations with a nephew of Arburola. The vicar refused to give permission" for the marriage (Blanco Segura, 1967: 258).

The social group that gave authorities the most headaches however, was composed of alcoholic women, prostitutes, and adulterous and incestuous women. In the 1700s, the Capitanía General de Guatemala condemned women alcoholics to be "exposed to public shame for two hours on three consecutive days," and in 1791 an institution was founded for the purpose of confining such women. (The *algodón* [cotton] that inmates were given to work with is the source of the term *algodonera* [cotton mill], which even today is applied to the women's prison.) Crimes such as adultery, incest, and prostitution were often given as reasons for arrest (AE, n.d., no. 37). María Porras, for example, owner of a procurement house and "the original Costa Rican 'Celestina' [procuress]," was condemned to exile in 1807 (Blanco Segura, 1967: 257).

Many women who were considered uncontrollable or deserving of punishment were sent into exile or put under the guardianship of another person. One place of exile was Boruca, near the Panamanian border, where some Talamanca Indian tribes were moved together with Cartago families, in 1705, to begin a new village. One document in the archives stated: "It would be appropriate in the Lord's service for women who because of their bad behavior cannot be properly controlled here [in Cartago], that the governor of this province order them expressly to pass their purgatory there" (Thiel, 1897, no. 112: 214). Other places of exile were Bagaces, near Nicaragua, and Matina, on the Atlantic coast, where the women were put under guardianship of a responsible person whom they had to serve. Reasons for punishment were always "scandalous behavior," "suspicious conduct," or "bad life." For instance, in 1725, María de la Portilla was put under guardianship because her reputation had been damaged by scandals. She had accused José Miguel González, a seventeen-year-old man, of seducing her and fathering her two children. María de la Portilla was condemned to four years of exile in Bagaces, where she was entrusted to a guardian for whom she had to work (Thiel, 1898, no. 118: 314).

When a woman was put under guardianship, she was confined to the house of a person of good renown. In many cases, the reason a woman was put under guardianship was that her parents would not permit a marriage. The woman's future husband would then request that the woman remain under guardianship to ensure her faithfulness, and that the trustees deliver her to him when he asked. In other cases, women were confined while complaints about scandalous behavior were under investigation or marriage judgments were being negotiated. In one such case, described in a 1723 document, "José Gómez and

Josefa Nicolasa were accused of cohabitation. Josefa Nicolasa was put under guardianship and José Gómez was put behind bars. Since they did not want to get married, José Gómez was sentenced to serve as watchman at the coast for half pay and the other half of his pay was to be applied to the cost of the trial and other church expenses. Josefa Nicolasa received permission to help her sick mother with the understanding that she would have to go into exile if she left the house or committed other offenses" (Thiel, 1898, no. 118: 312). A woman was expected to render absolute obedience to her guardian.

The treatment indigenous women received was particularly denigrating, despite the fact that the government prohibited doctrineros from punishing Indians. When an Indian woman married, the doctrinero required her to work in his kitchen, arguing that he was performing a work of charity by giving her the chance to learn. In fact, the true gain was on the part of the doctrinero, who gained a house worker in addition to the 6 or 7 pesos he charged the couple for the wedding he performed. The abuse was so great that in 1675 the royal inspector Don Benito de Novoa Salgado reported the practice to the king, calling it deplorable and alluding to other sinful things done to Indian women, which he did not dare to mention "in order not to offend Your Majesty's ears" (Fernández, 1889: 274).

A 1715 document narrates the story of an orphaned Indian woman named Dominga Liberada de Moya, a faithful parishioner of Ujarrás. In disregard of the law, Governor Lacayo de Briones had taken her from Ujarrás and put her under guardianship at the house of Sergeant Major Don Francisco de la Madriz Linares. When an ecclesiastic judge requested her return, the governor informed him that he would return her to Ujarrás only to marry her off. When he ordered a surgeon and a midwife to examine her, they both declared she was too weak from general maltreatment to be married. Such documents reveal the humiliations women suffered at the time (CD, 1985, no. 18: 49).

Not all pain was inflicted by strangers, however. Aggression within marriage was common, as evidenced by the number of times women cited mistreatment by their spouses as their reason for requesting a divorce. In many cases, women and children were abandoned if the husband could produce evidence of a previous marriage or other information that could serve to annul the marriage.

Women and Social Status

Seventeen of the Metropolitan Curia documents relate to women and social status. Most of them refer to women of a privileged class, within the framework of a colonial society that was not prosperous but was markedly patriarchal. Recovering information about the status of indigenous, mestizo, black, or slave women is more difficult.

During the colonial period, women related to the Spanish Crown were treated as if they were mythical figures. Celebrations of great solemnity honored such occasions as births, weddings of infantas, and pregnancies of the queen. Some of these near-mythical figures became models of womanhood for pious matrons of the upper class, who with their outstanding virtues counteracted the alternative model of women whose scandalous lives were highly visible—the "libertines and insolent ones," the lovers or protegées of governors or captains.

However, these high-status women also show up in archival records of legal controversies—altercations with priests, charges of slander or expropriation of goods, or other offenses. Thus, Doña Manuela Fernández de la Pastora, a lady from Cartago, was excommunicated for having "slapped a priest" who obstructed her view of the bulls at a bullfight (Blanco Segura, 1967: 202–03).

Domestic servants, slaves (most often mulatto or mestizo women), and Indians comprised the lowest social status. Their only option for moving up the social scale was marriage with masters or gentlemen or, in exceptional cases, receiving a dowry from a cofradía. The oldest documentation of such a marriage dates to 1720. It refers to the marriage of Diego de la Cruz, a mulatto, widower, and mail courier between Costa Rica and Guatemala, and Josefa Cabral, a mulatto slave owned by a lady in the colonial capital of Cartago. Women slave holders, like men slave holders, bought and sold their bondspeople. Slavery was institutionalized in Costa Rican society, and we can only assume that the life of women slaves was particularly hard. A black slave woman in the mid 1600s was sold for 280 pesos, "a little mulatto boy of a year and a half for 150 pesos" (CD, 1986, no. 22: 24).

Servitude existed particularly in the *doctrinas* (missions), as "doctrineros had to have in their service a cook, a tortilla maker, and a servant. The Indians had to give them minimally 30 fanegas [a cubic measure] of corn per year, a chicken every day, two reales [real=25 céntimos] of beef per week, and four reales of cacao. For feast days they had to give two pounds of fish and one or two reales of eggs and a botija [earthenware pitcher] of honey and another of fat every six months" (Blanco Segura, 1967: 140). Obviously, all Indians suffered grave exploitation, but Indian women even more so.

Some Indian women succeeded, though, in resisting colonial and religious intolerance. Consider the case of the four *picaronas zambas* (a black-Indian racial mix), the famous "Crafty Zambo Women," who were kidnapped in 1761 and taken before the priest in Esparza. Although he interrogated them about their people, he was unable to learn anything. He forced them to guide an expedition to the Guatuso Indians, and for eleven days the four crafty women led the priests astray, traveling on unknown paths without ever showing them the location of their villages (Blanco Segura, 1967: 199–200).

Conclusion

The unedited documents in the Metropolitan Curia of San José contain information that reveals the contours of the daily life of the women of colonial Costa Rica. These documents illustrate the fusion of the three patriarchal systems of the Spanish crown, the Spanish Catholic Church, and the autochthonous indigenous cultures. For these women, religion functioned as a weapon of conquest.

Like the documents themselves, the women of colonial Costa Rica have been quietly hidden from our view for a very long time. Now, however, the archives are introducing us to many different types of women. Some were active, enterprising, assertive, creative, and diligent in their enterprises. Others were despised, offended, and submerged in an ignominious anonymity. Many constantly rebelled against the yoke of patriarchal structures. One thing, however, is clear: In no way were they the demure and listless figures that commonly appear in illustrations of the time. They were strong, persevering, and intelligent human beings.

The lives and economic activities of all these colonial women centered around two great institutions, the church and matrimony, which controlled not only the women themselves but also the cultural, economic, and political development of their society. Much of the progress of this society seems to have been based on the riches and the daily labor of their women, who often were persuaded by their religious and familial beliefs to act against their own best interests.

The events reported in the archives—the anecdotes and even the silences—document violence against women. The very laws that were presumably dictated by intentions to protect them resulted in aggression against women's dignity and rights and constituted an instrument of manipulation of women's consciences and aspirations. At the same time, however, the events recorded in the archives show another facet of Costa Rican history. These records document the contribution of women to colonial values and daily life and to the struggles for justice and the construction of a more humane world.

Endnote

1. Ecclesiastic documents concerning colonial Costa Rica's religious and political affairs are kept in the Vatican; in Spain; in León, Nicaragua, the center of the archdiocese to which colonial Costa Rica belonged; and in Costa Rica itself. The San José documents underlying this study, stored in thirty-eight large boxes, are still mostly unexplored. Some were translated from the old Spanish by Bernardo Augusto Thiel, bishop of Costa Rica from 1880–1901, and were published in 1896, 1897, and 1898. Others were translated by historian Ricardo Blanco Segura and published in 1967. Some were indexed by the Facultad de Filosofía y Letras (School of Philosophy and Arts) of the Universidad Nacional in 1985–86.

Biodata

Cora Ferro Calabrese, born in Argentina and a naturalized Costa Rican, was one of the principal founders and the first director of the Instituto de Estudios de la Mujer (IEM) (Institute for Women's Studies); formerly the Centro Interdisciplinario de Estudios de la Mujer (CIEM) (Center for Interdisciplinary Women's Studies) at the Universidad Nacional (UNA) where she has been deputy director since mid-1993. Her academic work focuses on women's studies, ranging from comprehensive research to participatory work with women's groups. She was coordinator for the Comisión Nacional de Esperanza Solidaria (National Commission of Solidary Hope), an interdenominational organization which supported the work of the Consejo Latinoamericano de Iglesias (Latin American Council of Churches) on social service projects.

At IEM she participated in developing the Casa de la Mujer (Women's House) for outreach to women in the community, and in creating the journal *Casa de la Mujer*. She serves on its editorial board and as a contributor. She also wrote "Mujeres indias hacen teología" (Indian women do theology), which appeared in July 1994 in that journal, and "Mujeres en la Colonia. Entre la vida y la ley" (Women in the colony. Between life and law), which appeared in the *Revista de Ciencias Sociales* of the Instituto de Ciencias Sociales of the UCR. At the Congress on Women and Violence held in San José in 1993, she presented the study "La cara oculta de la crisis" (The hidden face of the crisis).

With Ana María Quirós Rojas, Ferro published *Mujer, realidad religiosa y comunicación* (Women, religious reality, and communication—originally published in 1988, second revised edition in 1993); and "Derechas y humanas: Confrontando un mito impostor" (Upright and human: Women face a deceitful myth), *Casa de la Mujer* 4 (December 1993).

Ana María Quirós Rojas, also a Costa Rican, has worked as coauthor with Cora Ferro on research for numerous publications and is currently completing her Ph.D in education with a dissertation on adult education and women. She has worked in consciousness raising and education among working-class women and is associated with the extension service for research of the Universidad Nacional, as well as in the Proyecto EduMujer (Women's Education Project), training women in technical high schools throughout the entire country in nontraditional occupations, under the joint sponsorship of the Costa Rican Ministerio de Educación Pública (MEP) (Ministry of Education) and the Organización Internacional de Trabajo (OIT) (International Labor Organization). She is a member of the Red Latinoamericana de Mujeres (Latin American Women's Network), a regionwide information exchange organization connecting individual women.

References

Archivo Eclesiástico (AE). n.d. Cajas nos. 1–38. San José: Curia Metropolitana.

Blanco Segura, Ricardo. 1967. *Historia eclesiástica de Costa Rica*. San José: Editorial Costa Rica.

Centro de Documentación de la Facultad de Filosofía y Letras (CD). 1985, 1988. *Boletín*, nos. 18, 22, 23, and unedited. Heredia: Universidad Nacional.

Dussel, Enrique. 1983. *Historia general de la iglesia en América Latina*. Pt. 1, vol. 1. Salamanca: Sígueme.

Fernández, León. 1889. *Historia de Costa Rica durante la dominación española 1502– 1821*. Madrid: Tipografía de Manuel Ginés Hernández, Impresa de la Casa Real.

Ferro, Cora, and Ana María Quirós. 1992. "Mujeres en la colonia. La historia leída desde la perspectiva de las mujeres." Mimeo. Heredia: IEM.

MacLeod, Murdo. 1973. *Spanish Central America. A Socioeconomical History, 1520–1720*. Berkeley: University of California Press. Trans. Luis Guillermo Solís, 1980.

Monge Alfaro, Carlos. 1976. *Historia de Costa Rica*. 14th ed. San José: Libr. Trejos.

Thiel, Bernardo Augusto. 1896, 1897, 1898. "Datos cronológicos para la historia eclesiástica de Costa Rica." *El mensajero del clero [San José]* 9 (1896; nos. 99–100); 10 (1897; nos. 102, 104, 105–07, 109, and 112); 11 (1898; nos. 117–20).

7 ✸ Contradictory Aspects
of Costa Rican Women's History
During the Nineteenth Century

Clotilde Obregón Quesada

In Costa Rica, as in many parts of the world, the role women played and the varied contributions they made to the nation's development during the nineteenth century have gone relatively unnoticed. However, the Costa Rican Archivo Nacional in San José contains extensive documentation that opens a window allowing a look at women's activities.

After briefly introducing the reader to nineteenth-century Costa Rica, I will show that although women's legal status was declining, their educational and economic activities were not only considerable but were even improving toward the end of the nineteenth century. Of course, the archives reflect a limited sample; they record primarily the activities of women who owned or were associated with certain resources. It is worth keeping in mind, though, that nineteenth-century Costa Rica was both relatively homogeneous and basically poor.

Historical Circumstances of Costa Rican Society

To understand women's role in Costa Rica, one must understand that Costa Rica differed from other Latin American regions. Toward the end of the eighteenth century, Costa Rica was characterized by relative political autonomy because of three factors: its distance from power centers; a small population, so that the society lacked an adequate labor force; and few cities. Farm people did not begin to move into towns in Costa Rica until the eighteenth century, when three new towns appeared in the western Valle Central (Central Valley) (Obregón Q., 1989: 179). During that time, civil and ecclesiastic authorities in the colonial capital of Cartago had encouraged the inhabitants of the Aserrí region to concentrate in towns, to facilitate government services. In response, the people of Aserrí founded the Villa de Bocas del Monte, under the protection of the patriarch of San José, today's capital. Though the decision had been imposed by outsiders, they began to take advantage of the unity town life brought, and they soon aspired to power and leadership in the province of Costa Rica.

Besides their unity of purpose, the Josefinos—the citizens of San José—had the economic resources to achieve their goal. They cultivated sugar cane and grains, and they traded cattle with the Pacific coast region of Esparza, Las Cañas, and Bagaces. That area was part of the district of Nicoya, which was administratively connected to Nicaragua. However, it earlier had been Costa Rican, and the cattle trade and tobacco cultivation kept it closely tied to Costa Rica. After 1805, tobacco cultivation depended upon the tobacco warehouse in San José (ANCR, no. 496). The economic ties would result in the annexation of the Nicoya district by Costa Rica on July 25, 1824 (Sibaja, 1978).

In 1821, Costa Rica became independent. Those who pushed for independence worked out an interim pact, the Pacto Social Interino del Estado de Costa Rica (Interim Social Pact of the State of Costa Rica), which was a system of governance that retained the Spanish constitution and legal codes. The country thereby began the new age in a constitutional setting. The inhabitants of San José took on the leadership in working out the Pacto Social, and in 1823 San José replaced Cartago as the capital (Obregón L., 1969).

In 1824, Costa Rica became part of the República de Centro América but remained autonomous and sovereign within that federation, as established by the 1825 Constitution of Costa Rica. Shortly thereafter, in 1827, in an early Costa Rican initiative in the Central American peace process, the Costa Rican government sent a peace mission to El Salvador. It also established the administrative institutions and practices of a constitutional government, which it would retain (Obregón L., 1974). Moreover, this period marked the beginning of coffee cultivation, through which Costa Rica established markets in Europe and the United States (Obregón Q., 1982).

The Federal Republic of Central America broke apart in 1838, and efforts to reestablish it failed. A difficult period in international relations followed. Costa Rica's strategic position on an isthmus between the world's major oceans, where canal construction was feasible, became a constant factor in its political and economic affairs. In the border region with Nicaragua along Lake Nicaragua and the San Juan River, Great Britain, the leading power of the time in the Caribbean and Central American region, faced a newly arising rival, the United States.

After 1854, aggressive U.S. policies provoked war. In 1856–57 Costa Rica faced the invading army of William Walker, who controlled Nicaragua and wanted to convert Central America into a territory with slavery, as a key port for international trade through an interoceanic canal. Costa Rica destroyed Walker's army at Santa Rosa in the Pacific Northwest and, in a beautifully executed maneuver, gained control of the San Juan River and its fortifications. Walker could no longer receive men and arms from the United States, even though the U.S. government had ignored Central American complaints and closed its eyes to shipments from New York and New Orleans in support of Walker (Obregón L., 1956).

Costa Rica's triumph saved the country but left it economically in ruins. The United States demanded damages for supposed destruction of U.S. properties. The payments were unfair: Costa Rica had not been the aggressor, it had merely defended itself. However, the obligation to pay reflected the new U.S.-British alliance in the Caribbean. The British would not oppose the United States, provided the latter fulfilled the conditions of the 1850 Clayton-Bulwer Treaty, which allowed Great Britain's presence on the Central American mainland. Thus, when in 1859 Belize became a British colony, which violated the Monroe doctrine, the fact was widely hailed in both countries (Rodríguez, 1964).

As a result of the war, Costa Rican plans for schools for males and females, for a university, and for an increase in musical education were partially paralyzed. The country could not return to these plans until the 1860s and after, when it founded several institutions. In the meantime, Costa Rica strengthened its political parties and the electoral system and modernized public services of water and electricity. In 1884, San José became the second city in the Americas to have electric lights. (Boston was the first.) In the 1870s, Costa Rica also built a railway to the Atlantic (Stone, 1976).

Meanwhile, economic dependence upon monoculture grew with the extension of banana plantations at the Atlantic coast. Early in the twentieth century, bananas, which originally had been a complementary crop, would compete with coffee as Costa Rica's principal export product.

Against this background of the political and economic development of Costa Rica in the nineteenth century let us now picture the contradictory aspects of women's lives.

The Deterioration of Women's Legal Situation

To a certain extent, studying the lives of nineteenth-century women is easy in Costa Rica because women retained their maiden name in marriage and, from the eighteenth century on, children carried both their mother's last name and their father's. This custom has permitted Latin American women to retain their identity and to avoid the trauma of being legally obligated to use the husband's name.

Moreover, along with the rest of Spanish America, Costa Rica inherited Spanish laws that clearly established women's dowry and inheritance, and their right to represent their husbands and to emancipate their children (i.e., to declare them legally of age). In fact, early Costa Rican laws protected women and allowed them to defend themselves, though they did not give them political equality. Thus, in the early 1800s we still find such cases as that of Concepción Palacios, who was authorized to manage the family's possessions because of her husband's bad behavior and despite his unsuccessful protests. Her husband had legally pledged the following: "Don Luis Castillo obligates himself to his wife, Doña Concepción Palacios, not to drink any more, and should he fail to live up to this commitment, gives her the right to divorce him or separate herself from him, for a time as may be convenient to her. He obligates himself in addition to help her with what he earns and not to give her any reason to suspect infidelity" (IPSJ, 1, 1750–1835).

As the nineteenth century progressed, however, French laws penetrated Latin America (Sáenz C., 1987); liberal politicians introduced the changes in their search for highly respected European "progress." One consequence of the change was that women lost their status, above all in family law. Toward the end of the century, women could, for example, be accused of infidelity and punished by being sent to prison, whereas husbands could be unfaithful for a period of up to a year before a woman could sue. Women's inequality grew in the 1880s but was hidden behind their relative equality in education. Despite women's advances in education, the legal status of Costa Rican women during the nineteenth century experienced a downward trend.

Advances in Women's Education

As the Josefinos prospered economically, they invested in education, hiring teachers to educate their children. With education came change, and it affected the position of women. In the still somewhat rural setting, distant from the urban customs of Cartago, San José women acted in less traditional ways. For example, they went out alone with young men, sitting behind the riders on their horses, something that seemed inappropriate to many foreign travelers who later visited the country (Marr, 1929). This and other customs would change during the nineteenth century.

Educational development in Costa Rica began with the founding of La Casa de Enseñanza de Santo Tomás (Santo Tomás high school), a secondary school that had been maintained since 1814 by private citizens in San José. In 1824, the first chief of state, Juan Mora Fernández, a teacher, made Santo Tomás a government-supported school. Both Santo Tomás secondary school and the Universidad de Santo Tomás (founded in 1843) educated only men; nevertheless, as men's education changed, so did the education of women (González V., 1989). In fact, women in Costa Rica advanced more than women in other Latin American countries.

At first, women's education was in the hands of private teachers, who were paid by the parents. Hence the educational level of the parent generation in part determined the decision to educate the child. After 1831, the state began to take an interest in women's education. In 1841, the government of Braulio Carrillo founded the first girls' high school, the Liceo de Niñas. Under Vicenta Baltodano's directorship, this girls' high school provided basic education in reading, writing, drawing, sewing, and embroidery. Parents insisted that an adult accompany the girls to the school, which was located next to the Santo Tomás university. It is interesting to note that the salaries of the director of the boys' school and of the directora of the girls' school were the same (Obregón Q., 1989).

The girls' high school received a warm reception from San José parents. It also awakened the desire for a more complete education for girls. In 1847, President José María Castro founded by decree an academically more ambitious girls' high school, which would teach reading, writing, accounting, religion, morals and virtue, urbanity, geography and history, world and natural history, physics, music, drawing, Spanish, French, and Italian. This new school functioned for a number of years, and during that time newspapers reported on the teaching and the speeches the young women gave at graduation. Education for women reached other cities, too; schools were established in Alajuela, Cartago, and Heredia during this period (Obregón Q., 1984).

A bill prepared by President Castro to expand primary education became law in 1869 under his successor, the physician Jesús Jiménez. The state declared primary education free and obligatory. This further widened educational opportunities for girls, even though their education still took place in private schools in the more important cities, at least until the 1885–86 Educational Reform. This reform brought a graded kindergarten-to-secondary-school educational system, with established curricula, and local education councils taking care of school buildings (González F., 1961).

More and more girls gained access to education. Rural communities established *escuelas mixtas,* public coeducational primary schools, obtained teaching materials from school supply stores, and created school libraries. The Colegio Superior de Señoritas, a girls' high school, was founded and included a normal school (i.e., a teacher-training program). This offered women the opportunity of acquiring a secondary education and becoming teachers. Moreover, a private secondary school, the Colegio de Nuestra Señora de Sión, existed, as well as numerous schools that taught young women music, languages, and painting. Thus, in terms of education, women advanced during the nineteenth century (Pacheco, 1971).

Women's Economic Activities

Women's economic activities in the nineteenth century were varied and more important than has generally been acknowledged. Early in the century, five women owned cattle ranches in the zones of Esparza, Las Cañas, and Bagaces. Among them was Filiberta Recio, who in 1810 still managed her ranch at the age of ninety-five (ANCR, no. 1390). In the Central Valley, women took an interest in agriculture, buying and selling coffee plantations or purchasing land from the government for growing coffee.

The women engaged in these activities belonged to the upper social strata; they had to plant coffee and cultivate it for five years before it produced any income. The 1848 list of coffee plantation owners shows that some were widows who, after their husbands' death, continued at the helm of coffee plantations that belonged to them either through dowry or inheritance from their husbands. Four such women were Dolores Oreamuno, Ana María Porras, Jerónima Fernández, and Jacinta Morales (IPSJ, 1, 1750–1835). Others were single or married women who owned capital, such as the Arlequí sisters, Feliciana Sáenz Ulloa, María Echavarría, Pilar Bonilla Navas, Joaquina V. Carrillo Valverde, Rafaela Carrillo Morales, and Trinidad Gutiérrez Peñamonge (IPSJ, 1, 1750–1835).

The capacity to manage their own capital allowed some women to form a true economic partnership with their husbands, with equal administrative functions and rights. Some partnerships comprised various economic activities. That of Camilo Mora and Ana Benito Porras handled real estate transactions and money lending; Nicolás Castro and Juana Ramírez were active in real estate transactions and cattle raising. Pilar Bonilla Navas maintained her economic activities separately from those of her husband, Manuel Mora F., as did Jerónima Fernández, who managed her own haciendas for decades until her death (IPSJ, 2, 1835–50).

Women also entered the tobacco and liquor business. The production and sale of liquor and tobacco had been state monopolies under the Spanish government, a practice the Costa Rican government continued. Licenses were sold at public auction, and many women, represented by men, obtained liquor and tobacco licenses. Women of well-known families often entered business to solve economic problems; Ana Fernández, for example, ran a tobacco store in San José after her father's death (IPSJ, 1, 1750–1835).

Numerous women are recorded in activities related to state-licensed liquor stores from the first decade of the century on. They participated in auctions throughout the country, from Guanacaste along the Pacific coast to the Central Valley. Their activity became important after the war against Walker's Filibusters in 1856–57. The returning troops brought with them a devastating cholera epidemic, in which more than six thousand people died—10 percent of the total population. Women whose husbands were in the war, or who had been widowed or had lost their fathers, took over the liquor stores the male family head had managed. In 1860, 75 out of 126 (nearly 60%) of the state-licensed liquor stores were in women's hands. A report requested by the general superintendent during the war stated the administrators had not made any mistakes, that "even the widows did very well" (Kierszenzon, 1983: 92). So did women who authorized sons or other relatives to participate in auctions for tobacco or liquor licenses or who claimed their inheritance or took over when their mothers married a second time. Some, like Rosario Fernández, became guardians of a husband who had been declared mentally incapacitated (IPSJ, 1, 1750–1835).

Still other women were traders during this period. An interesting case is that of Andrea Venegas of Puntarenas; she managed a liquor store, owned a department store, and in 1845 imported flour, plums, and raisins from Liverpool. Some women had stores in the Central Valley. Records of these women still exist because then, as now, owners had to pay fees to the municipality (ANCR, GM, no. 10971). Others catered for banquets, or prepared cakes for festivities or table decorations for important occasions, such as the banquets offered to the victorious troops of the 1856–57 war (Kierszenzon, 1983).

Conclusion

Although this account considers only women's legal status, education, and economic activities in the nineteenth century, we can draw some conclusions. First, documents do exist for reconstructing women's history. Furthermore, it is clear that "progressive" French legal patterns caused women to lose status, power over their own affairs, and protection during the nineteenth century. However, efforts to improve women's education grew, particularly after the 1856–57 war. In fact, women's education after 1888 would have permitted them active participation in the country's development, if they had had legal equality. Nonetheless, it at least provided a base for women's success in education in the twentieth century, when as members of the Educators' Association they would demonstrate publicly for their political rights. Finally, Costa Rican women's actions during war did not differ from those of women in other countries. In men's absence, women were responsible heads of family, both morally and economically.

In sum, the nineteenth century gave Costa Rican women advances and professional opportunities in education and a notable participation in economic activities. But it also was a time of decline in their legal status, when they had little if any political power. Obtaining at least the basic rights of citizenship would have to wait until the middle of the following century.

Biodata

Clotilde Obregón Quesada, a Costa Rican, holds a master's degree in history from the Universidad de Costa Rica. Her research focuses on Costa Rica and Central America. She has published numerous articles and three books: *Costa Rica: Relaciones exteriores de una república en formación* (1984), *Carrillo, una época y un hombre* (1989), and *El Río San Juan en la lucha de las potencias, 1821–1860* (1993). Her study on Carrillo won the Aquileo J. Echevarría National History Prize in 1989. She also received the Cleto González Víquez Award in History, bestowed by the Academia de Geografía e Historia de Costa Rica (Costa Rican Academy of Geography and History). In 1989–91 she chaired the History Department at the Universidad de Costa Rica. From 1990 to 1992 she was president of the administrative council of the Museo Nacional de Costa Rica (National Museum of Costa Rica) and is currently director of the Biblioteca Nacional (National Library) in Costa Rica.

References

Archivo Nacional de Costa Rica (ANCR). San José. Document nos. 496, 1390.
——. Guerra y Marina (GM). Document no. 10971.
González Flores, Luis Felipe. 1961. *Historia de la educación en Costa Rica*. Vol. 2. San José: Ministerio de Educación Pública.
González Villalobos, Paulino. 1989. *La Universidad de Santo Tomás*. San José: Editorial Universidad de Costa Rica.
Indice de los Protocolos de San José (IPSJ). Vols. 1 (1750–1835) and 2 (1835–50).
Kierszenzon, Frida. 1983. "El monopolio de licores en Costa Rica." Tesis de Grado, Universidad de Costa Rica.
Marr, Wilhelm. 1929. "Viaje a Centro América." In *Costa Rica en el siglo XIX*, ed. Ricardo Fernández Guardia, pp. 103–220. San José: Editorial Gutenberg.

Obregón Loría, Rafael. 1956. *La campaña del tránsito*. San José: Editorial Universidad de Costa Rica.

——. 1969. *Nuestra historia patria. Los primeros días de Independencia*. San José: Editorial Universidad de Costa Rica.

——. 1974. *Costa Rica en la federación*. San José: Editorial Costa Rica.

Obregón Quesada, Clotilde. 1982. "Inicio del comercio británico en Costa Rica." *Revista de ciencias sociales*, 24 (October): 59–69.

——. 1984. *Relaciones exteriores de una república en formación*. San José: Editorial Costa Rica.

——. 1989. *Carrillo, una época y un hombre*. San José: Editorial Costa Rica.

——. 1993. *El Río San Juan en la lucha de las potencias*. San José: Editorial UNED.

Pacheco, León. 1971. *Mauro Fernández*. San José: Ministerio de Cultura, Juventud y Deportes.

Rodríguez, Mario. 1964. *A Palmerstonian Diplomat in Central America: Frederick Chatfield*. Tucson, Ariz.: The University of Arizona Press.

Sáenz Carbonell, Jorge. 1987. *El despertar constitucional de Costa Rica*. San José: Editorial Libro Libre.

Sibaja, Luis Fernando. 1978. *Nuestro límite con Nicaragua*. San José: Editorial Don Bosco.

Stone, Samuel. 1976. *La dinastía de los conquistadores*. San José: Editorial Universitaria Centroamericana.

8 ❋ The Suffragist Movement in Costa Rica, 1889–1949

Centennial of Democracy?

Sara Sharratt

On November 7, 1989, Costa Rica celebrated the Centennial of Democracy, commemorating an 1889 uprising of citizens against the threat of fraudulent elections. José Joaquín Trejos, president of Costa Rica (1966–70), called the 1889 uprising a demonstration of "citizens, mostly campesinos, who gathered . . . carrying sticks and machetes, firm in their insistence that the will of the people be respected" (Trejos, 1989: 15a). The 1889 demonstration produced results: The outgoing president promised free elections, and the clearly favored candidate easily won the election.

Trejos supported this 1989 commemoration but strongly protested the notion that it signaled the *birth* of Costa Rican democracy. I agree, but for different reasons: Proclaiming 1989 as a centennial obscures the fact that by that year women had had the right to vote for only forty years. It also fails to consider the role women played in the fight for democracy and their struggle for women's political rights. Moreover, between independence in 1821 and women's enfranchisement in 1949, Costa Rica experienced periods of dictatorial rule and fraudulent elections, and not even men themselves were all equal.

These facts then beg the question of what our patriarchs call democratic rule. For sixty of the hundred years in the supposed centennial, women were not even considered citizens, as historian Fernando Volio confirmed when he proclaimed proudly: "For a long time, the right to vote, the right to political representation and to the practice of liberal theory have been *inherent attributes* of each one of our citizens who identify the above with the democracy which places us among civilized nations" (cited in Víquez, 1978: 13; emphasis added; the word *ciudadanos,* translated here as "citizens" is inherently masculine but neither explicitly includes nor represents women).

This study explores the unique characteristics of the suffragist movement

61

and its strategic struggle. Its intent is to dispel widely believed myths that women in Costa Rica were handed the vote on a silver platter. The study documents sixty years of courageous efforts by which women and a few sympathetic male supporters finally won for women the right to vote. While struggling for their political rights, women endured the contempt and ridicule of conservative and liberal patriarchs. Nevertheless, during those sixty years, women were deeply involved in all large grassroots movements aimed at preserving so-called democratic processes or ending wage discrimination against women teachers.

Women Under Costa Rican Patriarchy

To understand women's struggle during this period, one must first understand how three dominant institutions jointly and separately enforced and rationalized women's lack of political rights. Those institutions are the legal system, represented by all Costa Rican constitutions from 1821 to 1949; the educational system; and the Catholic Church.

Women and the Constitutions

Costa Rican democracy is a product of evolutionary change in the rules of political participation after independence. Between 1821 and 1949, eighteen different Costa Rican constitutional documents were drawn up, partly as a result of internal political unrest as one government replaced another.

Costa Rica was granted independence from Spain on September 15, 1821, a fact Costa Ricans did not learn until October 12, 1821. As the poorest, most isolated province in its region, Costa Rica had remained untarnished by political struggles. Indeed, its existence had been "duly ignored" by the empire, probably because its "wealth consisted of some cacao for domestic use which also served as currency, and tobacco of very poor quality which constituted, at times, the only export product" (Víquez, 1978: 20–21).

In the beginning, independence produced internal strife. Except for a brief period in which Costa Rica was part of a regional federation, the República Federal de Centro América (Federal Republic of Central America), it remained unaligned, seeking potential alliances with other provinces in the region. Not until 1848 did Costa Rica become a fully independent republic (Víquez, 1978: 95). Between 1824 and 1890, twenty-five governments held power. Seven took it by force, six were interim governments, and eleven were elected in uncontested elections. Only one made it to power with a campaign deserving the name of a true political battle (Vega, 1982: 90).

In its attempt to define the people who would be eligible to elect governments, Costa Rica at first chose indirect voting; electors would be selected—using criteria of personal wealth, morals, and education—by means of successive popular balloting based on territorial voting districts. This process required several stages, which invited corruption, intimidation, and fraud. Indirect voting was practiced until 1913, except for one direct election in 1844 (Vega, 1982: 88).

During this period, "democracy," exemplified by the right to vote and to be elected to office, was the domain of the male oligarchy. Costa Rican patriarchal thinking prevalent throughout most of this time is best assessed by viewing constitutional documents in terms of the way they defined three important terms: *Costa Rican, citizen,* and *voting citizen* (CA, 1946).

Before 1848, a critical distinction was made in constitutional documents between a citizen and a voting citizen. *Voting citizens* were defined in 1824 as all inhabitants, native born or naturalized, who were eighteen years of age, had an honest job or profession, and could exercise their rights (i.e., were not mentally incompetent or criminals) (CA, 1946). Note that this definition does not exclude women. (Even though women did not vote until 1950, they were not *explicitly* denied the right to vote until 1848; that right was again denied in 1917.)

By 1841, a voting citizen had to be twenty-one years old (twenty, if an educator or head of household); own a house *and* have property, capital, or an "industry"; and be self-supporting. To be elected to office, a voting citizen had to own a certain amount of capital; the amount varied with the importance of the office (CA, 1946: 90–93). Clearly, women were not the only Costa Ricans excluded by these criteria; uneducated or poor men could not be voting citizens either. As José Luis Vega (1982: 91) noted, these requirements left out about 80 to 90 percent of all citizens during the nineteenth century.

To illustrate: As late as 1884, the illiteracy rate in Costa Rica was 87 percent (Fallas and Silva, 1985: 114). By 1892, it was 80 percent in the country and 61 percent in the capital and main centers of provinces (Vega, 1982: 92). The 1927 census showed a total population of 471,524, of whom 47.3 percent were literate individuals above the age of nine. An additional 1 percent was semiliterate, and 23.6 percent were illiterate (Barahona, 1986, Annex 2: 52). The remaining 28.1 percent were under age nine. These figures make it clear that a significant number of poor males could not act in agreement with their "inherent attribute"—maleness—and exercise their citizenship. Consistent with prior practices, potential elected officials had to have a certain amount of capital to be elected to office.

In 1848, women were *explicitly* excluded from voting when a *citizen* was defined as a male, age twenty-one or over. This criterion was in force until 1859, when the word *male* was deleted and the voting age was lowered to twenty. The constitutions of 1859, 1869, and 1871 were identical on this point. To be a voting citizen, a person had to own property or have an honest job and had to know how to read and write. Only patriarchal interpretation decided that women were excluded from the above definition. The 1917 Constitution, twenty-eight years into our celebrated century of democratic rule, *specifically* excluded women, for the second time, from the definition of citizen and thus of voting citizen. In 1919 the 1917 Constitution was revoked, and the 1871 Constitution reestablished previous criteria for citizen and voting citizen, which were in force until 1949.

Of course, the right to vote was only one of many expressions of the patriarchal nature of Costa Rican society which considered women incompetent and in need of protection. In 1841, for example, a man's citizenship could be suspended if he abandoned his wife and children or failed to live up to his responsibilities toward them (CA, 1946: 91). Variations on this theme were maintained in 1847 and 1848; in 1869, however, it became a crime if a male was ungrateful to his parents, but not if he deserted his wife and children. Then by 1871, in addition to *explicitly* limiting women's political rights, Costa Rican patriarchs also eliminated sanctions against husbands' and fathers' irresponsible behavior, thus stripping women of the power to redress grievances. The situation became absurd in the 1917 Constitution, which required that if a foreign-born woman gave birth to an illegitimate child and the Costa Rican father of the child refused to acknowledge paternity, the mother would have to abandon the infant so that he or she could become a Costa Rican citizen (CA, 1946: 235).

Similarly, a Costa Rican woman who married a foreigner automatically became a citizen of the husband's country and lost her Costa Rican citizenship. She could remain Costa Rican only if she "was unable to receive her husband's citizenship" (CA, 1946: 233). Even today, a wife cannot grant her husband the right of citizenship, although a Costa Rican man can grant this right to a woman. This discriminatory clause (dating from 1841) constituted one of the arguments against granting women the right to vote, and it was taken as evidence that the patriarchs saw women as subordinate to men. Nobody ever suggested declaring this criterion unconstitutional, even though all Costa Rican constitutions since 1825 have claimed that "all Costa Ricans are equal under the law" (CA, 1946: 53). Cleto González Víquez, a leading liberal and twice-elected president of Costa Rica in the twentieth century, commented that voting was restricted only "by age, marital status, personal wealth, private and public morality" (Víquez, 1978: 75). And gender? It did not even occur to him to consider gender, nor did it occur to other liberals of his time.

As women lobbied and struggled for the vote, they assumed their civil rights were the same as those held by men. This was not the case, and it still is not, especially for married women. Under the 1844 Civil Code, for example, a married woman could not exercise the *patria potestad* (right of parental authority). After 1888, she could exercise it only when her husband was absent (Odio, 1989). In 1888, civil marriages and divorce proceedings were first instituted, as well as a woman's right to make a will and to enjoy identical civil rights (Fallas and Silva, 1985: 152–53). In 1888, women were also granted the right of *tutela* (guardianship). Yet, the male remained the head of the household, and a wife could not leave the country or sign contractual agreements without her husband's consent. These restrictions did not apply to single women. Thus, when a woman married, she lost her ability to make legally binding decisions. As Elizabeth Odio, twice minister of justice (1978–82, 1992–94), has stated, "The law treated married women as mental incompetents" (1989). Only in 1973 did the new Family Code—which came into force in 1974—establish *near*-equality of civil and political rights for women independent of marital status.

Given this context, it is not surprising that women were barred from professional roles. Angela Acuña, Costa Rica's first woman lawyer and later a leading suffragist, had to appeal to the Legislative Assembly in 1916 for her right to exercise her profession; women of that time could not act as witnesses in legal documents or wills (Calvo, 1989a: 80–81). Acuña argued that acts such as being a witness constituted civil and not political rights. After endless debates, Acuña's request to practice as a lawyer was approved, but her petition to be a notary was denied. (All lawyers are notaries in Costa Rica, and until recently there was no feminine form of *notario* [notary public].) The role of notary was considered the exclusive right of a voting citizen, and women were not voting citizens. The clause that a notary had to be a voting citizen was finally removed in 1922.

The position of women in Costa Rica was underscored by their absence from the committees appointed for the celebration of the Centennial of Independence in 1921. The patriarchs did not nominate even one woman to the organizing committee. Angela Acuña, already well on her way to becoming the leader of the suffragist struggle, suggested the formation of a National Congress on Women, but that motion, too, was defeated (Calvo, 1989a: 97). It seemed understood, though never stated, that this particular centennial celebrated men's—not even all men's—independence from Spain. Perhaps it is not so illogical that Nobel Prize winner President Oscar Arias Sánchez in 1989 celebrated one hundred years of democracy and forty years of women's voting rights in Costa Rica.

In 1921, Angela Acuña turned to women's rights in full, to the extent possible for her and her contemporaries. Before that struggle for the vote can be understood, however, we must explore the role of the educational establishment and of the Catholic Church. These essential forces also actively blocked women from obtaining their political rights.

Women and Education

Throughout Costa Rica's history, a common argument against granting women their political rights was their lack of education. But at the same time, the patriarchal system was limiting women's access to educational opportunities, even though education is another of those "inherent" citizen's attributes in Costa Rican civic tradition, "one of the central concerns of our founding fathers. Governments are evaluated depending upon how much they support educational endeavors" (Volio in Víquez, 1978: 8). The slogan "Costa Rica has more teachers than soldiers" ('policemen' after the 1949 elimination of the military) is an integral aspect of Costa Rican cultural identity. But what about women?

The first Costa Rican primary school was founded in 1812; the first secondary school, La Casa de Enseñanza de Santo Tomás, in 1814; and the Universidad de Santo Tomás opened its doors in 1843 (Fallas and Silva, 1985: 51). But only in 1847—thirty-five years after the founding of the first school—was a woman's right to receive an education formally recognized: "Education is a right of all citizens" and, specifically, "Public instruction of *both sexes* will be uniform throughout the nation" (CA, 1946: 148, Art. 169, 170). (The "uniformity" issue is not true even today, if one considers that the home economics course is still taught to women students only [CMF, 1988, p. 34].) In 1858, education became compulsory for *both* males and females, and Article 6 of the 1869 Constitution stated, "Elementary education of both sexes is compulsory, free and subsidized by the State" (Alfaro and Ríos, 1984: 25).

But education, although compulsory for both genders, was not the same for men and women. The Liceo de Niñas (first Girls' High School in Costa Rica), a private girls' school begun informally in 1841, changed in 1847 into a legitimate secondary school to train women to become elementary school teachers and to teach other important skills (Sherman, 1984: 18). In 1856 the school closed, stating that "it had accomplished its goal" of training forty teachers. It re-opened in 1858, its curriculum changed from elementary education to "prepa-ration for home life," with an emphasis on domestic chores so that women could learn their duties as men's companions. They were "taught" how to be frugal, run a household, and change diapers (Fallas and Silva, 1985: 157–66). Public schools were few, located mainly in capitals and inaccessible to most girls, who were not allowed to walk long distances. In 1856, only three of seventy-one public educational institutions were for girls (Sherman, 1984: 18). In 1871, a new law instructed school officials to admit only one girl per house-hold and to determine on the spot which of the female children in the house-hold had most potential (Fallas and Silva, 1985: 16).

Women's right to education was reiterated in the major educational reform of 1886. The Colegio Superior de Señoritas (Girls' High School and Normal School), the oldest public secondary school for women, was inaugurated in 1888 as a four-year teacher-training institute. It taught calisthenics, home eco-nomics, sewing, drawing, and hygiene, as well as reading, writing, arithmetic, geography, history, and pedagogy (Chacón, 1984: 4). A 1902 reform added typing and secretarial skills. In 1903, the Colegio suffered its worst blow: It became a professional school to grant teaching and "business" degrees, a eu-phemism for secretarial work. The curriculum was reduced to three and two years respectively (Chacón, 1984: 6). Consequently, young women who wanted to pursue university studies had to enroll in the boys' secondary school during the last two years to earn the high-school diploma that would qualify them to attend the university. Only in 1934 was the Colegio recertified as a regular secondary school (Barahona, 1986: 83). Private schools could not grant a high-school diploma until 1941; before that date, private-school women students had to transfer to the public Colegio Superior de Señoritas (Chacón, 1984: 7) to fulfill university entrance requirements.

In their education as in their marital roles, women were not treated as citizens whose full potential should be developed. Rather, women's education was seen primarily as an efficacious way of training future wives, mothers, and educators of potential politicians (*El Mentor Costarricense*, 1844: 251). Consis-tent with this hardly logical perception, the subject of civics was dropped from their curriculum and replaced with sewing, embroidery, domestic science, and candy making (Fallas and Silva, 1985: 166).

This model of women's "civilizing function" continued throughout most of the twentieth century. Moreover, many Costa Ricans viewed any kind of education for women as dangerous and contrary to women's nature: "Not only will they cease to bear fruit, but they will also bring shame and dishonor to their loved ones. We cannot help, therefore, but feel pity for those who encourage women to partake in reform movements and reproach those women who forget that they will lose their modesty and their delicacy, which are the building blocks of domestic tranquility. It is in this sphere where their true influence on society can be manifested" (*El Mentor Costarricense,* 1846: 271).

But in the end, advocates of girls' education won. An 1887 magazine article encouraged parents to send girls to school, stating that although a woman could not equal a man's abilities and natural rights, they could reach his level in the areas of arts and letters (cited in Sherman, 1984: 18). Even this education was tailored to support patriarchal ideology: "If they are an essential part of our society, what reason is there for not spending 50 pesos on their education if one is already spending 100 pesos on a boy's education?" (*El Mentor Costarricense,* 1844: 252). Another "supporter," the editor of *La Enseñanza,* a boys'-school magazine, could not hide his contempt when he visited the best girls' secondary schools. "The Colegio de Sión [a religious private school founded in 1878] besides the *usual infantile opening speech* delivered by the principal, tested its pupils. I must admit the teachers worked incessantly and well. This was most evident in the fields of *arts and decoration*. I suggested that they be taught in Spanish [they were taught in French]," and "the Colegio Superior de Señoritas taught its students writing, reading, grammar, and history. I was pleased by the beauty of the calisthenics classes. Sewing skills were unsurpassable" (*La Enseñanza,* 1887: 351; emphasis added).

When women were not being impelled to develop their domestic skills, they were encouraged to become teachers. Patriarchal ideology held that "inside every woman there is a teacher" (Chacón, 1984: 17). It worked. In 1890, there were 322 male to 407 female teachers. In 1940, comparable figures were 611 to 2,047. In the mid 1980s, the proportion was one male teacher to every eleven female teachers (Chacón, 1984: 28). Women provided a source of cheap educational labor. But when it came to providing scholarships for advanced training, women were not given preference or even parity: "The government will subsidize ten Costa Rican youngsters (eight men, two women) to go to the United States and Europe to pursue advanced training. The males will be trained in engineering and natural sciences in general. The women will be trained in professional feminine arts" (*La Enseñanza,* January 1887: 320).

The Universidad de Santo Tomás closed in 1888. It was reestablished as

Universidad de Costa Rica in 1940, and since that time women's admissions have not been restricted. But even today, parity in education is far from a reality. Women are still graduating in traditional careers and they still face considerable discrimination in the availability of postgraduate and professional training. (For a complete analysis see García and Gomáriz, 1989). Thus, not only was women's lack of education used to deny them the right to vote, the whole educational system treated them as noncitizens.

In spite of their poor education, however, women fought constantly in Costa Rica's political battles, even when they were considered too uneducated to engage in politics. Clearly, something was amiss.

Women and the Church

The third important force preventing women from obtaining the right to vote was the Catholic Church, the institution of the country's official religion. Like the state, the church was interested in maintaining women's subordinate position in keeping with the "natural order" of the world (Zúñiga, 1985). Throughout Costa Rica's republican period, religious leaders affirmed that women's place was in the home: "It is necessary for humanity that there be a subordination of one sex under the other as this presents God's will. . . . There are two pulses of human life, freedom and obedience. If obedience is not exercised, freedom will degenerate into the whims and tyranny of the stronger one" (Ferro and Quirós, 1988: 53–54). According to this belief, women by nature needed male tutelage or society would face economic and spiritual decay.

The church played a significant political role in Costa Rica and was courted by all political parties. Cora Ferro and Ana María Quirós (1988: 48) note that during women's struggle for the vote the church:

1. Was conservative and in a constant struggle against Protestantism, communism, and modernism;
2. Was dominated by an elitist oligarchy;
3. Was concerned with ethical and moral dilemmas and devoid of any discussion of social political problems;
4. Showed a European influence that tended to romanticize life for women; and
5. Was masculinist and androcentric.

Needless to say, the church totally opposed women's enfranchisement. In 1958, many years after the vote was won, priests were still lamenting, "Today, husband and wife belong to different political parties. This creates conflict. It is no good for women to participate in politics. . . . The delicate femininity and dignity of wives and mothers demand that they stay away from politics" (Ferro and Quirós, 1988: 83). Thus, religion was a vital force in maintaining the status quo by instructing women to be submissive, compliant, and solicitous. This is still true today.

Sixty Years of Suffragist Struggle

The Costa Rican suffragist movement shared much with movements in Europe and the United States, but it also displayed unique characteristics. As had been the case in Europe and the United States, the women of Costa Rica struggled for years—sixty years, in fact—to win the vote (DMF, 1982: 5). But in Costa Rica, the women's rights movement lacked the grassroots support from masses of people that similar movements enjoyed in, for example, the United States. Frequently, Costa Rica's profound class differences and highly patriarchal Spanish Catholic heritage isolated women suffragists as leaders of small movements who divided their attention between class struggles and women's rights.

As in Latin America in general, the Costa Rican feminist movement was started by women who had struggled for their education and who often shared specific characteristics (Gross and Bingham, 1985: 8). Costa Rican women in the movement tended to have the following characteristics:

1. One parent was an immigrant of European background.
2. They had studied in Europe or in the United States.
3. They had participated in international women's organizations.
4. They had professional training as teachers or doctors and were self-supporting.
5. They were often from the middle class.

Angela Acuña exemplifies these women. Her mother was half German. Acuña had studied at a girls' private school in England and had attended suffragist meetings in England (Calvo 1989a: 51). Although Acuña was not a teacher, as were most Costa Rican suffragists, she was a professional woman—a lawyer—and she was from the middle class. And she typified the suffragists in another way. Many suffragists took pride in their good manners and attempted to be as nonconfrontational as possible toward the patriarchs of the time. This certainly was not the case in England. Yet, as Yadira Calvo reasons, Acuña's key to success was, without a doubt, the manner in which she tried to minimize the affront to those who held the obsolete beliefs of the time, though it certainly slowed down the conquest of women's political rights (1989a: 64).

The role of female teachers in the movement was more central in Costa Rica than in Europe or the United States. Teachers often belonged to the Liga Feminista (Feminist League) that Acuña had founded in 1923 (see Calvo, chap. 1 above) and to the Worker's party, and they therefore endured the divided nature of the struggle. Yet, Costa Rican feminist groups created less political pressure around the vote than around other causes. Women often led protests in grassroots movements that were not concerned primarily with women's political rights. In fact, women never staged large protest demonstrations to gain their political rights. In patriarchal Costa Rica a deviation from pre-scribed roles was severely punished. Consequently, attacks on brave women who dared demand the vote were particularly vicious.

What Costa Rica's suffragist movement did share with almost all other women's movements in the world, however, was male opposition and the arguments men used to support that opposition.

Increasing Intensity over Fifty Years, 1889–1940

The struggle for women's political rights in Costa Rica became evident in 1889 when, for the first time, women's rights became an issue for an incoming president. After the election, newly elected President José Joaquín Rodríguez acknowledged women's participation in the November 7, 1889, uprising and endorsed their right to vote, the first time a Costa Rican president had made this concession. But he qualified the endorsement to ensure it would not go any further: "I consider this premature, and I am only a carrier of this message so that the Legislative Assembly, if it wishes to, may take it into consideration" (Barahona, 1986: 38).

In the early 1900s, Costa Rica's newspapers were filled with cables from the radical suffragist movement in England. This flow of cables had an impact on Costa Rican society, and local newspapers responded with sarcasm, mockery, and ridicule. "It has been rumored in the capital that in the province of Alajuela women are seeking to form a political feminist group. How ugly and bothersome to see women meddling in political campaigns. . . . Each home will become a political club where peace and security will be lost" (*La Información*, 1913: 2). Or "Isn't it ridiculous for women to discard their home obligations in order to do politics. Some would call this behavior immoral" (*La Informacion*, May 13, cited by Barahona, 1986: 53).

Against this background, Angela Acuña's long career as a suffragist began. The years when Acuña had been a student in England were among the most tumultuous in the struggle for the vote there. "I was aware of how they had broken the window of Parliament, of the kidnapping of Mr. Asquith, the prime minister, and of their intention of throwing him into the Thames" (Acuña, 1969: 343). She returned to Costa Rica in 1910; in 1912, with a special dispensation, she became the first woman to enroll in the boys' secondary school for certification to enter the university.

The political climate of 1912 was so conservative that even Acuña wrote under a pseudonym, avoiding the radical tone of the messages of her European sisters. She was a bit defensive about her feminism and was flattered by male appreciation of her femininity. "When I founded the Feminist Movement in Costa Rica, I could not be called an old maid. I was young, happy, gracious, and not at all ugly. . . . I never intended to discard femininity, the greatest beauty God has given us. . . . One great compliment was an inscription on a gift from a male friend: 'To the most feminine of the feminists' " (Acuña, 1969: 347).

Her first argument for the vote built on the premise that women would continue to outnumber men and marriage was therefore not an option for all women. Furthermore, she stated, women needed to be more independent and self-governing because they were less willing to enter the convent (the other plausible alternative), polygamy was detestable to all, and infanticide was practiced only by the "savages of Africa" (Acuña, 1969: 348). Obviously, Acuña's egalitarian feminism was not completely egalitarian, and certainly it was not free of a racism common to that time.

While a few brave women joined with Acuña to demand the right to vote, other groups emerged to fight for workers' rights under the leadership of María Isabel Carvajal (a teacher and renowned writer who wrote under the pen name of Carmen Lyra), Luisa González, and male intellectuals who founded the Sociedad Federal de Trabajadores (Federated Worker's Union) in 1912 (Chacón, 1984: 62; also see Calvo, chap. 1 above). In 1931, Carvajal was a founding member of the Communist party, the first Costa Rican party to put women's political rights on their platform. Actually, the party's commitment to women's struggle was minimal. Carvajal herself supported women's right to vote, but she fought primarily for workers' welfare and did not see feminist struggles as a separate issue. Acuña's and Carvajal's lives were curiously intertwined throughout this period and, in separate but related struggles, they were almost always on opposite sides in their political alliances. They never resolved their differences, and this affected the struggle for women's political rights.

The year 1917 marked the first time that a women's grassroots movement evolved around the struggle for the preservation of democratic practices. During Federico Tinoco's dictatorship (1917–19), the government seriously curtailed civil liberties and the freedom of press and assembly. The country went through a severe financial crisis, and teachers (most of them female) were among the most seriously affected. In addition to being poorly paid, they were paid in *tercerillas* (thirds), notes representing one-third of their salary, which were to be redeemed at a bank at a future unspecified date. Friends of the government (males) purchased the tercerillas at half their face value from teachers who needed the money immediately; later the "friends" exchanged the tercerillas for their full value at local banks (Barahona, 1986: 70). When teachers became vocal opponents of Tinoco, he threatened them with layoffs, firings, and the revamping of pension plans. They became the major leaders in the opposition to the government. María Isabel Carvajal was clearly one of those leaders.

Many violent demonstrations in 1919 against the Tinoco dictatorship were headed mostly by women and students, who were frequently beaten and hosed down. Carvajal herself was wounded in one such encounter (Chacón, 1984: 76). On June 13, 1919, women led by Andrea Mora, with support by Carvajal, burned the official newspaper *La Información* (Chacón, 1984: 80). They kept up the pressure, and Tinoco was overthrown. Throughout this period, Acuña had continued writing on women's political rights, but as an old friend of the Tinoco family, she backed him during these events. She was loyal especially to María Fernández Le Chappelain, her schoolmate and Tinoco's wife (Calvo, 1989a: 91)

In 1920 Tinoco's successor, Julio Acosta, became the second Costa Rican president to support women's right to vote. "In the last political battle, women showed their moral caliber and their willingness to die for their beliefs, and they gave men examples of their civic commitment," he said. "We need their cooperation in our struggles against alcoholism and other vices. Women proved their unselfishness, the purity of their passion, and the kindness of their souls" (cited by Barahona, 1986: 68). Although he recognized women's leading role in the restoration of democratic processes, he limited his enfranchisement proposal to municipal elections and to women who paid taxes. And what he was demarcating as women's projects clearly did not represent Acuña's vision in 1920.

President Acosta's 1920 proposal supported a measure that Acuña had sponsored five years earlier. In 1915, she had used somewhat similar arguments in articles in favor of the vote, which appeared in her newly founded literary magazine *Figaro*. "Don't you think it is unjust," Acuña asked at that time, "that men without economic resources are allowed to vote even though they don't pay taxes, and women who pay them cannot vote? If this is not unjust, I do not know what men call injustice" (Calvo, 1989a: 76). The response of opponents quickly followed: "For God's sake, Angelita, have pity on us: Don't you think it would be equivalent to tying a rope around our necks and jumping in the river if we were to tolerate a political campaign run by La Canduche and La Sevilla [famous "madams"]? I can just see a working session suspended because of the president's labor pains or because of the unexpected visit of an uncle at the vice president's house" (cited by Calvo, 1989a: 77).

President Acosta's motion was defeated on August 15, 1920 (Barahona, 1986: 72). Acuña later stated, "Up to this point, I had fought alone, protected and encouraged by a select group of distinguished gentlemen" (Acuña, 1969: 351). She then turned her attention toward women and, on October 12, 1923, founded the Liga Feminista, the first official suffragist organization in Costa Rica. She was its first president, and most of its members were teachers (Barahona, 1986: 72). "We knew that our activities were not taken seriously. There was around them a conspiracy of silence. We did not fool ourselves," Acuña later wrote (1969: 355). A teachers' dispute sparked the league's first organized move; in 1924, male teachers submitted a bill that would raise the salaries of men but not of women teachers. "*At that time,* I did work for the women teachers of the country" (Acuña, 1969: 357; emphasis added). Acuña was obviously feeling defensive about her lack of participation during the Tinoco period. After the league's active campaign, the male teachers lost their bill.

In 1924, Acuña began sending signed petitions to the Legislative Assembly, requesting women's enfranchisement (Chacón, 1984: 100–01). In 1925, the league, acting as a formal organization, asked the assembly to grant women the vote. The league presented its demand in the midst of an electoral reform that included an article listing—following European tradition—categories of people who would be ineligible to vote: children, the mentally defective, minors, criminals or those in jail until rehabilitated, and women (Calvo, 1989b: 4). The league proposed to remove women from this list, contending further that the language of the 1871 Constitution did not exclude women, and that they should therefore be granted the right to vote. The patriarchs did not intend to take this additional step.

It was at this point that opponents cited a woman's inability to grant citizenship to her foreign-born husband as evidence of women's subordinate status under the law. They also cited Article 73 of the Civil Code: "A wife must obey her husband, live with him, and follow him if he were to change residence" (Barahona, 1986: 106). Other arguments noted the dangers to a woman's "physical and moral beauty . . . whereby the vote would tarnish the white tunic covering her body" (*La Gaceta*, 1925a), or stated, "It is degenerate of men to say that human perfection means 'become independent, fight, educate yourself.' I will always prefer to see my daughters praying and asking God for enlightenment" (*La Gaceta*, 1925b).

Women lost again, but this time the patriarchs held out a carrot: "The day will come when a select group of women will be given the right to vote and be elected. . . . We don't think all should have it, because too many are uneducated" (Barahona, 1986: 101).

In 1926 Acuña returned to Europe (Calvo, 1989a: 113), where she would remain for three years. Her absence affected the suffragist struggle noticeably, and the Liga Feminista became involved in traditional feminine activities. Its new president, Lidia Fernández, joined other educated women, such as the noted writer Lilia Ramos, in deploring women's lack of education, which precluded their becoming voters (Anonymous, 1926). They also blamed the victims, women themselves. Fernández, for example, asserted that women's great demand for luxuries oppressed husbands and children (*Diario de Costa Rica*, 1931, September 14: 1a). No wonder that the same newspaper described the Liga Feminista as a charitable organization (*Diaro de Costa Rica*, 1926, July 16: 13). There were still strong feminist voices, but they seemed in the minority. The same paper quoted another suffragist leader, a Mrs. McCormick, as saying: "Every time we speak of women's liberation, there is considerable anxiety. . . . Men invent thousands of tricks to deny women their right. What do men think politics is all about? Who has given them the right to claim it only for themselves?" (*Diario de Costa Rica*, 1931, September 14: 1a).

Yet, the word *feminism* scared people. Atheism, for example, was a common accusation used against feminists. In 1929, the organization changed its name to the Cultural Society, and it also changed its objectives, which became those of encouraging the intellectual, physical, and moral education of women and guiding them in their duties, especially maternity (Barahona, 1986: 118). No wonder that after her return in 1931 Acuña said, "The suffragist movement declined during my absence. Women became involved in other activities" (1969: 360).

In 1931, soon after her return, the restored Liga Feminista, with Acuña again its president, sent to the assembly another bill to amend the constitution. This time, Acuña was joined by other prominent leaders, such as Esther de Mezerville, principal of the Colegio Superior de Señoritas (Calvo, 1989a: 135). The proposed amendment would grant the right to vote to the following women:

university graduates, teachers, typist secretaries, accountants, nurses, women who completed elementary school and could speak one foreign language, women who graduated from private schools, women who spoke two or more foreign languages, and, finally, women who owned land or property (Barahona, 1986: 132–33).

The suffragists were responding to the carrot the patriarchs had held out in 1924 and to their own privileged status. Hoping to placate men, they avoided a radical course and endorsed a classist and racist proposal. By now, the league was familiar with all the arguments opponents were publicly debating. Opposition was fierce. In a series of articles Acuña spoke out for the professional educated woman; in one, she stated, "Costa Rica has a large number of outstanding women. Denial of their political rights constitutes a violation of the principles of justice. The vote is for those of us who deserve it" (*La Nueva Prensa*, 1931). She poignantly accused male politicians of using women for their political benefit: "There are ladies in this country whom many gentlemen do not consider worthy of voting during times of political tranquility. Yet, when in trouble, they seek their support. . . . Many meetings in those ladies' homes were both private and political in nature" (*La Nueva Prensa*, 1931).

Action on the proposed amendment was delayed for one year. In a letter signed by Acuña on June 23, 1932, the league asked the assembly to discuss the question; they were informed that it had been submitted to a legislative commission and sent to the archives, i.e., tabled (Chacón, 1984: 105). No protests, no public demonstrations! But the matter had been put to rest for only a short time. On May 10, 1934, the Liga Feminista, spearheaded by Acuña, again demanded that women's right to vote be considered (Barahona, 1986: 137). A change in the long list of potential qualified women voters deleted those who had graduated from private schools.

By this time, opponents' arguments were well known: Women's place was in the home, away from the dirt and corruption of politics; women would lose their femininity and all those virtues men wanted them to have; women were not educated enough and would therefore complicate rather than simplify the political process; and of course, giving women the vote would destroy the family. The motion did not even make it to the plenary session. It was sent directly to the archives. However, the matter was intensely discussed, for the league was a well-run organization with numerous members. The proposal also did have the support of some legislators.

In 1939, the Liga Feminista submitted another demand to the legislature, arguing that the 1871 Constitution did not exclude women. Again, the request failed to make it to the plenary session. The system was so conservative and repressive that the struggle would last ten more years.

Women Defending Democratic Processes, 1943, 1947

The period from 1940 to 1948 is considered one of the most significant in Costa Rican history. In 1940, Rafael Angel Calderón Guardia became president, supported by his conservative predecessor León Cortés and the oligarchy. Cortés had staunchly opposed women's rights. Calderón, despite his previous political alliances, introduced broad social reforms that not only alienated the oligarchy but also won him the support of both the Communist party and progressive church leaders (Barahona, 1986: 168).

THE PROTEST OF MAY 15, 1943

On May 15, 1943, women and students organized to protest a proposed electoral reform. The demonstration was unparalleled in Costa Rican history.

In 1943, President Calderón was supporting the presidential candidacy of his protegé Teodoro Picado against León Cortés. Picado's party faction in the assembly, i.e., the faction of the executive branch, prepared an electoral reform to give the executive branch significant powers in overseeing the elections. On May 12, students led a demonstration (Calvo, 1989a: 182) and many women joined their ranks. On May 14—given that the proposed "reform" had been introduced, approved at first reading, and was ready for a vote count in one of the fastest moves ever seen in the Legislative Assembly—numerous women sent a letter to President Calderón asking him to veto the bill, pointing out that it would ensure fraud (Calvo, 1989a: 183). Calderón ignored them. Acuña and many others organized a major protest march for May 15. On May 14, candidate Picado asserted, "We do not need these hysterical women to win" (Calvo, 1989a: 184). The demonstration was so successful that the press noted, "We have never seen a feminine movement of this caliber before" (cited in Calvo, 1989a: 183). *La Ultima Hora* editorialized on May 16 that it was "a triumph of Costa Rican women" (cited in Calvo, 1989a: 185). The proposed electoral reform was withdrawn.

For women's issues, however, the victory was not so clear-cut. Carvajal and Acuña again found themselves behaving as political opponents, although they favored similar issues. As a leader of the Communist party, Carvajal was supporting, albeit partially, Picado's candidacy, and she was loyal to him, just as

Acuña had remained loyal to Tinoco from 1917 to 1919 and had remained silent during the huge grassroots movement against him.

Meanwhile, conservative-opposition candidate Cortés was now actively courting women by supporting their right to vote. His party pushed a reform to Article I of the Electoral Law (Ley de Elecciones, Artículo 1) to read: "The right to vote is essentially a political right and must be exercised by citizens, *male* or *female*, for whom it is a right and an obligation" (Calvo, 1989a: 188). Acuña and the league, realizing that the reform was losing, began an intense lobbying campaign. A countercampaign of ridicule and accusations of opportunism against Cortés mocked women's efforts to secure their political rights. Typical of this criticism was a new play, *Las Candidatas* (The women candidates), in which suffragists were ridiculed (Calvo, 1989a: 193). When the play's opening was announced, the league organized a protest meeting in which 560 women subsequently demanded its cancellation.

Although the league's efforts to close *Las Candidatas* were successful, its support of the reform was not. In what historians now label a fraudulent election (Vega, 1982), Picado became president, and the proposed modification of Article I of the Electoral Law was never discussed. Still, the official opposition party had supported women's right to vote. With that, the issue had finally become a part of the patriarchy's political games.

Looking back on this time, Manuel Mora, who was the leader of the Communist party in 1943, claimed in 1986 that the reformist Calderonistas had been against the women's vote in 1943 because they were afraid to alienate the Catholic Church, and that their conservative opponent Cortés had used it only as a political ploy against the ruling party (Barahona, 1986: 176). Mora also stated, "Women don't gain anything if we allow them to vote in a booth filled with capitalists. They must have the right to vote, but there are other rights, too, . . . to be mothers . . . to have their children protected" (Barahona, 1986: 234). Clearly, men of all political persuasions avoided making women's issues central in their struggles.

THE PROTEST OF AUGUST 2, 1947

The results of the 1946 midterm elections were met by a flood of accusations of fraud. The conservative opposition, now headed by Otilio Ulate, tried to form an alliance with President Picado on condition that Picado dissolve his association with the Communist party. When this failed, the conservatives launched a strike, demanding that the next elections be clean and that ex-president Calderón not run for reelection (Chacón, 1984: 132). The strike was prompted by police attacks on student demonstrators. Violence escalated and businesses that closed in support of the strike were looted (Chacón, 1984: 141).

Emma Gamboa, president of the teachers' union, emerged as a leader and coordinated a protest movement against the government (Chacón, 1984: 142). Once again, women's political rights were not the central issue, though by now they were on the platform of one of the leading parties. On August 1, 1947, a large number of women, headed by Gamboa, sent a proclamation to the press. They demanded an end to violence, asked Calderón to leave the country, and announced a demonstration. They declared that women carrying flags and singing the national anthem would march to the president's house in a peaceful protest against all the violence and political corruption.

On August 2, after receiving assurances of police protection, the women marched to President Picado's palace. He talked to them in the street and said sarcastically, "Since it is August 2 [the day of the Virgin Mary, the patroness of Costa Rica], ask her for a miracle" (cited by Chacón, 1984: 101). Gamboa and her demonstrators decided they would remain overnight in front of the president's house to continue the peaceful protest. That evening, the president sent a message that he would not sign anything unless they left. Not wanting him to use their presence as an excuse for his refusal to act to end the violence, they proceeded to leave (Chacón, 1984: 162). At that point, all hell broke loose. Army soldiers began shouting obscenities and striking the women with blackjacks. Margarita de Guzmán, a participant, reported, "Defenseless women were shot at with machine guns. We were returning home, singing the national anthem and then it happened. At that moment, they started shooting at us. . . . Finally, we broke into two groups . . . and had to tolerate the insults and obscenities soldiers yelled at us" (DMF, 1982: 33–34). At one point she was hit with a gun when she refused to lie on the ground. Elena López, who participated and was hit by a bullet, later said, "God wanted me to survive so I could see the women teachers and the Costa Rican ladies perform such incredible acts of courage" (*Diario de Costa Rica*, 1947, August 12: 1, 12).

On August 3, President Picado signed written guarantees for democratic free elections. The coalition—conservatives, teachers, and students—called off their strike. Thousands of women had demonstrated on August 2; they represented all political parties, social classes, and ages. At the head of this group were women teachers, led this time by Gamboa.

Meanwhile, Acuña had moved to Los Angeles, and the Liga Feminista had ceased to participate as an organization in the women's movement. A new generation of teachers and university students had emerged during this last confrontation. Once again, women leaders had worked for the survival of the democratic process during a period when Costa Rican democracy did not even recognize them as citizens. Yet teachers, students, and the middle classes had become the base of a new social democratic party under which they would finally win the vote in 1949.

THE FINAL PHASE

Matters worsened and led to a civil war in 1948. At the end of it, Calderón was exiled and Otilio Ulate, now supporting women's political rights, became president. On June 20, 1949, assembly member Ortiz Martín introduced a bill which redefined citizenship: "Citizenship is an aggregate of duties and political rights to which all Costa Ricans of *either sex* who are eighteen years or older are entitled." Ortiz called women's participation in the civil war "sufficient grounds to grant them the vote" (Barahona, 1986: 191). It appeared the bill would easily pass, but assembly member Chacón Jinesta asked for further discussion (DMF, 1982: 39). He said that in his own personal poll he had found that the majority of the women were against the vote, and he cited the familiar arguments that politics was dirty and women should not be polluted, that they were not educated enough for the vote, and so on. One amendment suggested, "Voting would increase divorces. I would be willing to grant the vote to those twenty-five years old, single, widowed, or divorced" (DMF, 1982: 32). Chacón finally agreed women should vote, but he warned, "The vote is not a reward but a cross to bear. I base this on my personal poll, which tells me that women do not want to vote" (DMF, 1982: 39).

In a 33-to-8 vote, the bill finally passed on June 20, 1949. All citizens, male or female, age twenty and over, could now vote (DMF, 1982: 35: see also *Constitución política, 1987* for age amendment). Costa Rican women cast their first votes on a referendum on July 31, 1950. The first woman to vote, Ramona Cruz, age 82, traveled on horseback for an hour and a half to get to the voting place (Chacón, 1984: 201). Three years later, in 1953, Costa Rican women voted for the first time in a presidential election.

Postscript

The early suffragists went on to varying experiences. On June 25, 1949, Acuña, then in Los Angeles, sent a congratulatory letter to the Legislative Assembly (Barahona, 1986: 200). She was named Mujer de las Américas in 1957, and later was the first woman ambassador to the Organización de Estados Americanos (OEA) (Organization of American States) (Calvo, 1989a: 219–20). Carvajal was forced into exile and died in Mexico in 1949, without having been allowed to return to Costa Rica. She is considered a pioneer and innovator in Costa Rican literature and one of its proudest citizens. Gamboa was minister of education in 1949 in the Ulate administration. She later became the founder and first dean of the Escuela de Pedagogía (School of Education) at the Universidad de Costa Rica.

In another ironical twist, the clause "citizens of either sex," which had been added in 1949, was found unconstitutional by the assembly on May 17, 1971; the assembly stated that by definition "citizen" included both women and men. Acuña had always been right!

When Acuña was named Woman of the Americas, Alberto Cañas, Costa Rica's ambassador to the United Nations, said, "The history of Costa Rica cannot be written without its women, and the history of women in Costa Rica cannot be written without Doña Angela" (cited in Calvo, 1989a: 214). To this statement we add, "nor without many others who are still waiting to be lifted from obscurity." It would have been so much easier if their voices could have been heard from the beginning.

Biodata

Sara Sharratt has a Ph.D. in clinical psychology and is a professor of counseling at Sonoma State University in Rohnert Park, California. In her private practice as a clinical psychologist she created the first women's counseling center in California. As Fulbright lecturer (1986–88) she taught the first graduate courses in women's studies at the Centro Interdisciplinario de Estudios de la Mujer (CIEM) (Center for Interdisciplinary Women's Studies), now the Instituto de Estudios de la Mujer (IEM) (Institute of Women's Studies), at the Universidad Nacional (UNA) in Heredia. She acted as a consultant in 1988–89 for the Universidad de Costa Rica and the Universidad Nacional in the development of a joint master's program in women's studies, which was inaugurated in the fall of 1993. She has written articles and books on family therapy and cross-cultural therapy and has done extensive research on sex roles and violence against women.

References

Anonymous. 1926. "Una regia velada." Newspaper clipping, private collection Lilia Ramos.

Acuña, Angela. 1969. *La mujer costarricense a través de cuatro siglos*. San José: Imprenta Nacional.

Alfaro, Carlos, and Francisco Ríos. 1984. *La educación: Fragua de nuestra democracia.* San José: Editorial Costa Rica.

Barahona, Macarena. 1986. "Las luchas sufragistas de la mujer en Costa Rica, 1890–1949." Thesis, Universidad de Costa Rica.

Calvo, Yadira. 1989a. *Angela Acuña: Forjadora de estrellas.* San José: Editorial Costa Rica.

———. 1989b. "El lenguaje y la ley." Paper delivered at the Seventh Interdisciplinary Congress of Human Rights. August 15.

Centro Nacional para el Desarrollo de la Mujer y la Familia (CMF). 1988. *Situación de la mujer en Costa Rica: 1975–85.* San José: Ministerio de Cultura, Juventud y Deportes.

Chacón, Carmen María. 1984. "Las mujeres del 2 de Agosto de 1947 en la vida política del país." Thesis, Universidad de Costa Rica.

Colegio de Abogados (CA). 1946. *Digesto constitucional de Costa Rica.* San José.

"Confrontación analítica." 1887a. *La enseñanza: Revista de instrucción pública, ciencias, literatura y arte,* no. 5 (January): 341–62.

Constitución política de la República de Costa Rica. 1987. Costa Rica: Imprenta Nacional.

Diario de Costa Rica. 1926. July 16, p. 13.

———. 1931. "Asamblea feminista." September 14, pp. 1a, 5a, 5b.

———. 1947. August 12, pp. 1, 12.

Dirección General de Mujer y Familia (DMF). 1982. *Algunos aspectos relativos al voto femenino en Costa Rica.* San Jose: Ministerio de Cultura, Juventud y Deportes.

"Disposiciones gubernativas: Decreto importantísimo." 1887b. *La enseñanza: Revista de instrucción pública, ciencias, literatura y arte,* no. 5 (January): 308–23.

El Mentor Costarricense. 1844. October 26.

———. 1846. "Educación." October 16.

Fallas Jiménez, Carmen Liddy, and Ana Margarita Silva Hernández. 1985. "Surgimiento y desarrollo de la educación de la mujer en Costa Rica, 1847–1886." Thesis, Universidad de Costa Rica.

Ferro, Cora, and Ana María Quirós. 1988. *Mujer, realidad religiosa y comunicación.* San José: EDUCA.

García, Ana Isabel, and Enrique Gomáriz. 1989. *Mujeres centroamericanas. Tomo I. Tendencias estructurales.* San José: FLACSO.

Gross, Susan Hill, and Marjorie Wall Bingham. 1985. *Women in Latin America: The 20th Century.* St. Louis Park, Minn.: Glenhurst Publications.

La Enseñanza. 1887.

La Gaceta. 1925a. March 6.

———. 1925b. April 2.

La Información. 1913. May 13.

La Nueva Prensa. 1931. June 12.

Odio, Elizabeth. 1989. Personal communication. September 10. Minister of Justice, 1978–82 and 1990–94, and Family Code reformer.

Sherman, Mary. 1984. *Costa Rican Women on the Threshold of Change.* San José: Canadian Corporation Program, Canadian Embassy.

Trejos, José Joaquín. 1989. "El alma de nuestra democracia." *La Nación*. August 27, p. 15a.

Vega, José Luis. 1982. *Poder político y democracia en Costa Rica*. San José: Editorial Porvenir.

Víquez, Cleto González. 1978. *El sufragio en Costa Rica ante la historia y la legislación*. San José: Editorial Costa Rica.

Zúñiga, Gil. 1985. "Un mito de la sociedad costarricense: El culto a la Virgen de Los Angeles (1824–1935)." *Revista de historia* 6, no. 11 (January–June): 47–109.

9 ❋ Unusual Costa Rican Women

Three Who Were Proclaimed "Distinguished Citizens of the Nation"

Ana Isabel Gamboa Hernández and
Sara Gurfinkiel Hermann

The Benemeritazgo de la Patria (distinguished citizenship of the nation) is the highest honor the Costa Rican state can bestow on a citizen who has contributed in extraordinary ways to the progress and welfare of the country. The title is conferred by the Comisión de Honores (Honors Commission), which is composed of members of the Legislative Assembly. It is confirmed by the whole assembly.

Since the award was established at the end of the nineteenth century, fifty-four citizens have been recipients, only three of them women (Fernández, 1987). This study describes the contributions these women made to the nation's history, identifies the reasons they were nominated, and suggests explanations for why so few women received the award. It concludes with a proposal for developing fitting criteria that will open the selection process to more women nominees.

Originally, the Benemeritazgo was awarded only to presidents of the republic, while they were in power. A significant contribution to society's well-being was not an essential criterion—the award was somewhat congratulatory in its early years. The Benemeritazgo was accompanied by other titles, some of them military, so that one would address a recipient of the award as "Your Excellency, General and Distinguished Citizen, Señor . . ." (Fernández, 1987: 6). The award process has changed since its nineteenth-century origin. The four members of the Comisión de Honores now determine the criteria, which have differed markedly over time. Thus, for example, the title has been awarded posthumously in recent years. To nobody's surprise, no woman has ever been a member of the commission. In our research we found no continuous documentation or systematic analysis of the award or of the selection process. We hope this presentation will stimulate interest in further inquiry.

Three Distinguished Female Citizens

The three women who were named distinguished citizens were María Emilia Solórzano Alfaro, a president's wife who is believed to have supported measures of social benefit; Emma Gamboa Alvarado, an educator of great national and international stature; and Angela Acuña Braun, Costa Rica's first woman lawyer and an ardent civil rights activist.

María Emilia Solórzano Alfaro (1835–1914)

Little is really known about María Emilia Solórzano. She came from the province of Alajuela, where she was a member of one of Alajuela's leading families; this had instilled in her "piety, compassion for the needy, good work habits, simplicity, and kindness" (Acuña, 1969, 1: 92–93). She married Tomás Guardia, who in or out of the presidency controlled Costa Rica from 1870 to 1882.

As Guardia's wife, María Emilia Solórzano traveled widely. She returned from one of her travels, a trip to France, having made the decision to establish a girls' high school, El Colegio de Nuestra Señora de Sión, in the city of Alajuela. According to tradition, another of her achievements was that she collaborated efficiently in favor of, and probably was the inspiration for, the suppression of the death penalty in Costa Rica. Little more has been written about María Emilia Solórzano. No records tell whether she had to struggle to achieve her goals of girls' education or the abolishment of the death penalty. She was awarded the Benemeritazgo de la Patria (award for distinguished citizenship) on April 10, 1972 (Acuña, 1969, 1: 92–93).

Emma Gamboa Alvarado (1901–1971)

Emma Gamboa was also from the province of Alajuela, where she obtained her early education. She then attended a teacher's training institute, the Escuela Normal de Heredia (Heredia Normal School), which later became the Departamento, now is the Escuela de Pedagogía at the Universidad de Costa Rica. Gamboa earned a B.A. in education; an M.A. in education; and, in 1947, a Ph.D. in philosophy from the University of Ohio in Columbus, Ohio. She returned to dedicate herself "to teaching, as preschool, elementary, and secondary teacher, minister of public education, dean of the now Escuela de

Pedagogía, at the Universidad de Costa Rica, and as founder of the Escuela Laboratorio (laboratory school)" (Fernández, 1987: 115).

Gamboa published widely. Her first book, published in 1935 was the *Nuevo silabario* (New reader), which changed teaching in all of Costa Rica. In *Nuevo silabario*, Gamboa emphasized that a book to teach reading must have meaning for a child and must lead the child to reading gradually, without losing the connections between the written word, the spoken word, and the child's world. She used as her themes the home, games, school, nature, and Costa Rican folklore. Gamboa also wrote children's books, such as *Lectura activa* (Active reading) (1936), and the famous *Paco y Lola* (1960). Her stories and verses for children were well loved.

In her scholarly work, Emma Gamboa proposed a holistic democratic education, with attention to the country's history. She stressed the dignity of the individual and the dynamics and creativity of the child. She taught that knowledge is not education and that learning has to be "motivated by experience, acquired through experience, and connected to later experience to be incorporated into our lives" (Gamboa, 1976: 29).

In 1950, she was declared Woman of the Year by *Mademoiselle* magazine, and she figured among the ten most outstanding women in different parts of the Americas. She received the Benemeritazgo de la Patria on May 27, 1980 (Fernández, 1987: 20ff).

Angela Acuña Braun (1888–1983)

Angela Acuña came from Cartago and graduated in 1916 from law school in San José. The country's first woman lawyer, she fought for women's legal equality and against prejudice, even before she had graduated from law school.

In 1915, Angela founded the review *Figaro,* to which the best writers of the Americas contributed. In 1916 she presented to the Legislative Assembly a first petition to broaden women's options for practicing law (Calvo, 1989: 79). In 1924 she conducted a campaign in support of women school teachers, who fought against proposed salary differences between men and women. She also presented to the assembly for the first time the demand for women's right to vote (see Sharratt, chap. 8 above). She addressed many presidents in the Western hemisphere in her demands for this right (Soto, 1975). Years later, she achieved her goal of seeing Costa Rican women serve as notaries, judges, mayors, and Supreme Court justices (Calvo, 1989).

In 1940 Angela Acuña founded the Costa Rican branch of the Panamerican Roundtable, an early human rights organization. This was followed a year later by her appointment as delegate to the Comisión Interamericana de Mujeres (CIM) (Inter-American Commission of Women) in Washington, D.C. (Fernández, 1987: 41).

At about this time, Acuña also began to write her historic study *La mujer costarricense a través de cuatro siglos* (Costa Rican women in four centuries), which was published in 1969. In 1953 she did a comparative study of legislation on women for the Unión Panamericana. She was named ambassador of Costa Rica before the Organización de Estados Americanos (OEA) in 1957 and, in that same year, was named Woman of the Americas. On June 7, 1982, Angela Acuña was awarded the Benemeritazgo de la Patria (Calvo, 1989: 236).

A Request to the Comisión de Honores

In view of the importance of the contributions of these three women, why has the Comisión de Honores not awarded the honor of Benemeritazgo de la Patria to more women?

One major reason is that society has prevented women from taking an active part in the nation's affairs. Compared with men, women had only limited access to education until recent years. And those women who were educated were not encouraged to participate in public life. What a woman needed to know, according to commonly held beliefs, was to run a house, educate children, and prepare food for her family.

But there is a second and more important reason why so few women received the Benemeritazgo de la Patria. The Comisión de Honores has always had an exclusively male membership. This all-male board of judges has consistently ignored or undervalued women's contributions to the national well-being—and there were such contributions!

We therefore request that the Comisión elaborate publicly its criteria and rules for considering candidates for distinguished citizenship. We further request that these criteria be appropriate for assessing the contributions both of outstanding Costa Rican men and of outstanding Costa Rican women. In recent years, two women have been proposed for this award (Fernández, 1987). The first is Pancha Carrasco, the nineteenth-century heroine of the war against William Walker (Calvo, chap. 1 above). The second is María Isabel Carvajal, twentieth-century political leader, suffragist, and informal adviser and friend of Costa Rican presidents. Carvajal, who is also a famous writer under the pen name of Carmen Lyra, was recognized by the Legislative Assembly as Benemérita de las Artes (distinguished person in the arts, in this case, distinguished writer), a title created especially for her (Sharratt, chap. 8 above). We suggest that the Comisión de Honores reconsider the candidacies of these two women and identify other meritorious women so as to give women their rightful place among Costa Rica's distinguished citizens.

Biodata

Ana Isabel Gamboa Hernández, a Costa Rican, received an M.S. in psychology from the Universidade Católica do Minas Gerais, Belo Horizonte, MG, Brazil. She pursued graduate studies at the Centro Interdisciplinario de Estudios de la Mujer (CIEM) (Center for Interdisciplinary Women's Studies), now the Instituto de Estudios de la Mujer at the Universidad Nacional. She works as a clinical and industrial psychologist and consultant for industrial enterprises.

Sara Gurfinkiel Hermann, a Costa Rican, completed a licenciatura in psychology at the Universidad de Costa Rica and did graduate work at CIEM. She taught at the Universidad Autónoma de Centro América and conducted research at the Instituto del Niño, Centro de Investigación y Docencia en Educación (CIDE) (Children's Institute, Center for Research and Training in Education) at the Universidad Nacional. In 1992 she went to pursue graduate studies in Mexico and is currently working there.

References

Acuña Braun de Chacón, Angela. 1969. *La mujer costarricense a través de cuatro siglos.* Vols. 1 and 2. San José: Imprenta Nacional.
Calvo, Yadira. 1989. *Angela Acuña. Forjadora de estrellas.* San José: Editorial Costa Rica.
Fernández Rivera, Felipe. 1987. *Beneméritos de la patria.* San José: Imprenta Nacional.
Gamboa, Emma. 1935. *Nuevo silabario.* San José: Imprenta Lehmann.
——. 1936. *Lectura activa.* San José: Imprenta Lehmann.
——. 1960. *Paco y Lola.* San José: Imprenta Atenea.
——. 1976. *Educación en una sociedad libre.* San José: Editorial Costa Rica.
Soto, Jorge Luis. 1975. *Galería de valores femeninos.* San José: Litografía A.B.C.

Acknowledgments

The authors did this study as participants in the graduate seminar "Women in History: From Invisibility to Visibility" at the Centro Interdisciplinario de Estudios de la Mujer, now Instituto de Estudios de la Mujer (IEM) (Institute of Women's Studies), at the Universidad Nacional in the fall of 1988. Emma Gamboa, one of Costa Rica's distinguished women citizens, is the first author's aunt who made a deep impression upon her when she was a child. Both authors thank Professor Clotilde Obregón of the History Department of the Universidad de Costa Rica, and Felipe Fernández Rivera, chief of archives of the Costa Rican Legislative Assembly, for comments on an earlier draft of the paper.

10 ❀ Peasant Women's Autobiographies

Women's Double Contribution to the Rural Economy

Zaira Escamilla Gutiérrez and Lorena Vargas Mora

This study is an analysis of five farm women's autobiographies selected from the twenty-six included in the five-volume *Autobiografías campesinas* (AC), published in 1979 by the Escuela de Planificación y Promoción Social (School of Planning and Social Development) of Costa Rica's Universidad Nacional (UNA). To encourage the expression and collection of experiences of rural people, UNA had asked farmers to submit entries in a competition for the best campesino autobiographies. Many more entries arrived than could be selected for the final published selection.

These five exceptional women were born between the end of the nineteenth century and the middle of the twentieth. They are identified as *ERGP,* born in 1889 (AC, 1979, 4); *Angelita,* born in 1906 (AC, 1979, 1); *Rosalinda,* born in approximately 1938 (AC, 1979, 4); *CMS,* born in 1947 (AC, 1979, 4); and *Campesina Feliz (happy woman farmer),* born in 1948 (AC, 1979, 4). They had the audacity to consider their life histories important and worthy of being told, so they grasped the opportunity of making them known.

The autobiographies of the five farm women are historic documents of great value; they offer a wealth of detail that permits a closer look at the way of life, the feelings, and the thoughts of Costa Rican peasant women. Although the autobiographies are rich sources of information about many other aspects of these women's lives, this analysis limits its focus primarily to their economic contribution to the survival and well-being of their society. The autobiographies offer a rare view, often hidden by traditional literature and historiography, of the work women have done as basic participants in the economic process throughout history. From these writings one can glean the importance of women's twofold contribution to the agricultural economy through their work in the fields and their reproductive contribution to their families' survival, first in their families of origin (their parents' families) and thereafter in their families of orientation (the families they and their husbands founded).

Women's Economic Lives Within Their Parents' Families

The information about the organization of the economic enterprise in the women's families of origin can be assessed according to landholding; agricultural production; the division of labor into women's work, children's work, and men's work; and the control of the product of this labor. The five parental families—the women's families of origin—were rural, composed usually of biological father and mother, though one family had a stepfather. The families were large, with an average of seven children; all five women referred to the constant pregnancies of their mothers. Each family had a house in the village, where the mother remained to take care of the small children, animals, and produce and grain processing. The father constructed a little hut wherever he worked the land and took his older sons and daughters to live there with him.

Landholding

The families either raised their crops on unoccupied plots of land that they did not officially own, or they rented lands. The land was basically virgin forest land, which the whole family cleared for cultivation without mechanical tools. Having cleared the land, the families then often acquired ownership of it by gradually purchasing small plots. In all cases, the transactions were handled by men and the property eventually was held by the men.

Agricultural Production

The crops the families cultivated were basically subsistence crops: rice, corn, beans, legumes, and vegetables. They had a few animals to provide eggs, milk, and meat for home consumption. The father of the family usually sold the small quantities of excess products to acquire other items the family needed in its daily life, such as spices, clothes, candles, and medicines.

Division of Labor

The women's workweek included many activities. They washed clothes in the river and carried water from it. They took care of children. They cooked, ironed, and swept and cleaned the house. They prepared the soil for planting, and they also cultivated and processed by hand the farm products: coffee, sugar cane, rice, beans, and tubers. In addition, they salted meat, milked cattle, fed domestic animals, and cut and carried wood. When their men went to other parcels of land to plant or were away selling cattle or other agricultural products, the women had to take on the additional tasks of maintaining the fields and taking care of the remaining cattle and horses, moving them from one pasture to another.

Such multiple tasks were the building blocks of the lives of these women: "I picked coffee and planted bananas, yucca, sugar cane, beans, corn, yams, ñampi [a type of yucca], and rice. I cut fire wood. I planted cucumbers. I threshed beans and peeled rice. I raised chickens. I handled a rifle of sixteen shots. I cleaned fallow land with a machete. I cooked, washed, ironed, took care of children, ran errands, and did the housecleaning" (CMS, 1979, 2: 42).

Children had to participate in fieldwork as well as housework. They cared for younger siblings, ironed, carried water, washed clothes in the rivers, herded and cared for animals, dried grains in the sun, gathered fruits and vegetables, fished, husked and shelled corn, milked cows and made cheese from the milk, cooked, cleaned the house, and weeded fields. They also helped the farmhands, which meant going to the field, preparing food, fetching water, and keeping the fire going.

The women wrote in their autobiographies about the repeated pregnancies of their mothers, and how they resulted in the daughters' permanent participation in housework and in taking care of younger brothers and sisters. Even very young daughters lent a hand:

One day, my mother had just been given another daughter. My father had gone to work. He was late, and mother was crying because she was hungry. I could not cook—I was barely five years old. But father had prepared a pot with green plantains [cooking bananas] and beans. When I saw it I decided by myself to climb on a chair, and thus took her a plate. When father came, mother had finished it all (CMS, 1979, 2: 26).

Another gave a glimpse of the role of the oldest daughter:

I had to help my mother with the housework, because we were many brothers and sisters, and my mother bore children like a good fruit tree bears fruit. Since my sisters were younger than I, they were not of much help, and I had to go to the river with the heavy wooden washboard piled high with dirty clothes from the entire week, for there were many men (ERGP, 1979, 4: 119).

Balancing education and work at home was not always easy. After school, the young girls had to work hard to help, sometimes replacing the mother so that she could move on to other work: "I used to go to school and then come home to wash the diapers of my little brothers, clean, put on the water for coffee. . . . When Mother went to work, she left me to take care of my little brothers" (CMS, 1979, 2: 27). At least one farm daughter did not think that education was a priority, however. Angelita wrote, "When I finished fourth grade and entered fifth, I was eleven years old. I did not want to go on . . . because I thought I was too old to continue going to school. What happened then was that I went to cook for men who worked in the fields." (Angelita, 1979, 1: 11). Others liked going to school and believed they did well. Campesina Feliz finished the six years of primary school, and Rosalinda completed three of the four years of secondary school and also took music lessons. CMS completed her studies in the 1970s by means of extension work. (Extension courses have been and are still widely available in Costa Rica, at all levels—primary, secondary, and university.)

The one woman who had never attended school, ERGP wrote about the school she and other parents built for their own children: "Now at least the children will not be as illiterate as their poor parents who never even went to school" (ERGP, 1979, 4: 128).

Men specialized basically in fieldwork, scouting virgin land, selecting crop-land, preparing the soil, sowing, harvesting, and transporting the products.

Control of the Product of Family Labor

Men controlled the family's income through acquiring properties and carrying out transactions related to these properties. They also handled small-scale commercial activities, such as the sale of farm produce and grains, and the purchase of clothing, some foods, and some household utensils. None of the women writers stated that their mother managed any money.

Women in the Families They Formed with Their Husbands

The authors of the autobiographies married peasants who worked as farm laborers. The families they formed with these men were their families of orientation. CMS married at age fourteen, but the other women were married at a later age—ERGP and Angelita each at age thirty, Rosalinda and Campesina Feliz each at age twenty-one.

The women's own families were smaller than those of their mothers, with an average of five children. In their stories they speak about moving frequently because of the scarcity of available lands in their home villages and their lack of inheritance. Angelita was the only one who did not move; she inherited a small property from her parents.

Throughout their lives, these five women did many different types of work: housework, farm work, paid employment, and political and communal activities. Some of them experienced significant changes in their social situation, given that they had to assume, temporarily or permanently, the maintenance of their families, and thus had to carry out many different tasks. Rosalinda worked as a seamstress, saleswoman, and office worker before finally becoming a public defender, a paralegal position that educated laypersons in rural areas could achieve through much experience. She also participated in communal activities. In one entry, she wrote, "At the moment, I continue with my office work for the Guardia Rural [rural police force] station. I like that, and about two months ago the Supreme Court decided to name me public defender. I do work a lot, because really I have many things to do in the house and outside. I have two sons in high school, three in elementary school, and the smallest one in kindergarten" (Rosalinda, 1979, 4: 147–48).

CMS's marriage broke up, and she assumed the responsibility of maintaining her two children. She joined her mother and one of her sisters working as a maid, cook, and dishwasher. Campesina Feliz stayed in agriculture, but with the help of a loan, she managed to establish a farm operation growing rice. She also participated actively in community organizations, in which she took on leadership roles:

> I must say I very much like working for the well-being of our community. Right now I am secretary of the Integrated Development Association of this community, president of the school board, president of the 4-H Club, and coordinator of the Social Aid Commission. I am president of the Women's Organization of the Liberación Nacional party [equivalent to the Democratic party in the United States—Ed.], and a few days ago I was elected as coordinator to represent the Integrated Development Association in the Youth and Sports Committee in this community. Well, in all these committees I work hard and am delighted, because if there is anything I like, it is to work for the progress of our town (Campesina Feliz, 1979, 4: 155–56).

Only ERGP and Angelita remained simply farm women throughout their lifetime.

Women's Problems in Costa Rican Farm Life

The information these five authors provide in their autobiographies about the working conditions for farmers and the participation of women as producers and reproducers of the rural labor force allow us to draw certain conclusions about the role women have played in the Costa Rican farm economy.

The primitive subsistence economy of the farm families, governed as it was by a scarcity of land, resources, and mechanical tools, accounts for the fact that family labor was the only method by which these families survived. Land was cultivated for production through the joint efforts of men, women, and children who had to invest a great amount of time and physical labor to achieve a basic subsistence. As their circumstances did not permit families to produce many goods beyond those they needed for their own survival, an accumulation of resources was practically impossible.

This form of economic production led to a division of labor through specialization of men's and women's activities. Men were responsible for fieldwork, selection and preparation of land, and sowing, transport and sale of crops. However, women did not enjoy a clear separation between housework and fieldwork; they, too, participated in sowing, harvesting, and processing crops. Moreover, adult women and girls were exclusively responsible for housework. When men were absent—out scouting for new land or involved in business transactions—women and children had to carry the entire work load in house and fields.

As many details and anecdotes about childhoods full of work, deprivation, and suffering illustrate, child labor acquired vital importance in this production scheme. The authors emphasized their mothers' hard work in house and field, which their own apprenticeships perpetuated from early girlhood on.

Since transactions to obtain access to land and to acquire property were open only to men, the marginalization of farm women did not result from the work they did but rather from their restricted capacity to control the product of their labors. As women's work was part of nonremunerated family work, their relation with agriculture was demonetized. This in turn put them at a disadvantage in a production process in which they invested untold hours and a substantial amount of physical effort. Moreover, farm women's domestic work, because of the physical conditions under which it took place—given the quality and location of housing and the absence of public services such as electricity, potable water, and transport—did not permit the use of household technology. Thus, the intensity of the work farm women had to do, together with their frequent pregnancies, created precarious health conditions for them.

Comparing the Older and Younger Women Across Time

Table 10.1 compares these five women across time, and it reveals fewer differences than might be expected between those born around the turn of the century and those born in the middle of the twentieth century. The older

Table 10.1. The Five Farm Women Compared

Name	Date of Birth	Years of Education	Age at Marriage	Number of Children	Work Experience Other Than House, Farm	Residence
ERGP	1889	none	30	4 and 1 stepchild	none	farm
Angelita	1906	4 (elem.)	30	9	none	from farm to country town at old age
Rosalinda	1938?	3 (second.)	21	6	sales, seamstress, office work, public defender	from farm to country town
CMS	1947	3 (elem.) finished through extension studies	14	5	housemaid, work in restaurant as cook and dishwasher	from farm to country town
Campesina Feliz	1948	6 (elem.)	21	2	housemaid	from farm to country town

women married later in their lives than did the younger ones, which may relate to the relative isolation of farm families during the earlier period. As to number of children, only one of the older women—Angelita—had many. She had nine, the others from two to five.

The greatest differences occurred in the type of work the women did. The older ones never worked for pay outside of the home. Of the three younger ones, only one—Rosalinda—worked as a semiprofessional. The others did housework, even though they did it for pay outside their own homes.

All except one have moved around a good deal, accompanying fathers or husbands who seemed constantly on the lookout for better ways to make a living, and for new land. Even though all of these women worked from a very early age, only one reported owning property, and she inherited it (Angelita, 1979, 1: 37).

Conclusion

The five autobiographies offer us insights into Costa Rican farm women's lives for the period between approximately 1910 and 1975. During this time, women made a twofold contribution to the farm economy, carrying the entire load of productive and reproductive work in the home and sharing responsibility, or sometimes assuming it completely, for the farm operation as well. Farm women envisioned this as natural—as what they had to do. And throughout their lives, they did so without obtaining control or even sharing in the control over the product of their labor. The continuity and invisibility that characterize the domestic and agricultural work of farm women has not traditionally been subsumed under the concept of La Doble Jornada (The Double Work Day), which has been used rather to characterize the condition of women who work outside the home in urban, industrial settings. However, the stories of the five farm women fully illustrate that the concept fits their obligations equally well. After all, their workday began long before daybreak and did not end until long after dark.

Thus women contributed as the men did to their families' economic success and to the extension of agricultural cultivation. In addition, they ensured their families' physical reproduction and well-being. Unfortunately, traditional analysts of agricultural processes and rural life have failed to see this and simply have not acknowledged the vital productive contribution of farm women to what theoreticians have called "economic development." Consequently, these women did not share as they deserved to in the financial benefits from the fruits of their labor.

The autobiographies also suggest that only in more recent years have farm women branched out to nonfarm activities for wages, as well as to communal involvement. Perhaps this is a first step on the part of these women toward obtaining control over their own earnings.

Even though the present analysis limits itself to describing women's work in agricultural communities or rural towns of Costa Rica, the *Autobiografías campesinas* offer much additional information about other aspects of farm women's lives. They are a rich source, for example, of women's knowledge about their bodies and physical health, and about women's experience with incest, violence, aggression, and abandonment. The *Autobiografías campesinas* may lend an insight into women's growing consciousness of their being exploited. All of these topics deserve closer attention and would complement the present analysis.

In essence, the lives of these women revolved around their children, husbands, and work. One of them, Angelita, closes her autobiography by saying, "I have twenty-six grandchildren, nine greatgrandchildren—what more do I want?" (Angelita, 1979, 1: 40).

Biodata

Zaira Escamilla Gutiérrez is a Costa Rican psychologist and a professor at the Universidad Nacional (UNA) in Heredia. She did graduate work in women's studies at the Interdisciplinary Women's Studies Center (CIEM), now the Institute for Women's Studies (IEM).

Lorena Vargas Mora is a clinical psychologist. Until 1992 she taught at the Universidad Nacional and has since been working in her own private clinic.

References

Escuela de Planificación y Promoción Social. 1979. *Autobiografías campesinas*. Vols. 1, 2, and 4. Heredia: Editorial Universidad Nacional.

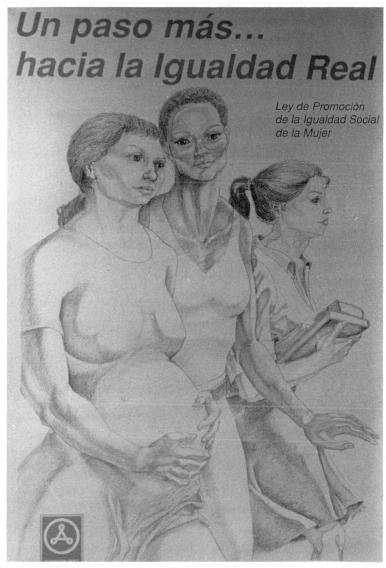

"One step further . . . toward true equality." A poster that praises the passage of the Law for the Promotion of Women's Social Equality

THE LAW IS an important component of Costa Rican life. Costa Ricans' confidence in their nonmilitarized democracy is based on their expectation that the law should and will regulate the interaction of individuals and groups. You cannot buy or sell a car or a house without a lawyer guiding you through the myriad of formalities connected with such a transaction.

This does not mean, of course, that Costa Ricans always respect or obey their laws, particularly if the latter contradict age-old cultural traditions or patterns. In fact, knowing how far one can go in bending the law without breaking it is a true survival skill. Moreover, diverse—frequently foreign—roots often make Costa Rican laws, codes, or legal stipulations inconsistent with one another. Yet laws do proclaim ethical standards and ideals that may someday become reality.

This background also applies to the question of women's legal status and legal gender equality. This important aspect of human rights is still more a long-term goal than a reality in Costa Rica. However, as the public debate continues and grows stronger, not only government policies but also government institutions are changing in response, and Costa Rican women are making real gains. Thus, for instance, in October 1993 the Defensoría de los Derechos Humanos (Office of the Defender of Human Rights), including that of the Defensoría de los Derechos Humanos de la Mujer (Office of the Defender of Women's Human Rights), was removed from the Justice Department to ensure complete independence of decision making and actions, and it was renamed Defensoría de los Habitantes (Office of the Defender of the Inhabitants, or Office of the Ombudsman). As before, the Office of the Defender of Women's Rights remains part of this larger institution.

The present section of this *Reader* explores some of the complex recent manifestations of the struggle for women's legal equality.

The Law and Women's Lives: Contradictions and Struggles, by Tatiana Soto Cabrera

Tatiana Soto sets the stage for the discussion of women's legal status by offering an overview of the Costa Rican legal framework. She reviews obstacles to women's rights in Costa Rica, such as the inadequacy of Costa Rican law and the inconsistency of its administration, women's ignorance about their rights, and the cultural tradition of denying basic rights to women. The author examines formal and informal dynamics affecting women's rights in the public sphere—including the formal judicial framework, government institutions, and the broad, nongovernmental elements of the public sphere—and presents the unequal power dynamics in the private sphere.

Soto discusses the increasing institutionalization of processes that serve women's needs and notes the surprising international effect the Thomas-Hill congressional hearings had on Costa Rican women's readiness to denounce sexual harassment. She presents a feminist rationale for the necessity of a total transformation of society, and she sees some hope both in the increasing governmental recognition of women's needs and in women's departure from a traditional pattern of acquiescence.

Negotiating Women's Legal Equality: Four Versions of a Law, by Aixa Ansorena Montero

Aixa Ansorena presents the first of two accounts of the debate that raged from 1989 to 1990 in the Costa Rican Legislative Assembly over a famous bill designed to achieve *igualdad real*—true equality—for women, a bill that finally passed in modified form. Both accounts of the debate document the patience required to obtain long-term gains for women. Ansorena offers a short description of the political negotiation process that led to the bill's passage—the bargaining and the give and take. In addition, the author analyzes the four versions of the bill that emerged during the Legislative Assembly's two-year debate. In March 1990 the Proyecto de Ley sobre la Igualdad Real de la Mujer was passed as the Proyecto de Ley de la Igualdad Real de la Mujer (Law for the Promotion of Women's Social Equality). The debate weakened some of the original provisions, but in other areas the proposal retained its original content.

Leading Arguments Against Women's Legal Equality: Highlights of a National Debate, by Ana Elena Badilla Gómez

This second account of the Proyecto de Ley sobre la Igualdad Real de la Mujer analyzes the national debate that followed the bill's introduction into the Costa Rican Legislative Assembly. The four principal objections to the bill were that (1) its provision mandating gender proportionality in politics was unconstitutional because it discriminated against men; (2) the bill was not needed because no discrimination against women existed; (3) the name of the bill was inappropriate, since true equality between women and men was not a politically desirable outcome; and (4) the provision mandating shared financing of day-care centers by working parents, employers, and government was unfair to employers. The objections stimulated a societywide discussion about women's subordination, which contributed to strengthening the feminist movement in Costa Rica.

Redefining Political Equality: More Than Including Women, by Alda Facio Montejo

Alda Facio concludes the section on the quest for women's equality by raising the fundamental theoretical-philosophical question of whether legal equality of the genders can ever be achieved. She contends that it cannot, unless seriously flawed basic concepts are redefined. True political equality for women is impossible without a redefinition of essential components of Western legal thinking, such as "human being," "citizenship," "equality of men and women," and "equality before the law," all of which are based on the erroneous androcentric assumption that white, middle-class, heterosexual males constitute the quintessence of "human being." She further argues that men and women are "equally different," and any valid definition of the above concepts must include the respective differences of both genders.

11 ❊ The Law and Women's Lives

Contradictions and Struggles

Tatiana Soto Cabrera

Throughout most of its history, Costa Rican society has denied women their basic rights. Although women have made some progress in the formal legal arena, such as achieving the right to vote in 1949 (see Sharratt, chap. 8 above) and the promulgation of the Family Code in 1974, these measures often were not consistent, frequently were not implemented, and certainly had little effect on women's daily lives—particularly the lives of poor women. During the 1980s, new incentives inspired women of all strata to renew their efforts to obtain their rights, often by initiating consciousness-raising and self-help activities.

This analysis first highlights the obstacles to women's rights in Costa Rica and then surveys the formal and informal mechanisms and structures, in both the public and private spheres, that form the framework for women's struggles during the 1990s.

Obstacles to Women's Rights

Understanding the obstacles to women's rights is the first step in planning a strategy for the future. In Costa Rica, the obstacles that now exist are (1) the inadequacy of the legal framework, in terms of laws and institutions, and the inconsistencies in the administration of the law; (2) women's ignorance about their rights; and (3) a cultural tradition that denies women basic rights.

The Costa Rican Legal Framework and the Administration of the Law

Compared with other Latin American societies, Costa Rica's legal framework for women's rights is relatively advanced. Problems arise, however, in the protection of women's established rights. The legal codes are weakened by inconsistencies and voids, which are coupled with inadequate institutional processes and adverse interpretations on the part of the authorities. For instance, under the laws of the Patronato Nacional de la Infancia (PANI) (National Agency for Child Protection), a battered woman may leave her home if the agency gives her permission to do so. Under these circumstances, the law prohibits her husband from accusing her of abandoning her family; he therefore cannot withhold economic support. Under the Family Code of 1974, however, that same act of leaving might cause the wife to lose some or all of her economic rights. Unfortunately, National Agency officials often fail to apply their own rule and, instead, ask the husband to sign a permit allowing his wife to leave. I know of no case in which the husband consented to his wife's leaving.

Women's Ignorance About Their Rights

We must attribute women's failure to exercise their recognized rights in part to their ignorance of the codified laws. Awareness of this problem has been growing in recent years and multiple efforts are now under way to provide training and information. In one such effort, the Universidad Nacional (UNA) offered the course "Women and Power" in 1987 (Ferro, chap. 28 below). In 1988, the Comité Latinoamericano para la Defensa de los Derechos de la Mujer (CLADEM) (Latin American Committee for the Defense of Women's Rights) organized the seminar "Women and the Legal System." An outgrowth of this seminar was feminist input into the formulation of the Proyecto de Ley de la Igualdad Real de la Mujer, which was debated in 1988–90 in the Costa Rican Legislative Assembly (see Ansorena, chap. 12 below; Badilla, chap. 13 below; Facio, chap. 14 below). That committee also sponsored in 1989 the first International Conference on Women, Law, and Development in Central America and México, which provided a regional perspective and contributions on family law, labor law, and laws regarding violence against women. That same year, UNA offered a free survey course, "Women Facing Life and Law," to non-professionals, and a working session of professionals produced policy proposals on human rights (Facio, 1989). Formal studies have analyzed the administration of justice (Molina, 1989) and the legal mechanisms that fail to protect victims of sexual aggression, largely because of male biases in issues of rape and in legal proceedings (Peralta, 1986; Soto, 1988). Another instance of growing awareness was, of course, the wide public debate over the Proyecto de Ley sobre la Igualdad Real de la Mujer discussed in the Assembly (Ansorena, chap. 12 below). Though greatly modified before it passed, the new law nonetheless constituted an advance for women's rights in some fields (CMF, 1990).

Efforts to increase women's awareness of their legal rights have met with some success in recent years. Nevertheless, most of the advances in knowledge and awareness have benefited highly educated women, leaving the great majority of Costa Rican women ignorant of their rights under the law.

A Cultural Tradition of Denying Basic Rights

Advances in women's legal awareness, however, do not alter the absence of protection for women's specific needs within the Costa Rican cultural system. Vast discrepancies exist between the few legal benefits women enjoy and the daily realities they encounter. The limitations on women's enjoyment of a better life, and their fears and weaknesses as they struggle toward that life, confirm that the exploitative system of our culture is deeply embedded in our national psychology. Countless husbands still dictate even the arrangement of furniture in the home and the style of their wives' hair or dress. Some also refuse to grant their wives permission to work outside the home, to study, or even to leave the house for shopping or social occasions.

Women's Rights in the Public Sphere: Formal and Informal Dynamics

The Formal Judicial Framework

In Costa Rica, most laws that govern social problems are contained in the Family Code, the Labor Code, and the Penal Code.

FAMILY CODE

The Family Code offers few appropriate procedural mechanisms. For example, presumably to protect the family from state intervention, parties in a disputed family case have to hire their own legal counsel except in cases that involve children or child support issues. (In such cases, the Patronato Nacional de la Infancia, PANI, is an interested party.) Legal services require financial resources, which women often do not have. Furthermore, as a matter of principle, both parties to the conflict are considered equal, which ignores differences in power and economic resources between men and women, which are often quite large.

LABOR CODE

Unlike the Family Code, the Labor Code recognizes the inequalities between the parties to the conflict—the employer and the employee. The code therefore provides support to the worker in order to balance these inequalities. However, through segregation of certain categories of workers, many women are excluded from the general protection of the Labor Code. For example, domestic workers, most of whom are women, are an excluded category.

PENAL CODE

The penal system is a complex governmental organization. In public interest issues, the state carries all the cases, offering defendants state-paid public defenders. Cases that concern family matters, however, are defined as within the private domain, and in such cases the woman must hire her own legal representative. Thus, in not paying legal services for private problems, the state is, in fact, perpetuating male dominance.

Government Institutions

Government efforts to advance the status of women have grown over the years. President Oscar Arias (1986–1990) confirmed the institutionalization of the Centro Nacional para el Desarrollo de la Mujer y la Familia (CMF) as part of the Ministerio de Cultura, Juventud y Deportes (MCJD) (CMF, 1990). He also created, by executive decree, the Office of the Women's Defender (*La Gaceta*, 1989). After the Proyecto de Ley sobre la Igualdad Real de la Mujer was revised and passed as the Ley de Promoción de la Igualdad Social de la Mujer, this Office of the Women's Defender became, as part of the Ministry of Justice, a more permanent institution than one created only by executive decree. Then, in October 1993 it and the parallel offices that protect the interests of consumers, children, the elderly, indigenous people, and other minorities were removed from the Ministry of Justice to allow more independence of action and were placed under the renamed Office of the Defender of the Inhabitants. In addition, the Delegación de la Mujer in the Ministerio de Gobernación y Policía accepts and channels women's complaints about violence or aggression. In 1991, the Office of the Women's Defender served twenty-five hundred women, according to a press conference of April 13, 1992. The Delegación de la Mujer in early 1992 stated that it was at that time receiving an average of three hundred to four hundred complaints each month.

AUTONOMOUS GOVERNMENT INSTITUTIONS

Nevertheless, many autonomous government institutions that are not dependent on any of the governmental ministries continue to implement procedures that discriminate against women. For example, the regulations under which the Instituto de Desarrollo Agrario (IDA) (Agricultural Development Institute) selects beneficiaries consider women to be less qualified to receive land, technical training, loans, and other benefits. The Instituto Nacional de Aprendizaje (INA) (National Institute for Occupational Training) will not train women in nontraditional occupations or skills.

The Broader Public Sphere

Dynamics and mechanisms in the nongovernmental, more informal public sphere also create obstacles for women and diminish women's rights. These obstacles take the form of sexual harassment and discrimination at work, union repression, discrimination in political parties or processes, discrimination or exploitation in popular organizations, social censorship of critics of sexual discrimination, and perpetuation of stereotypes of submissive feminine behavior propagated by the media and by educational materials. Women's limited presence in leadership positions in unions, cooperatives, or political parties is notable, and it inspired the original proposal in the Proyecto de Ley sobre la Igualdad Real de la Mujer for a quota system for candidates for election (CMF, 1988). (This component of the bill was later eliminated.) Moreover, it is common knowledge that many women are coerced into complying with employers' sexual demands in order to obtain promotions or employment or to avoid being fired. Because no sanctions exist, few women sue for sexual harassment, and many women have been ostracized in the workplace for defending themselves or refusing advances. Many have lost their jobs, ostensibly through a "restructuring" of the organization. However—and this is a hopeful sign—ever since the Clarence Thomas–Anita Hill hearings in the United States, the number of complaints of sexual harassment in the workplace filed by Costa Rican women with the Office of the Women's Defender has increased dramatically.

WOMEN'S ORGANIZATIONS

Even though most women's organizations believe that women's power is built on communication, on solidarity with other women, and on their collective understanding of the mechanisms of oppression, the power of most such organizations is limited. They are dispersed and do not communicate well, even though they pursue identical objectives. Thus the female part of the population is politically less strong than it could and should be.

Unequal Power Dynamics in the Private Sphere

Probably the highest level of conflict—the conflict that most hampers women in the exercise of their rights—is also the least documented and most complex. Its domain is the home. Most women carry out the greatest part of their activities in the private sphere and consider it the most important dimension of their lives. Yet there they learn conformism; there they have to face the most direct aggression; and there they must begin the struggle for their human dignity.

Many women who live with a husband or *compañero* (common-law husband) face grave problems. It is still common in Costa Rica for men to be interested not in sharing life with their partners but only in receiving benefits. Housework remains the exclusive obligation of many women, who are threatened by physical violence, sexual or psychological aggression, affective indifference or devaluation, and economic exploitation. According to a recent study, one of every two women who turn for services to the National Agency for Child Protection (PANI) has suffered domestic violence (PANI, 1990).

In the case of divorce, negotiations, if they take place at all, commonly end in an unequal settlement and a decline in the woman's status. This happens because the woman is exhausted from pressure and uneducated about how to fight for her rights. In addition, the laws are contradictory; family law, for example, contributes to the decline in a divorced woman's status by permitting her to give up her economic rights, whereas under the Labor Code her economic rights are inalienable. In other words, labor legislation clearly defends the economic rights of all workers, women included, whereas the Family Code allows women to renounce their right to financial support, particularly to child support. As men are almost without exception poorly educated about their obligations as fathers, in the power struggle of divorce proceedings they often make the grand concessionary gesture of relinquishing custody of their children, leaving the mother with the right, but also with the burden, of caring for their children, usually without any economic support that would enable her to do so.

Women in Costa Rica go through an enormous crisis at the moment of divorce. Viewing themselves as failures, they assume the blame for the end of the marriage, continuing to worry about their partners who humiliated them. They are afraid of being alone, dread the criticism of society, and find it agonizingly difficult to make decisions, particularly about their own legal situation. Few worry about their sexuality and their future in that respect.

Finally, the levels of violence within Costa Rican families are often comparable to tortures inflicted under dictatorships. Many women have a long history of abuse that began with incest during their childhood (see Batres, chap. 19 below, and Carcedo, chap. 18 below). The dimensions of the problems of abuse are still unquantifiable in Costa Rica. Even among intellectuals we do not yet find an understanding that these humiliations constitute a human rights violation and we must fight against them with the same commitment with which we oppose political oppression and torture. This is and will continue to be a woman's problem. So far, however, only feminist organizations such as the Comité Nacional por la No Violencia Contra la Mujer (National Committee for the Prevention of Violence Against Women) have taken up the problem of the invisible domestic war against women.

Conclusion

In sum, the emerging picture of women's rights in Costa Rica is mixed. The enjoyment and exercise of basic rights by Costa Rican women still leaves much to be desired. The state, law, customs, and informal system of social controls are full of sexist obstacles to the goal of women achieving their rights. There is an astounding incongruity between, on the one hand, the achievements of the Costa Rican legal system and, on the other hand, the inconsistencies of its application and the miseries of the daily realities of Costa Rica's women citizens— most of them poor, without power, and without state protection of their interests.

Yet some progress has taken place. The government is making an effort to establish institutions and processes designed to devote attention to women's needs and resolve their legitimate complaints. And women themselves are not as quiet as they were ten years ago.

Biodata

Tatiana Soto Cabrera, a Costa Rican, received a licenciatura in law from the Universidad de Costa Rica and is one of the original members of Ventana (Window) (see Camacho, Facio, and Martín, chap. 2 above). Since 1987 she has been a legal consultant on legal and gender questions for various feminist organizations. She is the author of *Los Mecanismos Legales Desprotectores de la Víctima de Agresión Sexual* (The legal mechanisms that fail to protect victims of sexual aggression; 1988). In 1989–91 she acted as a legal consultant for the Casa de la Mujer de los Barrios del Sur (Women's House in the Southern Suburbs [of San José]), whose work with battered women is supported by the Fundación Acción Ya (Action Now Foundation), a nonprofit organization helping low-income women. She worked with the Programa Interdisciplinario de Estudios de Género (PRIEG) (Interdisciplinary Gender Studies Program) at the Universidad de Costa Rica in 1991, and in 1991–92 was a legal consultant for the Defensoría de los Derechos Humanos de la Mujer, Ministerio de Justicia. She is now at the Defensoría de los Derechos Humanos de las Internas del Sistema Penitenciario Nacional (Office of the defender of the human rights of women prisoners in the National Prison System).

References

Facio, Alda. 1989. "De derechos del hombre a derechos humanos." *Mujer/Fempress*, no. 91 (May): 6–7.

Centro Nacional para el Desarrollo de la Mujer y la Familia (CMF). 1988. *Proyecto de ley de igualdad real de la mujer*. San José: Ministerio de Cultura, Juventud y Deportes.

———. 1990. *Ley de promoción de la igualdad social de la mujer*. San José: Ministerio de Cultura, Juventud y Deportes.

La Gaceta. 1989. Decreto no. 19157. No. J-166. September 1.

Molina Subirós, Giselle. 1989. "La mujer frente a la administración de justicia." Licenciatura thesis. Facultad de Derecho, Universidad de Costa Rica.

Patronato Nacional de la Infancia (PANI). 1990. "Características de la mujer agredida atendida en el PANI, propuesta de intervención." Computer-produced internal document (September).

Peralta Cordero, Lydia. 1986. "Síndrome de la mujer agredida." Licenciatura thesis, Facultad de Derecho, Universidad de Costa Rica.

Soto Cabrera, Tatiana. 1988. *Los mecanismos legales desprotectores de la víctima de agresión sexual*. San José: Ministerio de Cultura, Juventud y Deportes, CMF.

Acknowledgments

This article is based on the author's participation in feminist organizations, years of work with support groups for women who suffered violence, and her legal consulting to help women defend their rights. Both the author and the translator wish to thank Alda Facio for her comments on an earlier version of the translation of this article.

12 ❈ Negotiating Women's Legal Equality

Four Versions of a Law

Aixa Ansorena Montero

In March 1988, the Proyecto de Ley sobre la Igualdad Real de la Mujer (Bill for Women's True Equality) was introduced to the public; one month later, it was sent to the Legislative Assembly of Costa Rica (CMF, 1988–89). Two years of intense public debate about women's political and social rights followed before the bill, substantially changed, was passed as the Ley de Promoción de la Igualdad Social de la Mujer (Law for the Promotion of Women's Social Equality) (*La Gaceta*, 1990; see Badilla, chap. 13 below).

It may come as a surprise that Costa Ricans were discussing women's equality while the rest of Central America was torn by political and military conflicts. But we must consider both the bill and the debate in the context of the stable democracy and relatively high living standard of Costa Rica. The nation's political stability is based on a number of reforms that have been achieved through social legislation dating back to the 1940s, including the nationalization of banks, universal extension of social security, incentives for cooperative and community organizations, and general access to primary and secondary education (Contreras and Cerdas, 1988; Rojas, 1982).

At the same time, however, the Costa Rican social system has preserved strong and deeply rooted social inequalities between men and women, which persist despite a tradition of struggles for women's rights dating from the beginning of the century.

Women's Continuing Inequality

The Ley de Promoción de la Igualdad Social de la Mujer was a response to women's continuing low participation in politics, in the labor market, and in the administration of justice. Table 12.1 illustrates the gender imbalances in the assembly, municipal governments, community organizations, and the labor force. It also shows the low level of women's income compared with that of

Table 12.1. Indicators of Female Inequality

Area of Inequality	Women	Men
Political Representatives		
National Assembly (1953/–86)	6%	94%
Municipalities (1953/–86)	11	89
Community organizations (1986)	17	83
Labor		
Economically active population[a] (1987)	28	72
Administrators, managers (1985)	22	78
Income		
Mean national salary 1987 (men's salary=100%)	82	100

a. Percentage of working-age population that was employed, looking for work for the first time, or unemployed. This category excludes housewives and students (PRIEG, n.d.; García and Gomáriz, 1989).

men. These data are easily quantifiable, but other types of inequalities cannot be so readily measured. In judicial proceedings, for example, most cases of violence or sexual aggression against women are still considered lesser offenses, even though the number of women treated in the Clinic of Forensic Medicine from 1983 to 1987 had doubled within the five-year span (Molina, 1988). Women also suffer discrimination in terms of access to property, particularly in social programs for rural areas, where land is routinely assigned to men.

The Objectives of the Bill

The Proyecto de Ley sobre la Igualdad Real de la Mujer voiced demands in six areas:

1. *Political rights and the exercise of public office,* to ensure women's increased political participation;
2. *Social and economic rights,* to establish mandatory child care, financed by employers and users, and to ensure equal rights to property for legally married or common-law husbands and wives;
3. *Protection of women while they denounced aggression or sued* to ameliorate procedures in cases of sexual abuse and aggression;
4. *Education,* to eliminate sexist content from teaching materials;
5. *Advocacy* through an Office of the Defender of Women's Rights;
6. *Reforms of existing laws.*

The bill did not intend, however, to modify radically the social, economic, or political conditions that underlie women's inequality; thus it did not include reforms in all areas in which women experience discrimination. Nor did it pretend to resolve immediately all the forms of women's domination that are so deeply embedded in Costa Rican culture.

Processes in Support of Women's Rights in Historical Perspective

The Proyecto de Ley sobre la Igualdad Real de la Mujer is not the first case in which Costa Rican women mobilized to pursue their social, economic, or political rights. In the past, women acquired rights through legal processes. These processes generally took three forms, only one of which arose exclusively from women's feminist consciousness and mobilization.

In some cases, the state adopted measures that lacked a strong social mobilization in their favor. This was the case when Costa Rica recognized divorce through the Civil Code of 1888. In such instances, the state anticipated social conflict and acted to control it. Rights acquired by this type of process did not necessarily translate into reality. In the case of the divorce code, for example, a long time passed before either women or men claimed their right to divorce, primarily because of the existing religious sanction of excommunication.

In the second process by which women acquired rights, the state adopted measures in response to pressures exercised by broad social and political forces. Although the measures produced results that extended women's socioeconomic rights, and women's groups and outstanding women leaders may have participated, the movements cannot be considered feminist either in goals or in social composition. Historic examples of the second process are the social reforms of the 1940s; the passage of the Social Security System, which in principle guaranteed "equal salary for equal work, without distinction of sex"; various public health programs that paid attention to maternity; and, in 1943, the Labor Code (Contreras and Cerdas, 1988; Rojas, 1982).

At times, however, the state did adopt certain measures as a direct result of pressures exerted primarily by mobilized women. Feminist movements expressed and directed these demands, even though other groups may have participated in the struggle. One prominent example of this third type of process was women's mobilization in the struggle for the vote during the first half of the twentieth century (see Sharratt, chap. 8 above); that movement continued until the vote was granted to women in 1949.

The Different Versions of the Bill

The Proyecto de Ley sobre la Igualdad Real de la Mujer was inspired by the United Nations Convention on the Elimination of All Forms of Discrimination Against Women (Badilla, chap. 13 below). It was further aided by the commitment during the 1985–86 electoral campaign of Oscar Arias (president from 1986 to 1990), who promised to support women's demands for the elimination of discrimination.

The bill went through four versions (see table 12.2). The first version was made public by the president's wife, Doña Margarita Penón Góngora de Arias, on International Women's Day, March 8, 1988. Version 2 (April 1988) became the first text actually sent to the assembly. Version 3 (September 1989) evolved during the debate. The final version (February 1990) reflects the political compromise that enabled the bill to become law. Table 12.2 outlines some of the important changes in content that took place between the first and fourth versions. The most controversial changes were those related to women's political participation, economic and social rights, and protection from sexual abuse and aggression. The changing titles of the bill indicate the direction of the process.

In some cases, the final version weakened earlier proposals. For example:

- Version 1 proposed a quota system for women candidates in elections to the assembly and municipal governments. This provision was abolished, but the political parties were charged with adopting measures (including the expenditure of funds) for encouraging women's active political participation.
- The financing of child-care centers for workers, proposed in Version 1 to be shared by private enterprises and users and made obligatory for all enterprises, was in Version 4 turned over to the government and no longer termed obligatory.
- Version 1 proposed measures for the protection of women engaged in judicial processes involving sexual abuse or aggression. Version 4 left such women only the possibility of being accompanied to forensic exams by a person of their choice and the right to make complaints about aggression in front of a woman functionary. Version 4 also stipulated training of judiciary personnel to sensitize them to deal more adequately with victims of crimes of violence.

In other cases, however, the final version maintained or strengthened the original proposals:

- Version 4 retained the original proposal making it obligatory for any property provided through public welfare programs to be registered in the name of both legally married spouses or, in a common-law union, solely in the woman's name.

- Version 4 upheld the elaboration presented in versions 1 and 2 to eliminate gender-role stereotypes from teaching materials, and the obligations added in Version 2, namely to teach shared responsibilities of the genders, to cover women's contribution to history, and to finance occupational training for women.
- Version 4 changed the Office of the Defender of Women's Rights proposed in Version 1 into the Defensoría General de los Derechos Humanos, charged with ensuring protection of human rights, especially those of women, children, and consumers.

Other provisions strengthened the bill over the earliest version, but weakened it in relation to intermediate versions. For example, Version 4 established reforms to the Labor Code restricting dismissal of pregnant or nursing women and maintained the prohibition of contracting women for unhealthy work, but the final provisions were weaker than those of Version 2. Diverse groups in the country participated in the national debate over the bill, through the media, roundtables, workshops, and lectures, all of which prompted modifications.

In the aggregate, the changes of the principal components of the bill show regressive tendencies. Though on some aspects, such as employment and protection of workers, the newly approved law is broader than the 1988 proposal, early demands for political participation through quotas, and for socioeconomic rights such as child-care obligation were lost. In several instances, specific measures were replaced by general statements without practical details and obligatory compliance (CMF, 1990).

Every Little Step Counts

When the bill was moving through the assembly so slowly that passage seemed doubtful, the executive, President Arias, established an Immediate Action Plan for Equality, to respond by way of executive decree or interinstitutional agreements to at least some of the originally formulated demands. This brought, for instance, the creation of the Office of the Defender of Women's Rights in the Ministry of Justice; an agreement with the Ministry of Public Education to reform textbook content; and agreements to make credit available to women, train women workers, extend social security coverage, and ensure women's access to sports (Badilla, pers. comm., September 15, 1989). The Immediate Action Plan created better conditions for women during the difficult debate, though several of the measures would not survive the change of government in the spring of 1990.

In the end, the Ley de Promoción de la Igualdad Social de la Mujer is a

Table 12.2. Selected Dimensions of the Four Versions of the Equality Bill

Topic	Version 1 (March 1988) Bill for Women's True Equality	Version 2 (April 1988) Bill for Women's True Equality	Version 3 (Sept. 1989) Bill for Equality of Rights of Men/Women	Version 4 (Feb. 1990) Law for the Promotion of Women's Social Equality
Political rights: Voting and election to public office	Proportional selection of male/female electoral candidates in relation to distribution of voters by gender; 25% of election funds to be used to stimulate women's participation	Eliminated proportional selection of electoral candidates by gender; retained use of funds; 30% of top posts must go to women during next ten years, 50% following 10 years; if two candidates are equally qualified, woman to be preferred	Each political party is to use its own discretion for use of percentages of funds to increase women's political participation; maintained preference for women candidates	Each party will spend a percentage of election funds to improve women's participation; eliminated preference for women when candidates are equally qualified for top posts
Social, economic rights	Obligatory provision of child care workers and employers to share costs; gave women heads-of-family right to health care coverage; women co-owners with husbands of public housing, owners if union is common-law	Duplicated version 1; further stated that child care also will receive government support; maintained right to health care coverage for women heads-of-family	Private enterprise not obligated to share cost of child care centers; state obligated to offer child care, parents to share in cost; women heads-of-family may extend health care coverage to family members; co-ownership of public housing for married and common-law partners	Duplicated version 3; maintained right to child care, health care coverage for women heads-of-family, and co-ownership of public housing for married and common-law partners

Protection against sexual abuse and violence	No pardon for rapists; female official, judge to preside at rape trials; nonpublic hearings; woman can choose person to go with her to forensic medical exam	Duplicated version 1; specified that judicial employees must be retrained to deal adequately with victims of violence	All version 1 and 2 provisions were eliminated; woman can choose to be accompanied to forensic medical exam	Duplicated version 3 but restored right to declare sexual aggression before a female judicial official; restored retraining of judicial officials
Education	Eliminated stereotypes of male/female gender roles from educational materials	Duplicated version 1; required teaching of shared responsibility of genders; women's history; provided financing for occupational training	Duplicated version 2	Duplicated version 2
Women's legal defense	Created women's legal defense agency: Office for the Defense of Women's Rights	Duplicated version 1	Created Office for the Defense of Human Rights of Women, Children, Consumers	Duplicated version 3
Reform of family, penal, civil, labor codes	No specific item for legal reform	Protected pregnant and nursing women against dismissal and against being hired for dangerous jobs	Duplicated version 2, but dropped some sanctions against employers who terminate employment of pregnant women under such pretexts as restructuring	Weakened restrictions against terminating employment of pregnant and nursing women; confirmed women's and children's rights in common-law united families

Sources: CMF, 1988/89; CMF, 1990.

political compromise, but it is also another step in the direction of providing equality in women's lives. Some Costa Rican feminists are disappointed, but others say that every little step counts.

Biodata

A Costa Rican, Aixa Ansorena Montero is an anthropologist and a consultant and investigator in the fields of rural development, health, and family welfare for the Ministerio de Cultura, Juventud y Deportes (MCJD), the European Economic Community, and CEFEMINA, the Feminist Center for Information and Action. Since fall of 1993, Aixa has been doing graduate work in Anthropology at the University of Indiana in Bloomington. She obtained a M.A. degree and is approaching the Ph.D.

References

Badilla Gómez, Ana Elena, personal communication. Sept. 15, 1989.

Centro Nacional para el Desarrollo de la Mujer y la Familia (CMF). 1988–89. Proyecto de Ley de Igualdad Real de La Mujer. Three versions. San José: Ministerio de Cultura, Juventud y Deportes.

——. 1990. Ley de Promoción de la Igualdad Social de la Mujer. San José: Ministerio de Cultura, Juventud y Deportes.

Contreras, Gerardo, and José Manuel Cerdas. 1988. *Los años cuarenta. Historia de una política de alianzas*. San José: Editorial Porvenir.

García, Ana Isabel, and Enrique Gomáriz. 1989. *Mujeres centroamericanas*. Vol. 1. San José: FLACSO.

La Gaceta. 1990. No. 59 (March 26).

Molina, Giselle. 1988. "La administración de la justicia en la violencia conyugal." *Mujer*, no. 5: 13–16.

Programa Interdisciplinario de Estudios de Género (PRIEG). n.d. "Situación de la mujer en Costa Rica: Un perfil de su discriminación." Mimeo. San José: Universidad de Costa Rica.

Rojas, Manuel. 1982. *Lucha social y guerra civil en Costa Rica 1940–1948*. San José: Editorial Porvenir.

13 ❀ Leading Arguments Against Women's Legal Equality

Highlights of a National Debate

Ana Elena Badilla Gómez

The years 1988 and 1989 were an important period for feminism in Costa Rica. During this time we witnessed a national debate following First Lady Doña Margarita Penón Góngora's presentation to the public, on March 8, 1988, of the Proyecto de Ley sobre la Igualdad Real de la Mujer (Bill for Women's True Equality). The two years of debate that followed in the Legislative Assembly were comparable to the struggle before 1949, the year in which Costa Rican women finally obtained the vote (see Sharratt, chap. 8 above).

The debate over the Proyecto de Ley sobre la Igualdad Real de la Mujer was carried on in the assembly; in the media; within political parties, unions, and feminist organizations; and among citizens in general. In all these places, defenders and opponents of the bill voiced their opinions, which ranged from total to partial support to opposition, and from superficial to profound criticism.

Those who opposed the bill cited four principal arguments (CMF, 1988):

- The proposed gender proportionality in politics was unconstitutional.
- There was no need for the bill because there was no discrimination against women in Costa Rica.
- The term *true equality* was inappropriate because the bill might indeed provide a practical mechanism for achieving equality, which was not a politically desirable outcome.
- The provision of shared financing of day-care centers should not be a concern of employers.

This article analyzes these criticisms in order to identify the bill's virtues and defects, its social significance, and its value for the Costa Rican feminist movement.

Rejection of Gender Proportionality in Politics:
The Fear of Shared Power

The first chapter of the Proyecto de Ley sobre la Igualdad Real de la Mujer, which dealt with women's political rights, was without a doubt also its best-known part. It was extensively analyzed and debated by the press and the members of the assembly. The intent of the chapter was to promote greater participation of women in positions of political decision making, whether as elected officials or presidential nominees. This chapter was watered down through a legalistic discussion that, in the last analysis, reflected the fear of the patriarchal powerholders that they might lose their hold on the reins of the political system and be required to relinquish to women a democratic share of men's decision-making powers.

La Prensa Libre (1988b), one of the major national newspapers, ran an editorial on March 11 stating the following:

> The principle of nondiscrimination which our Political Constitution embraces rests upon the true equality of opportunity for both sexes. Thus, all can be nominated as candidates or elected as officials, according to their true or presumed abilities, regardless of gender. Only when an individual—man or woman—with qualifications and enough support to be nominated as a candidate is denied the candidacy, and another, without better qualifications or support becomes the candidate solely because he or she belongs to the correct gender to ensure the proportionality which the law demands—we repeat, only at that moment—would we be witnessing discrimination on account of gender, which would go against the spirit of the Constitution.

In the same vein, the newspaper *La Nación* (1988), a counterpart and competitor of *La Prensa Libre,* argued on March 31: "We think it dangerous to require that political parties distribute representative positions on the basis of proportionality between men and women in the country. Individuals are not qualified, intelligent, or service-minded only because they are either men or women."

We heard the suitability argument also from women who held important public office and opposed the bill for political or ideological reasons. As Marcelle Taylor, member of the opposition, said (1988), "With a law proclaiming the equality of women, we do not seem to take into account women's training, qualifications, loyalty, and other values but merely weigh the fact that they are women."

The Colegio de Abogados (National Lawyers Association), the national professional organization to which practicing lawyers are required by law to belong, named a Commission for Women's Affairs which stated, "Changes like those suggested by the bill would violate the rights of male and female citizens who in truth are the persons who decide candidacies with their vote" (CA, 1988).

More interesting still is the statement of the Tribunal Supremo de Elecciones, the independent body that supervises the honesty of elections in Costa Rica. Upon inquiry by the Social Affairs Commission of the Legislative Assembly, the Tribunal Supremo responded, "To acknowledge the need of reforming Article 60 of the Electoral Code so as to eliminate discrimination—in accordance with the bill under consideration—would mean accepting that clear constitutional and legal dispositions which prohibit any kind of discrimination on account of gender have been violated" (TSE, 1988).

This was a very surprising comment for the tribunal to make. Political discrimination against women is probably so overwhelming that the tribunal preferred not to acknowledge reality: Costa Rican women constituted more than 45 percent of the electorate in the 1980s, but their participation in the assembly since 1953 has been only 6 percent (PRIEG, n.d.), and only fifteen women were ministers or vice ministers between 1970 and 1989 (CMF, 1989). Is that not discrimination? But that is not the only surprising aspect of the tribunal's comment. Even stranger is that following the Tribunal Supremo's statement, the press and many members of the assembly began to criticize the bill as unconstitutional—a judgment reserved for the Supreme Court. Moreover, many critics alleged unconstitutionality without asserting the reasons in support of their view.

Finally, of course, the argument was made that the bill's promoters were "politically frustrated women." Sadly enough, the author of that phrase was none other than the chairman of the assembly's Social Affairs Commission, which studied the bill (Carvajal, 1988).

The Refusal to Acknowledge Discrimination:
A Vote Against the Essence of the Bill

Besides their objection to proportionality, critics questioned whether the bill was necessary. "The bill happens to be not only polemic but also unnecessary. It will disturb and upset what has already been established in our Constitution and our laws," editorialized *La República*, another of San José's principal daily newspapers, on March 14, 1988, echoing what opposition assembly member Marcelle Taylor had written in *La Nación* on March 12 (1988). The argument was that the principle of equality is firmly established in the Constitution, and the nation cannot legislate equal opportunities for women because it is impossible to establish equality by force.

The commentators ignored completely the United Nations' definition of the concept of discrimination against women, which includes "any distinction, exclusion or restriction made on the basis of sex which has the effect or purpose of impairing or nullifying the recognition, enjoyment, or exercise by women . . . of human rights and fundamental freedoms" (United Nations, 1988). Accordingly, a piece of legislation is discriminatory not only when it expressly discriminates but also when its application may have discriminatory effects. Further, the United Nations Convention on the Elimination of All Forms of Discrimination Against Women obligates the signatory states to adopt the principle of equality between women and men in their constitutions, and its Article 4 states that the adoption by participating governments of special measures of a temporary character, with the goal of accelerating the actual equality between men and women, is not considered discrimination (United Nations, 1988).

In agreement with that principle, a mere formal constitutional declaration, such as the one provided in Article 33 of the Costa Rican Constitution that "all men are equal before the law," is not sufficient. It will be necessary to establish expressly that *women and men* are equal before the law. The creators of the Proyecto de Ley sobre la Igualdad Real de la Mujer envisioned it as one of the special measures mentioned by that very convention.

In the wake of the refusal by the press and by assembly members to acknowledge the existence of discrimination against women, one of the specific proposals that evoked most opposition to the bill was the proposal to create an Office of the Defender of Women, the Defensoría or Procuraduría de la Mujer. Opponents protested the creation of the office in *La Prensa Libre* on March 12 (1988a): "We believe that today flagrant violations of the rights of certain groups of the citizenry may exist. But we could not identify these groups by gender. Besides, even if we accepted that violations of the rights of women take place simply because women are women, we doubt that the creation of a new Procuraduría is the way to overcome those violations."

Assembly commission members who studied the bill shared this opinion. Not even the visit of the ombudswoman from Norway—one of the few countries in which such an institution exists—managed to convince commission members of the importance of the office. Thus, the text approved by the commission eliminated the proposal for an ombudswoman's office and introduced in its place a proposal to create an office for the defender of human rights, in which would be included a specific ombudsperson for the defense of women, children, and consumers. At that point, the government by executive decree created the Defensoría de la Mujer (Office of the Women's Defender) (*La Gaceta*, 1989).

Changing the Name of the Bill:
A Vote Against True Equality

During the discussion in the assembly, the element that weighed most heavily against the bill was its very name. All opponents agreed that the bill's title could not be the *Proyecto de Ley sobre la Igualdad Real de la Mujer*. For some, the most threatening idea was that women wanted a law that not only spoke theoretically of equality, but that would also be an instrument that would contribute to creating equality in practice. Therefore, at the very moment that the assembly sent the bill to commission, assembly member Mario Carvajal suggested a name change to the Bill of Women's Rights (1988). Later another legislator, Jorge Rossi, proposed calling it the Proyecto de Ley de Igualdad Esencial de la Mujer (Bill for the Basic Equality of Women) (1988). Finally, Norma Jiménez, the only woman member of the commission, moved that the bill be renamed the Proyecto de Ley sobre la Igualdad de Derechos entre Hombres y Mujeres (Bill for the Equality of Rights Among Men and Women) (1988).

Regardless of that change, defenders of the bill continued to call it the Proyecto de Ley sobre la Igualdad Real de la Mujer, and the public continued to identify it as such.

Day Care: The Worst Threat to Private Enterprise

Rarely in our society has an article adopted on behalf of children generated so much opposition as that generated by the proposal for shared financing of day-care centers.

Some groups in Costa Rican society feared that we women might forget that our essence is to be mothers and our basic responsibility is to bear and educate our children. Others viewed the article for the creation of day-care centers for workers' children under seven years of age as a statist and leftist measure. This group seemed to have forgotten that maternity is an option, not an obligation, and that women working outside the home do not forget their responsibilities toward their children. On the contrary, women bear the brunt of an unequal distribution of household and child-care responsibilities. Women, not men, suffer from the effects of the double or triple day, with one workday for housework, another for child care inside the home, and a third for outside work.

Nonetheless, the press focused on private enterprise opposition to the creation of such centers. The proposed financing divided the cost among the state, the users, and private entrepreneurs, who were opposed, of course, because they did not wish to consider a reduction of the profits they obtained at the expense of poorly paid employees.

Response to the threat of mandated sharing of the cost of day care was immediate. Emergency meetings were held, and newspapers ran editorials with such titles as, "New Tax on Businesses Causes Alarm" (*La República*, 1989); "Urgent Meeting of Chamber of Commerce Presidents: Private Sector on the Alert" (*La Prensa Libre*, 1989); "Objections to Surcharge on Business Accounts: Chambers of Commerce Propose Changes in Bill on Women" (*La Nación*, 1989). The representatives finally gave in and determined that day care should be financed by government appropriations and user fees.

The Objections Strengthen Women's Desire to Fight for True Equality

In the last analysis, all the objections against the bill grew out of a patriarchal conception of society. In some cases, the patriarchs refused to recognize that discrimination against women exists, and in others they admitted that women's participation has been limited and attempts should be made to raise it. Those who admitted that attempts should be made, however, proposed to tailor the solution to the efforts and capacities of individual women, without considering the social, cultural, and ideological factors that maintain discrimination and hinder the full access of all women to politics, credit, and civil rights.

During this discussion of the bill, some profound and constructive criticisms emerged. One in particular stands out: After the analysis of its technical faults and the recognition of its importance, the bill became too modest, and more substantial measures should have been proposed to achieve a true change in the situation of Costa Rican women (DiMare, 1988). The bill as such failed to address many issues that contribute to the gravest types of implicit or explicit discrimination women experience daily. Many of the proposed measures were at most timid first attempts toward a real solution.

Most of those who defended the bill did not deem it a legal instrument that was going to solve all of women's problems; rather, they saw it as a means of beginning a discussion that previously had never taken place in Costa Rica. There was agreement—not only within the feminist movement and the most progressive sectors of society but also among men and women of the left and the right, among workers and intellectuals, among housewives and professionals—that the approval of the bill was an unavoidable step for further social development. The feminist movement therefore assumed a position of critical approval for a government-sponsored bill, which went beyond the limits the government originally envisioned. In fact, this initiative, promoted by First Lady Doña Margarita Penón, totally escaped the control of the president's office and was embraced by all those women who identified with it.

Even in the most distant rural communities, women came to know about the Proyecto de Ley sobre la Igualdad Real de la Mujer. They analyzed it and felt that through it they claimed their basic rights. The growth of women's organizations, the unification of those organizations around a common goal, and, above all, the expression of the feminist movement as a representative actor in society with its own voice were undoubtedly the main achievements of this much debated bill. This process of debate cleared a path toward true equality for women.

Biodata

Ana Elena Badilla Gómez, a Costa Rican, holds a licenciatura in law from the Universidad de Costa Rica. She also did graduate work at the Centro Interdisciplinario de Estudios de la Mujer (CIEM)(Center for Interdisciplinary Women's Studies) (UNA). She was a legal adviser for the Centro Nacional de Desarrollo de la Mujer y la Familia at the Ministerio de Cultura, Juventud y Deportes (Ministry of Culture, Youth and Sports), and for the program Mujer No Estás Sola. She was the coordinator for diffusion of the law's text and information about the Law for the Promotion of Women's Social Equality at the Fundación Arias para la Paz y el Progreso Humano (Arias Foundation for Peace and Human Progress) and currently is the director of the foundation's Centro para el Progreso Humano (Center for Human Progress), which focuses exclusively on women. She coordinates the center's programs for women with a regional, that is, Central American, scope.

References

Carvajal, Mario. 1988. "Declaraciones, Sesión de la Comisión de Asuntos Sociales de la Asamblea Legislativa." *Expediente 10605, Tomo I.* September 28.
Centro Nacional para el Desarrollo de la Mujer y la Familia (CMF). 1988. *Proyecto de Ley de Igualdad Real de la Mujer.* San José: Ministerio de Cultura, Juventud y Deportes.

——. 1989. *Situación de la mujer costarricense*. San José: Imprenta Nacional.

Comisión de Asuntos de la Mujer, Colegio de Abogados (CA). 1988. "Documento presentado a la Comisión de Asuntos Sociales de la Asamblea Legislativa." *Expediente No. 10605, Tomo I.*

DiMare, Alberto. 1988. "Igualdad real de la mujer." *La Nación*. San José. September 15.

Editorial, *La Nación*. 1988. "Igualdad para la mujer." San José. March 31.

——. 1989. "Objetan recargo en planillas. Cámaras proponen reformas a proyecto sobre la mujer." San José. February 14.

Editorial, *La Prensa Libre*. 1988a. "Observaciones a magnífica intención." San José. March 12.

——. 1988b. "¿Qué es igualdad real?" San José. March 11.

——. 1989. "Reunión urgente de presidentes de cámaras. Sector privado en estado de alerta." San José. February 14.

Editorial, *La República*. 1988. "La igualdad real de la mujer." San José. March 14.

——. 1989. "Alarma nuevo impuesto sobre las planillas." San José. February 14.

Jiménez, Norma. 1988. "Moción, Sesión de la Comisión de Asuntos Sociales de la Asamblea Legislativa." October 19.

La Gaceta. 1989. Decreto 19157. No. 166 (September 1).

Programa Interdisciplinario de Estudios de Género (PRIEG). n.d. "Situación de la mujer en Costa Rica: Un perfil de su discriminación." Mimeo. San José: Universidad de Costa Rica.

Rossi, Jorge. 1988. "Moción, Sesión de la Comisión de Asuntos Sociales de la Asamblea Legislativa." December 13.

Taylor, Marcelle. 1988. "Ley de la mujer: Esa no es la ley que esperamos las mujeres." *La Nación*. San José. March 12.

Tribunal Supremo de Elecciones (TSE). 1988. "Pronunciamiento presentado a la Comisión de Asuntos Sociales de la Asamblea Legislativa." *Expediente No. 10605, Tomo I.*

United Nations. Center for Human Rights. 1988. *Human Rights—A Compilation of International Instruments*. New York: United Nations.

Acknowledgments

I am grateful to Alda Facio for comments on an earlier draft of this paper. This analysis represents the author's position and does not constitute a statement by the Fundación Arias para la Paz y el Progreso Humano.

14 ✸ Redefining Political Equality

More Than Including Women

Alda Facio Montejo

Toward More Perfect Justice

The legal concepts or philosophical principles that form the underpinning of laws may seem universal and eternal, but in fact they are constantly changing. As concepts and principles are reinterpreted in the light of historic realities, they evolve, keeping pace with humans' search for a more perfect justice. A case in point is the principle of legal equality, as expressed in Chapter 1 of the first version of the Proyecto de Ley sobre la Igualdad Real de la Mujer (Bill for Women's True Equality) (see Ansorena, chap. 12 above), which was passed in revised form by the Costa Rican Legislative Assembly in 1990 (CMF, 1990). The first version of Chapter 1 never reached the assembly floor because the bill was revised by the executive before it was submitted to the assembly's Social Affairs Commission for analysis.

The first version of Chapter 1 proposed that all political parties be required to present a ratio of women-to-men candidates identical to the ratio of women-to-men registered voters in the party. For women, that number is about 49 percent. This affirmative-action proposal raises serious questions about three concepts related to the principle of legal equality: *citizenship, political equality of men and women,* and *equality before the law.* Throughout the philosophical-legal history of Costa Rica, nobody has ever dared to question the accepted definition of these three concepts. Doing so now constitutes a first-ever challenge to traditional thinking to which most Costa Ricans, including women, are not yet ready to respond.

The following analysis examines how we must reconceptualize these three components of our legal thinking, to arrive at a more just principle of equality. However, before we can do that, we must first redefine an even more basic concept—*human being.*

Redefining *Human Being*

Even though the principle of equality underlies most contemporary formulations of human rights, these formulations fail to account for essential differences between human beings. They use "man" as the prototype or model of "human being," and thereby favor men, specifically men of a certain class, race, and professional status. Thus, when we speak of "equality of the two genders," we have been conditioned to think of raising woman's condition to that of man, who personifies the essence of what it means to be "human." Yet, an assessment of the continued discrimination women suffer, as Latin American feminists and international organizations urge, reveals a need for redefining the term *human being* as the basis for the "principle of equality," in order to ascribe to both concepts a new content that responds to the needs and aspirations of all humans.

One way to approach redefining the androcentric *human being* is to examine arguments against Chapter 1 of the bill. Did male lawmakers deny women the opportunity to debate this bill because they understood the danger to themselves—that of losing the power to define principles and values underlying Costa Rican laws? Or did they prevent debate out of a reasonable concern for its constitutionality, as many argued? Given that a legislative debate—through which all bills must pass—can never be unconstitutional (the Constitution, after all, establishes this process), the answer may well rest with the first explanation. Thus, the refusal to discuss Chapter 1 shows that we women have been naïve in thinking men would consider our needs and would be willing to share power if only we show we are capable or have been discriminated against. On the contrary, the refusal proves that we cannot assume we can gain power without having men lose a good share of it in the process.

Meanwhile, the prototypical human continues to be the male, and patriarchal ideology has made us believe that this is natural, normal, and unchangeable. Women are the "other," the specifically different. Laws directed at the male are presumed to be directed toward humanity as a whole, to be generic and gender neutral, whereas laws directed toward women are seen to be specific to their gender only. Thus, laws intended to correct sexual discrimination are perceived as benefiting only one gender. Although we affirm this as correct, we do not accept the notion that other laws, legal principles, or values based on men's experiences are gender neutral.

Depending on how one analyzes universally accepted principles of citizenship or equality before the law, one must take a stand for or against the corrective measures proposed in Chapter 1 of the Proyecto de Ley sobre la Igualdad Real de la Mujer. That bill required, for the first time, "affirmative" action in election policies in order to achieve the goal of incorporating the above-mentioned three fundamental concepts of *citizenship, political equality of men and women,* and *equality before the law* into the desired reconceptualized, more just principle of equality.

Redefining *Citizenship*

The concept of citizenship shared by probably all Western countries implies that the status of "citizen" transcends all differences in civil society. That is, one can assume that if Costa Rica's Political Constitution establishes that native-born and naturalized Costa Ricans are citizens, all of us are guaranteed the same opportunity to ascend to positions of political decision making. A corollary of this assumption is that laws are neutral and can be applied to all with the same effect. Obviously, if we use these concepts of citizenship and neutrality of laws, we must oppose any affirmative action because such action would by nature be discriminatory by making distinctions between groups of citizens. Moreover, if we believe in the neutrality of laws—i.e., that laws are directed at all of us without distinction of gender, class, or other characteristics—we must contend that legal equality has already been achieved.

If we accept that women are citizens just as men have been for years before them—though women had no role in defining the rules about the rights and duties of citizenship—we must logically also accept that women have not achieved popularly elected office because we women are not qualified, not because the existing rules make it difficult to do so. And that is just what opponents to Chapter 1 of the bill argued: that there were not enough qualified women to fill the quotas that the chapter required. Furthermore, the bill's opponents claimed that any measure to revise the rules was discriminatory because existing rules are gender neutral.

Another argument raised in opposition to the call for corrective measures to achieve true equality of citizenship is the myth that Costa Rican women have lived for the last one hundred years in a democracy with free elections. Few Costa Ricans realize that the struggle for women's citizenship had barely begun by the late nineteenth century, and that women did not receive the formal status of citizen with pseudo-equal political rights until the Constitutional Assembly of June 29, 1949. Thus, women have acted under these pseudo-equal rights only since they participated for the first time in local elections in

1950—a little more than forty years ago. How strange! Even those who are familiar with this history do not always see a conflict with the myth of one hundred years of free-election democracy. Obviously, if the myth is so widely believed, Costa Ricans will not question the equality of opportunity regarding elective office.

Moreover, women have exercised only part of the rights they gained in 1949. They have voted in numbers fairly similar to those of men, but they have held elective office at the national, regional, or local level in only minimal numbers. Records for 1987 show that, although women have constituted from 45 to nearly 50 percent of the voters since 1953, their presence in the Legislative Assembly has never exceeded 6 percent (PRIEG, n.d., Tribunal Supremo de Elecciones, 1985, 1989, 1991).

Redefining Political *Equality of Men and Women*

Conscious of this real, though not formal, discrimination, the women who proposed Chapter 1 of the Proyecto de Ley sobre la Igualdad Real de la Mujer suggested an affirmative-action measure to establish proportionality of the sexes by requiring political parties to include among the candidates for local, provincial, and national assemblies a number of women proportional to the number of women party members. Yet most Costa Ricans believed the measure would establish a quota of nearly 50 percent for women candidates and would unconstitutionally discriminate against men. The proposed chapter did not even guarantee that women would actually arrive at the legislature, as their candidacy would not ensure their election.

Unfortunately, proponents of Chapter 1 did not think to defend their argument by pointing out that human rights concepts develop continually as different generations, cultures, classes, ethnic groups, and genders constantly redefine abstract, universally acknowledged principles according to new needs. The incorporation of economic and social rights into what we today consider human rights is one such example. The workers' movement achieved economic and social rights at the end of the nineteenth century. If the workers' movement was able to reconceptualize bourgeois rights and freedoms from the workers' perspective, can not the women's movement also reconceptualize the right to political equality—which we have never enjoyed fully—according to women's needs?

The Costa Rican Political Constitution of 1949 establishes in Article 33 that "All men are equal before the law and discrimination against human dignity cannot be permitted." This article prohibits discrimination only against human dignity. No article explicitly prohibits measures to undo discrimination—whether by quotas, affirmative action, or any other corrective measure—unless we interpret an action to eliminate centuries of discrimination to be an act against human dignity, or unless, of course, human dignity is understood to be the dignity of men, and only men of a certain race and class.

Those who interpret Article 33 as prohibiting affirmative action harbor a concept of equality that grew out of the French Revolution, a bourgeois concept that we have to transcend because it fails to account for true differences between genders, races, ethnic groups, classes, etc. Those who criticize affirmative action firmly believe that if action were taken to eliminate discrimination against women in political elections it would establish another type of discrimination. They fail to acknowledge that current discrimination against women violates the Constitution, which prohibits discrimination against human dignity. Since women have never been the model of the human being who has the right to vote and be elected (a right established by men for men), women have never had the same opportunity to be elected, even after formally obtaining that right. Moreover, since we have neither participated in developing rules for political electoral activities nor enjoyed total citizenship, we also have not been able to reform concepts developed without us.

Redefining "Equality Before the Law"

Men, who have seen themselves as representing the human species, have traditionally considered themselves qualified to decide everyone's fate without any input from women. The French revolutionaries who proclaimed their well-known "Liberty, Equality, and Fraternity," for example, did not permit women to enter the General Assembly. French women did not achieve the political rights for which so many of their sisters died until more than a century after the revolution, yet nobody considered this a violation of the principle of equality. Similarly, in Costa Rica, Article 33 was part of constitutions long before and after women obtained the right to the vote. Earlier, women were "equal before the law" but could neither vote nor be elected; today we women are "equal before the law" and can vote, but for all practical purposes we still cannot be elected.

In Costa Rica, most people believe that for women equality before the law is limited to receiving the rights and duties elaborated and promulgated by men. Consequently, legal equality between men and women is believed to be guaranteed by proclaiming it, instead of by ensuring it through measures that truly permit the participation of women in defining national priorities. We women have not yet understood that despite having achieved the nominal right to be elected to positions of political decision making, we have not become true citizens actively executing the political rights and duties granted to those eighteen years and older by Article 90 of the Constitution. Even after the revocation of the constitutional articles establishing that only males are citizens, Costa Rican culture continues to support the belief that men can represent women's interests in the public sphere, just as husbands could—and in some parts of our country still can—legally represent wives' interests in the private sphere.

During the pseudo-debate over Chapter 1 of the Proyecto de Ley sobre la Igualdad Real de la Mujer, opponents insisted that it did not matter whether political functionaries were men or women because the offices represented humankind, not one gender or the other. Interestingly enough, those same individuals also opposed affirmative action to bring women into decision-making positions. They argued that if such measures brought a majority of women to decision-making positions, men would be the subjects of discrimination. This is a double standard: On the one hand, it is not discriminatory against women if 94 percent of the representatives are men, because being male or female does not matter in political activities. On the other hand, it would be discriminatory against men if more than 51 percent of government representatives were women. Just as grammar establishes that the masculine form can include females but the feminine form represents only the "not masculine," in the androcentric mentality of politics, men may represent the human species, but women may represent only women.

Thus, a law that benefits only men (even if not targeted explicitly at the male population) is not understood as discriminatory against females, whereas a measure that eliminates unfair male privilege in political elections, though it does not benefit only women, is seen as discriminatory against males. We must clarify: No law ever targets specifically the male part of the population, as this part is commonly called "the people." The irony of androcentrism in political participation is that it produces an effect directly opposite from the effect it strives to establish. Historically, men have represented only the interests of men, but most women in power positions have also represented only the interests of men, as only men's interests were considered representative of all the people. But even if it were certain that women, once in power, would represent only the interests of women (thus a majority of women in political decision-making positions would discriminate against men), why would it be discriminatory, if proportionality had been established between women voters and the number of women candidates for such political decision-making positions? It would still remain the case that not all women candidates would be elected.

Returning to the argument of the unconstitutionality of quotas, which may have influenced the decision of the executive branch to withdraw the bill in its first version, one must remember that every society has written and unwritten laws. An unwritten law in Costa Rica places the upper limit for women's participation in the Legislative Assembly at 6 percent. That means that women have a quota for political power of 6 percent. Hence, the proposal in Chapter 1 was not to introduce quotas but to make existing quotas more equitable by elevating women's share of power from 6 percent to 50 percent. Those of us who want to create quotas of 50 percent have another concept of what constitutes human beings and give a different content to the principle of equality. We believe that we women are equally or more qualified to make decisions in the name of the human community. Thus the problem is not one of establishing quotas but of raising the low quotas to reasonable ones.

Those who opposed proportionality also argued that it would permit an individual to get to the Legislative Assembly solely on the basis of the biological fact of being a woman, without regard to qualifications for wielding power. But this argument, too, must be disqualified. Who can guarantee that men, with their unwritten quota of 94 percent, were not elected merely because of their biology rather than their qualifications for governing? The lamentable state of the Costa Rican Legislative Assembly certainly makes this idea a possibility, if not a logical conclusion.

Given that it is nearly impossible for Costa Rican women to be elected to positions of political responsibility, extending to women the right to be elected is not enough. The procedures that rule the electoral process must also be changed. It is not enough to establish formal legal equality between beings who live in conditions of inequality. Legal equality between men and women will never be achieved merely by declaring some point in time when they will be equal before the law. We must also ask to precisely what condition of men do we wish to raise women? Trying to establish legal equality by legislating that women will be treated as if they were men would only legalize and institutionalize existing inequalities.

Allowing Women and Men to Be "Equally Different"

We must base a reconceptualized principle of true equality on the understanding that men are as different from women as women from men—i.e., that we are equally different. Laws—especially laws that govern access to positions of political decision making—must acknowledge this difference. Acknowledging differences is not the same as discriminating or creating new inequalities; rather, it uses as the baseline for redefinition the reality of women's present inequality, which has been amply demonstrated.

Those who favor the notion of being "equally different" understand that to achieve the principle of equality, we must eliminate inequality and hierarchicalization of men and women, not eliminate the differences between us. One of the arguments against the Proyecto de Ley sobre la Igualdad Real de la Mujer was that it wanted to deny the natural differences between the genders and impose by force a horrible "unisex" world of uniformity. Those who think that the only way to eradicate inequalities is by eliminating differences between human beings merely show an entirely androcentric vision of the world; they are still relying on the paradigm of the representative human being as a Western, white, heterosexual male with no visible disabilities. They cannot imagine that a world without inequalities could instead be populated by beings of different races, beliefs, ethnic groups, genders, sexual preferences, who have different qualifications and limitations. For those unimaginative people, equality means agreement with their stereotype of human being, and anyone who moves away from that stereotype necessarily moves away from the concept of human being.

Unfortunately, those of us who favor an equality based on being equally different lack power to redefine the principle of true equality and give it content. The only way to obtain power in this system appears to be through instituting measures that directly benefit women, and to obtain such measures more women with gender conscience must occupy political decision-making positions. Yet, women who rise to such positions often have no gender conscience and hotly defend androcentric equality.

It is also true that the women who proposed Chapter 1 of the bill did not achieve the conceptual clarity that would have allowed them to defend their position. Instead of acknowledging that by giving more opportunities to women the proposal was taking privileges away from men, they argued that Chapter 1 did not propose affirmative action, that these measures were temporary, and so on. We women have generally made the mistake of avoiding confrontation with those in power, believing we can achieve more equality if we do not imply that men will lose their gender privileges. Thus, to those in power our discourse sounded either insincere or, minimally, confused.

If women had had weightier arguments, Chapter 1 of the Proyecto de Ley sobre la Igualdad Real de la Mujer would have been, if not approved, at least discussed in the Legislative Assembly. We must learn from our failures, and we must think more profoundly about achieving equality. We must propose solutions to women's inequality which do entail loss of privileges by men, without deeming this loss unconstitutional. We must understand, as men understand, that achieving a more egalitarian society cannot mean that everybody gains. If they really want a more just society, the privileged, dominant ones must be willing to give up privileges. If they are unwilling to lose privileges, we must unmask them for what they are and not permit them to overwhelm us with talk about democracy for all humanity. We must accustom ourselves to seeing the loss of male privilege not as discrimination against men but as a necessary step toward equality. Their advantaged condition is based on gender privileges and not on superior qualifications or a natural division of power.

Chapter 1 of the Proyecto de Ley de la Igualdad Real de la Mujer, which was intended to provide more opportunities for women to participate in the electoral process, will not be part of the laws in this republic in the near future. But that must not discourage us. The knowledge that those in power did not want to discuss true political equality will point us in new directions, in order to change the world so that it adjusts itself to our measure also.

We live in a patriarchal world, and women by definition have no power to legislate our equality. But we can develop solid arguments and organize ourselves effectively. We can put pressure on men and women who say they favor equality, so that they will eliminate the discrimination from which women suffer. One important step we can take is raising consciousness about the extent of androcentrism, which until now has imbued our principle of equality. Being conscious of our exclusion, we women are not going to accept an equality that leaves men at the center of political power. Women will have to gain more political power to push for laws—rights for *all* human beings—not only for those of white, Christian, middle-class, heterosexual, Western males with no visible disabilities.

Biodata

Alda Facio Montejo is also one of the authors of "The Group Ventana," earlier in this *Reader*. Her biodata are given there (see chap. 2 above).

References

Centro Nacional para el Desarrollo de la Mujer y la Familia (CMF). 1989. *Situación de la mujer costarricense.* San José: Imprenta Nacional.

——. 1990. Ley de Promoción de la Igualdad Social de la Mujer. San José: Imprenta Nacional.

Constitución Política de la República de Costa Rica. 1949. San José: Imprenta Nacional.

Tribunal Supremo de Elecciones. 1985, 1989, 1991. *Estadísticas del Sufragio.* San José: Imprenta Nacional.

Newspaper headlines demonstrate different problems that cause discrimination against women (from back to front): two women every week infected with AIDS; Ticas earn less than men; ten women per day abused; 100 women [so far this year] lose their jobs because of pregnancy; 42.7% single mothers in 1994

PART III PRESENTED the legal, political, and philosophical arguments for equality. We turn now to a series of readings that offer an insight into ordinary everyday instances of inequality and varied experiences of discrimination in Costa Rican society. By showing how women cope, the selections prove the strength of the individual-efficacy root of feminism. The presentations are ordered according to types of discrimination: by race or class, sexual preference, physical disability, and domestic violence, including incest. This approximates the sequence in which different types of discrimination have risen successively into public consciousness, first through self-help efforts at the grassroots level, thereafter through scientific investigation of the phenomenon, then through discussion in the political and legislative arena, and finally through a society-wide debate in groups, organizations, and the media.

Women Heads of Household in Costa Rica's Limón Province: The Effects of Class Modified by Race and Gender, by Eugenia López-Casas

Eugenia López-Casas presents the situation of low-income women in Limón as an example of socially based discrimination against poverty intensified by race and gender. López-Casas's article deals largely with aspects of the women's movement; in women's fight for survival, they continue to accept the patriarchal society but begin to assess critically the social structure of which they are a part.

After a brief overview of the background and characteristics of Limón Province on Costa Rica's Caribbean coast, the author demonstrates, through the women's own words, how class, race, and gender affect poor female heads of household in the local setting. Of the total population of the region, these women are most threatened by poverty; nevertheless, they develop effective survival strategies that in turn bring them self-confidence and empowerment.

The Lesbian Feminist Group Las Entendidas, by Paquita Cruz

Paquita Cruz traces the growing sense of identity among lesbian feminists, who firmly refuse to continue to be labeled a socially deviant group. She describes their increasing readiness to identify themselves openly with their sister lesbians and discusses their explicit desire to take the initiative in cooperating with heterosexual feminists in areas of mutual needs and interests.

The analysis provides a short history of the lesbian feminist group Las Entendidas (Those in the Know), founded in 1987. The group has given Costa Rican lesbians a nucleus around which they can develop their sense of identity, self esteem, and solidarity. Various lesbian groups meet with Las Entendidas, which coordinates local activities including lectures, recitals, theatrical presentations, and international events such as the April 1990 Segundo Encuentro de Lesbianas Feministas de América Latina y el Caribe. Las Entendidas has helped make it possible for lesbians to join with heterosexual feminists in the struggle against patriarchy. Participants at the Encuentro Centroamericano Feminista in Nicaragua in March 1992, for example, decided that topics related to lesbianism were to be a regular feature at all future meetings.

Women with Disabilities: Between Sexism and Handicappism, by Paula Antezana Rimassa

Costa Rican society, Paula Antezana argues, cannot provide accurate statistical information on people with disabilities. Such individuals face rejection, repulsion, pity, and aggression. This situation is a double burden for women with disabilities, who experience a twofold discrimination through sexism (which puts gender before the human qualities of the individual) and handicappism (which focuses on the disability before acknowledging the individual's humanity). The author offers six hypotheses about the effect of handicappism and sexism on women with disabilities and asserts that these hypotheses should be investigated and tested in Costa Rica.

Never to Cry Alone Again: Women and Violence in Costa Rica, by Ana Carcedo

Discrimination through violence is the focus of Ana Carcedo's study. It is the first of two articles on violence against women in the family, and it deals with women battered by rape and aggression. Carcedo traces the history of attempts by the organization Mujer No Estás Sola to deal with the problem. Many Costa Rican institutions and organizations cooperate with the group, among them the Centro Feminista de Información y Acción. The center and its partners rejected the model of battered women's shelters, popular in other parts of the world, on the rationale that they require unavailable resources and yield relatively limited results.

To counteract the traditional pattern of women's dependency, they developed a program of support groups that allow women to share their experiences and to develop self-confidence and decision-making capacity. In many communities, they sponsor workshops for the prevention of violence through women's empowerment, education in alternative forms of communication, and the discrediting of violence.

Father-Daughter Incest: Case Studies in Costa Rica, by Gioconda Batres Méndez

In Costa Rica, the emergence of yet another topic—incest—from taboo and silence encouraged research, discussions among concerned social scientists and feminists, and reports and editorials in local newspapers. Gioconda Batres offers a small sample of her path-breaking research on father-daughter incest and self-help groups for the young victims and their mothers. She reports on the work of the new Fundación Ser y Crecer, which is institutionalizing the treatment of victims of incest, the training of professionals, and further research.

Drawing on years of research with incest victims and their families and of therapy with sex-abuse victims, the author analyzes the dynamics of incestuous families. She summarizes more than one hundred sessions with adolescent victims of father-daughter incest and their parents. She delineates the construction of masculinity, the experiences of the victims and their mothers, the psychological effects, the social reality, and the therapeutic recommendations for the treatment of problems resulting from father-daughter incest. Research and therapy, including self-help group therapy, are continuing.

15 ❋ Women Heads of Household in Costa Rica's Limón Province

The Effects of Class Modified by Race and Gender

Eugenia López-Casas

Costa Rica is famous for variations in relief, climate, flora, and fauna, and it shows a physical diversity that belies its size. This diversity translates into a variety of socioeconomic conditions, despite the unifying experience of Spanish colonization, nineteenth-century independence, and twentieth-century development of dependent capitalism.

At present, Costa Rica is experiencing an economic crisis resulting from several factors; these include, but are not limited to, the external debt, the decline of coffee prices (coffee being one of Costa Rica's two principal export crops, the other being bananas, though both have recently ceded first place in export earnings to tourism), and the constant political upheavals in countries of the Central American region. Only 40 percent of Costa Rican wage earners earn the cost of the *canasta básica* (market basket), the minimum food required for subsistence for a four-person family (Méndez M., 1989). This general impoverishment particularly affects the female population, and above all women who are heads of households.

Female heads of household have been the focus of extensive analysis during the last few decades. Cross-cultural studies indicate that throughout the world, the economic position of women is low where the proportion of female-headed households is high (Seager and Olson, 1986). Analysts have attributed this finding variously to historical, cultural, social, or economic causes; recently they have also considered the effects of the international division of labor and the global political economy on changing family forms. But global factors do not act alone; they play themselves out in local settings. This study examines the phenomenon in Limón Province, a marginal region in many ways, to demonstrate the interaction of local time- and case-specific factors of class, modified by race and gender, among poor, single, black women who are heads of household.

The Afro-Caribbean Background on Costa Rica's Atlantic Coast

Limón Province has always been the least populated of Costa Rica's seven provinces. Located on the Atlantic coast in the Caribbean lowlands, formerly covered with humid tropical forest, the region today is full of banana and cacao plantations. Some forests remain in the region away from the coast, but much terrain has been cleared for ranching. The area was settled in the 1800s by Jamaicans and other English-speaking Protestants. Thousands of Afro-Caribbeans came as contract labor to build a railroad that would open the Atlantic port of Limón for coffee export. At the same time, banana producers also employed many Afro-Caribbeans to develop large plantations. In the 1930s, the banana companies relocated to the Pacific coast because of crop diseases, but the Costa Rican government prohibited Afro-Caribbeans from migrating there or to other areas—probably because Costa Ricans, proud of their European ancestry and despite substantial Indian admixture, considered themselves as whites who compared favorably to their darker-skinned neighbors in Central America and hoped to stay that way (Seligson, 1980).

The limitation on their free movement caused considerable economic hardships for the Afro-Caribbeans of Limón Province. Moreover, the province was ignored politically and marginalized economically. Though President José ("Pepe") Figueres after the 1948 Civil War eliminated these discriminatory measures and continued the crucial social welfare reforms of his predecessors, no important changes were evident until the early 1970s. Those changes included the construction of roads, expansion of commerce, improvements in health and education services, promotion of tourism and cattle raising, and reappearance of banana plantations. Accompanying those advances, however, was deforestation, resulting from logging and environmentally unsustainable agricultural practices. During this time, there was also a rapid influx of non-Afro-Caribbean migrants from other areas of Costa Rica and Central America, which altered the social structure of many communities. Throughout, Afro-Caribbeans have been least favored economically, and Afro-Caribbean women, especially single heads of household, were among the most seriously affected.

Female Heads of Household in Limón Province

In Limón Province, female heads of household experience a harsh daily reality affected by all the distant causes analysts suggested, but also reflecting local patterns of interaction based on class, race, and gender. One can best assess these factors by looking first at class and then examining the effects of race and gender in conjunction with class, as the women talk about their lives in poor peasant and urban families (López-Casas, 1990).

Early socialization into patterns of women's work and subordination are characteristic of many female heads of household, who had to give up schooling to go to work and supplement the family income. Nancy, thirty years old, describes her experience: "I attended primary school for four years. I wanted to go on and study nursing in a hospital. I like it! But my mother said, 'You cannot study, you have to help me, I got a lot of children.' So I had to stop going to school to help her iron other people's clothes. I would take the bundle of clothes, and I would iron, and iron, and iron, and often I could not manage the irons; they were made of cast iron and very heavy. Sometimes I could not grip the iron, it would turn over my hand and burn my arm. Then my mother would grab me by the hair, shake me, and say, 'You have to learn to be a woman.'"

To be a woman means housework. Olga, a black woman of thirty years, comments on women's primary task: "Well-trained *good* women [able to perform domestic labor properly], even if they have the disgrace of not marrying or of being abandoned, they can fit in any home. It is not the same for men 'cause they can't do these things. This is why women are wished for in other people's houses. Women are fitted for housework, because women are for households. It's a woman's destiny."

But Costa Ricans value education. The women always refer to it, even though they have to give it up, generation after generation. Hear forty-eight-year-old Samantha talk: "I wanted my children to study, not to be like I was, but I had to take them out of school, because what I earned was not enough to keep us alive, let alone buy books and school uniforms. I needed one to take care of the little ones, and the other to go into the street and sell fruit while I went to work."

Nidia, who is thirty-five, provides another example: "My children had to leave school to help me, you know; I can't afford their education. I wanted them to learn skills, become mechanics or electricians. Roberto is very clever, he works selling newspapers. He is very good at business. If I give him one hundred colones, he turns them into three hundred."

By the time children reach eight or ten years of age, they become an income-producing resource for the women, who develop small family enterprises in which all help. Earlier, though, when the children are small, the women have to rely on the help of the extended family, particularly their mothers and grand-mothers, who take care of the children while the woman goes out to work.

Race plays a peculiar role in child care in Limón. The custom is to leave children with the maternal grandmother, but many black women from Limón, even grandmothers, go to New York to work as cooks. So mothers leave their children with maternal grandfathers, and the old men bring up the children. Prohibited from moving to the Central Valley, black people moved abroad—many to the United States—and this became the prevalent pattern.

Gender is another factor that creates difficulties through discrimination in earnings. Whether they do permanent, part-time, or piece work, women earn less than men! Costa Rican labor laws have outlawed this type of discrimination since the 1950s, but employers have found ways of circumventing the law. Moreover, women are at a disadvantage since they cannot work overtime because they must care for children. Also, they are often illegally deprived of their true wages by unfair accounting and underhanded swindles.

Margarita, thirty-eight years old and a rural worker, tells this story: "I have worked in the countryside, alongside men, producing more than they did. But I always had a woman's luck, and they paid me a peseta [1/4 colón] less per hour. On payday, my check was the smallest, and if I complained they would not hire me again."

Marielena, a twenty-five-year-old worker reports: "They hire me every three months, and then they make me resign. They send us to work in a different section every three months, and in that way they do not have to pay us *prestaciones* [severance pay]."

In view of such effects of class, race, and gender, Limón Province women who are heads of household have created defense mechanisms through inge-nious survival strategies: (1) households in which mother and children work together for income; (2) hidden prostitution, by which women do sexual favors to get work, obtain rent, etc.; (3) family networks among mothers and daughters to trade goods and services; and (4) neighborhood solidarity when women heads of household organize small enterprises that provide them with a system of exchange of goods and services, including child care.

Survival Strategies Foster Self-Reliance

The factors of class, race, and gender interact to make Limón women who are single heads of household highly vulnerable to poverty. Yet, being alone, hav-ing a space of their own, allows them to make decisions, control their own money, and become aware of their capabilities and rights.

Bethany, an urban black woman of twenty-five years tells us: "A companion? It would have to be somebody with whom one could share all—he would have to be understanding, share housework, income, the responsibilities with the children. If not, I prefer to be alone and be responsible for my children. Thank God, I have taken care to make myself a future for my children. I studied—true, not the career I would like [she is a secretary], but it was the one within reach. I have worked hard to improve my income and to help my children advance, without needing the help of their father."

Bethany participates in a church group and a community organization for housing. This has given her self-esteem and a certain influence, and she enjoys the respect of the community. Many women heads of household who belong to women's organizations are also achieving the community status Bethany gained. Those are the women who are organizing themselves, who have supported, for instance, the movement for the Proyecto de Ley sobre la Igualdad Real de la Mujer (Bill for Women's True Equality) that was recently passed in Costa Rica (see Ansorena, chap. 12 above, and Badilla, chap. 13 above). These Costa Rican women, capable of making decisions, aware of their rights, have become awakened before many of their sisters on the continent.

Biodata

Eugenia López-Casas is a Costa Rican born in México City. She has a Ph.D. in anthropology from the University of Durham in England and is a professor of social anthropology at the Universidad de Costa Rica. She has had a long-term interest in women, and in 1974 she was the first to do research on women heads of household, a subject on which she has written widely under the name of Eugenia López de Pisa. She is one of the founders of the Programa Interdisciplinario de Estudio de Género (PRIEG) (Interdisciplinary Gender Studies Program) at the Universidad de Costa Rica (UCR) and was involved with the recently established M.A. program in Women's Studies. She also served as director of Género y Envejecimiento (Gender and Aging), a university program in which students can fulfill their social-service requirement for graduation by working in eight senior citizens' day centers. Employing a gender focus, the centers offer recreational and educational activities, thereby increasing solidarity and mutual support among the senior citizens. At the moment she is teaching Gender and Gerontology in UCR's interdisciplinary M.A. program in Gerontology.

References

López-Casas, Eugenia. 1990. Analysis of Life Stories of Fifty Women Heads of Household on the Atlantic Coast of Costa Rica. Research in progress.

Méndez Mata, Rodolfo. 1989. "Verdad y realidad en Costa Rica." La Nación. September 8, p. 18A.

Seager, Joni, and Ann Olson. 1986. Women in the World. London: Pan Books.

Seligson, Mitchell A. 1980. *Peasants of Costa Rica and the Development of Agrarian Capitalism*. Madison, Wis.: University of Wisconsin Press.

Acknowledgments

This study draws on research in progress. It presents the analysis of fifty life stories of Limón Coast women heads of household. The author thanks these Limón women, who bravely face their problems and have taught her how they are turning their disadvantages into assets.

16 ❋ The Lesbian Feminist Group Las Entendidas

Paquita Cruz

Lesbian feminists founded Las Entendidas (Those in the Know) in early 1987 as a base from which we could struggle against our particular oppression. Although some of us had participated in other feminist organizations, we had never been able to entirely identify with them because they never discussed topics that concern us, such as the problems of lesbian mothers; homophobic attitudes, both among heterosexual feminists and ourselves; job discrimination; or the images patriarchal society projects of lesbians. Even when we participated in support groups alongside heterosexual feminists, our sexuality and our daily life with our partners were always pushed aside.

Yet, belonging to those groups raised in us a feminist consciousness and showed us how our daily independence from men makes us a threat to the domination patriarchy exercises over women. Our life-style demonstrates that it is possible for women to be self-sufficient, and it proves that women are not dependent beings. But our most dangerous characteristic, the one for which we are punished the most, is that we do not obey the mandate of obligatory heterosexuality, that we tell all women that life offers other options—not necessarily lesbian options, but nonetheless options for fulfillment and independence. To militate against the danger lesbians present to the stability of patriarchy, its institutions keep us invisible, dispersed, guilt-ridden, and homophobic. We realized that if we were to become free and independent, we would have to find our own identity through a feminist interpretation of patriarchal reality.

We decided therefore to form our own support groups, in which our political and erotic relations with other women could be openly expressed and even encouraged. We looked for other lesbians who had not joined feminist groups, and we began to meet. Initially uncertain of how to proceed, we found that our need to talk, to offer each other affection and solidarity, supported us and gave us strength to act. We gathered to read together, to speak of our intimacies, to express doubts and fear, and to laugh together. About ten to fifteen women were in the original group of Las Entendidas. In our early meetings in the home of one of our members, we met many restless lesbians who brought us new ideas. The group began to stabilize.

We soon found that the first battle we had to wage was within our own group, and we fought this battle on three fronts: against our weak self-esteem, which we had acquired from a society that rejected us; against our own homophobia, which we had absorbed throughout a lifetime of disrespect; and against our passivity, which caused us to tolerate the discrimination we suffer in all areas.

Having clarified and worked out these issues among ourselves, we decided to extend the scope of our activities to the larger lesbian community. We began by going to the bar La Avispa (The Wasp), which at that time was the only public place in San José where we could get together and be ourselves. The women bar owners and many women customers supported us. They understood.

In La Avispa we soon organized evenings "for women only," to build up our self-esteem. These events now take place on the last Wednesday of every month, and in recent times several of the meetings were sponsored by the owner of La Avispa. On some evenings we offer lectures on various topics related to women and lesbians. On others we stage recitals of poetry, classical or popular music, or lesbian theater. Still others feature events focusing on dance, painting, or narrative literature. During our evenings together we have learned that the more united we are, the better we can fight against the ruling homophobia that supports patriarchy.

In 1989 we began to publish a quarterly bulletin, *Las Entendidas*; in it we comment on feminist activities inside or outside Costa Rica, reproduce lesbian and feminist texts, and provide a forum for lesbians to express themselves. As of late 1993, fifteen issues of *Las Entendidas* have appeared.

We also started a reading group, open to any woman who wants to attend. We read and discuss literature on the oppression of all women, and we ponder the importance of heterosexuality for patriarchy and the ways in which patriarchy also oppresses heterosexual women. As we read lesbian literature, essays of lesbian feminists, and articles about the experience of other lesbians, we let go of our own homophobia and build our self-esteem. Politicizing ourselves, we gain strength to defend our life-style against a society that represses us and forces us to live our lesbianism in hiding, feeling guilty.

In addition to these activities, which reached hundreds of Costa Rican lesbians, Las Entendidas organized the Segundo Encuentro de Lesbianas Feministas de América Latina y el Caribe (Second Encounter of Feminist Lesbians of Latin America and the Caribbean) in mid-April 1990 in San José. (The First Encounter took place in Mexico.) About two hundred lesbians of the region participated in the Second Encounter, which featured workshops on such topics as sexuality, alternative law, violence, feminism and lesbianism, aesthetics, the political implications of coming out of the closet, lesbian mothers, and myths about lesbianism. New topics also appeared during the meeting. Recreational activities included antipatriarchal beauty contests, feminist talent shows, concerts of music by women composers, and games to heighten our solidarity and strengthen our lesbian identity.

This Second Encounter brought an important amplification and consolidation of the international network with other lesbian consciousness-raising groups throughout the continent. The open discussion of so many different topics with women of so many countries over the span of a few days gave us new points of view and contributed to developing fully our lesbian consciousness.

The Lesbian Community Before Las Entendidas

The importance of the bar La Avispa as a meeting place for lesbians throughout the years before the foundation of Las Entendidas cannot be stressed enough. Among gay bars, La Avispa was one that was predominantly feminine. We went there in groups when we wanted to be lesbians in public, our only goal that of enjoying ourselves, dancing, and having a few drinks. It was one of the few places in which we occasionally met with women from different socioeconomic backgrounds. Yet, those of us who somehow had in part managed to overcome our homophobia considered the bar a sordid, dark, maybe even dangerous place. Its decoration was dismal. It was, and still is, frequented by the police. When the police were coming, a white light advised us to stop dancing in pairs, and we all returned to our seats. The bar was also frequently visited by heterosexual men, who came to satisfy their sick interest in a conduct they consider sinful. We accepted both kinds of visits without comment.

Except for gatherings at La Avispa, lesbian women had no community. We formed small groups, banding together according to similar cultural, economic, and social conditions, often meeting at private parties. The various groups coexisted, but not without a certain rivalry: there were Las Deportistas (The Athletes), Las Intelectuales (The Intellectuals), and Las Plásticas (The Plastic Ones) who were less political and more consumer-oriented, both in appearance and possessions, than were the other groups. Las Tractoras (The

Braves) were the more daring "butch" lesbians who displayed their lesbianism in dress and behavior. In contrast, Las Enclosetadas (The Hidden Ones) remained "in the closet," formed very closed groups, and never attended gay parties. Only rarely did we meet lesbians from outside these groups, and when we did, we felt no sense of solidarity. We were nearly invisible, comfortably hidden in our small friendship groups, some more closed than others. Most of us carried on a double life in our work and with our families, and we paid a high emotional price in a situation from which we saw no escape.

Our lack of lesbian-feminist consciousness made us accept the social discrimination and police repression in the bars as a matter of course. It exhausted us, but because of our self-rejection, which we had learned in a discriminatory, gynophobic as well as homophobic society, we suffered the situation without rebellion.

Changes for Costa Rican Lesbians

We cannot yet speak about a complete revolution in the society around us. We could not in the short span of less than a generation change the profoundly antifemale attitudes of men and, unfortunately, also of many women. We have not yet concluded the stage of consciousness raising within our own lesbian community, and we are still far from celebrating the day on which we can move openly through society without any fear, claiming our rights equally with other citizens of Costa Rica.

But we do see changes and hope. Aware of the need for a solidarity that we must offer to all women in this gynophobic society, we have tried to establish a closer relationship with heterofeminists. This has not been an easy relationship, and the movement has always been initiated by us. They did not search us out or invite us to participate in their parties or events. Even today, most Costa Rican heterofeminists are still at a stage long since abandoned by feminists in other societies—the stage in which they try to convince men that all feminists are not "like those women who are not feminine." Thus many heterofeminists have fallen into the patriarchal trap of refusing to join with us for fear of being labeled lesbians. Because of that fear we probably have gained only a limited rapport, and that with only a few of the women outside our lesbian community. The great majority of the heterofeminists still only tolerate us, provided we are silent and almost invisible. The more heterosexual we appear, the more they accept us. In their fear and internalized heterosexuality, some have acknowledged their worry that we might move into a large number of places in their sessions, meetings, and other activities.

When we have asked for the support of other feminists, only a small minority have responded, which has tended to make us feel that our lesbian-feminist group is isolated within the larger Costa Rican feminist movement. Still, we do note slight changes, and our international success is beginning to have repercussions at home. A few heterofeminists feel they can learn from and with us, and some even acknowledge that heterosexism may affect them more than it affects us.

Despite the lesbophobic attitudes and behaviors of the heterofeminists, we continue to believe that the first step outside of our lesbian community must be toward them, because both groups fight against patriarchy. And, though we understand that their homophobia stems from the same source as ours, namely patriarchy, we expect more from them than from other women, because only together can we build an egalitarian society without discrimination against any human group.

In fact, after we had organized the Second Encounter and weathered the repression unleashed by press, church, and government, many heterofeminists did recognize the magnitude of the discrimination directed against us. Today, the topic of lesbianism and the participation of our group in the activities of the feminist movement are increasingly accepted. In March 1992, Costa Ricans brought to the Meeting of Central American Feminists in Nicaragua six sessions on lesbianism, among others on topics such as internalized lesbophobia, lesbian sexuality, and relations between lesbian and heterosexual feminists.

Thus, being organized has not only helped the members of Las Entendidas grow but has also brought wider acceptance of our activities in Costa Rica. We have received support from lesbians of many different ages and socioeconomic levels; the face of the lesbian community has changed considerably over the last few years.

For the moment, we are happy to have begun to move, to recognize that we have changed internally. We now have an important center in the remodeled La Avispa, with more light, more windows, better music, and more lesbians who want to exercise their right to occupy a dignified place in the world. When police officers enter, we no longer run to our seats feigning "not me." We now dare to continue dancing and to ignore them. They will continue to exercise their small power, but we will see to it that this power diminishes.

The members of Las Entendidas and the lesbians who join in our activities enjoy extensive support, through which we provide for many of our social needs. Our dear friend continues to offer her home for celebrations of Christmas, the New Year, birthdays, and anniversaries. Such dates are no longer associated with the pain of pretending to be who we are not or of being separated from our partners and far from our true lesbian family. And at every celebration, we see new faces joining us.

Other friends have offered new spaces for meetings and encounters. We celebrate magically feminine ceremonies to chase away the bad spirits of patriarchy or to summon the forces of peace and beauty to sweeten our lives. This new freedom we are enjoying leads us to discover time and again new and more creative forms of being together, which we want to share with other women. We sense that with this type of energy we can win out over patriarchy. Most important, this form of resistance is certainly more fun.

We have recently achieved greater solidarity among the different groups that coexist within the lesbian community. We are many now, sharing various spaces and many concerns, joining women of all ages and from all possible backgrounds. We marvel every day about what and how much we have achieved. We have been able to affirm our existence in a moving and energizing way. The struggle has brought us joy and has made us feel stronger and more able to face what is to come. Our road will not be easy, but it will not be as hard as the one we have already traveled. Now that we have taken our first steps we will continue to move, sometimes slowly, at other times more quickly—but always now with greater assurance because of our newly achieved identity.

Biodata

Paquita Cruz, a Costa Rican, studied museography in Mexico, photography in Italy, and art at the School of Fine Arts at the Universidad de Costa Rica. While living in Italy and France, she also traveled to the Middle East. For a time she had her own art restoration studio in San José. Recently she has returned to painting and is doing videos on women.

17 ❀ Women with Disabilities

Between Sexism and Handicappism

Paula Antezana Rimassa

We live in a society with room for only one kind of human being. All aspects of life are shaped to satisfy the needs of people who are male, forty-five years of age or younger, white, and middle class; who have no apparent physical limitations; and who are characterized by the aggressiveness and motivation required to maintain the status quo. People outside of these parameters face rejection, discrimination, repulsion, pity, and aggression. Their very existence is an offense, a threat against society. Individuals with disabilities are an example of such outsiders.

In antiquity, children born with physical or mental limitations were often eliminated by means of socially accepted practices that ranged from cold-blooded assassination to abandonment. Over time, this practice changed, and people began to believe that these children deserved pity and that benevolent institutions should take care of them.

Both conceptions influence the actual image of persons with disabilities: They are either rejected or pitied. Society has converted disability into a stigma that affects men and women and inhibits their full development as total human beings.

Some Thoughts on Terminology

Language, an important manifestation of culture, can be oppressive. To free ourselves, we must search for new terms to replace sexist and discriminating ones. We must equally avoid using euphemisms. Individuals with disabilities have been labeled by such degrading terms as *handicapped, crippled, disabled,* or *invalid.* However, to see the individual as a total person, we must stop focusing first on her or his physical or mental capacities. Thus, I use the term *individuals with disabilities,* which carries a clear social and political connotation, instead of *disabled individuals,* which immediately identifies individuals by their physical or mental capacities. "Women with disabilities" are first and above all women, though circumscribed by disabilities that socially condition their lives. Therefore, the expression *women with disabilities* constitutes more than just a technical term.

Studies in countries other than Costa Rica clearly conceptualize the situation of women with disabilities (Fine and Asch, 1984; Hannaford, 1985; Saxton and Howe, 1987). Such research has identified a close relationship between sexism and what has been called handicappism. Both sexism and handicappism constitute truly oppressive ideologies. Just as we differentiate between sex and gender, we can speak of disability as merely a physical or mental condition and of handicappism as its social expression. The inability to gain access to education, health care, political and community participation, employment, or an independent, dignified life does not stem from a physical disability in itself. Rather, this restricted access has its origins in a society whose structures not only ignore but specifically marginalize individuals with disabilities. That is, society expressly nourishes handicappism. In Costa Rica we do not yet have any studies or debates on this relationship.

Disability and Gender

For an individual with a disability, considerations of gender, race, ethnicity, sexual preference, or social class seem to become irrelevant. It is as if the disability in itself eclipsed other human dimensions. Nevertheless, and here arises one of many contradictions, even though the importance of gender seems to disappear in the face of disability, men and women do not receive equal treatment. In fact, gender can alleviate or exacerbate the impact of disability.

Yet, disability does not affect men and women in the same way. If discrimination and undervaluation of women is something we learn in early childhood, how does this affect women with disabilities? To say that women with disabilities are doubly discriminated against is more than mere rhetoric.

Men and women are socialized differently. A disability weighs more heavily on women in a society in which physical attributes largely determine whether they will be accepted. The fact that an organ or sense does not function fully mutilates women internally, so they consider themselves incomplete. The absence of that function of their body becomes an absence of their sense of self-worth.

The media sell an image of women that is a stereotypical ideal of beauty that few women attain. At some point all women have suffered the frustration of not being like media images. From girlhood, women have learned to feel uncomfortable with their bodies. Yet, an important difference defines the group of women with disabilities: For them those frustrations are not temporary.

Moreover, women with disabilities are also excluded from the traditional roles of women, though certainly not by their own choice. Maternity, for example, is inconceivable for many women with disabilities. Similarly, interpersonal relations, and particularly couple relationships, are especially difficult, if not impossible. Society has likened disability to asexuality, particularly regarding women. Studies show clearly that sexual experiences of women with disabilities are extraordinarily limited and that few of them will marry (Fine and Asch, 1984; Hannaford, 1985). Most men are repelled by the idea of becoming romantically involved with a woman who, in their minds, is not healthy or whose dependence, a trait basically accepted as feminine, would be so accentuated that the man would become a caretaker, which typically is a feminine role. In the few isolated cases in which the woman does enter into a couple relationship, the man is often considered either a saint or a loser.

Women with Disabilities in Costa Rica

Costa Rica does not provide statistics about the exact number of people with disabilities, nor does it provide statistics about their living conditions. The Consejo Nacional de Rehabilitación (National Council for Rehabilitation) publishes a *Registro Nacional de Minusválidos* (National Register of the Handicapped) (meaning invalids!), which reports a total of forty-five thousand individuals with disabilities (1989). Nevertheless, the same institution acknowledges that those data do not reflect the true magnitude of the population with disabilities. It prefers to use the projections of the Organización Mundial de la Salud (World Health Organization), whose data indicate that at least 10 percent of the population worldwide have some disability. According to such estimates, three hundred thousand individuals with disabilities live in Costa Rica.

Consequently, it is difficult to estimate the number of Costa Rican women with disabilities. According to the *Registro Nacional de Minusválidos,* 42 percent of the reported people with disabilities are female. However, if we consider that Costa Rica, like all of Central America, experiences the feminization of poverty and that disability is intimately related to poverty (UNICEF, 1981), through lack of access to early or continued treatment, for instance, we can hypothesize that many more women than men must be affected by disability.

Not only do statistical summaries ignore women with disabilities in Costa Rica, most people who consider themselves dedicated to the struggle for the rights of individuals with disabilities or for the rights of women have not even imagined the specific situation of women with disabilities. Those who did so contemplated the situation in theory only. It is no accident that the topic of disability compounded by gender has only recently been acknowledged in Costa Rica; many people customarily avoid facing the reality of the daily life of a woman with disabilities, preferring to view that reality through the opaque lens of such euphemisms as *physically challenged* or *differently abled*. As a result, the problems women with disabilities face have not been recognized by those engaged in recent social struggles. In the remainder of this essay, I propose some hypotheses that should be tested by future research.

Some Hypotheses in Need of Testing

Although general projections about the living conditions of individuals with disabilities exist for Costa Rica, they are not disaggregated by sex. Nevertheless, I have combined data from other countries with personal experiences and observations to propose hypotheses about living conditions of women with disabilities in Costa Rica.

Hypothesis 1: Few Costa Rican women with disabilities have joined the work force in the last decade. Despite the fact that many women have entered the work force during the past decade, women with disabilities have not participated in that process. In general, women with disabilities of working age are unemployed or underemployed, living on meager government pensions or surviving with the help of their families. Yet, even in cases of severe disabilities, those women who live with their families frequently do housework. This does not happen to men with disabilities; if they stay home, they usually do not do any housework. Women with disabilities who must seek work outside the home in order to survive face extremely discriminatory treatment at the worksite.

Hypothesis 2: Women with disabilities do not participate to any great extent in formal or informal education. In Costa Rica, women participate widely in formal and informal education, yet women with disabilities do not. Furthermore, most efforts to increase their participation have not met with success. For example, in 1989 the Instituto Nacional de Aprendizaje (INA) (National Institute for Occupational Training), which regularly serves people without any apparent disabilities, wanted to begin a training project for women with disabilities from poor urban areas. The well-intentioned project never became a reality for lack of institutional political will. However, the planners had already carried out two sessions with a group of women with disabilities to ascertain the kind of training they desired. (This was an unusual step, for many professionals believe they fully understand what the needs of women with disabilities are.) The women in the group responded almost unanimously that they wanted, as one phrased it, "a training program that will teach me to be somebody." Another stated, "I want to learn an occupation, finish school, and be somebody." These responses eloquently demonstrate the women's thirst for opportunities. Even those who never learned to read and write knew that only with occupational preparation would they be *somebody*, with all that this term implies.

When they were asked why they believed such a project for women with disabilities was necessary, one of them replied, "if women without our limitations find it difficult to obtain the opportunity of training for occupational skills, how much more will women with disabilities? Rarely if ever are we given a chance to show our talents, however humble they may be."

In response to the question of how such a goal could be accomplished, two replied, "We must speak about each of our plans and dreams that are within the realm of possibility," and "I want to know more about how discrimination against women with disabilities affects their families." Such replies reveal the need for women to escape from the four walls in which they are often imprisoned and their need to express their dreams, frustrations, suppressed tears, and legitimate anger. Though these needs may seem unrelated to training, they actually are closely related. A training program must take into account the individual as a whole person.

Hypothesis 3: The health-care experiences of women with disabilities are generally related to care by specialists for the individual's specific disability. In the field of health care, our experiences with the medical profession and with health services have been strictly limited to specialists for each woman's functional limits. Often we are reduced to inert bodies that are subjected to observation and medical experimentation.

We are systematically exposed to medical oppression. The doctors—almost always men—believe they know what we need. Those of us who have experienced (and I believe almost all of us have) being in a hospital under medical observation understand what it means to see the most intimate space of our privacy invaded. Our "cases" are described in copious reports, which are written about us but to which we never have access. We are rarely informed about the different treatments specialists prescribe. Everybody pretends to know our bodies better than we do, and we are reduced to mere physiological entities.

U.S. activist Marsha Saxton refers to medical oppression as a type of oppression with its own characteristics, according to which we must deliver ourselves to the medical system and deny our own much more exact and realistic knowledge of our own bodies and experiences (Barrett, 1990).

Hypothesis 4: Most women with disabilities are poor. To affirm that the majority of the women with disabilities are poor is no exaggeration. Disability is strongly associated with poverty.

Hypothesis 5: Women with disabilities are not taken into account. In Costa Rica, women's needs are not taken into consideration in rehabilitation policies, be they concerned with prevention, rehabilitation, or occupational health. Sexism, exacerbated by handicappism, characterizes those who formulate policies, and who, of course, do not have any visible disabilities themselves.

Hypothesis 6: Freedom of movement is prohibited by architectural barriers. Architectural barriers in the capital as well as elsewhere have turned Costa Rica into a country that is practically inaccessible to individuals with disabilities. They are entirely robbed of the option of moving independently.

Conclusion

At a time when topics relating to women evoke special interest, the situation of women with disabilities fills the void left by the progress of feminism. The topic of women with disabilities should be analyzed and discussed by society in general and by women with disabilities in particular. We women with disabilities must cast off our invisible status and know and respect ourselves and our own value so that we can participate fully in society.

Biodata

Paula Antezana Rimassa was born in Cochabamba, Bolivia, but now lives in Costa Rica and is a Costa Rican citizen. She had polio at age one, and she uses a wheelchair. She completed graduate studies in law at the Universidad de Costa Rica and worked as legal consultant in the Arias government (1986–90). Thereafter, she served as program officer for the Fundación Arias para la Paz y el Progreso Humano (Arias Foundation for Peace and Human Progress); in 1992 she took on the function of director of the foundation's Centro de Filantropía (Center for Philanthropy).

References

Barrett, Carolann. 1990. "A Network for Disabled Women, an Interview with Marsha Saxton." *Woman of Power,* no. 18.

Consejo Nacional de Rehabilitación. 1989. *Registro nacional de minusválidos*. San José, Costa Rica.

Fine, Michelle, and Adrianne Asch. 1984. *Women with Disabilities*. Philadelphia: Temple University Press.

Hannaford, Susan. 1985. *Living Outside Inside*. Berkeley, Calif.: Canterbury Press.

Saxton, Marsha, and Florence Howe. 1987. *With Wings*. New York: Feminist Press at the City University of New York.

UNICEF. 1981. "Pobre entre los pobres." Internal document. Mimeo.

Acknowledgments

In Costa Rica, we as yet have no studies about the relationship between handicappism and sexism. This is a first exploratory analysis of the topic; it constitutes a statement by the author only. It is not a statement of the Fundación Arias para la Paz y el Progreso Humano.

18 ❈ Never to Cry Alone Again
Women and Violence in Costa Rica
Ana Carcedo

This does not pretend to be a history, even less *the* history, of the movement against aggression toward women in Costa Rica. It simply revives memories of a process I lived, alone and together with other women and men, as a member of various organizations concerned about the violence against women.

1982: Beginning of a Collective Concern

In the early 1980s graffiti crying "Death to the Rapists" appeared on walls in San José. They looked alike, which seemed to indicate the campaign of an organized group, though one indignant individual could have been behind it. This was probably the first time anybody publicly registered the need for collective action to stop the violence against women in Costa Rica and to put an end to the impunity with which perpetrators could act. The slogans did not provoke uprisings, and no one ever claimed authorship of the campaign. But the cry against rape fed the concern about aggression of individuals and groups.

Centro Feminista de Información y Acción (CEFEMINA) (Feminist Center for Information and Action) as well as Ventana, the two feminist organizations of the time, stated that laws and legal procedures were entirely inadequate (see Carcedo, Sagot, and Trejos, chap. 3 above, and Camacho, Facio, and Martin, chap. 2 above). Often in trials about rape the victim ended up the accused, as the first issue of the review *Mujer* (Women) (1983a), published by CEFEMINA, documented. In its second issue, *Mujer* (1983b) denounced the increase of rape and the existence of gangs of rapists. CEFEMINA began a campaign, with complaints and action, to bring about changes in legislation, government protection, and women's self-organization for defense in neighborhoods and communities.

Although rape was a taboo topic, in April 1983 CEFEMINA organized a roundtable on the problem, thereby provoking a heated debate. The attempt to organize community groups against rape, though, was a failure. Nobody wanted to participate. Women said the mere fact of belonging to such a group made them suspect of having been raped.

Yet the concern grew, and with it grew the effort to make people aware and to promote changes in legislation, institutions, and public opinion. Meanwhile, attention was focusing increasingly on rape within marriage and on sexual aggression within the family. Feminist and professional organizations began to show concern for women battered by their spouses. In 1982, a first meeting, the Seminar on Battered Women, took place, with seventy-five persons attending. Most participants at that meeting heard for the first time about analyses and responses from the movement against violence in the United States and Europe. Some participants decided to go on meeting to discuss proposals to deal with the problem.

The Debate About the Shelter

The Seminar on Battered Women began the debate about the best way of dealing with domestic violence against women in Costa Rica. Shelters, the general response of the movement in the United States and England, became the central issue. The rationale for a shelter is simple. The battered woman must leave home to be safe, particularly in an emergency. She must be able to count on—at least for a certain span of time—sufficient space in which to think about and organize her future without worry, tension, fear, or the risk of further aggression. A shelter can offer a safe haven for her and her children, time to look for work and housing, and time to file a complaint.

Most Costa Rican women who had decided to develop an action plan viewed a shelter as an unsatisfactory answer if it was meant only to house and protect the women and their children. In a proposal to the Primer Congreso Universitario de la Mujer (CUM) (First University Congress on Women) in May 1984, these women tried to enlarge the scope of the topic, proposing a women's center for attention to *or* sheltering battered women, and for involving the community in the prevention of violence (Facio F., 1985). Members of CEFEMINA discussed and finally threw out this alternative. Some professionals shared this position, totally or in part. Unfortunately, no written records of the discussion remain.

CEFEMINA rejected the idea of the shelter as an alternative for action for four reasons. First, entering a shelter does not allow women to break the pattern of dependence with which they were raised and which was reenforced through their relationship with the aggressor. On the contrary, the support of the shelter strengthens this pattern. No doubt, the woman's living conditions and daily activities change, but the change is not a result of her own decision. Other people become responsible for her.

Second, in Costa Rica the combined effort of the feminists at that time was small, and the resources they could muster would have served only a small number of mistreated women. The physical, emotional, and material cost of maintaining a shelter is enormous. Even though CEFEMINA had no alternative to offer, it decided to search for something that promised a greater yield for its efforts. CEFEMINA's members wanted to reach more women—the entire society—and besides, they wanted an answer that included prevention. Without prevention, one would never get to the roots of the problem.

The third reason CEFEMINA hesitated to adopt the model of a shelter relates to women's subjective expectations. A shelter offers tremendous options for providing material and legal services to women. New ideas about legislation emerge. Personnel learn to raise and administer resources. But CEFEMINA reasoned that what was most needed was an understanding of the women's personal needs. A shelter offers battered women many possibilities for leaving the battering relationship behind, but is that what the *women* wanted? When we listened, we found their emotional world was a crucial factor.

Finally, CEFEMINA rejected the notion of charity for the victim inherent in the shelter alternative. Charity would institutionalize and marginalize the women as well as the problem, instead of helping women to create their own survival strategies and making society responsible for offering them comprehensive options.

The debate about the shelter did not, incidentally, remain at a level of words. In 1984, professionals of the Asociación Centro de Orientación Integral (Center for Comprehensive Counseling) obtained foreign financing to open a shelter, the Albergue Belén (Shelter Bethlehem), in San José. They took in battered women and their children and provided legal aid, dealing with an average of six new cases daily. The status of the Albergue was precarious, and in the end, the program closed in April 1985. Unfortunately, the insights and lessons of its staff did not ever become widely known.

This experience strengthened CEFEMINA's stand against aligning itself with the idea of shelters. Above all, the Albergue experience confirmed the gigantic organizational effort required for maintaining a shelter and the limited return from the energy and resources expended. During 1984, two CEFEMINA members had been able to observe firsthand twenty U.S. shelters, which made CEFEMINA even less supportive of the shelter alternative. We found some very perturbing results. Many women left the shelters and renewed their relationships with their aggressors. Moreover, the time in the shelter ended before many women had found work or a source of income. Did they end up in the street?

CEFEMINA decided not to mortgage its future and refused to participate in any project that involved shelters. Among professional women concerned with the problem, and even among some women affected by the problem, the popularity of the shelter alternative began to dwindle. Nevertheless, many others continued to propose shelters as the primary response to aggression within the family (Ugalde, 1989). Of course, if nobody could offer an alternative that in practice would be more viable, the debate would remain highly unbalanced.

The Search for Other Alternatives

After 1985, a cloak of silence fell over the topic of aggression within the family. The proposal presented to the 1984 University Congress of Women did not obtain financing, and the group that had developed it dispersed. Yet the concern over the problem remained, and each member carried that concern to her respective organization and daily work. Nationally, the problem had not been brought to public attention nor had it provoked institutional or governmental preoccupation. It remained hidden, nonexistent in the eyes of society and its institutions. Foreign organizations also seemed uninterested in financing projects related to aggression against women in Costa Rica. People working either alone or collectively on this problem did so exclusively with their own resources.

But if this was a relatively quiet time nationally, it was not characterized by passive acceptance. In those years, violence against women became a popular topic for research and theses for lawyers, psychologists, social workers, and others (e.g., Armas, Caravaca, and Conejo, 1986; Esquivel, González, and Zúñiga, 1988; Molina, 1989; Peralta, 1986; Soto, 1988), and for graduate courses taught at Costa Rican universities (see Ferro, chap. 28 below; Guzmán, chap. 29 below; Jiménez, H., chap. 30 below).

Moreover, through daily work with women in communities and centers of social services, we at CEFEMINA learned at the micro level about the problem's material and subjective dimensions. Some of our current reasoning dates back to that time. One of the most important issues relates to women's struggle to obtain title to their houses. These women represent about 80 percent of all those who supported self-construction housing projects and had built their own houses (see Sagot, chap. 22 below). From discussions about this right to property, which the state had been reluctant to accord to women, came comments such as "Now [that I own the house] he cannot mistreat me any longer and throw me out of the house. Now, *he* has to leave if he touches me." Indeed, why should society permit the aggressor, in addition to mistreating the woman, to stay in the home and send the woman and her children into the street? Such thoughts had been used as a reason to justify the shelter alternative. Consequently, CEFEMINA began to take as its baseline for all planning and action that if anybody had to leave the house, it would be the aggressor.

In addition, much that sounded persuasive in theory did not fit what we observed in daily life. As a rule, women did not want to give up their relationships with their aggressors, nor did they want to take legal action against them. True, they were seeking the intervention of someone with authority, but they wanted that individual to demonstrate to the aggressor that he was behaving incorrectly, so that he would change and the man and woman could develop a good relationship. Illusions? Maybe, but this reality, rather than some other ideal that we might wish to see as the attitude of the battered woman, had to be our point of departure.

Moments of Pain and Reflection

Part of the focus CEFEMINA has given its work on violence against women is closely linked to several particularly painful events that took place in 1986 and 1987. On April 6, 1986, seven women were brutally assassinated with firearms, and three of them were raped. One victim was an adult, the others minors. This event had an enormous impact upon public opinion, though there never was a satisfactory investigation. Nevertheless, the wish to stop the aggressors' impunity grew among individuals and concerned groups. Then, a year later, in February 1987, a series of systematic assassinations began—eleven to date— generally of couples, in which the murderer was particularly merciless against the female victim. Here again was evidence of an impunity against which it seemed impossible to fight.

CEFEMINA plunged anew into discussions about how to deal with the problem of violence against women. Members decided to seek direct intervention in support of women; to orient the work toward criticism, sensitizing, and prevention; and to discredit violence. They reasoned that the aggressors' impunity had persuaded society to accept its own impotence and passivity and to accord little value to a woman's life.

In August 1987, CEFEMINA began to conduct "meetings of small groups of women, without the presence of men, so as not to inhibit them as they vent their experiences" (Caravaca, 1987). Simultaneously, CEFEMINA offered lectures to larger groups to sensitize them to the problem, to women's rights, and to prevention of aggression against women and children. The dynamics in these groups quickly moved beyond legal questions as the complex realities of fear, anguish, and illusion emerged. For six months these meetings brought new elements of the aggression pattern to CEFEMINA's attention.

As a result, in 1988, CEFEMINA developed a sensitizing workshop "Conflict Among Spouses, Aggression in the Home, and Mistreatment of Minors"; we carried the workshop to work and study centers in various cities and communities and to professionals and functionaries of different institutions. In our travels across the country we met many people seeking to confront the problem, both individually and in groups. Some were independent professionals, some had the support of institutions, and others were individuals sharing their own resources. This exposure gave CEFEMINA an informal inventory of activists and additional insights.

Our work complemented the actions of a growing number of people who worked to demystify violence and dedicate themselves to the defense of battered women—in lawyers' offices, consulting rooms, work places, or teaching posts. The strengthening of feminist currents and a growing general preoccupation with the situation of women undoubtedly favored this new level of activity, even though the topic remained taboo for the general public and officially existed neither for the law nor for governmental institutions.

Finally, a Plan for Comprehensive Action: "Mujer No Estás Sola"

By the end of 1988, conditions seemed ripe for a significant step forward. This at least was how it appeared to CEFEMINA, and its president so declared at the inauguration of the Segundo Congreso Universitario de la Mujer (CUM) (Second University Congress on Women) in September (Carcedo, 1989). A working session proposed a Comité Nacional por la No Violencia Contra la Mujer (National Committee to Prevent Violence Against Women and in the Family) to integrate previously dispersed efforts and promote new activities. At the beginning, the committee included members of CEFEMINA and of the Comité del Niño Agredido (Committee for Battered Children); functionaries of different institutions, such as the Patronato Nacional de la Infancia (PANI) (National Agency for Child Protection) and the Centro Nacional para el Desarrollo de la Mujer y la Familia (CMF) (National Center for the Development of Women and the Family) of the Ministerio de Cultura, Juventud y Deportes (MCJD) (Ministry of Culture, Youth, and Sports); professionals working in private practice with battered women; and women and men who simply wanted to participate. In the end, a stable core emerged.

The first task this committee assumed was that of celebrating, for the first time in Costa Rica, the Día Internacional de la No Violencia Contra la Mujer (International Day for the Prevention of Violence Against Women), on November 25, 1988. It was a success. Most of the diverse women's groups, government institutions, and programs specially directed toward women participated. For that occasion, the committee published "Mujer No Estás Sola" (Woman, You Are Not Alone; 1988), a pamphlet directed at women who suffer mistreatment. Thereafter, this pamphlet became one of the most important instruments for communication among the women.

A few days later, "Nuestro Mundo" (Our World), a popular TV program with a viewing audience made up mostly of housewives, began a series of open telephone interviews. When the topic of family violence against women came up, many viewers called and asked for immediate help. The testimonies we heard, and the anguish with which the women spoke, had a tremendous impact. Not being able to offer counseling, the two presenters called for an open meeting of all women who felt affected, to face together the problem of aggression.

On December 1, 1988, about fifty women squeezed into a room at CEFEMINA, and a new form of support group was born which became decisive in the development of the movement against mistreatment of women. Support groups strengthen the self-respect of every woman and her capacity to make decisions and carry them out.

In August 1989, the National Committee for the Prevention of Violence Against Women and CEFEMINA, working together, began the program Mujer No Estás Sola, with help from the Centro Nacional para el Desarrollo de la Mujer y la Familia (CMF). The program established support groups and working groups for sensitizing and prevention in communities. Today, it carries out and fosters research, training, and counseling, and it also promotes changes in public attitudes through the media. Within institutions it works to further a change of attitude in treatment and regulations, and on the national level, promotes changes in legislation.

Between December 1988 and December 1991, more than three thousand women, in groups or through individual consultation, have received help from Mujer No Estás Sola. We respond to an average of 110 monthly phone calls from women asking for support and counseling, and about 100 calls from professionals and institutions requesting information and coordination. We have reached more than six thousand families in different communities through programs of sensitizing and information. The women have the option of joining working groups to solve specific problems or participating in workshops for empowerment.

The comprehensive approach to the problem and the individual support we give each woman have contributed to the popularity of Mujer No Estás Sola. The program has had a considerable impact because it is the first in Costa Rica to offer direct attention to battered women. Results so far go beyond the mere count of women who received services and information, or the experience our organization gained. The Ley de Promoción de la Igualdad Social de la Mujer (Law for the Promotion of Women's Social Equality), approved in March 1990 (see Ansorena, chap. 12 above; Badilla, chap. 13 above; Facio, chap. 14 above), the Defensoría de los Derechos Humanos de la Mujer (Office of the Defender of Women's Human Rights), formerly in the Ministry of Justice and now part of the Defensoría de los Habitantes (Office of the Defender of the Inhabitants), and the Delegación de la Mujer (Women's Delegation) in the Ministerio de la Gobernación y Policía (Ministry of the Interior and Public Safety) (essentially a police station for gender crime where women can file complaints about violence) provide important support for attention to women and prevention of aggression against them.

A Network of Related Efforts

Aggression against women in the family is now a publicly accepted topic, and part of the responsibility for its acceptance rests with Mujer No Estás Sola. As the wall of silence and prejudice crumbles, others have amplified our network of related efforts, through new organizations, training programs for official personnel, or international gatherings.

Some of these organizations and their work with victims include the following: The Comité del Niño Agredido has for years carried on the almost impossible task of abuse prevention in local communities. The Fundación de Solidaridad (Solidarity Foundation) works with women who have been operated on for breast cancer, who are often mistreated physically and emotionally by their families. Individual pioneers in therapy with groups of women victims of incest have organized since April 1990 the Fundación Ser y Crecer (FUNCRESER), a private nonprofit organization that works in programs of prevention and treatment, teaching victims that they are not guilty and that they can learn to cope with their experiences (see Batres, chap. 19 below). The Fundación Promoción, Capacitación y Acción Alternativa (PROCAL) (Foundation for Advancement, Training, and Alternative Action) has been active since 1985, beginning by helping street children and later moving into work with pregnant adolescents, who are usually victims of incest or rape. For them it has created shelters called María Chiquita.

In the effort to sensitize and train officials of public institutions to the problem of violence, CEFEMINA and Woman, You Are Not Alone have cooperated with FUNCRESER to provide training courses or workshops for members of the Ministry of Justice, the judiciary system, and police forces. CEFEMINA does continuous training of personnel of health organizations.

Finally, CEFEMINA and Woman, You Are Not Alone have been responsible for national and international conferences in the area of violence against women, in order to further raise consciousness and develop policy proposals. The meeting of the Primera Consulta Nacional para Elaborar Propuestas de Políticas Públicas en Relación a la Violencia Contra la Mujer (First National Conference for the Elaboration of Public Policies Regarding Violence Against Women) on November 25, 1991, produced a list of ninety policy suggestions addressed to all governmental and public institutions that are in any way responsible for dealing with the problem of violence (CEFEMINA, 1991a). With that same objective, the Primer Encuentro Centroamericano y del Caribe Sobre Violencia Contra la Mujer (First Central American and Caribbean Meeting on Violence Against Women) convened on December 1–8, 1991—with representatives from more than forty programs in Canada, the United States, Mexico, Guatemala, El Salvador, Honduras, Nicaragua, Costa Rica, Panama, the Dominican Republic, Puerto Rico, Brazil, Peru, and Ecuador—and proposed similar measures for the region (CEFEMINA, 1991b).

Finally, we must not forget the dispersed and anonymous collective of professionals, mostly women, who at every state institution and in hundreds of marginalized communities seek new ways of facing the problem and struggle to persuade their institution to assume responsibility. But today, as we witness diverse approaches to the problem of violence, we see no single solution. We accept the challenge and continue searching for new and better ways.

Biodata

Ana Carcedo is also a co-author of "Improving the Quality of Women's Daily Lives: Costa Rica's Centro Feminista de Información y Acción," which appears earlier in this *Reader* and carries with it her biodata (see chap. 3 above).

References

Armas Romero, Rossy Bell, Adilia Caravaca Zúñiga, and Juan Bautista Conejo Badilla. 1986. "La mujer frente al sistema legal costarricense." Licenciatura thesis, Facultad de Derecho, Universidad de Costa Rica.

Caravaca Zúñiga, Adilia. 1987. Internal report. CEFEMINA. August 15–September 1.

Carcedo, Ana. 1989. "Palabras de bienvenida." *Mujer* 5: 8.

CEFEMINA. 1983a. *Mujer* 1 (March).

CEFEMINA. 1983b. *Mujer* 2 (April).

CEFEMINA. 1991a. "La política contra la violencia ha sido no tener políticas. Violencia en la convivencia familiar contra la mujer y los niños." Draft of final document. Mimeo. San José, Costa Rica: CEFEMINA.

CEFEMINA. 1991b. "Políticas públicas para enfrentar y prevenir la violencia contra las mujeres y en la familia. Propuestas por el I Encuentro Centroamericano y del Caribe Sobre Violencia Contra la Mujer." Mimeo. San José, Costa Rica: CEFEMINA.

Comité Nacional para la No Violencia Contra la Mujer. 1988. *Mujer No Estás Sola*. San José, Costa Rica.

Esquivel, Ana Luisa, Patricia González, and Patricia Zúñiga. 1988. "El incesto: Un estudio casuístico de seis familias." Licenciatura thesis, Escuela de Psicología, University of Costa Rica.

Facio Fernández, Tatiana. 1985. "La mujer agredida." *Mujer* 1 (June): 39.

Molina Subirós, Giselle. 1989. "La mujer frente a la administración de justicia." Licenciatura thesis, Law Department, Universidad de Costa Rica.

Peralta Cordero, Lidia. 1986. "Síndrome de la mujer agredida." Licenciatura thesis, Law Department, Universidad de Costa Rica.

Soto Cabrera, Tatiana. 1988. *Los mecanismos legales desprotectores de la víctima de agresión sexual*. San José, Costa Rica: Centro Nacional para el Desarrollo de la Mujer y la Familia.

Ugalde, Juan Gerardo. 1989. "Síndrome de la mujer agredida. Síndrome de la agresión familiar." *Mujer* 5: 41–43.

19 ✻ Father-Daughter Incest

Case Studies in Costa Rica

Gioconda Batres Méndez

This study is based on the author's research with victims of incest and their families since 1988 and on her work as therapist with victims of extrafamilial sexual abuse and intrafamilial incest, with adult male victims of brother-brother incest, and with other sexual offenders who reported offenses during therapy. The author treated at different times the abusing fathers, the mothers of the victims, and the adolescent victims of father-daughter incest.

The phenomenon of incest in Costa Rica has been reported over a long period. Only recently, however, has the accumulated evidence permitted a systematic assessment of the complex dynamics of incestuous families and an identification of the phenomenon's social links with the structure of patriarchy in Costa Rica.

Guided by a feminist vision of the problem, the author used more than one hundred individual, family, and group therapy sessions with victims of incest and their families in compiling this report. With the agreement of the victims, the sessions were taped, transcribed, and then revised by them, so as to be true to their testimonies. The study analyzes the statements of the victims and their families and relates the findings to other investigations. It is a first attempt to transmit the experiences of the author and her male and female patients. The patients testify with courage about the process, sharing their pain in an effort to clarify what is going on in Costa Rican families. All participants authorized publication. The names of the victims have been changed to protect their identity.

In this study we define *incest* to be any form of sexual caresses or sexual gestures shared with a minor to satisfy the sexual needs of an adult whose authority derives from the affective ties that connect him to the child. Although this does not necessarily imply physical sexual relations, it can include, beyond the use of pornography and sexual gestures, masturbation or sexual relations between fathers and daughters.

The Costa Rican Context

As part of the research, the author studied Costa Rican historic documents in the Archivo Nacional (National Archives) to determine whether cases of incest were reported in the past. Those who finally admitted that the problem exists in Costa Rica insist that it developed very recently, but this was not the case. Even before 1817 reports were recorded in the archives. One case, for example, was that of Lieutenant Matías H., who was suspected of incest with María Gertrudis, his ten-year-old daughter. The father declared his daughter provoked him, as she had "the inclination to be bad." The father's lawyer accused the victim of having tried to threaten conjugal and familial tranquility and, in the end, the judge absolved the father of all guilt (ANCR, no. 1105).

More recently, various public institutions and private organizations, such as the Comité del Niño Agredido of the Hospital de Niños (Committee for Battered Children of the Children's Hospital) and the Fundación PANIAMOR (Foundation for Bread and Love) have revealed that sexual abuse and incest in Costa Rica are growing alarmingly. Both the press and various research organizations now publish statistics that formerly remained hidden. These statistics do not take into account the hundreds of cases that remain anonymous in families that cover up the problem to avoid denouncing the offenders.

The Construction of Masculinity in Patriarchy: How an Offender Is Formed

The true significance of father-daughter incest cannot be understood unless the analysis parts from the perspective of patriarchy, in which men prevail over women and women are subordinate. This unequal system ensures the reproduction of a masculine psychology of domination and a feminine psychology of victimization, through which fathers exert great power over their daughters (Herman, 1981, p. 55).

In contemporary Costa Rican society, the qualities considered masculine in men do not differ much from the characteristics of the fathers in all the incestuous families of the author's clinical practice. Society expects men to show strength, power, domination, and competitiveness. Sex is the arena in which these concepts of masculinity are played out. Men are pushed to separate affection from sex, are socialized into sexual activities and fantasies apart from the context of a relationship, and are attracted to younger partners with less power than their own. Diane Russell calls this the mysticism of masculinity, reinforced by media images and pornography (1984, p. 119).

The construction of this mystic masculinity within the family and its transmission from generation to generation were defined by one of the victims in the following manner:

> My father's father was also a *machista* (domineering male). Ever since he married my grandmother, he cheated on her with other women and beat her up. He spoke to my father of those women, of his adventures, and took him to prostitutes when he was still young, to make him a man. Then my grandfather left my grandmother and married another woman. My Papá hated his mother because she remarried. He said she should have remained unmarried to raise her children, but for his father he feels an obsession—his father is the only one he accepts as better than himself. It is the same story with my brother, he is already like my father. He thinks women are dirty. When I had a boyfriend, he began to cry and said I was a prostitute. He hits my mother and my sisters, learning that one can hit women. Papá says he soon has to take him to the prostitutes. But he is only twelve years old, and Papá shows him naked women. He took another son to prostitutes when he was only twelve years old. For my little brother, Papá is the greatest. He always says he wants to be like him.

In this family, the hidden messages the young boy receives create in him stereotypes of masculinity and an interpretation of the relationship between men and women which implies that women are dirty sexually and must be controlled. He learns that one way to control them is to hurt them—attack them and humiliate them. He is beginning to know that if he wants to be strong and have control, he must imitate his father. He has also learned that sex and gentleness towards women do not go together.

In other families, three of the victims' fathers read pornography and used pornographic magazines during the incest with their daughters. The relationship between pornography and sexual violence is sufficiently proved, and offenders believe it can rationalize the sex act with children (Russell, 1986). It is not surprising to hear incestuous fathers say that what they did with their daughters did not harm them.

The Mothers

The author's research revealed, as did that of others (Sgroi, 1982, p. 192), that the mothers of the victims showed patterns of behavior consistent with one of two models. The first model is that of women with low self-esteem, with a history of abuse in their childhood and with few social relations. These women are submissive and dependent on their husbands and have no power within the family. Because they do not think of themselves as capable of living without their partner, these mothers find it most difficult to leave their husbands when they discover incest.

The second model of mothers corresponds to women who have less serious problems of childhood aggression or family pathology and who maintain familial and social relations that give them support. These women can more easily make decisions to leave, or to make their husbands leave the home when the incest is discovered.

Carmen fits the first model, as her testimony shows:

Theresa was my foster mother. She had three single, embittered daughters. They beat me with sticks and always complained about the sacrifice they had to make for me. When I was about five, my mother took me to collect rent for a few rooms she rented, and I remember when she was talking to one of her tenants, a man picked me up and kissed me on the mouth and touched my genitals. When I was twelve years old, my mother became sick with arteriosclerosis and was not quite coherent. I felt very alone, she was the only one who had given me a little bit of affection. The second daughter had 'attacks'; they said she was schizophrenic and had to be committed to the former Asilo Chapuí [psychiatric hospital]. When I met the man who is now my husband, it was a great success for me. I never believed I could have anything, and this was the first thing I had. Besides, my sisters said we should not let go of men when we are 'fishing.' I was very grateful someone like him paid attention to me.

A weak powerless mother who cannot decide to leave, or ask her partner to leave, creates conditions for a constant mother-daughter confrontation in which the daughter feels betrayed and abandoned by the mother, and the mother feels overwhelmed by a feeling of guilt for not protecting her daughter. This is reinforced by a father who constantly belittles the mother and psychologically abuses her. Yet, at the same time, the daughter also feels annoyed with her mother for being weak and unable to protect herself against sexual aggression, and for needing to be protected. One adolescent said, "I do not think I can ever get married. How could I leave my mother with my father? She says, what would happen to her if I left? I hate that she is so dumb and lets herself be managed by Papá."

The mother-daughter interaction always presents two reproaches, one that the daughter abandons the mother if she leaves, and the other that the mother abandons her daughter when she tries to separate the daughter from the father. On one occasion, when Carmen's husband had to leave the house, she cried and lamented all day long, clearly blaming her daughter. Consequently, the daughter's depressive symptoms became severe as she, the victim, felt guilty for having hurt others and having broken up the family.

The study indicated that victimized mothers must be an important focus in the treatment of incest and that they need support. As a rule, mothers initially offer resistance to any kind of treatment, especially group treatment, because with their low self-esteem and feelings of guilt they find it difficult to face others.

The Victims

Five young women, ages thirteen to twenty-one, participated in the research. All of them reported the incest to their mothers during adolescence. Four went to, or are still undergoing, individual therapy with the author and participate in a self-help group for victims of incest. The group is the first of its kind in Costa Rica, and treatment is free. The young women belong to all social classes. The earliest age of abuse was four years, the oldest eighteen years. One was raped four times by her father; the contacts with the remaining four did not include coitus. The average time they remained silent without commenting on the incest to their mothers was seven years.

Taken together, these five victims represent a typology of different behavior models toward incestuous sexual abuse. Their differences in behavior seem to depend on personal, social, and family history, though they also display characteristics similar to those of sex-crime victims—e.g., feelings of lack of control over their own bodies, damage to their sexuality, guilt, shame, and a reduced capacity to establish affective relationships. As already indicated, the primary evidence for the study is the testimony of the young women. They themselves, through their testimonies, related what incest has meant in their lives. Here are three such testimonies:

Elena (twenty-one years old)

> I do not remember when it began. I must have been seven years old. He pulled my pants down and said vulgar things. When I was older, he asked me to put on sexy, provocative clothing and to masturbate or watch him masturbate. I felt Papá did this because he was the person who most loved me. He said it was a secret between the two of us and made me feel important. I became disillusioned when he told me he had given money to other girls to have sexual relations, and when he insulted me when I went out with my friends.

Elena came for treatment for other reasons. During treatment she said an unknown person had offered her work and asked her if she had been abused, promising to cure her of her trauma with a sexual relationship in which he would do exactly the opposite of what her father did. She was not aware that this was also a sexual abuse until someone close to her said she was behaving strangely and made her seek therapy.

Many women who experience incestuous abuse and its associated betrayal lose the capacity to correctly judge the honesty of others or to recognize the difference between what may and may not be dangerous for them. Once that capacity has been damaged, incest victims become vulnerable to later abuses. They have repressed their deep, painful feelings of fear and rage and have divided themselves into two parts. One part maintains an appearance of normality, the other denies the painful experiences and the feeling that they are bad. This compartmentalization later keeps them from recognizing other abusive situations.

María (fifteen years old)

Mother and Father were separated. When I was thirteen, Mammi sent me to my father. Whenever I went, he touched me. The second time I went, he raped me. It happened about four times. He was always drunk and forced me. I did not tell Mammi because I was afraid she would not believe me. Since this happened with Papá, I am like this. I was different. I misbehaved, but not extremely. I went for walks and came back, never did I do the devilish things I do now. All has changed completely. I hate the world; I tell myself that I am an idiot that this had to happen to me, that nobody would believe I am that stupid. It never entered my mind that my father would do this to me. My Papá produces in me at the same time love, pity, and resentment. I do not care if they lock him up.

This adolescent's sexuality is associated with violence, repulsion, fear, rage, shame, guilt, and a feeling of being dirty and hurt, which is typical for most victims of sexual abuse (Russell, 1986). After her experience she began to show signs of a chaotic sexuality, of sexual interests inappropriate for her age. She fled from home, had sexual relations with a stranger, had behavioral problems, and was put in a juvenile center. Some victims like María learn to identify themselves as sex objects, to develop sexual relations like those they experienced in childhood (Norwood, 1988, p. 117).

Cecilia (fifteen years old)

I remember when I went to kindergarten, Mammi sent me to Papá, so he would teach me how to write. I was four years old. He did not tell me not to say anything, but I never told Mammi because I did not know if it was okay or not. He told me this was nothing rare, that fathers in the whole world had to do this. As I was only four years old, it did not mean anything, I believed it was normal since it was in a magazine Papá showed me. I confused things, I thought what he did to me was because he loved me, and I adored him. When we are little, we believe what daddies say. I could hit him, but he never hit me. I believed that was because he loved me; I was all mixed up. I preferred to leave things alone and think of other things. Today I feel sorry for my dad, but I do not want to see him again.

From age four until she was fifteen, when she reported the incest, Cecilia was silent about her abuse. Then in school at lectures about sexual abuse she had to confront her confusion again. Her grades suffered. She locked herself in her room until she could stand it no longer, and then she told her mother. Together they sought therapy.

Some children cannot recognize sexual gestures during abuse and interpret them as affection. They are in no condition either to evaluate or to consent, given the difference of power between father and children (Finkelhor, 1980, pp. 76–77).

Keeping the secret of having been a victim of sexual abuse for so many years can increase the feeling of being stigmatized and the psychological impact of guilt, shame, and low self-esteem. As Robin Norwood points out, the trauma of incest consists in "the violation of confidence, the imposition of secrecy, the negation of protection, the invasion of borders, be they physical or psychological, or both" (1988, p. 153).

The Relationship with the Father

Ambivalences between loyalty and betrayal and between affection and annoyance characterized the father-daughter relationships of the young people who participated in this study. They also reported compassion toward their fathers, focusing less on their own pain and on that of their mothers.

For some, at least initially, the incest was important because it was the only kind of affection or love they could have from their fathers. They expressed love for their fathers but not for the abusive act. Two of them perceived the sexual relations as a privilege that made them important through a relationship in which they were special to their fathers. Although this relationship with the father gave them a certain power over their brothers, sisters, and mother, it also carried with it an oppressive power to unite the family or tear it apart if the victim revealed the secret. This sense of power in individuals who have neither any control over their own lives nor any power within the family is the only access to power and control they can derive from their experience. At the same time, such sentiments increase their feelings of guilt and shame. For another victim, the incest had an abusive meaning from the very beginning. She clearly stated her annoyance with her father: "I would not have liked to love him, because in this way I feel less betrayed. I feel better that I did not love him so much. I never saw him as father, even before he abused me."

The young women internalized a psychology of masculine supremacy, which from generation to generation produces boys and girls who admire the father's power. Having subordinate women educate and raise boys and girls guarantees that the psychology of masculine supremacy will be reproduced in the next generation. Under such conditions, father-daughter incest will be frequent (Herman, 1981).

The Family Dilemma

Costa Rican society values the family highly, and many incestuous families confront the possibility of a break-up when they discover incest. They face a dilemma: They can separate the victim from the home, a decision that creates in her the sense of being castigated and revictimized, or they can separate the father from the home, which produces in the victim a feeling of having betrayed or destroyed the family.

As long as the abuse is not acknowledged, the family can act out the social farce of being united and well and can therefore retain society's approval. When the victim reveals the secret, the family may disintegrate. To defend themselves against dissolution, many families require the victim to keep the secret (Norwood, 1988). The author's clinical experience has confirmed that the victims in such families are the people who have the greatest difficulty recuperating. Their feeling of double betrayal against the mother and the father, their rage, and the control others maintain over them do not permit them to take control of their own lives. This pattern is totally opposed to the goal of therapy with the victims of incest, which is to help them to achieve just this control.

Therapy for the Victims of Incest and Their Families

The self-help groups for victims of incest and their families, particularly the mothers, are a treatment option that is beginning to show positive results. Frequent in other countries, those groups are not as yet common in Costa Rica. The two self-help groups of victims and mothers about which we are reporting are a beginning. The insight from this study indicates that we must use all therapeutic means to treat these families and that self-help groups have great value for the victims, mothers, and offenders in those families.

As for treating offenders, experts are debating whether therapy can modify behavior. In the author's experience, offenders do not accept therapy without some coercion, though definite results are not yet available. An offender who was referred to a male therapist, the only one who has accepted a year of therapy, has made some behavioral changes but, in his therapist's opinion, he shows great resistance and little sensitivity for what has happened.

The Institutionalization of Treatment

In 1990, in an effort to institutionalize the treatment of victims of incest, a group of concerned social scientists and health care professionals created the Foundation for Life and Growth (FUNCRESER), a nonprofit organization that through its program Amor Sin Agresión offers services to victims of incest, sexual abuse, and other forms of aggression, and to the families of such victims. As of the spring of 1992, the foundation has been receiving an average of three calls daily for help, and it is providing ongoing treatment for one hundred individuals, children, adolescents, and adults.

However, the goals of FUNCRESER are not limited to the comprehensive treatment of victims, their families, and the offenders. Among its goals are consciousness raising among professionals of public and private institutions who work with children and women to foster a better understanding of the problem, and an increase in research and the distribution of information about incest.

This is a first report of an investigation in progress. The facts here reported will be enriched as the research continues. At the moment of this writing, the adolescent victims of incest and their mothers are continuing individual and self-help group therapy. We, the researchers and therapists, are constantly learning more about the victims' plight and how to help them.

Biodata

Gioconda Batres Méndez obtained an M.D. from the Universidad Nacional Autónoma de México (UNAM) and has a postdoctoral specialization in psychiatry from the Universidad de Costa Rica. She did graduate work in women's studies at the Centro Interdisciplinario de Estudios de la Mujer (CIEM) (Center for Interdisciplinary Women's Studies) at the Universidad Nacional. She has taught graduate gender studies courses sponsored by the Consejo Superior Universitario Centroamericano (CSUCA) (Council of Central American Universities) and United Nations Development Fund for Women (UNIFEM). She was a consultant for the Fundación PANIAMOR, a member of the editorial board of the Colegio de Médicos (a professional organization of medical doctors) writing about women-related topics. She was founder and president of the Fundación Ser y Crecer (FUNCRESER) (Foundation for Life and Growth). Currently, she is a private therapist and the director of the Training Project for Domestic Violence of the Instituto Latinoamericano para la Prevención del Delito y el Tratamiento del Delincuente (ILANUD) (United Nations Latin American Institute for the Prevention of Crime and Treatment of Offenders). Through ILANUD, she published in 1992 *La violencia contra la mujer en la familia Costarricense (Aggression against women in Costa Rican families)*, and in 1993 *La silla de la verdad (The chair for telling the truth)*, a guide with cartoon-like drawings to put at ease children who must testify in court in domestic violence or incest lawsuits.

References

Archivo Nacional de Costa Rica (ANCR). Document no. 1105.

Finkelhor, David. 1980. *El abuso sexual al menor*. México: Editorial Pax.

Herman, Judith Lewis. 1981. *Father-Daughter Incest*. Cambridge, Mass.: Harvard University Press.

Norwood, Robin. 1988. *Cartas de las mujeres que aman demasiado*. Buenos Aires: Javier Vergara, editor.

Russell, Diana. 1984. *Sexual Exploitation*. Beverly Hills, Calif.: Sage Publications.

——. 1986. *The Secret Trauma. Incest in the Lives of Girls and Women*. New York: Basic Books.

Sgroi, Suzanne. 1982. *Handbook of Clinical Intervention in Child Sexual Abuse*. Lexington, Mass.: Lexington Books.

Acknowledgments

To the adolescents with whom I work, their mothers, and all those individuals who support my efforts to understand the reality of incest in Costa Rica and to contribute to the recuperation of those who survive incest and of their families.

Elizabeth Gómez M., staff member of Mujer No Estás Sola (Woman, You Are
Not Alone), on the hotline with a woman who is reporting abuse and aggression

As Costa Rican women have expanded their participation in society and moved beyond traditional individual struggles for family survival, they have taken a greater role in public leadership in work, community, and political settings, from women's movement types of activities to feminist concerns. At the same time, governmental and nongovernmental organizations—domestic and foreign—are beginning to pay greater attention to women's needs and contributions.

Adapting skills that have served them well in the microenvironment of the family or small enterprise, women are creating large institutions with elaborate leadership hierarchies, handling complex administrative and financial processes, participating in extended negotiations, making effective decisions for large constituencies, and taking part in imaginative long-term planning.

This section first provides an impressionistic description of some of the original humble, small-scale experiences of women and then demonstrates—bypassing diverse intermediate stages—some of the ways women are learning to master the challenges of large-scale organizations.

Peace Corps Volunteers See Working-Class Women's Realities, by Jessica Brown, Cynthia K. Green, Linda Pearl, and Vilma Pérez

The authors, Peace Corps volunteers, open this section with four vignettes relating their experiences with working women's problems in Costa Rica. The authors draw upon their work in primarily poor rural and inner-city areas to provide glimpses into women's daily lives. The volunteers describe the perceptions, attitudes, and aspirations of these women and offer examples of women's resourcefulness, creativity, individual efficacy, and increasing consciousness.

Women as Leaders in the Costa Rican Cooperative Movement, by Mireya Jiménez Guerra

Mireya Jiménez reports on efforts to enlarge the participation of women in the leadership of cooperatives through training programs and consciousness raising. The author provides a brief overview of the slowly increasing participation of women in the upper ranks of the Costa Rican cooperative movement. Although in theory the movement supports women's integration into its political, economic, and educational leadership, in practice traditional patterns of discrimination still prevail. Women still struggle to gain a leadership presence that corresponds to their active involvement in cooperatives.

Training provided by the Asociación Programa Nacional de Asesoría y Capacitación para la Mujer is increasing the number of women who qualify for leadership positions, though the program leaders anticipate an uphill fight.

Two other organizations, the Comité Regional de la Mujer Cooperativista de Centroamérica y del Caribe and the Fundación para el Desarrollo de la Mujer Cooperativista (FUNDACOOP) provide technical or management training to women cooperativists.

The Struggle for Housing in Costa Rica: The Transformation of Women into Political Actors, by Montserrat Sagot

Montserrat Sagot reports on her analysis of the efforts of lower-class women to obtain adequate housing through a concerted and highly organized self-help movement. The struggle converted participating women into self-confident, successful political actors at the grassroots level. The study examines the activities of women members of the Comité Patriótico Nacional (COPAN), the country's most effective organization in the struggle for housing, as a case study of women's political participation in Costa Rica during the 1970s and 1980s. Sagot reviews the factors responsible for the rise of new social movements in Latin America, specific socioeconomic conditions that promoted the Costa Rican housing movement, the growth of the movement and its influence on government policy, and the implications of women's political participation for their personal and family lives.

Long-Term Survival of a Costa Rican Women's Crafts Cooperative: Approaches to Problems of Rapid Growth at CASEM in the Santa Elena-Monteverde Region, by Ilse Abshagen Leitinger

Many income-generating projects for women in Latin America involve the production of crafts. They often fail after varying periods of operation. By contrast, the Comisión de Artesanos Santa Elena-Monteverde (CASEM), a women's crafts cooperative, survived serious challenges during its ten years of operation and now plays a substantial economic, social, and policy-making role in its region. It has experienced impressive growth (from 8 to nearly 150 members) and achieved substantial product diversification. The analysis describes the historic background of the region and discusses CASEM's origin, rapid growth, training and marketing programs, and its social mission for women's empowerment. The article concludes with a summary of CASEM's five-year plan.

Reconceptualizing the Theory of Women in Organizations: Contributions of Feminist Analysis, by Laura Guzmán Stein

The final article in this section contributes to the theoretical-philosophical basis of feminism. Laura Guzmán presents an argument for improving all organizational analysis by integrating women's positive, creative, and characteristically female contributions to organizational efficiency. The study probes four assumptions about women in the classic Weberian theory of organizations: (1) women do not participate in organizations; (2) women are incapable of resisting exploitation and subordination; (3) in some organizations, women are already integrated; and (4) the structural informality of women's organizations creates problems as well as potential. The author argues that women's experiences in organizations cannot be subsumed under men's experiences. Analyzing and understanding women's experiences requires a redefinition of concepts and models and the incorporation of the concept of gender into a revised theory of organizations.

20 ❀ Peace Corps Volunteers See Working-Class Women's Realities

Jessica Brown, Cynthia K. Green, Linda Pearl, and Vilma Pérez

Maruja and María (Ciudad Quesada, Northern Lowlands, Caribbean Coast)

"Ooh! I wonder if Gonzalo left any money in his pants," says María as she checks her brother's trousers before washing them. "Hmph," she snorts, "only 40 colones [50 cents U.S. at the time of the story]. Well, whatever he leaves in his pockets is mine to keep."

I'm a bit stunned at this, feeling it's dishonest. "Do you really keep the money?" I ask. "How much do you find?"

"Oh, once I found 200 colones, and another time, Papi left 400 colones in his pocket. '¡*Salado!* [Your tough luck!],' I say. After I find the money, I tell the boys, 'I clean, cook, and wash—and only sometimes do you pay me for the washing.'"

María's mother, Maruja, lets out a big sigh as she eyes the pile of clothes to be ironed. She's already ironed seventeen shirts, I count, amazed. "Oh," says Maruja, "if Carlos José [Maruja's husband] didn't leave his wallet around I wouldn't have a thing, and neither would the children. Not a thing. This morning, he left his wallet. I took 1,000 colones to buy a thermos for Pablo when he starts high school. It's not fair! Yesterday Carlos went to the bank and withdrew 20,000 colones for his brother and 5,000 colones to lend his friend. And he makes me beg for every penny he gives me and then justify where I spent it. He says women don't need money—that our work in the house isn't really work. There are six males in this house, with just María and me to do all the housework. He pays his sons for work in the field—even the six-year-old— but doesn't pay his daughter or wife for work in the house. No, Jessie, taking money from his wallet is not a sin. It's not a sin."

"You're right," I think to myself, "it's not."

Jessie Brown

Locha (Sámara, Nicoya Peninsula, Pacific Coast)

Eloisa Jirón López, known as Locha, is at times a typical Tica, yet she is fiercely independent. She was born and raised in a small pueblo, Sámara de Nicoya, in Guanacaste Province. Married at the age of fifteen, Locha found herself divorced at the age of twenty-five, homeless and facing the task of raising three boys, ages five, seven, and nine. She returned to her mother's house to seek shelter and food for herself and the children, but within a week she knew she needed to find some way to support herself. She found work, and for two rigorous years worked from 6 a.m. to 9 p.m. cleaning and cooking for fifteen people and from 9 p.m. to 2 a.m. serving food and drinks in a small bar. During this time, Locha saved as much money as she could. She was lucky because her mother helped her by watching the boys.

When Locha had saved enough money, her mother, who owned some land, gave her a small plot on which to build a house. Locha's house initially was just two sleeping areas. Further work on the house had to wait and was done as she could pay for it. She found another job with better pay for fewer hours. Even as busy as she was, she still made time to teach her children good work habits and moral values.

It has taken more than twelve years, but Locha now has a beautiful rancho house with three bedrooms and a kitchen with a brand new stove and refrigerator. Her current project is having a new toilet and shower installed. And all around her house are beautiful trees, plants, and flowers that she planted and tended over the years.

Her boys are grown now. Two completed high school, which was difficult because Locha had to pay room and board for them in another town two hours away. Her three sons do not smoke or drink and are well-adjusted young men. To clothe them over the years, Locha learned to sew, and she now owns two sewing machines and makes clothing. She uses the income from making clothes, and some from cutting hair, to supplement her social security support payments. Her mother is now building a new house, and Locha is helping out financially when she can.

Many Ticas in Locha's situation would never have achieved what she did, especially more than a decade ago. Most would have been content to live with their parents and look for another husband to support them. Locha never remarried, and she is proud of the fact that she accomplished everything on her own. She is not rich, but she has a roof over her head, clothes on her back, and food on her table—good food, meat and vegetables, not just rice and beans. She is free to come and go as she pleases. She is not afraid to leave the house at night and can be seen frequently at the dances here and in Nicoya. Locha is well liked and respected in the community, and she has set a good example, showing that a Tica can survive alone and well.

How do I know all this? I am a Peace Corps volunteer. When Locha heard I needed a place to live, she opened both her heart and house and said, "Come, live with me."

Cindy Green

The CoopeVegan Soccer Team (CoopeVega de Kutris, Near Ciudad Quesada, Caribbean Lowlands)

CoopeVega is located thirty-five kilometers south of Nicaragua, near the San Carlos River. When I joined the community, I tried to decide how I could help. I found the town lacked public facilities, such as a park or a clean cemetery. The townspeople were poor, and an income-generating activity, perhaps a bakery, seemed a good project. I tried to generate interest in my ideas among the women, but after several failed attempts to motivate them, I realized it was time to listen instead. I asked the women what they wanted to do. They wanted to play soccer.

In fact, a fair number of women wanted to play soccer, but they never had tried it because they thought it was a man's sport. I insisted that if they wanted to play they could. Once the women learned that the "gringa" not only knew how to play soccer but had played it in the United States, they decided they could play, too. Our team began with several women, and they invited others. Gradually more and more women showed up, until the team finally had seventeen members—some married, some single, all between the ages of twelve and twenty-six. After practicing for several months, the women wanted to play against another team, and they organized a game against a local men's team. The women won!

When the women first started practicing, the men didn't have any objections. They figured the women would lose interest quickly, so it was easier not to say anything. After the game against the men, however, the team members' husbands and fathers said the women could continue to play, as long as they competed only against other women. There are no other women's teams near CoopeVega, but this didn't discourage the women; they simply invited other women's teams from the region.

To encourage support from the CoopeVega community, the women decided they would also invite men's soccer teams to come and play against the CoopeVegan men's teams. This way, the town members would turn out to watch the men, but they would also get to see the women. After the first game, the townspeople realized that the women were pretty good, and thereafter they came to support both the women and the men. When the women wanted to travel to other communities, the town helped to arrange transportation, and husbands and fathers allowed the women to go and play. This was a wonderful thing, since in many rural areas women are still not permitted to leave the house.

At first, CoopeVegan uniforms consisted only of matching shirts—team members wore their own shorts. The women's team shared the shirts with the men: After playing their game, the women would quickly change shirts so the men could play. The women soon decided they wanted their own uniforms, and they set out to raise money, selling food during home games and holding a dance. Their work paid off: They accumulated enough money to buy fifteen complete uniforms—shirts, shorts, and socks.

The CoopeVegan women's soccer team is still going strong. All they needed was someone to listen and to support them. Seeing that they could start and succeed with an activity gave the women strength to organize games, travel, raise money, and buy uniforms. This strength carried over to other aspects of their lives. For the first time, women are now on the governing board for CoopeVega. They are more actively involved with community enhancement groups, such as one that works with the local health center. Through playing soccer, the CoopeVegan women learned that if they want to, they can do things. They are now using this knowledge to help themselves and their community.

Linda Pearl

The Women of Limoncito (Shantytown in the Center of Limón, Costa Rica's Principal Port on the Caribbean Coast)

The center of Limón has two shantytowns: Cieneguita and Limoncito. They reflect the social problems of big cities: underemployment, poverty, drugs, and distrust toward one's neighbors. People who need a favor probably won't ask and are more likely to steal. I was sent to help Limoncito's women alleviate their economic and social problems.

Most women in Limoncito are married. Their husbands work six-day workweeks for Envaco, a carton factory; Instituto Costarricense de Ferrocarriles (INCOFER) (Costa Rican Railway Institute); or Junta de Administración

Portuaria y de Desarrollo Económico de la Vertiente Atlántica (JAPDEVA) (Board of Port Administration and Economic Development of the Atlantic Coast), the port authority. Women fix their husband's noonday meal and send it to them in a thermos. They take care of children and do housework, and most of them also do crafts to bring in extra income. In cases of severe economic need, they hold part-time jobs, though few such jobs are compatible with the women's already busy days.

The first income-generating project I proposed was one for making tortillas, but it failed—the women were not motivated, because large factories turn out good tortillas. Then I came up with the idea of working bamboo to make furniture and crafts. With increasing deforestation, the government and international agencies are promoting the use of bamboo for building houses and other structures in many parts of Costa Rica. At the first meeting I called, only eight women showed up, and those eight needed a job desperately. It was four weeks before I could convince additional women to join the bamboo project.

Even if they came, could I teach the women the art of bamboo work? I had no experience with bamboo. But when I was young, I used to do carpentry work with my father, and I relied on that memory. So I adapted tools to working with bamboo, which is a common material in the area. I improved my skills, I taught the women what I knew, and we made bamboo products, polishing our techniques and sometimes finishing the bamboo pieces with bits of wood or wire. Our work sessions became times of comradeship as we shared a lot of small talk, trading jokes and talking about our lives. We ended up trusting each other.

After three months we had created several prototypes. We made flower bases and hanging flower containers, differently shaped supports of horizontal hollowed parts of bamboo trunks, or vertical pieces of trunks with several inserted protruding spout-like holders for individual flowers or vines. In the Limón climate, you can put plants into holders without soil, and they will thrive on only air and water, be it rain or spray, and flower every year. We also developed table, wall, and ceiling lamps; letter holders; picture holders; a purse; and two types of beaded curtains for doorways. We exhibited the prototypes in a souvenir shop where we could gain feedback from customers. The exhibit was a success, and the women then decided to explore the bamboo crafts market. We wanted to create a local market for bamboo goods; if we could do this, then we would integrate personnel to help us export our products. First, however, we wanted to ensure the local market by talking to owners of several furniture stores and gaining their support for our products, which they agreed to give. Our next step will be to work out a marketing plan. We'll determine which parts of town offer a market, and which items will be most profitable. We'll also discuss whether we need to modify any of the items or to discontinue production of some.

But we needed to consider another problem. Who would take care of the children? All the craftswomen have small children; the mothers would rather give up their jobs than neglect their home duties. We therefore planned a workplace with a small playground where the women could work and keep an eye on the children at the same time.

As we worked, we discussed women's right to a better life and better treatment. These were new thoughts. The women even considered such an idea an excess of freedom, which could disrupt family ties. In their view, women must be devoted to the home, and the women of Limoncito want to be housewives forever. They do not want to change their status; they believe in the division of labor by sex. My coworkers distinguished two kinds of women: women and true women. A woman is a female, but a true woman is a female who can do hard work without failing in her main duty of being a housewife. Although the women of Limoncito said they consider carpentry men's work, they did not think they were invading the men's area by working with bamboo. In fact, they said, carpentry with bamboo does not reduce their femininity, it exalts it because they do it in addition to taking care of their home.

In the coming months, the women will add other crafts to their bamboo work—knitting, crocheting, embroidery, and fabric painting. They want to produce a variety of items to satisfy different clients' needs and to avoid saturating the market with a few items. Eventually, they plan to train other women to meet the demand for bamboo products.

Right now, the project looks workable. The group needs additional tools, a permanent workplace, product storage space, and some support from government agencies. But the women of Limoncito have already enjoyed their first success: They feel strong enough to face these problems, and they are confident they will succeed with their enterprise.

Vilma Pérez

Biodata

Jessica Brown is from Albuquerque, New Mexico, and holds a B.A. (1987) in political science and Latin American studies from Colorado College in Colorado Springs. As a Peace Corps volunteer, she was stationed between 1989 and 1991 in Esquipulas de Aguas Zarcas, San Carlos.

Cynthia K. Green, from Muskegon, Michigan, has a B.S. (1983) in business administration from Grand Valley State College in Allendale, Michigan. She did graduate work in business administration at Western Michigan University in Kalamazoo, Michigan. Between 1989 and 1991, she was stationed in Sámara de Nicoya.

Linda Pearl, from Denver, Colorado, holds a B.A. (1986) in economics and business administration from Fort Lewis College, Durango, Colorado. She was stationed in CoopeVega de Kutris between 1988 and 1990.

Vilma Pérez is from Toa Alta, Puerto Rico. She completed a B.A. (1979) in social anthropology and geography at the University of Puerto Rico and an M.A. (1983) in applied anthropology, linguistics, and bilingual education at the University of Florida. She taught at the Colegio Universitario Tecnológico de Bayamón (Bayamón Technical College), University of Puerto Rico, and was stationed in Los Corrales, Limón, between 1989 and 1991.

Acknowledgments

The four authors were part of the Women in Development program of the Peace Corps in Costa Rica between 1988 and 1991. Like all Peace Corps volunteers, they were generalists, open to different tasks, flexible and adaptable, even though each had her own special interests. As a rule, Peace Corps volunteers are involved in more than one activity, e.g., working with women in small income-generating enterprises, such as bakeries, medicinal or vegetable gardens, or crafts cooperatives; teaching English or other subjects; helping with or developing educational programs, kindergartens, sports, or early childhood stimulation programs; or participating in diverse communal activities.

21 ❋ Women as Leaders in the Costa Rican Cooperative Movement

Mireya Jiménez Guerra

The goal of the cooperative movement in Costa Rica is to improve the socio-economic situation of its members. In 1993, the movement consisted of four hundred cooperatives, involved in a great variety of productive enterprises and comprising approximately 300,000 members. They represented nearly 10 percent of the total population of the country and 30 percent of the economically active population.

To understand women's situation in the Costa Rican cooperative movement, we must know something about the socioeconomic and political situation of the country. In Costa Rica approximately 51 percent of all households are headed by women, yet women workers earn less than men. The average monthly salary for women working in manufacturing or in the *maquila* (assembly) industries, for instance, came to approximately 8,000 colones from 1988 through 1990 (about $90–95 U.S. in early 1990). In comparison, the average monthly salary for men during that period was 10,000 to 12,000 colones (about $115–140); men, however, almost always perform more skilled or prestigious tasks, often of a supervisory nature. This gender discrepancy between salaries remains essentially the same today.

Life expectancy for Costa Rican women is eighty years. After a long marriage, many women are widowed or divorced in middle age. Although in theory women are free to finish their studies or take up some employment to make themselves independent, it is unfortunately true that many succumb to cultural pressures and instead search for personal security in a second marriage. Tradition has made women believe they are without value if they have no man at their side.

In view of these cultural pressures, it is a great struggle for a woman who wants to achieve identity through her own capacity and initiative, to become an actor and a leader instead of remaining an object. At the same time, women do occupy important political positions in government, though their participation in regional politics, municipalities, and political parties is smaller (PRIEG, n.d.). A few examples: Under President Oscar Arias (1986–90), the second vice president of the republic, Victoria Garrón, was a woman. During those years, women also accounted for 12.5 percent of the membership in the Legislative Assembly, and for 7 percent in the leadership in municipalities. Under President Rafael Angel Calderón (1990–94), both the minister of justice, Elizabeth Odio, and the minister of culture, youth, and sports, Aida Faingezicht, were women. Women made up 10.5 percent of the Legislative Assembly, and, again, 7 percent of municipal leadership (Jiménez, 1994). Moreover, a woman, Margarita Penón, the wife of ex-president Oscar Arias, ran for nomination for president of one of the two leading political parties. Although she was not nominated, she forced other candidates to address issues that otherwise might have been neglected.

Women in the Costa Rican Cooperative Movement

Women represent about 40 percent of the total membership in the Costa Rican cooperative movement, in all parts of the country. Originally, women were passively associated with cooperatives, as followers; rarely did they hold leadership positions. Many factors limited women's active participation, the more important ones being male domination or machismo, women's limited education, the work load of the Double Day, women's fear of asserting themselves, and inadequate preparation for leadership.

Since 1985, however, women have begun to ascend to leadership positions. The cooperative movement has given them opportunities to incorporate themselves more effectively into its political and decision-making structures, mainly through the work of three organizations. The Asociación Programa Nacional de Asesoría y Capacitación para la Mujer Cooperativista (APROMUJER) (National Advisory and Training Program for Women Cooperativists), founded in 1985, is training and advising women on various aspects of cooperativism. The Comité Nacional de la Mujer Cooperativista (National Committee of Women Cooperativists), established in 1987, receives support from the Norwegian government's Alianza de Cooperativas Internacional (International Alliance of Cooperatives) and has counterparts in all other Central American countries; it is helping with the organization of women's cooperatives. The most recent, the Fundación para el Desarrollo de la Mujer Cooperativista (FUNDACOOP)

(Foundation for the Development of Women Cooperativists), which dates from 1990, is focusing particularly on educating women cooperativists for management and for attention to environmental questions (Jiménez, 1994).

The following is a brief analysis of the increase in women's participation in the cooperative movement's leadership to document the advance of women as leaders in the political, economic, and educational activities of the movement.

Women in the Political Leadership of Costa Rican Cooperativism

At the beginning of the 1989–91 period, seven women were elected to the political leadership structure of the cooperative movement, the plenary of the Consejo Nacional de Cooperativas (CONACOOP) (National Council of Cooperatives). Given a total of forty-one seats in the plenary, the seven women accounted for 17 percent of the total. The same percentage holds for the 1991–93 period. Earlier, in the 1987–89 period, five women so elected represented 13 percent of the total membership of thirty-eight. This compares to the years 1979–81, when the first woman ever elected to the plenary constituted 4 percent of the total membership of twenty-five (INFOCOOP, 1990; Jiménez, 1989, p. 5; Jiménez, 1994). Since the plenary distributes the power for the development of cooperatives, women's increasing participation at the top level of the movement is clearly important.

APROMUJER, which has been charged with preparing women cooperativists for political participation, has established as a goal for 1993–95 raising women's participation in the plenary to 30 percent. Though women's participation did not reach that goal it rose to above 21 percent, the highest rate ever achieved (Campos and Jiménez, 1995).

Women as Managers of Cooperatives

Within the economic management of cooperatives, women participate as leaders in the *maquila* and ready-to-wear textile industries in 2 percent of all cooperatives in the country. However, cooperatives administered by women are not always women's cooperatives.

Since early 1990, women's cooperatives have been establishing themselves in the southern zone of the Pacific coastal lowlands, in Limón at the Caribbean coast, and in San Carlos in the northern Caribbean lowlands, all of which are in full operation under women's leadership. Women's participation in economic management often is hindered by the *machista* (male-dominant) pattern of Costa Rican society and by women's lack of training in business administration (INFOCOOP, 1990).

Women Leaders in Cooperativism's Educational Structures

One of the findings of the 1989 study was that women cooperativists have had little access to the educational structures of Costa Rican cooperativism (Jiménez, 1989: 13). Cooperativist leadership has, however, become aware of women's limited participation. Through its training programs, APROMUJER has been pursuing the goal of increasing the representation of women in the education for leadership.

Consequently, in 1989–90, APROMUJER provided training for one hundred women leaders in management courses, for ten women in marketing courses, and for three women in the upper administration in the Centro Nacional de Educación Cooperativa (CENECOOP) (National Center for Cooperativist Education). These women also participated in seminars on current economic problems of the country (INFOCOOP, 1990). Currently, these training programs continue, and new women cooperativists are enrolled in them.

The Future of Women as Leaders in Cooperatives

In Costa Rica, as in most Latin American countries, women have been discriminated against in the formal work force. In many government institutions, discriminatory beliefs and practices inhibit the use of women's skills under conditions equal to those of men. In the private sector similar discrimination prevents women from participating in the work force. And in the informal private sector, we find such discrimination is intensified by a scarcity of capital, a lack of knowledge about women's abilities, an absence of skills training for women, and a lack of protection through legislation (Jiménez, 1989: 13).

Moreover, the staffing of executive positions in the cooperative movement itself reflects this inequality. Since its inception in 1973, every executive secretary of CONACOOP has been a man. Recommendations of the plenary or the executive to consider women have been recommendations in theory only. Even in second-level positions, in federations and unions, the leadership consists only of men (Jiménez, 1989: 13).

This gender inequality occurs despite the fact that the few women leaders in the cooperative movement demonstrate a higher level of general schooling than men. Among women leaders, 47 percent have had university training, compared with 28 percent of men (Jiménez, 1989: 25). But women are still marginalized by the leadership and are denied an opportunity to ascend to higher positions.

In sum, this analysis shows that although women have made strides in the cooperative movement in Costa Rica, the leaders of that movement have backed women's participation in leadership roles more in theory than in practice. Male leaders still hold and enact traditional sociocultural beliefs. APROMUJER argues that the more effective incorporation of women into the political and decision-making ranks of cooperativism will not only advance women but will also strengthen and consolidate the movement as a whole. At the same time, APROMUJER knows that if women cooperativists want to join these ranks, they face an up-hill struggle requiring the training, initiative, and persistence of many women. Two organizations—the Comité Regional de la Mujer Cooperativista de Centroamérica y del Caribe and FUNDACOOP—reinforce and extend the work of APROMUJER in response to the perceived need for training in order to prepare women cooperativists for leadership.

Biodata

Mireya Jiménez Guerra has a bachelor's degree in psychology from the Universidad Autónoma Centroamericana and a licenciatura in sociology from the Universidad Nacional. She has done graduate work in planning, in the joint program of the Costa Rican Ministerio de Planificación Nacional y Política Económica (MIDEPLAN) (Ministry of National Planning and Economics) and the Chilean Instituto Latinoamericano de Planificación Económica y Social (ILPES) (Latin American Institute for Economic and Social Planning), and in agricultural administration and extension at the Centro de Cooperacíon Internacional para el Desarrollo Agrícola (CINADCO) (Center of International Cooperation for Agricultural Development) at the Israeli Ministry of Agriculture. She participated in the international seminar, "The Role of Women and Youth in the Cooperative Movement," sponsored by the Adenauer Foundation in Cali, Colombia. She was the first president of the Comité Regional de la Mujer Cooperativista de Centroamérica y del Caribe (Regional Committee of Central American and Caribbean Women Cooperativists) and is a member of the Planning Department of the Instituto Nacional de Fomento Cooperativo (INFOCOOP) (National Institute for the Development of Cooperatives), which plans the development of cooperative activities. She is also the president of the Foundation for the Development of Women Cooperativists (FUNDACOOP), the first foundation of its kind in Central America. Among her publications are *Situación del movimiento cooperativo en Costa Rica* (1989) and *Mujer y desarrollo en Costa Rica* (1994).

References

Campos Méndez, Marta, and Mireya Jiménez Guerra. 1995. *Diagnóstico de la participación de la mujer en el sector cooperativo costarricense.* San José, Costa Rica: Asociación Nacional de Asesoría y Capacitación para la Mujer (APROMUJER).

Instituto Nacional de Fomento Cooperativo (INFOCOOP). 1990. Internal documentation.

Jiménez Guerra, Mireya. 1989. *Diagnóstico de la participación de la mujer en el movimiento cooperativo costarricense.* San José, Costa Rica: APROMUJER.

——. 1994. *Participación de la mujer en las estructuras socioeconómicas de Costa Rica.* Parts 1 and 2. San José, Costa Rica: FUNDACOOP.

Programa Interdisciplinario de Estudios de Género (PRIEG). n.d. "Situación de la mujer en Costa Rica: Un perfil de su discriminación." Mimeo. San José, Costa Rica: Universidad de Costa Rica.

Acknowledgments

The article is based on a 1989 study carried out by the author for APROMUJER, with updates to 1992. The author would like to thank Marta Campos Méndez, president of APROMUJER, for years of cooperation in the struggle to empower women in the cooperative movement.

22 ❊ The Struggle for Housing in Costa Rica

The Transformation of Women into Political Actors

Montserrat Sagot

This study examines the political participation of women in the struggle for housing in Costa Rica from the late 1970s to the 1980s, focusing on the women members of the Comité Patriótico Nacional (COPAN) (National Patriotic Committee), the most effective organization in the housing movement. The study attempts to show the consequences of the housing struggle on (1) government social housing policy, (2) the design and organization of new communities, and (3) the personal and family lives of participating women.

The study divides into four sections. Section I reviews factors that brought new social movements to Latin America and emphasizes that women have been centrally involved, even though their presence has been ignored or even denied. Section II describes the socioeconomic conditions that promoted the appearance of one such movement, the housing movement in Costa Rica. Section III examines the growth of the housing movement, its influence on government housing policy, and the impact of women's views on the design of the new communities and on the organization of communal life. Finally, Section IV addresses the implications of political participation in the housing movement for women's personal and family lives.

I. Women, Political Activism, and Social Movements in Latin America

After the Second World War, the capitalist system underwent a rapid structural transformation that included the creation of a culture of mass consumption, the destruction of the traditional social milieu, the break-up of the working class, an increasing process of individualization, and an accelerated destruction of environmental resources (Hirsch, 1988). Out of these changes grew new forms of social and political conflict, particularly during the 1960s and 1970s. In Central America, the 1960s witnessed the opening wedge of a serious economic crisis that led to state crises during the 1970s (Torres-Rivas, 1981). Central American governments, unable to propose an economic plan in response to the new conditions, found their credibility threatened (Portantiero, 1981). Political conditions brought violent changes, among them overt repression and electoral fraud. Traditional political parties and organizations displayed a lack of political efficacy to deal with the new social conditions during this critical period (Falk, 1987). The so-called new social movements, led by women, students, peasants, and citizens are, then, the concrete ways in which social subjects organized to face the new conditions, and are an expression of the complex social dynamics that go beyond mere class conflicts.

Women have been centrally involved in such movements, be they resistance movements in workplaces and neighborhoods (Ackelsberg, 1988), or urban movements—particularly housing movements—in Latin America, a fact often ignored or denied (Chant, 1987; Moser, 1987a; Vance, 1987). Such denials stem from the tradition of interpreting social movements and their politics as reflections of the public, i.e., the masculine, world (Schneider, 1988). Deeming political activity to be inherently masculine, students of social movements have neglected the influence of patterns of gender relations, which also shape processes of social change. During economic crises, for example, gender as well as class inequalities are likely to increase rather than decline (Edgell and Duke, 1983).

The failure to see women as social actors has been reinforced by a parallel tendency, the failure to consider communal activities as political (Schneider, 1988). Political theory in the Western world has identified the public realm with politics, limited to men, and has identified the private realm with the home and close community, assigning these areas to women. This ideological separation has circumscribed the agenda of politics and the range of likely participants (Ackelsberg, 1988). Yet women, in the role of sustainers of networks of human relations inside the community and primary providers for their families, are potentially the main builders of some new social movements. Caroline Moser (1987b) has estimated that more than 50 percent of households of the Third World are headed by women; in the specific Costa Rican communities I studied, that figure rose to 75 percent.

In the Latin American context, researchers have recently become increasingly aware of the political impact of grassroots organizations and, through them, the political mobilization of women (see for instance, Jaquette, 1991), although much research is still needed to document these processes (Adler Hellman, 1992). Empirical studies on the political action of Costa Rican women are virtually nonexistent, which can be attributed in part to the Marxist tradition, which tends to see political events and social movements' activity as epiphenomena resulting from deeper economic forces (Sagot, 1991).

However, because the housing movement concerns matters of daily survival, it does easily "politicize" the so-called private domain and transform women into "public" actors. In the light of this reasoning, the remainder of this study will demonstrate how women have been the main organizers of the Costa Rican housing movement and how they, through their participation in the movement, have been transformed into social and political actors.

II. The Costa Rican Socioeconomic Reality

Given Costa Rica's democratic tradition, the economic crisis of the 1970s did not provoke a political crisis, yet it did create serious social disarray. One of the most severely affected areas was housing and its related problems, i.e., access to basic services like water, electricity, and transportation. By the 1980s the country faced a deficit of 270,000 houses, which means that 61.7 percent of the population was affected by lack of housing (Sojo, 1988).

The lack of decent housing, above all in urban areas, was a direct consequence of the structural transformation that began in the late 1950s and early 1960s. At that time, Costa Rica experienced a dramatic reduction of its agricultural frontier, a rapid concentration of property, and the first steps in the industrialization process (Rovira, 1982). Consequently, by the late 1970s and early 1980s, 30 percent of the general population and 45 percent of the rural population was living in poverty (FLACSO, 1984; Sojo, 1988).

Historically an agricultural country, Costa Rica faced rapid but uneven growth of urban areas because of massive migratory flows from rural areas to major cities, a pattern that continues today. This growth, particularly of metropolitan San José, brought serious urban problems like *tugurios* (squatter settlements), a dramatic increase in property prices, invasion of nearby agricultural land, indiscriminate urbanization (such as the creation of industries in residential areas), industrial pollution, and lack of recreational areas—in sum, a general deterioration of urban life.

The appearance and continuing growth of squatter and shanty settlements surrounding major Costa Rican cities—such as those of San José, Limón, and Puntarenas—became a serious and major source of social conflict. From the unsatisfied needs and anger of families in these communities arose a strong movement for decent housing during the late 1970s. Women and children constituted approximately 90 percent of this movement.

III. COPAN's Housing Movement: Old Tactics and New Solutions

The 1970s in Costa Rica also witnessed an intense ideological debate among leftist parties (Camacho and Mejívar, 1985). Voters questioned both the political line, means, and forms of the struggle and the effectiveness of traditional leftist organizations. New leftist parties like the Movimiento Revolucionario del Pueblo (People's Revolutionary Movement), the Partido Socialista (Socialist Party), and the Frente Popular (Popular Front) proposed solutions for social problems, addressing what they termed the "real needs of the people." During this period women members of a new Trotskyite party, the Organización Socialista de los Trabajadores (OST) (Socialist Workers' Organization), formed the country's first feminist organization, the Movimiento para la Liberación de la Mujer (MLM) (Women's Liberation Movement). From this union COPAN would be born.

MLM began its work in the mid-1970s with women from San José's poorest communities. In the southern suburbs, the Barrios del Sur, MLM organized women to fight against a bill that was to prohibit the use of intrauterine devices (IUD). The bill's sponsors, some of Costa Rica's most conservative political and religious forces, considered the IUD an abortive device. MLM leaders decided that the best way to fight the bill was to organize those most directly affected, the IUD users. In the end, the bill was defeated, and MLM took advantage of its new organization to form the first self-help health groups in Costa Rica (see Carcedo, Sagot, and Trejos, chap. 3 above; Carcedo, chap. 18 above). During this period of focusing on health issues, MLM members discovered that the most important unsatisfied needs among women from the poorest communities were housing and related services. People were unhappy with the alternatives proposed by government agencies, and they expressed a willingness to form independent housing committees; in response, OST and MLM began organizing the committees in 1978 in search of a program to satisfy the needs of the lowest-income people.

The government, through the Instituto Nacional de Vivienda y Urbanización (INVU) (National Housing and Urbanization Institute), had proposed a self-help program called Site and Services, which would provide infrastructure, land, and materials, and the people would build their own houses. International agencies widely accepted this type of program. For example, the governments of Mexico, Brazil, Ecuador, Kenya, and Sri Lanka had recognized "self-help" housing as beneficial for a city's economy because it reduces the state's responsibility to provide conventional housing to large working-class groups in urban areas (Moser, 1987b). Members of early housing committees found, though, that the Costa Rican government was not carrying out the program. The first housing committees organized with the goal of obligating the government to implement the Site and Services program, efficiently, and on a large scale.

In 1980 MLM founded the Coordinadora Nacional por Vivienda Digna (National Coordinating Committee for Dignified Housing), an umbrella organization for all housing committees. By 1981, both the OST and the MLM had changed names. OST had become the Comité Patriótico Nacional (COPAN), and MLM, the Centro Feminista de Información y Acción (CEFEMINA) (Feminist Center for Information and Action). By changing their names, the two organizations acknowledged that they had become grassroots organizations with more short-term practical goals for political action, i.e., obtaining decent housing for the poorest strata of the population and general improvement of their daily lives.

A massive presence of women characterized these housing committees. Men's participation was neither regular nor reliable. Women consistently constituted nearly 90 percent of the members. It is not surprising that women's involvement was more intense. Women spend more time in the house than men do, and they experience the need for decent housing more directly. Even with an outside job and a husband or companion, women carry the main responsibility for activities related to social reproduction—i.e., the satisfaction of their family's material and emotional needs. Thus women are more likely to participate in movements aimed at improving the conditions of their daily lives.

COPAN and its feminist arm, CEFEMINA, developed a decentralized organization with housing committees in the most important cities, San José, Alajuela, Heredia, and Cartago; intermediate "sectorial" or "regional" leadership; and a general coordinating committee, La Dirección, composed of intellectuals and major organizers charged with overseeing the regional committees.

COPAN's tactics combined legal and illegal forms of political action, such as staging peaceful demonstrations and hunger strikes, taking over public buildings, and constructing barricades to close major streets. The years 1979 to 1983 were characterized not only by rather confrontational forms of COPAN's political action but also by a peak in popular movements. The government response to these popular protests was repressive.

Thereafter, COPAN decided to avoid direct confrontations between women and children and the police, and it employed other forms of political action. In 1984, four women and five men, all members of housing committees, went on a hunger strike, demanding a rapid solution to the housing problem. After eighteen days, the government accepted their demands and signed the first agreement with COPAN.

In 1985, COPAN made an agreement with Oscar Arias Sánchez, then presidential candidate of the Partido Liberación Nacional (PLN) (National Liberation Party): COPAN would support him in the 1986 presidential election if he would commit himself to solving the housing problem. Arias promised to build eighty thousand houses for the lowest-income people. Housing was included in the National Development Plan as the "most important unsatisfied basic need in the country" (MIDEPLAN, 1986, p. 32).

Finally, in 1986 COPAN began building what its members call "new communities." Up to 1993, COPAN had been involved in seven construction projects for a total of more than five thousand houses. This involvement included three types of work: upgrading projects based totally on self-help; projects in which the government had urbanized a location and partially built the houses, providing a "wet core" which future residents finished through self-help; and communities that have been entirely designed and built by the people themselves.

Part of COPAN's long struggle has been to obtain the right to design and build houses and communities according to women's needs. Housing committees had found that government bureaucrats just wanted to build cheap houses. The first communities, designed totally and constructed partially by the government, were expensive, laid out in straight monotonous lines, with building walls so thin that people had no privacy. The communities also lacked recreational areas. Women complained that kitchens were too small and that faucets were too hard to reach, which caused them back pains. They showed that housing design and settlement layout negatively affected domestic labor and their daily lives.

Based on these insights, COPAN developed three principles:

1. To earn the right to a house, each inhabitant must participate in a communal self-help program, and each family has to accumulate a minimum of nine hundred hours of work on the housing project.
2. COPAN emphasizes the building of whole communities, not individual houses. It considers houses not only a place to sleep but a place to live, and COPAN therefore promotes recreation to foster better human communication.
3. In the construction of new communities, COPAN insists on preservation of environmental resources.

The organization of COPAN's self-help construction implied an enormous effort and much creativity. Although members were willing to work, most of them, particularly women, had no construction skills. Through communal construction in joint building groups, those who had skills and knowledge taught and supervised the others. The women soon acquired the necessary skills and became successful builders.

COPAN also developed a whole support system for the construction projects, including day-care centers, communal kitchens, warehouse controls, and temporary shelters. Older women and disabled people staffed these support centers, and their labor counted toward the nine hundred hours required for the allocation of a house.

The new communities developed an organizational structure for social relations. People formed support groups for the unemployed and for battered women, and committees for prevention of violence against women and children, for improving basic services, and for health services. Three communities even organized their own clinics for women and children, managed by health committees that promote campaigns against drugs and "for a better life without violence." Issues like child abuse and domestic violence against women are no longer private concerns; they are communal matters. When, for example, a woman leader's husband abused her, the community threatened to expel him. When he did not desist, the woman threw him out, and the men of the community escorted him outside of the community's boundaries.

Although over time, more men have become involved, particularly in construction, women are still overwhelmingly the main participants in community activities. In addition to their responsibilities for social reproduction, they have assumed responsibility for improving their family's living conditions through communal activities.

Thus, the presence of women has had a strong impact on community organization. Women's issues have become a focus of attention and action, and women's needs and ideas have led to specific designs and construction. As Sonia, a woman leader, says, "The new communities have a woman's soul" (Sagot, 1989).

IV. Effects of Women's Participation on Their Personal and Family Lives

Between December 1988 and June 1989, I interviewed sixty women from these new communities; all sixty acknowledged joining housing committees out of a sense of desperation over their living conditions and the poor solutions offered by government agencies (Sagot, 1989). One woman shared these feelings:

I really needed a . . . decent place to live. A house I rented close to a river washed away in a flood. . . . I went to Instituto Nacional de Vivienda y Urbanización (INVU). They asked for 7,000 colones, just to put me on the waiting list. Then I went to a housing committee, they asked me for 3,000 colones. I gave them the money; it was stolen. Finally, I heard about COPAN . . . and discovered that it was the only group helping us to get a house without asking for money.

Women joined COPAN and the housing movement as part of their struggle for survival. For the first time in their lives, the women I interviewed had joined a movement that involved them in attending meetings, participating in demonstrations, building barricades, and drawing graffiti on the city's walls to call attention to their struggle. For the first time, they were becoming visible, exposing themselves to political hostility and repression.

The women saw these actions as the only way they could obligate their government to pay attention to their demands. They found the activities exciting—an opportunity to break out of the monotony of their daily lives. Because of their living conditions, they abandoned traditional ideas of "proper" social roles and engaged in political action, even to the extent of jeopardizing their personal safety. However, the hope of better housing does not by itself adequately explain why these women continued their fight. They struggled for years with nothing more than hope because the association provided them the opportunity of creating bonds with other women. The massive presence of women, their dense network of social ties, created a sense of common identity, shared fate, and a strong solidarity group. Participating and discussing their needs, the women began to recognize that the lack of decent housing was a social problem. As one interviewee commented, "If you are alone, nobody pays attention. . . . I had tried for years to get a house all by myself. . . . It was only through the struggle with all the other people that they paid attention to us. We were so many . . . finally they had to listen" (Sagot, 1989).

The word *struggle* has become part of the women's vocabulary, associated with collective political action. Their involvement in the struggle for housing gave them the chance to link their own lives with those of others and to link issues affecting them and their families with state policy. These linkages created new collective identities.

The women also faced opposition from their husbands or partners, who did not approve of the women's participating in housing committees, and they had to win the right to go to meetings and become members. Many were actually abandoned by their male partners when they remained involved with COPAN despite the men's opposition. The women also faced opposition from some

male committee members who did not want women to be leaders and organizers. This became a major issue of discussion at all levels of the organization.
One woman leader described it as follows:

> We women had to "infiltrate" COPAN. In an organization with mostly women
> members, only a few of us were in leadership positions. We had long discussions in
> the directorate about it. Male members were very understanding. But it was not a
> matter of "understanding"; it was a matter of COPAN's power structure, which
> reflected the power structure of society. As women quickly began to assume respon-
> sibilities, they became leaders. Now most of the main leaders are women (Sagot,
> 1989).

In fact, during the struggle of the 1980s, the women assumed all the important tasks. Few men participated at that stage. However, when construction
began, more men started to show up. Women's dreams were becoming a
reality, and they wanted to participate. Men's increasing participation brought
with it the danger that they would control the communities, given their construction skills and physical strength. But joint building groups with similar
tasks for everybody reduced the inequality between women and men. That was
an important factor in women's empowerment, as they came to see themselves
as capable of doing anything and of controlling their own lives.

However, the time and effort women dedicated to construction work also
was detrimental. They were responsible not only for most of the housework—
and at times for outside jobs—but also for the heavy work of building the
houses. Though many women's ideas about their role in society have changed,
and many now believe women have a crucial role to play in community development or even in the country's destiny, women's subordinate position
inside the home has remained virtually unchallenged. Those still living with
husbands or partners have won the right to go to meetings, to participate in
community activities, and even to make some decisions about their personal
lives. However, they are still responsible for all the housework.

Regardless of the problems they still face, the women acknowledge that
their participation in the housing movement has completely changed their
lives and their self-perceptions. Most of them recall feeling worthless, useless,
and isolated, and they describe themselves as shy and quiet before they joined
the movement. Now they not only have discovered their own worth, but they
also perceive themselves as outspoken and capable of facing difficult situations.
They describe themselves as "knowing their way around" bureaucracy. They
feel powerful because nobody from a governmental agency can get away with
lying to them anymore. Finally, the fact that they are now seeing the concrete

results of their long struggle makes them feel like real achievers. That has completely changed their perspective about what they are capable of doing and accomplishing in life.

Conclusion

The housing movement has had a strong impact on the social struggles in Costa Rica's recent history. It has affected both government social policy and the lives of the participating women. Though it could be argued that for these women participation in the struggle for housing has been only an extension of their traditional roles in the "domestic domain," this participation did change them. They acquired new perceptions of themselves, new attitudes about their abilities, and new roles in formerly male-dominated activities. All of these constituted important steps in their empowerment.

Furthermore, these women recognize that issues they formerly considered private or individual were instead social problems. Through their community activism, women politicized the private domain, became visible through political action, and transformed themselves into conscious political actors. Women's new community activism—using realities as a starting point for political action and moving formerly private issues into the political arena—allowed them to build collective identities.

Moreover, women members of housing committees, with their commitment, discipline, and efficient organization, created a gender-conscious movement that influenced the design of communities and focused on specific issues of concern to women. They linked their individual lives to those of other women, their own families to other families, and their access to resources to government policy. For the women of the housing committees, everyday life became the basis for political work and personal transformation, which made them social and political actors.

Biodata

Montserrat Sagot is also a co-author of "Improving the Quality of Women's Daily Lives," which appears earlier in this *Reader* (Carcedo, Sagot, and Trejos, chap. 3) and carries her biodata.

References

Ackelsberg, Martha. 1988. "Communities' Resistance and Women's Activism." In Ann Bookmann and Sandra Morgen, eds., *Women and the Politics of Empowerment*, pp. 297–313. Philadelphia: Temple University Press.

Adler Hellman, Judith. 1992. "Making Women Visible: New Works on Latin American and Caribbean Women." *Latin American Research Review* 27, no. 1: 182–91.

Camacho, Daniel, and Rafael Mejívar. 1985. *Movimientos populares en Centroamérica.* San José, Costa Rica: EDUCA.

Chant, Sylvia. 1987. "Domestic Labour, Decision-making, and Dwelling Construction: The Experience of Women in Querétaro, Mexico." In Caroline Moser and Linda Peake, eds., *Women, Human Settlements, and Housing,* pp. 33–54. London: Tavistock.

Edgell, Stephen, and Vic Duke. 1983. "Gender and Social Policy." *Journal of Social Policy* 12, no. 3 (July): 357–78.

Facultad Latinoamericana de Ciencias Sociales. 1984. "El movimiento popular: 1970–1983." Mimeo. San José, Costa Rica.

Falk, Richard. 1987. "The Global Promise of Social Movements: Explorations at the Edge of Time." *Alternatives* 12, no. 2 (April): 173–96.

Hirsch, Joachim. 1988. "The Crisis of Fordism, Transformations of the 'Keynesian' Security State and New Social Movements." In Louis Kriesberg and Bronislaw Misztal, eds., *Research in Social Movements, Conflicts and Change, Vol. 10.* New Haven, Conn.: Jai Press.

Jaquette, Jane S. 1991. *The Women's Movement in Latin America. Feminism and the Transition to Democracy.* Boulder, Colo.: Westview Press.

Ministerio de Planificación Nacional (MIDEPLAN). 1986. Plan Nacional de Desarrollo. San José, Costa Rica.

Moser, Caroline. 1987a. "Mobilization Is Women's Work: Struggles for Infrastructure in Guayaquil, Ecuador." In Caroline Moser and Linda Peake, eds., *Women, Human Settlements, and Housing,* pp. 166–94. London: Tavistock.

——. 1987b. "Women, Human Settlements, and Housing: A Conceptual Framework for Analysis and Policy-making." In Caroline Moser and Linda Peake, eds., *Women, Human Settlements and Housing,* pp. 12–32. London: Tavistock.

Portantiero, Juan Carlos. 1981. "Sociedad civil, estado, sistema político." Mimeo. San José: Facultad Latinoamericana de Ciencias Sociales.

Rovira, Jorge. 1982. *Estado y política económica en Costa Rica.* San José, Costa Rica: Editorial Porvenir.

Sagot, Montserrat. 1989. Sixty Women's Oral Communications. Unedited, unpublished.

——. 1991. "Women, Political Activism, and Housing: The Case of Costa Rica." Ph.D. dissertation, Department of Sociology, The American University.

Schneider, Beth. 1988. "Political Generations and the Contemporary Women's Movement." *Sociological Inquiry* 58, no. 1 (Winter): 421.

Sojo, Ana. 1988. *Morfología de la política estatal en Costa Rica y crisis económica.* San José, Costa Rica: Universidad de Costa Rica, Instituto de Investigaciones Económicas.

Torres-Rivas, Edelberto. 1981. "La nación: Problemas teóricos e históricos." In Norbert Lechner, ed., *Estado y política en América Latina,* pp. 71–107. Mexico: Siglo 21.

Vance, Irene. 1987. "More than Bricks and Mortar: Women's Participation in Self-help Housing in Managua, Nicaragua." In Caroline Moser and Linda Peake, eds., *Women, Human Settlements, and Housing,* pp. 139–65. London: Tavistock.

Acknowledgments

The study is part of a Ph.D. dissertation in sociology written while the author was at The American University. It is based on more than five years of personal involvement with COPAN and CEFEMINA and on six months of extensive field work, from December 1988 to June 1989. The United States Agency for International Development (AID) provided the resources for tuition and expenses during coursework and the writing of this study.

23 ❋ Long-Term Survival of a Costa Rican Women's Crafts Cooperative

Approaches to Problems of Rapid Growth at CASEM in the Santa Elena-Monteverde Region

Ilse Abshagen Leitinger

The history of the Comisión (originally Comité) de Artesanos de Santa Elena-Monteverde (CASEM) (Artisans' Commission of Santa Elena-Monteverde) represents a ten-year process in which women in a remote rural setting of Costa Rica, struggling to improve their lives, joined together in a crafts cooperative and transformed it into a flourishing enterprise. They went through good and bad periods and had some lucky breaks, but—more important—they were remarkably persistent.

In what follows, I describe the historical and socioeconomic setting within which CASEM developed, and I record the interplay of relevant factors, focusing on six major themes:

1. The cooperative's beginning and growth;
2. Its evolving institutional format and affiliation with the multiple-service cooperative CoopeSanta Elena;
3. Its struggle to ensure high-quality production in sufficient quantities;
4. Organizational trouble shooting;
5. CASEM's social mission of empowering women—both its members and, increasingly, other women in the community;
6. The leadership's planning for the mid-term future and CASEM's emergence as a community force.

Weighing the individual factors of this process, I offer some conclusions on the sources of CASEM's success.

The Santa Elena-Monteverde Region in the Twentieth Century: The Rise of Diverse Economic Interests and a Multicultural Community

The greater Santa Elena-Monteverde region stretches in a northwest-southeast direction along the mountain range called the Cordillera de Tilarán that divides Pacific Costa Rica from Atlantic Costa Rica. Inhabited areas lie at altitudes from roughly 2,300 to 4,800 feet, with peaks rising above 6,000 feet (Rodríguez M., n.d.).

The altitude moderates the tropical temperatures. The region's climate divides into a dry season and a wet season. The dry season—November through April—is characterized by high winds and flying dust in areas where land is no longer forested, but with a beautiful view over the terrain sloping down to the Gulf of Nicoya and over the distant mountains of the Nicoya Peninsula. The rainy season—May through October—is marked by intermittent downpours, dramatically low, fast-moving clouds, and spectacular rainbows, when you rarely see Gulf or mountains but can savor the fresh fragrance of the lush green slopes that give Monteverde its name. Santa Elena is an agricultural center; Monteverde is best known for its Cloud Forest, a private virgin-forest reserve, but there is more to the region than that.

During the early twentieth century, the area was still isolated, forested, and sparsely populated, with logging and hunting activities supplementing subsistence agriculture. Adding to the isolation was the fact that the region cut across several administrative districts but remained far from their respective centers (Rodríguez M., n.d.).

In about 1915 or 1916, a few people hacked their way through the forest from the Guanacaste lowlands to what later became the town of Santa Elena, but after exploring the area, they did not stay. In the late 1920s, local subsistence farmers built liquor stills, using the remote place as a safe haven for their illegal activities. In the early 1930s, the first colonists came from the village of Guacimal and founded Santa Elena. Around 1930 to 1935, a man named Lindor lived in Lindora, a ribbonlike village along the upper stretch of the access road that branches from the Pan-American highway (Rodríguez M., n.d.). In 1951, a group of twelve Quakers arrived from the United States (Trostle, 1991a). Having left the United States to avoid the Korean War draft, they settled in Costa Rica, which by then was a democracy without a military. They bought a considerable tract of land to the southeast of Santa Elena, founded the Monteverde community, and decided on dairying for economic survival.

Three major economic activities developed. The first was cattle raising. Farmers in the area already had begun to raise cattle, using open land or cutting forests to expand pastures. The Quakers in 1953 created Productores de Monteverde, the *lechería*, or cheese plant, thereby encouraging a shift from beef to dairy cattle, which allowed farmers to develop today's principal enterprise (Trostle, 1991a). The second economic activity stemmed from the Quakers' landholding, which included a sizable piece of virgin forest that had been set aside to protect the water supply. Increasing danger of invasion by squatters led the Quakers to create the protected Reserva del Bosque Nuboso Monteverde (Monteverde Cloud Forest Reserve) in the early 1970s (Guindon, 1991; Trostle, 1991a). The reserve began to attract tropical biologists wanting to do research and, through them, growing numbers of people became interested in conservation. As the Cloud Forest Reserve attracted nature lovers interested in the forest's flora and fauna, the third economic activity began—today's international tourist industry, providing seasonal and year-round jobs through construction and maintenance work, multiple tourist services, and the artisans' production we are exploring in this article.

The most common occupations in the early years were dairy cattle raising, agriculture, and unskilled labor. Analyst Carmen Rodríguez (1992), reported 92 percent of the farms as owner occupied in 1973. Under commercial enterprises for that time, she mentioned two sawmills, two general stores, one hardware store, one grocery store, five bars, two dance halls, four *fonda-hoteles* (inns), one hotel, and two butcher shops. In 1980, Santa Elena, Cerro Plano, Monteverde, and outlying communities had eleven elementary schools with 900 students, according to Rodríguez. The Colegio Agro-Pecuario, Santa Elena's agriculturally-oriented technical high school dating from 1977, had 105 students. The total population of the region numbered approximately 1,600.

In the 1970s, the *lechería* was the most important business in the area. Farmers delivered their milk to it daily and depended on its successful operation for a major part of their livelihood. In time, however, overgrazing on the steep slopes reduced soil fertility and brought serious erosion. The dairy industry faced increasingly less favorable conditions, requiring costly management. Today, milk production has shifted to outlying areas, moving as far as twenty miles away, to the so-called milk shed. Farmers in the original Monteverde area have begun to focus more on tourist-oriented activities (Stuckey, 1991). The *lechería* does not want to expand operations beyond its current milk suppliers, but it is interested in increasing high-quality milk production by improving output per unit of land. It supports activities designed to counteract erosion and to stabilize pastures, and it aims at increased production through environmentally sound management, quality control, and efficiency at the plant (Vargas L., J. L., 1991).

The conservation movement and tourism, and to some extent the dairy industry, have been responsible for integrating the Santa Elena-Monteverde region into national and international networks of governmental and nongovernmental institutions and organizations, such as the Costa Rican ministries of education, agriculture, and public works; the World Wildlife Fund; the Nature Conservancy; the Canadian Development Agency; the Inter-American Foundation; and countless tourist enterprises.

By the early 1980s, diverse interest groups had established a number of community organizations with contradictory goals. Among them were the Cooperativa Múltiple Santa Elena, a multiple-service cooperative dating from 1971 (Vargas L., C. A., 1991); the Reserva del Bosque Nuboso Monteverde, managed since 1972–73 by the Centro Científico Tropical (Tropical Science Center) in San José (Guindon, 1991); the Asociación Conservacionista de Monteverde (Monteverde Conservation League), popularly La Liga, created in 1985–86 to preserve Pacific slope forests and ensure sustainable development of the region (LaVal, 1991; the Instituto Monteverde (Monteverde Institute), established in 1987 to carry out environmental education (Trostle, 1991b); the Cámara de Turismo ([Monteverde] Chamber of Tourism) to represent tourist business interests; and several local development associations (Stuckey, 1988) that attest to the people's "strong sense of overcoming difficulties and organizing themselves" (Rodríguez M., n.d.). Of growing importance has been the Plan de Desarrollo Integral Monteverde 2020 (Plan for Integrated Development of the Monteverde Region by the Year 2020), commonly known as MV 2020, an umbrella organization to negotiate community-wide decisions for maintaining the quality of life and making development truly sustainable (Plan de Desarrollo Integral Monteverde 2020, 1989).

Finally, over the last few decades, the Santa Elena-Monteverde region has become a multicultural community, although Costa Ricans remain in the majority (Rodríguez M., n.d.). Besides the Quakers, other non-Costa Rican residents of the region include retired U.S. couples who alternate between homes in Monteverde and the United States, scientists or professionals working for environmental and other community organizations, Canadians, Europeans, and various Central Americans. Although still mostly Roman Catholic, several communities have established fundamentalist Protestant churches of the Jehovah's Witnesses, Seventh Day Adventists, and Evangélicos, the Church of God (Stuckey, 1988). Current estimates put the region's population at three thousand. The international element extends into the larger community through educational institutions. The Quakers support a Friends' School with bilingual education, and in 1991 the Centro de Educación Creativa (Creative Learning Center), popularly Centro Creativo, began operating a bilingual school for residents who want their children to learn English to improve their occupational chances.

Thus, in about half a century, people in the formerly isolated region have been integrated into national and international networks that have had wide repercussions. These networks have also had a remarkable impact on women.

The Beginning and Growth of CASEM

In the mid-1970s, when these trends were becoming apparent, dairy plant officials thought it unhealthy for dairying to be the only major business. Knowing that dairying could threaten the environment and that it alone would not ensure the economic health of outlying communities, they began to look for other sources of income (VanDusen, July 15, 1992, pers. comm.). At the same time, the Central American economic crisis of the late 1970s was causing single-income families to lose their former standard of living.

The dairy plant encouraged a study to explore economic diversification for local farmers and craftsmen and to search for income-generating options for women. The CoopeSanta Elena (CoopeSE), itself in a refocusing phase (Vargas L., C. A., 1991), carried out the study with funding from the Inter-American Foundation (IAF) and the Canadian embassy (Vargas L., C. A., July 14, 1992, pers. comm.). Two anthropologists assisted by a local dairy plant employee— all women—did the study.

As the researchers visited the *caseríos*, the small outlying communities, they explored options for economic diversification—forestry or fruit tree nurseries, or collection and storage centers for agricultural products (VanDusen, July 15, 1992, pers. comm.). They noticed that everywhere they went, women were producing a variety of handicrafts. The researchers inquired if the women would like to organize a fair to sell their creations. About thirty women supported the idea. With funding from CoopeSE and IAF, the fair was held during Easter week of 1982, at the Pensión Quetzal in Monteverde (Jiménez, 1991); it offered a medley of wares for sale, such as doilies, embroideries, pressed-flower cards, and more.

The fair was a success. Eight women who even before the fair had been working together decided they would seriously begin crafts production, and the organization slowly took shape. They received small loans from CoopeSE and IAF for setting up both a shop and an office (Vargas L., C. A., July 15, 1992, pers. comm.), and other women's cooperatives offered advice on operations and merchandizing (Jiménez, July 14, 1992, pers. comm.; Rodríguez, July 15, 1992, pers. comm.).

At first, the women exhibited and sold in the house of Patricia Jiménez, one of their members who ran a second-hand-clothing store, "Artemás" (meaning "art and then some"), out of her kitchen in Santa Elena. They simply added their crafts to the wares in the store. Patricia's husband, a guide in the Cloud Forest Reserve, brought tourists looking for souvenirs. One of them, Jean Andrews, an artist from Texas, was to have a major influence upon CASEM's growth in later years; she returned frequently with materials, stayed to teach art and design, and helped with outside funding (Jiménez, July 14, 1992, pers. comm.).

As the operation flourished, more women joined, and the initial informality had to give way to increasing formality. In cooperation with their adviser from CoopeSE, business manager Carlos Vargas, the women developed an organizational structure and began to keep a written record in successive Libros de Actas (LA), official record books, that reflect discussions and decisions made in general assemblies and executive committee meetings (Libro de Actas, 1 to 6 [1982–84 to 1991–92]). The first Libro de Actas (LA) begins in late May 1982. From then on, the records give a detailed picture of the organization's successes, concerns, and problems—not the least of which was learning to keep adequate financial accounts (see, e.g., LA, 1 [October 6, 1982, February 25, 1983] and 2 [June 1985]). In July 1982, the women named their enterprise Comité de Artesanos de Santa Elena y Monteverde (CASEM), the Santa Elena and Monteverde Artisans' Committee. Later, "Comité" changed to "Comisión," but it remained CASEM, the name by which it is known everywhere.

Patricia's kitchen soon became too small. CoopeSE offered CASEM space in its Santa Elena office, but even before moving there in 1984 (Jiménez, 1991) the artisans had begun to talk about establishing a CASEM store in Monteverde, closer to the reserve, where tourists would find shopping easier (LA, 1 [March 25, 1983]). In 1986, CoopeSE made available a space in its Monteverde building. The new location immediately led to more sales (LA, 2 [May 1986]). By mid-1986, CASEM members were seriously considering building their own store, and by late 1986, they were planning the details (see, e.g., LA, 2 [October 1986] and 3 [December 1986]). It became a joint undertaking: CoopeSE made available the land, the Monteverde community provided sand and gravel, the lechería donated paint, and Jean Andrews transmitted via the Episcopal Church a U.S. donation of $10,000. (This transmission by way of a religious institution permitted the donation to remain tax free.)

Not everything went smoothly, however. The Canadian Development Agency rejected CASEM's application for funds, arguing lack of promise for economic success in this women's enterprise (Jiménez, July 14, 1992, pers.

comm.; Vargas L., C. A., July 14, 1992, pers. comm.). Nonetheless, the women persisted. Many donated time to clean the land in preparation for construction. Husbands contributed physical labor, and the artisans raised the percentage of their sales that they contributed to the cooperative's operating fund from 10 to 15 percent (Jiménez, July 14, 1992, pers. comm.).

Finally, in 1987, CASEM moved into the building it currently operates. Again, in keeping with the pattern, CASEM discussions already center on enlarging facilities or building additional ones to keep pace with growth and product diversification. Past improvements included restructuring the use of the building to provide better customer access; moving storage space for materials away from the sales area so as to channel deliveries to artisans away from tourist traffic; and replacing the wooden entrance door with wide glass panels to allow tourists a view of the exhibits even when the store is closed (LA, 4 [December 1, 1991]). Leaders are now exploring the possibility of further improving conditions for artisans by providing a lunchroom, restrooms, and, in the future, child-care facilities (LA, 6 [June 2, 1992]). They also are planning to construct additional work space for some new production processes used in the CASEM workshop.

During this time, CASEM experienced not only a consistent rise in production and sales but also a substantial increase in members. From 8 members in 1982, membership grew to 50 when CASEM moved to the CoopeSE building in Santa Elena in 1984 (CSE, Departamento de Artesanía, 1992). By the time of the transfer to Monteverde, the count stood at 73, and when CASEM moved into its own building, membership exceeded 80 (Jiménez, 1991). As of this writing, the count is near 150. At almost regular intervals, CASEM has had to fix new upper limits on membership—100 artisans in 1990, 125 in 1991, and 150 in 1992 (Vargas L., C. A., July 14, 1992, pers. comm.). These figures are surprising when one considers that throughout these years, the Libros de Actas reflect a continuous turnover in membership.

CASEM's Institutional Format and Affiliation with CoopeSE

The history of CASEM would be incomplete without a discussion of its relationship with CoopeSE. Initially, CASEM gladly accepted CoopeSE's support and advice on how to administer the enterprise, and Carlos A. Vargas L., CoopeSE's business manager, also helped manage CASEM. Most women had no experience with running a business, in fact, most had no experience with *any* work outside the home. The local economy had always offered jobs for cash only to men, and most men thought that was as it should be. However, as Costa Rica's currency, the colón, lost value through inflation, many men welcomed their wives' economic contribution. Yet, even though women wanted to work for an income, they felt uncertain; they therefore appreciated the group support. Thus, when CoopeSE introduced them to the mechanics of a cooperative enterprise that met their needs perfectly, they readily decided on a cooperative format for their crafts-producing enterprise as well (Vargas L., C. A., July 14, 1992, pers. comm.).

In successive deliberations, the women refined the objectives for CASEM. They decided it should offer employment opportunities for women; offer its members training in production and diversification of crafts; and, most important, offer the members an overall understanding of business operations (LA, 1 [October 6, 1982]). For CASEM's leaders, another crucial (though less formalized) objective was that this experience would lead to women's empowerment by providing the women with mutual support, a social meeting place, and an outlet for their creativity, thereby enhancing their self-confidence and decision-making ability (LA, 4 [October 21, 1988]; Rodríguez, July 15, 1992, pers. comm.). Meanwhile, the cooperative structure would help spread the economic risks.

As for women's empowerment, the documents establishing CASEM speak simply of "economic and social improvement" of artisans' families (CSE, n.d.[a]; 1987 n.d.[b]), with leaders consistently emphasizing that the social goal is as important as the economic one (see, e.g., LA, 4 [October 27, 1988]; Jiménez, July 14, 1992, pers. comm.; Lobo, July 17, 1992, pers. comm.; Rodríguez, July 15, 1992, pers. comm.).

To support the cooperative infrastructure, members contribute part of their earnings for maintenance and the purchase of raw materials. After various changes in the early years (LA, 1 [October 6, 1982]), membership and financing rules evolved (Jiménez, July 14, 1992, pers. comm.; Vargas L., C. A., 1987): Members now must live in the region, know some craft, participate in the general assemblies of CASEM, and sell only through CASEM. Each month, members are required to produce six items of their choice and to deliver those items in person to obtain an evaluation of quality and design. Members do their own pricing, incorporating the cost of materials, the cost of their labor, their contribution to the operation of CASEM and of CoopeSE, and their own profit. They receive their earnings only after their product has sold; if it has not sold after nine months, they must either take it back and upgrade it or withdraw it from the store. Such rules ensure that the artisans will have a say over what they produce. This is important because "artisans don't want to be told what to produce, because '*nos estamos dando el gusto*'—we enjoy what we are doing" (Lobo, July 17, 1992, pers. comm.).

Currently, artisans receive 65 percent of a given price for an item; 25 percent goes to CASEM for infrastructure, full-time employee costs, and CASEM's contribution to CoopeSE. The remaining 10 percent—the *capital social*—is a tithe that goes into a short-term fund for operating expenses where it earns no interest. CASEM uses these funds to buy material for sale to artisans or to provide loans with interest to the Savings and Loans part of CoopeSE. When artisans leave CASEM, they can withdraw their accumulated *capital social*.

If at year's end, CASEM shows an operating-fund surplus, the organization must decide how to use it. Initially, surplus money was invested at interest in CoopeSE's Savings and Loans operation. More recently, and particularly when the surplus has become rather sizable, the general assembly has paid out such gains to members, proportionate to each artisan's sales during the year (CSE, Departamento de Artesanía, 1992). Some regard these payments as a weakness, concerned that they may deflect members' attention from social benefits to financial ones. As one woman said, "CASEM must insist on members' commitment to the group. . . . It must train for group spirit, responsibility, decision making, self esteem . . . [and] remain an educational institution" (Rodríguez, July 15, 1992, pers. comm.). Others welcome the distribution, since the artisans' savings were losing value through inflation (Salazar, July 18, 1992, pers. comm.).

In 1987, with CASEM a successful operation, CoopeSE suggested that the organization either become a full member of CoopeSE or operate independently. A hard decision! Many members spoke for affiliation, and many others warned against it. The document "¿Con la Coope? ¿O sin ella?" (With the Coop? Or without it?) summarized arguments for and against, reflecting the agonizing negotiations (Anonymous, n.d.[a]). It also detailed the members' decision—to join formally with CoopeSE. Reasons in favor of joining included CASEM's savings in administrative expenses, the benefit of belonging to a legally established organization, the reputation and administrative expertise of CoopeSE, the social benefits of membership (e.g., right to training, loans, and household purchases), and the contribution CASEM could make to the well-being of CoopeSE, to which it felt deeply indebted. Today, CASEM is the "most consolidated, the strongest member" of CoopeSE (Anonymous, n.d.[b]). It earns 40 percent of CoopeSE's income, thereby paying 40 percent of the cooperative's administrative expenses. By comparison, the commercial services operation accounts for 45 percent, the coffee production unit of CoopeSE for 10 percent, and the savings and loan operation for 5 percent (Vargas L., C. A., July 15, 1992, pers. comm.).

Ensuring Adequate Crafts Production

CASEM's most difficult daily challenge is maintaining adequate production, in quality as well as quantity. Various policies focus on this problem, including frequent training courses to foster artisans' environmental awareness and enhance originality of design, measures for quality control, constant efforts toward product diversification, the establishment of a workshop at the store site, and successful marketing to take into account the newly arising competition in the Santa Elena-Monteverde region.

Design Courses

The challenge of ensuring sufficient production is magnified by the uninterrupted growth in the number of artisans in need of training, their constant turnover, and their special household obligations (Baum, 1990; Hoffschmidt, 1990). Moreover, the typical seasonal business cycle affects production. The peak of production should occur before the December-to-April high season of tourism, but that is also the period when artisans earn least and yet must invest most in buying raw materials.

From the beginning, training for artisans has been one of the leaders' major concerns, for which they obtained extensive support. Such training was originally offered by qualified CASEM artisans or by nonaffiliated community members, several of them Quakers who had particular artistic skills and served largely on a volunteer basis. They also taught problem solving, conflict resolution, and other socially relevant topics to advance CASEM's social goals. Some community women volunteered such services for many years and had a formative artistic influence on crafts production (Rodríguez, July 15, 1992, pers. comm.). With their help, rural artisans improved skills they already possessed—for instance, embroidery—or learned new skills, such as painting on cloth or elaborating their own designs (Jiménez, July 14, 1992, pers. comm.).

Originally, the Cloud Forest's flora and fauna provided the subject matter for all craftwork. Lately, the theme of sustainable development has also inspired many designs. CASEM acquired reproductions in which colors and shapes were true to nature (see, e.g., LA, 1 [August 1984]) and it allowed artisans to copy patterns of popular designs (LA, 1 [May 13, 1983]). As a matter of principle, however, CASEM designs cannot be reproduced outside the cooperative. According to the rules, each artisan may decide what item she will produce and how she will design it. CASEM therefore does not dictate production; leaders do, however, encourage artisans to produce items that sell well. From the mid-1980s on, the artist Jean Andrews returned many times. She brought materials and offered classes on art, design, or the functionality of products.

CASEM recently contracted with outside professionals to teach design. With growing artistic sophistication, artisans have gone beyond mere reproduction of nature to allow imagination and stylizing a role in their designs, thus achieving creations of art inspired by nature, in what some have called a characteristic "estilo Monteverde" (VanDusen, July 15, 1992, pers. comm.). These creations brought greater satisfaction to the artisans and better sales (CSE, Departamento de Artesanía, 1992; Rodríguez, July 15, 1992, pers. comm.; VanDusen, July 15, 1992, pers. comm.). They also emphasized environmental conservation, thereby serving all goals of the organization (CSE, n.d.[a]; n.d.[b]).

Quality Control

All Libros de Actas reflect the consultants' urging to maintain high quality. They also support the rules that artisans must deliver their products in person so that they can consult with the shop manager about quality, and that they will receive payment only after their products have been sold. Early on, CASEM established an Evaluation Committee to assess quality (LA, 1 [October 6, 1982]), and CASEM's courses also address the issue of quality production. Today's leaders refer to quality control as one of their principal objectives (Jiménez, July 14, 1992, pers. comm.; Salazar, July 18, 1992, pers. comm.; VanDusen, July 15, 1992, pers. comm.). In that context, they even confront technological issues, such as sewing machine repair (LA, 6 [June 3, 1991]), optimal quality of available electricity to ensure efficient machine operation (LA, 6 [April 3, 1991]), and overall streamlining of operations (LA, 6 [July 10, 1991]).

Product Diversification

Training not only emphasizes quality but also encourages product diversification, either through changes in the design of a popular item or through the use of entirely different materials, such as natural fibers, wood, paper maché, or ceramics (LA, 6 [September 2, 1991]; VanDusen, July 15, 1992, pers. comm.; Vargas L., C.A., July 14, 1992, pers. comm.). Some observers have suggested further steps. A visiting Peace Corps volunteer spoke of printing shirts instead of embroidering or painting them, and she discussed working with ceramics

(LA, 6 [September 2, 1991]). Art teachers Carlos Jiménez and Carolina Barrientos suggested introducing a folk art section in CASEM (LA, 6 [November 4, 1991]). They offered to teach a course on gourd preparation (LA, 6 [February 3, 1992]). Still, stand-by items, such as painted T-shirts, embroidered or painted blouses or skirts, reversible jackets with designs on both sides, earrings, necklaces, painted cards, letter paper, table cloths, potholders, wall hangings, and woven belts continue to be big money makers.

I have returned to CASEM at regular intervals over the last few years, and on almost every visit I have noted new products or new designs on display. Wooden crafts produced by the few male and some women members of CASEM, paper maché or stuffed animal toys have become popular offerings.

The Workshop

In response to the increasing demand for several popular items, CASEM leaders decided in 1985 to establish a workshop (LA, 2 [November 1985]). Today, the workshop is staffed by three full-time employees and a full-time supervisor, who earn a regular salary but do not receive *capital social*. The workshop uses the same pricing mechanism used by the independent artisans, so it also contributes to the overall operating fund. At times, workshop workers do receive bonuses from the yearly surplus (LA, 6 [December 23, 1991]). Currently, shop earnings pay the training costs for all artisans (Vargas L., C. A., July 15, 1992, pers. comm.). In addition to the full-time employees, twelve artisans work for the shop at home and are paid according to the number of items they complete. Artisans' personal designs cannot be used in the workshop, nor may the artisans working at home employ workshop designs except under contract by the workshop. Since its beginning, the workshop has consistently accounted for 30 percent of the sales at CASEM (Vargas L., C. A., July 15, 1992, pers. comm.).

Marketing

"CASEM has never had to worry about a market; that makes planning for proper marketing difficult," said Carlos Vargas (July 15, 1992, pers. comm.). However, several competing enterprises have recently sprung up in the region, e.g., the Hummingbird Gallery near the entrance to the Cloud Forest, the Butterfly Garden and La Galería in Monteverde, shops at local hotels, a shop in Cerro Plano, and one next to the popular restaurant El Trapiche in Cañitas, four kilometers west of Santa Elena (Jiménez, August 26, 1992, pers. comm.).

Consequently, CASEM leaders have taken steps to enhance marketing: As noted earlier, one of these steps is making better use of space in the CASEM store through separating the traffic of tourists from that of artisans (LA, 6 [January 12, 1991]). Another is the annual gift of a T-shirt, featuring a design not to be reproduced that year, to guides in the Cloud Forest, hoping the walking advertisement will encourage tourists to visit CASEM where the shirts were created (Huertas, July 15, 1992, pers. comm.; LA, 6 [June 3, 1991]; LA, 6 [July 1, 1991]). Further anticipated steps include adding new products, such as a calendar featuring Cloud Forest designs; improving presentation through more informative, better designed product labels (LA, 5 [May 8, 1990], 6 [January 12; July 1, 1991]); and creating attractive fliers with information about CASEM (LA, 6 [January 12, 1991]).

CASEM has also considered marketing nationally, should fewer tourists visit the Cloud Forest. Possible options include selling in other Costa Rican locations, such as San José hotels, the international airport, and the beaches (LA, 6 [October 7, 1991]), or selling to local customers. Such changes are not easy. Right now, the volume of production does not justify seriously considering these options; moreover, most local customers cannot afford the prices CASEM must charge. The recent addition of a serigraphy machine for printing substantially less expensive shirts may be a way of approaching the national market (LA, 6 [December 3, 1991; January 25, 1992; June 10, 1992]).

Finally, CASEM has been exploring options for export, especially to the United States, either through outlet stores—the owners of one such store in Boulder, Colorado, visited CASEM as tourists (LA, 6 [May 2, 1992])—or through a mail order catalog (LA, 6 [December 1, 1991]). Plans for such a catalog are still on the drawing board.

Clearly, diversified marketing requires greater production. To encourage that, CASEM in the last few years has carried out a design competition with cash prizes for the best designs (LA, 6 [July 1; October 7, 1991; February 3, 1992]). Much remains to be done on this issue.

Organizational Trouble Shooting

Despite its successes, the CASEM operation has not been trouble-free. Some problems relate to logistics and CASEM's rapid growth; others are human and attributable to inadequate communications or the nature of cooperative enterprises.

Given the steady turnover of artisans, executive committee meetings must constantly consider membership applications and withdrawals. In 1990, thirty-six new members joined and twelve withdrew (Gómez and Vargas L., 1991). In 1991 forty-seven new memberships and fourteen withdrawals were recorded (Gómez and Vargas L., 1992). Thus, in two years, withdrawals equalled nearly one-third of new memberships. Obviously, resources devoted to training people who soon will leave the organization contribute to CASEM's goal of improving women's lives, but they don't advance its business interests.

Another quandary is that many artisans who most need to earn money do not even produce the required monthly items, let alone increase their production. Alisa Baum (1990) and Kristin Hoffschmidt (1990) identified the following possible causes of low productivity:

1. The artisans' difficult working conditions, such as inadequate work space and large family obligations;
2. Women's traditional perception of craftwork as recreation, not as work that merits an income;
3. Women's tendency to think neither in terms of a cash economy nor of their own labor as deserving financial reward.

Baum and Hoffschmidt suggested improving the physical work space or other home working conditions. CASEM has made an excellent effort to modify artisans' homes through providing construction funds for attachments or structural changes (see, e.g., LA, 6 [January 12; May 6; August 5; August 31; October 7, 1991]). Recently, this policy was somewhat curtailed by limited funds. Nonetheless, fifteen artisans, slightly over 10 percent of all members, did benefit from work-space improvement.

One attempt to help low producers think in terms of money management has been the course "How to Earn Money with CASEM." It taught proper organization for production and basic accounting principles (LA, 6 [May 24, 1991]). The course is not given regularly, but leaders have recently integrated the material into the crafts courses the cooperative offers in many villages.

Other organizational problems are not so easily addressed. Several artisans sold items to the competition at other crafts stores or they independently sold items they had made with material bought from CASEM (see, e.g., LA, 5 [January 22, 1990]). CASEM does not want to curtail competition, but to keep its operation intact it has to enforce its rules among members (Salazar, July 18, 1992, pers. comm.).

Communications is another troublesome area. In such a large group, misinterpretations of information and personality clashes unavoidably occur. Yet, CASEM leaders have built on their conflict-resolution training and have met criticism openly. For instance, after an anonymous group complaint that CASEM operated in favor of "insiders" at the expense of "outsiders," leaders invited all members feeling any discontent to an open discussion session (LA, 6 [February 5; February 22, 1991). Unfortunately, only three artisans attended. The leaders may take comfort in knowing that they are dealing with a characteristic phenomenon of Costa Rican culture. CASEM's women exemplify what observers have identified as the desire of all Ticos to "*quedar bien*" (to get along, appear amiable) (Biesanz, Biesanz, and Biesanz, 1982: 11–12) and the "pervasive national tendency to avoid conflict and extremes of violent confrontation" (See Leitinger, Introduction).

CASEM leaders also acknowledge a social reason for misunderstandings: As a rule, most leaders have more education, better access to the outside world, and more varied experiences than most of the dissatisfied women artisans. The latter tend to live in isolated places and to be tied down by family constraints, easily feel discriminated against, and lack the leaders' self-esteem. They are unable to take advantage of options for training or participating in meetings or excursions and, with limited education, have difficulty understanding the complexities of accounting and the underlying principles of management in the cooperative. CASEM recognizes this problem and tries to improve communications with outlying areas, where transportation is essential if women are to connect to others. "Availability of family transportation is crucial to women's participation in employment," commented a woman from an outlying village (Lobo, July 17, 1992, pers. comm.).

Given membership turnover and constant growth, communication will continue to challenge CASEM leaders. "When we were twenty, we felt very close and had time to talk about everything," a founding member observed, "but now that the organization has become so big, there doesn't seem time for it" (Salazar, July 18, 1992, pers. comm.). Moreover, despite offering training for management and accounting, CASEM wants to avoid the image that its members are working exclusively for economic gain. Its leadership remains deeply committed to the organization's social mission.

The Social Mission of CASEM: Women's Empowerment

As stated earlier, in the view of its leaders, one of the most significant results of CASEM's operation has been the social effect of offering women options for income generation, training, education, and, simply, the opportunity to join with other women in a supportive social setting. These processes inspire self-confidence and lead women to take the initiative in community affairs, to speak up, and to learn to make independent decisions. In short, these opportunities empower women to contribute to the well-being of the community and to their own fulfillment. This was all the more important in the early years, when no alternatives existed for women in the area. Today, the expanding tourist industry presents other options. In fact, "if CASEM were starting today, who knows if we would become as successful as we have been," said one of its eight founders (Salazar, July 18, 1992, pers. comm.).

Some men have not been happy with the artisans' success. Many husbands welcomed the addition of their wives' cash income to their own—"The women's success could be measured in colones," noted Carlos Vargas (July 14, 1992, pers. comm.). Others, however, did not want women to take time out from home and child-care obligations in order to produce, learn, succeed, and maybe even travel or have fun with CASEM. Undoubtedly, men feared that women would become too independent and that men would lose control. One of CASEM's founders noted that "women were not used to taking on responsibility. They had been taught to obey fathers, brothers, husbands; they were not ready to make decisions or demand room for their own personal development." And she confirmed that "CASEM has changed men's attitudes . . . somewhat" (Rodríguez, July 15, 1992, pers. comm.). Sadly enough, not all men's attitudes changed. In one case, a father would not permit his daughter to go to CASEM to submit her craft items. When CASEM invited him to hear an explanation of the rationale for this requirement (LA, 6 [April 3, 1991]), he refused the invitation. In the end, the daughter left home and today is a single mother (Jiménez, August 26, 1992, pers. comm.).

Despite such difficulties, CASEM has profoundly changed the way women see themselves and the way others see them. In fact, some suggest CASEM's social achievements outweigh its economic ones (VanDusen, July 15, 1992, pers. comm.). To be sure, gender still determines community participation, but many women have gained confidence through their business success with CASEM or on their own (Drake, 1991; Hanson, 1991; Marsh, 1991; Vargas L., C.A., July 14, 1992, pers. comm.).

CASEM's efforts are also producing another satisfying result: By recreating the natural beauty of their environment, many rural women have developed a new perspective on the natural world around them, which they might not otherwise have examined so intensely (Gómez M., July 18, 1992, pers. comm.). As a result, the environmental concern expressed by CASEM's formal declaration to "foster the conservation of natural resources of the zone through the sale of crafts" has become a personal mission for these women (CSE, n.d.[a]; n.d.[b]).

Other aspects of CASEM's social mission include its many offerings of non-craft training, through courses on subjects important to rural women, such as health, nutrition, household management, and education (Jiménez, July 15, 1992, pers. comm.). Recently, in cooperation with the Monteverde Institute, CASEM has begun offering women's courses and workshops on diverse issues (LA, 6 [February 10; May 11, 1992]). Also, with the help of the Centro Nacional de Educación Cooperativista (CENECOOP) (National Center for Cooperativist Education), women at CASEM have studied organizational management (LA, 5 [February 26, 1990]). Beyond that, the contribution of local Quaker women, particularly the training in nonconflictive negotiation for problem solving, has been essential for the cooperative's management (Jiménez, July 14, 1992, pers. comm.).

An unexpected yet understandable side effect of CASEM's contribution to women's growing independence has been that some of the most enterprising, gifted members have found it difficult to accept conditions for membership over time. Among them are several excellent artists who devoted years to building up CASEM, provided training for artisans in outlying villages, and did exceptionally well with sales through CASEM. They have left the cooperative, feeling that their own creative initiative was stifled by rules such as the one requiring members to sell or exhibit only through CASEM. In fact, only three of the original eight founding members remain with CASEM today (Rodríguez, July 15, 1992, pers. comm.).

Leaders have agonized over having to impose conditions such as the rule of only selling through CASEM or of protecting the use of designs. They argue, however, that this is a legitimate price members must pay for the support, training, marketing, infrastructure, attention to well-being, and other social benefits membership offers (Salazar, July 18, 1992, pers. comm.). To promote such benefits, leaders also arrange purely recreational events, such as frequent fairs and community parties like CASEM's tenth anniversary party in May 1992. It has also sponsored occasional trips to other regions for fashion shows at hotels in San José or for outings at the beach (see, e.g., LA, 5 [January 27; February 26; May 8, 1990]; 6 [February 3, 1992]).

In the community, CASEM's role has changed noticeably. People ask CASEM for help and advice. Interested groups want to visit CASEM, ask CASEM trainers to visit their communities, and invite CASEM members to visit (see, e.g., LA, 5 [January 4; February 12, 1990]; 6 [March 12, 1991; May 11, 1992]). Despite its limited capacity to comply, CASEM responds judiciously to such requests. Recently, a new CASEM outreach program has begun to train non-members, Santa Elena high-school students, and interested participants in outlying communities. The previous manager of CASEM's store, Nery Gómez, now runs training programs in outlying communities (LA, 6 [May 11; June 10, 1992]).

CASEM is also a partner in community affairs. It contributed 60,000 colones (approximately $500 at then current exchange rates) to the twentieth anniversary celebration of CoopeSE (LA, 6 [July 1, 1991]), and it is working with the Asociación Conservacionista de Monteverde, the Reserva del Bosque Nuboso Monteverde, the Cámara de Turismo, the Centro de Educación Creativa, and the Plan de Desarrollo Integral Monteverde 2020 on various projects (see, e.g., LA, 6 [February 3; February 10; May 11, 1992]).

CASEM Looks Toward the Future

In its early years, CASEM responded primarily to its own problems, most of which resulted from constant growth in membership and sales and from the need for a permanent location. But as its operation has consolidated, as CASEM has become an economic force and has taken on responsibilities for the well-being of its own members, its leaders have become aware of the need not merely to respond to what has happened but also to anticipate what will happen, so as to plan appropriate action.

CASEM leaders have charted plans of action for different future scenarios, taking into consideration changing numbers of tourists, plans for marketing locally or internationally, and new production trends and products. They also have been asking how they can continue to improve the lives of the women working for CASEM and how they can contribute to the well-being of the community.

The current five-year plan (see table 23.1) provides an insight into the goals of CASEM's management (LA, 6 [January 13, 1992]). Highlights include streamlining the operation and doubling its present size (with an enlarged proportion of male members); improving training, technical processes, and social services to personnel and customers; expanding marketing options; and implementing careful financial planning. The plan represents an organization that is under control and aware of its setting, potential, and where it wants to

Table 23.1. CASEM's Five-Year Plan, 1992–96

| | | Proposed Activity Area | | |
Goals by Period	Personnel	Members	Community	Production	Organization
1 Consolidation (1992–93)	Get promotion agent to work with members Stabilize workshop personnel; minimum of seven employees	Give lunch to executive committee (Comisión de Apoyo) when meetings too long Separate tourists from artisans who buy material, receive pay, deliver items Offer high-fashion course Explore paper produced from fiber	Help the high school Support different CoopeSE departments (credit, coffee)	Printing of shirts, two employees Marketing Evaluate usefulness of sale by consignment Import raw material to make shirts Produce pure art	Continue General Assembly and social activities Train members and personnel in organizational processes Use microphone in meetings Find appropriate meeting hall

2 Assessment of future (1994)	Train personnel for export production	Improve management of *capital social*; put top limit on use; redistribute remainder Develop pension plan Establish workshops in community and outlying villages	Work with school in San Gerardo Create branch of CASEM in San Gerardo Take products to beaches	Open cheap cafeteria for women employees Child care at shop, training, and meetings Exports Product diversification Invest *capital social*; Buy vehicle Do industrial imprinting of paper	Create committees in outlying villages Evaluate relations with other parts of CoopeSE
3 Advance (1995–96)		Membership can go to 300 Number of male members should reach a minimum of 20%	Student production in San Gerardo	Offer communal workshops Encourage export diversification	Raise profits to 12% over sales + inflation; raise *capital social* to 30% Up individual sales to average inflation + 10% Distribute gains

Source: Actas VI

be five years hence. The plan also shows that CASEM is considering ways to deal with contingencies beyond its control, such as changes in the local, national, and international markets.

The Interplay of Factors

This reconstruction of CASEM's establishment and ten-year trajectory has identified a number of circumstances that have affected CASEM's growth and survival. Even if some of its successes served CASEM's social goals while hurting its economic ones, the major positive factors in CASEM's growth and survival seem to be a favorable physical and socioeconomic context; a clear mandate for job diversification expressed by local business leaders; a constantly growing market; access to business advice, guidance, and occasional outside financial support; a female population with no options for productive activities and no social interaction other than through family-related tasks; and a team of women with artistic and leadership potential and a vision of the double goal of women's economic and social empowerment.

The growth process produced problems, though. CASEM struggled continually to maintain quality and consistent production in the face of a growing demand for its handicrafts. Membership turnover has been very high, creating a constant need for training of new artisans in a variety of media. CASEM leaders also faced the logistic problems of a membership spread over a wide, topographically broken area; seasonally varying demands for artisans' production; and the task of constantly adjusting organizational and administrative structures to handle the rapid growth.

Which of these factors were crucial? The evidence allows only a preliminary assessment. It seems that in terms of the setting, the growth of tourism—which produced an ever-increasing demand for CASEM's products—and CoopeSE's continued support with sound business advice were essential and were responsible for major stages in the development. In terms of internal processes, CASEM's drive for quality, its development of the "estilo Monteverde" in response to the timely concern with the environment, and its conscious commitment to a double social and economic mission appear decisive. In addition, the capacity of the leadership to step back and reflect, to ask themselves uncomfortable questions, to face reality, to negotiate and be immensely persistent throughout a ten-year period—in sum, CASEM's leadership style—represents a condition without which the growth and survival of this organization would have been impossible.

Some of these conditions or factors are unique to the Monteverde setting and the time; others can be replicated elsewhere. Women who plan to embark on similar endeavors may want to study CASEM's experiences carefully. CASEM leaders will contribute to women's empowerment if they share their experiences with other Costa Ricans who have the courage to start their own enterprises.

Biodata

Ilse Abshagen Leitinger is a German-born, naturalized U.S. citizen. She has a Ph.D. in international studies from the University of Denver and has taught comparative sociology and Latin American studies at Grinnell College in Iowa. She was a Fulbright lecturer at the former Centro Interdisciplinario de Estudios de la Mujer (CIEM) (Center for Interdisciplinary Women's Studies), now the Instituto de Estudios de la Mujer (IEM) (Institute of Women's Studies) at the Universidad Nacional. She is a founding member of the Instituto Latinoamericano de Investigación Feminista (ILIFEM) (Latin American Institute for Feminist Research). She has been interested in Latin American women since she first explored the region from Mexico to southern Chile and Argentina in 1958 and 1959 (with Hans Leitinger), traveling by amphibious jeep and bridging gaps in the Pan-American highway by sea, using the jeep as a boat. Her research has focused on women's legal status, social history, Central American feminism, and women in development.

References

Albán López, Mary. 1991. "Situación de la mujer costarricense y su integración al desarrollo económico-social del país." Mimeo. San José, Costa Rica: Centro Nacional para el Desarrollo de la Mujer y la Familia (CMF).

Andersen, Sue. 1991. "The Women's Solar Oven Group of Oriente: A Multifaceted Approach to Women and Development in Costa Rica." Honors thesis, Department of Global Studies, University of Iowa.

Anonymous. n.d.(a). "CASEM—¿Con la Coope? ¿O sin ella?" Mimeo.

Anonymous. n.d.(b). "Información sobre CASEM." Mimeo.

Baum, Alisa L. 1990. "Factors Affecting Artisans' Productivity at CASEM, a Crafts Cooperative in Monteverde, Costa Rica." Mimeo. San José, Costa Rica: Associated Colleges of the Midwest Tropical Field Research Program.

Biesanz, Richard, Karen Zubris Biesanz, and Mavis Hiltunen Biesanz. 1982. *The Costa Ricans*. Englewood Cliffs, N.J.: Prentice Hall.

Castro Leitón, Cristina. Personal communications. July 18, 1992, August 25, 1992.

CoopeSanta Elena R.L. n.d.(a); contents indicate date of 1987. "Reglamento del Comité de Artesanas de Santa Elena de Monteverde (CASEM)." Mimeo. Santa Elena: CoopeSanta Elena.

——. n.d.(b) contents indicate date of 1987. "Reglamento Interno del Comité Artesanal de Santa Elena y Monteverde." Mimeo. Santa Elena: CoopeSanta Elena.

——. 1992. "Trabajamos para ser su mejor alternativa." Edición I.I. July. Mimeo.

CoopeSanta Elena R.L., Departamento de Artesanía. 1992. "1982–1992." July 26, 1992. Mimeo.

——. n.d. "Metas Período 91–92." Mimeo.

Drake, Melanie S. 1991. "Women's Multiple Contribution to the Community of La Cruz in the Santa Elena–Monteverde Region of Costa Rica: A Comparison Between Members of La Campesinita, a Women's Canning Cooperative, and a Group of Non-Members." Mimeo. San José, Costa Rica: Associated Colleges of the Midwest Tropical Field Research Program.

Gómez M., Nery. Personal communication. July 18, 1992.

Gómez M., Nery, and Carlos A. Vargas L. 1991. "Informe anual de la Comisión de Apoyo de CASEM. Enero 1990 a Enero 1991." Mimeo.

——. 1992. "Informe anual de la Comisión de Apoyo de CASEM. Departamento de Artesanía. Enero 1991–Diciembre 1992 [sic]." Mimeo.

Guindon, Wolf. 1991. "Reflections on Monteverde's Contribution to Conservation and Forest Protection 1951–1990." In Monteverde Family Album Volunteer Committee, eds., *Family Album*, vol. 13 (April 17), pp. 22–23.

Hanson, Joel C. 1991. "Community Creation Seen from San Luis: Bringing into Focus a Vision of the Future for the Santa Elena–Monteverde Region of Costa Rica." Mimeo. San José: Associated Colleges of the Midwest Tropical Field Research Program.

Hoffschmidt, Kristin J. 1990. "Crafts, Cooperation, and Confidence: A Productivity Study of CASEM, the Artisans' Cooperative of Santa Elena and Monteverde, Costa Rica." Mimeo. San José: Associated Colleges of the Midwest Tropical Field Research Program.

Huertas, Damaris. Personal communications. July 18, 1992, August 25, 1992.

Jiménez de Diller, Patricia. 1991. "CASEM." In Monteverde Family Album Volunteer Committee, eds., *Family Album*, vol. 13 (April 17), p. 117.

——. Personal communications. July 14, 1992, August 26, 1992.

LaVal, Richard. 1991. "Forming of the Monteverde Conservation League." In Monteverde Family Album Volunteer Committee, eds., *Family Album*, vol. 13 (April 17): p. 77.

Leitinger, Ilse Abshagen. 1990. "Changes in the Santa Elena–Monteverde Region in the 20th Century: The Rise of Competing Interests." Mimeo. San José, Costa Rica: Associated Colleges of the Midwest Tropical Field Research Program.

Libro de Actas, vols. 1 (May 25, 1982–November 8, 1984), 2 (November 8, 1984–November 26, 1986), 3 (November 26, 1986–July 7, 1988), 4 (July 27, 1988–August 3, 1989), 5 (August 3, 1989–January 12, 1991), and 6 (January 12, 1991–June 10, 1992).

Lobo Lobo, Lila. Personal communication. July 17, 1992.

Lyman, Timothy R. 1990. "Artisan Development: A Craft in Itself." Report of Aid to Artisans Research Associate, Second Round of Research. Mimeo.

Marsh, Anna L. 1991. "Women's Contribution to the Well-Being of Santa Elena, Costa Rica: Effects of Self-Image, Motivation, Consciousness, Feasibility, and Organizational Management." Mimeo. San José: Associated Colleges of the Midwest Tropical Field Research Program.

Monteverde Family Album Volunteer Committee, eds. 1991. *Family Album*, vol. 13 (April 17). Monteverde.

Plan de Desarrollo Integral Monteverde 2020. 1989. "Summary of Statutes." September 24. Mimeo.

Rodríguez, Bertalía. Personal communication. July 15, 1992.

Rodríguez Mora, Carmen María. n.d. (contents indicate date of 1983). "Información básica para el estudio de la comunidad de Santa Elena/Monteverde." Mimeo.

Salazar, Marta Iris. Personal communication. July 18, 1992.

Stuckey, Joseph. 1987. "Analysis of the Grassroots Development Process as It Occurred in Monteverde, Costa Rica, 1950–1987." Working draft of paper. Mimeo.

———. 1988. "Monteverde Area Groups and Institutions 1988: Who They Are; What They Do. A Report to Monteverde Town Meeting from the Planning Committee." April. Mimeo.

———. 1991. "Dairy Farming—The MV Cloud Times." In Monteverde Family Album Volunteer Committee, eds., *Family Album*, vol. 13 (April 17): 61–67.

Trostle, John. 1991a. "One Quaker's View of Monteverde." In Monteverde Family Album Volunteer Committee, eds., *Family Album*, vol. 13 (April 17): 8.

———. 1991b. "The Origins of the Monteverde Institute." In Monteverde Family Album Volunteer Committee, eds., *Family Album*, vol. 13 (April 17): 89–90.

VanDusen, Katy. Personal communication. July 15, 1992.

Vargas Leitón, Carlos A. 1987. "Memorandun: Relación anterior y actual de Coope-Santa Elena R.L. con el Comité de Artesanos." July 8. Mimeo.

———. 1991. "Coop Santa Elena." In Monteverde Family Album Volunteer Committee, eds., *Family Album*, vol. 13 (April 17): 55–57.

———. Personal communications. July 14, 1992, August 26, 1992.

Vargas Leitón, José Luis. 1991. "Dairy Plant Expansion." In Monteverde Family Album Volunteer Committee, eds., *Family Album*, vol. 13 (April 17): 43.

Villalobos H., Eduardo, and Mara V. Jiménez G. n.d. "Convenio para la construcción y operación de un local para la producción, exhibición y ventas de artesanías en Monteverde." Mimeo. Santa Elena.

Acknowledgments

Thanks to staff and members of CASEM, the CoopeSanta Elena, the Monteverde Cloud Forest Reserve, the Monteverde Conservation League, the Monteverde Institute, Monteverde 2020, and Productores de Monteverde, especially Cristina Castro L., Nery Gómez M., Damaris Huertas, Patricia Jiménez, Jan Lawther, Julia Lawther, Lila Lobo, Luis Monge, Bertalía Rodríguez, Marta Iris Salazar, Ree Sheck, Joe Stuckey, the Trostles and others of the Monteverde Friends Meeting, Katy VanDusen, and Carlos Vargas L. for insight and information; to my students Alisa Baum, Karin Bellomy, Melanie Drake, Meghan Fuchs, Joel Hanson, Kristin Hoffschmidt, Ellen Lock, Anna Marsh, Wendy Powers, Karen Stocker, Carol Weirs, and Jessica Wodatch, for sharing their understanding of the community's struggles and successes; to Grinnell College, Grinnell, Iowa, for continued research support; and to ACM and ICADS, off-campus study programs that allowed me to work with the region's communities and CASEM.

24 ✸ Reconceptualizing the Theory of Women in Organizations

Contributions of Feminist Analysis

Laura Guzmán Stein

This study probes certain assumptions that have generated a large volume of research on women's organizations and efforts to organize women in Latin America. The analysis of women's organizational capacity has in the past been based on theoretical and methodological schemes that fail to capture the feminine experience. Studies have taken the male as model and have denied the validity of interpretations women themselves provide. Yet women's experience is qualitatively different from that of men. Thus, I propose the introduction of feminist analysis into the theory of organizations.

The discussion on this topic has barely begun. We women are just now tearing down idols and myths presented to us for centuries as absolute and undeniable truth. Though this process of criticism and self-criticism is in its first phase, we must fortify it, encouraging sane reflection to eliminate theoretical dogmas still considered valid by many female and male researchers and activists, feminist or not. Only then can the groundwork be laid for new theories and methods for participating in the transformation of factors that heretofore have made true equality between women and men impossible. This will substantially improve organizational analysis.

Four Assumptions Dominate Research and Work with Women's Organizations

We must assess several assumptions for research on, or work with, women in organizations from a feminist perspective. Here are the four most generally accepted:

1. Women are reluctant to participate in organizations; this reluctance stems from their strong individualism and passivity, the result of socialization processes intended to prepare women for housework and motherhood.
2. Women have little capacity for resisting the oppression and exploitation to which

they are subject as women. When they face violence or marginalization because of being female, they do not resist; rather, they accept the situation passively, afraid to act to change it.

3. Some analysts object in principle to women's organizations on the rationale that these marginalize women even more. The principal assumption is that women can gain access to power and resources men control only through institutions legitimized by society and dominated by men, and that, if women unite to fight, society will not take them seriously.

4. Finally, critics evaluate women's organizations negatively because they lack formal hierarchical structures and legal identity; critics argue that such organizations are valid only if they are characterized by formal structures and modeled after Max Weber's legitimate authority (1944).

Toward a Feminist Theory of Organizations

According to Weber (1944), bureaucratic organizations organize individuals and tasks to guarantee continuity and stability by eliminating ambiguities in relations between members, even though internal conflicts may create a political territory in which struggles for power, prestige, personal value, and survival are endemic.

Feminist theory criticizes this bureaucratized organization of political, social, and economic life (Ferguson, 1985). Feminist analysis indicates the following:

- Understanding the patterns of domination and subordination between men and women makes us understand the subtleties of power and control that operate inside bureaucratic organizations, including social organizations such as unions, cooperatives, communal associations, and social service organizations.
- Acknowledging notions of personal identity and social interactions that prevail in women's experience suggests a debureaucratized vision of collective life.

A feminist theory of organizations is based on a nonhierarchical orientation. It reduces the chasm between private and public life and rejects hierarchical forms of organization in favor of a different vision of personal and collective life. This theory wants to rescue the organizational experience of women by asserting values important for a democratic society that is free of gender inequalities.

Assessing the Four Dominant Assumptions

Women's Absence from Community Life and Organization
In contemporary society, the sex-gender system dominated by men is strongly associated with the division of labor by sex, in which special significance is

accorded to the terms *public* and *private*. The "public" realm is the area of decision making par excellence, in which women have a subordinate position; the "private" realm is the area of everything domestic—tasks assigned to women, such as biological reproduction; reproduction of the work force; and the care of children, the aged, and the infirm (Sojo, 1985).

The community is perceived as part of the "public" world, which belongs to the male. Yet, this is where women interact actively with other individuals outside the domestic nucleus, though their presence and social interactions may not be recognized by patriarchal society, which conceives of them as being in the home, unaware of other spheres. Anybody can discover this reality in our Costa Rican neighborhoods.

Patriarchal ideology conditions female involvement in economic, social, cultural, and political organizations, as well as in community development projects (Nash, 1980; Romero, 1989). It influences the selection of research models to interpret the dynamics with which these groups enter into the life of their community and society. Consequently, women appear passive in communities, whereas men rise, as naturally prepared actors, to guide others and make the great decisions (Nash, 1980). Hence, this image of women largely determines not only the social condition of females in the community but also the quantity and quality of women's participation in communal life.

Moreover, women's participation in organizations or communal groups is inspired principally in areas seen as extensions of domestic roles: family planning, nutrition and health, child care, school committees, and religious and volunteer groups in general. Most if not all members of those groups are women, who participate as volunteers after completing their household obligations. Of course, groups or organizations in which most members are women have low national and communal prestige and often lack legal identity.

In contrast, male efforts are channeled toward institutionalized organizations, such as community development organizations, cooperatives, unions, sports associations, and others. The men control important posts that give them prestige and power.

Household responsibilities constitute a substantial limiting factor for women's participation in communal groups and organizations, since they take much time and energy that women cannot dedicate to other activities. Even less time remains for those who have to work for pay, so that *La Doble Jornada* (The Double Work Day) becomes a crucial obstacle.

Unfortunately, most research on women's organizational participation has focused on formal, institutionalized, and bureaucratized organizations. This bias has produced serious distortions in the assessment of the organizational capacity of women. However, some Costa Rican studies have contributed to clarifying the discrimination women face in gaining access to positions of decision making in formal social organizations, such as communal development organizations, unions, and cooperatives (e.g., Carro and Picado, 1980; Escalante, Barahona, and Guzmán, 1989; González, 1977; Jiménez, 1988). These studies also analyze factors that result in women's limited participation. Yet, the analysts rely on studies done in the context of organizations representing the masculine patriarchal model, and from these studies they generalize to all women's organizational activities. This practice is just as inappropriate as extrapolating from statistics about the so-called economically active female population to make generalizations about the female working population.

How can organizational analysts dare to state that women do not organize or participate in organizations because they are not massively represented in the ones institutionalized by the state and recognized by patriarchal society as worthy of the name *organization*? Such a sweeping generalization corresponds to recognizing as "work" only the "labor" that men do. The bias is serious: Women tend to join regularly in informal organizations (without legal identity) and women's groups. Excellent Costa Rican examples are groups that struggle for housing, in which 80 percent of the members are women (see Sagot, chap. 22 above); committees of rural education and nutrition centers; health centers; voluntary groups; production-oriented women's enterprises; and women's associations. The female membership in such organizations is high, despite the factors that limit women's participation in organizations outside the home.

The organizational forms those women employ to solve vital problems defy the orthodox postulates that dominate organizational analysis. The daily application of these forms, moreover, demonstrates their effectiveness for solving, through collective action, the problems affecting women and their families.

In part, women turn to informal organizations because they offer flexible hours and structures corresponding to the time many have available. Furthermore, organizations such as committees fighting for specific demands or associations for income generation respond to women's needs and priorities. They offer concrete benefits over the short term. In contrast, organizations controlled by men do not take care of the needs of their members because men, given the privileged position patriarchal society offers them, believe themselves qualified to interpret what benefits others and to consider solutions as universally beneficial, according to their masculine perspective.

Women's organizations also offer advantages to women with husbands or partners. When a woman partner participates in predominantly male groups, most men feel threatened, fearing they will lose control over her life. When a woman joins a female group, most male partners put up little or no resistance against her activity outside the home.

Women are also well represented in volunteer organizations. Laura Guzmán, Lorena Vargas, and Carmen Blanco (1985) found that in Costa Rica, voluntarism fulfills important social, economic, and political functions. But even when patriarchal society fosters the incorporation of women into volunteer organizations, it does not consider their activities to be "work" nor does it recognize the true value of the tasks that organizations of this type perform for national development.

Voluntarism attracts women because it allows them to use their time in an activity that society recognizes as useful and that does not generate much opposition from men. In addition, voluntarism permits women to obtain positions of prestige without having to compete with men. As a rule, the tasks allow flexible schedules, thus adjusting to the limits women face. State and private welfare institutions also support women's voluntary participation in certain programs. In some cases, participation is obligatory for those who obtain food, housing, or clothing in return. In others, it guarantees the permanent functioning of services through unpaid but qualified workers, inasmuch as the functions are similar to those the workers practice in the domestic realm.

One must conclude, therefore, that the female presence in groups and organizations is a reality, and all that remains is to make it visible, to capture its dimensions and implications. We can do so if we modify our way of envisioning organizations, assessing the female capacity to organize and our way of doing research. Organizational analysts must rediscover from the women themselves where, when, how, why, and with whom women join groups; what they think of themselves as actors in organizational processes; and what limits and satisfaction they find. Organizational theory must stop considering women as an extension of men and instead must see women as they are and attribute value to what they do.

On Women's Inability to Resist Exploitation and Subordination

Liberal and Marxist theories tend to see women, particularly poor women, as victims of structural forces. Yet, recent investigations seem to contradict this view and to offer evidence about how women resist and manage exploitation in the family, at work, and in the community.

Janet Everett and Mary Savara (1987) argue that women are capable of adapting to the contradictory context of capitalist development in societies stratified by class, gender, ethnicity, race, or caste. Although most women react against discrimination or oppression, they also understand—intuitively or consciously—their vulnerability in a society that discriminates against them as second-class citizens.

For instance, many women are aware of the degree to which their partners exploit them, but they understand that they need the partners as providers or as caretakers for the children while they, the women, work. Many studies confirm that working women recognize the abuses to which they are subjected in the workplace. Nevertheless, they cannot always resort to conventional forms of resistance—such as joining unions or filing suits against the Labor Ministry—because they would risk losing an income they desperately need. In cases of sexual abuse, consequences of denouncing the abuse can be worse for the woman than for the aggressor (Guzmán et al., 1985).

Women who work in transnationals and *maquila* industries know they will quickly lose their jobs if they participate in union negotiations. They also know from experience that no union will provide them with the income they need to maintain themselves and their families. Therefore, to withstand the oppressive conditions under which they carry out their jobs, they have developed subtle tactics that most investigators fail to perceive but that nonetheless allow them to reach their goals (Peña, 1982).

In some cases, women turn saboteurs to obtain obligatory leave, operating so skillfully that neither supervisors nor technicians can detect them. In other cases they generate massive hysteria to paralyze a factory. The technique of using rumors as a means of ending the violation of the rights of women workers by supervisors, directors, or owners has been very effective both in work centers and in communities (Guzmán et al., 1985).

Similarly, when facing situations of domestic violence, women have displayed a capacity to resist intelligently in a setting that opposes them and judges them on the basis of sexist prejudices. In various sections of metropolitan San José, in Costa Rica, women have organized a sign campaign during the hours of darkness. Houses with abusive men are labeled with placards stating, "Here lives a man who beats his wife," or "Here lives a rapist." To be thus exposed produces negative reactions that frequently act as control mechanisms. Case studies of women's life histories and testimony suggest that they do not enjoy subordination, as some say. Rather, they express the opposite feelings (Moritz, 1988; Osorio, Torrico, Guido, and David, 1986).

These practices show that women do not submit passively to men's domination or exploitation. When they cannot resist actively, they employ nonconventional mechanisms, which allow them to survive in an adverse environment without surrendering their active functioning.

Together, Yes—But Integrated or Not Integrated?

Organizational theory clearly defines two positions regarding women's organizations:

1. Proponents of integrated organizations argue that organizations exclusively for women add to women's marginalization because society limits their access to resources and can more easily discriminate against members of women's organizations.
2. Defenders of the existence of women's organizations contend that "integrated" organizations fail to integrate women because such organizations continue to be dominated by men, and women's interests are therefore subsumed under general, i.e., male, interests.

Other analysts confirm (Yudelman, 1987) that even when women can join mixed, i.e., integrated, organizations under conditions of equality, the need for women's organizations has not been eliminated. Experience shows that the latter offer better opportunities for developing self-confidence and skills in a solidary environment of participation, without competition or imposition, allowing access to resources and the achievement of economic or political independence (Osorio et al., 1986).

Some say that women's organizations are more vulnerable than men's organizations, that they are more easily manipulated and controlled by the state, political parties, or private agencies. Such statements lack support and reflect a sexist conception that denies women's capacity to act independently. However, the disadvantages that women's organizations suffer from in Latin America and Costa Rica occur with almost all organizations in the region.

Potential and Problems of Structural Informality in Women's Organizations

Informal, nonbureaucratic organizations do not correspond to Weber's model (1944)—the dominant model in Western society—of the legitimate authority of bureaucratic structures and processes, in which authority is granted on the basis of formal, legalistic rationality, tradition, or leadership charisma.

Yet, Kay Ferguson (1985) posits that organizations with structural informality foster consciousness raising and skills training of women, because they change relations that perpetuate social and gender inequality. Traditional bureaucracies strengthen and increase such inequalities, giving power to a few privileged members and limiting opportunities for the development of skills of subordinate members. Consequently, organizations that reproduce hierarchical structures reinforce patriarchal notions of gender relations, thereby favoring the subordination and exploitation of women as human beings.

According to Ferguson, women's unbureaucratic vision of the world and organizations is deeply rooted in their experience of being responsible for the care of others. Through that experience as female members in patriarchal society, women have acquired values of solidarity, empathy, responsibility toward and connection with others, which gives them both strengths and weaknesses. She further argues that women's responsibility to anticipate and respond to the needs of others requires sensitivity and empathy toward others, solidarity, and cooperation. Women therefore function best in informal contexts in which primary relationships and flexibility predominate.

Larissa Lomnitz (n.d.) found in Latin American society, in all social classes, systems of informal exchange functioning parallel to the formal economy, on the basis of long-term social relations. They create networks that convert social resources into economic benefits, such as security, prestige, or power. Women are the principal actors for creating and maintaining the networks that form the basis of the exchange system. Men have proved less capable than women in manipulating such social mechanisms, whereas women play an essential role in developing solidarity among participants and in maintaining a constant flow of goods and services.

Similarly, Devon Peña (1982) observed that women in *maquiladora* operations organized themselves successfully through informal dynamics based on personal networks that responded to their interests, needs, and limits, and thus were more efficient in resisting exploitation.

Nevertheless, these values and behaviors also contain enormous weaknesses which must be analyzed if they are to be understood and corrected within a feminist framework.

When individuals see their lives as being closely related to those of others, they develop a need for others. This creates dependence and vulnerability and explains why women often avoid risks or conflict (Ferguson, 1985). These attitudes become problematic in nonbureaucratic environments, where male and female actors must face conflicts between different personalities or interests; take on financial, social, and emotional risks; and solve problems of interpersonal relations, productivity, and efficiency.

Experience has taught women to subordinate themselves in the family and outside the home. This experience and the supporting ideology have deformed women's self-image and their notion of others, of social relations, and of interactions. They have developed a sense of incompetence in the public sphere, a sense of fear that their projects have no value in that context (Ferguson, 1985). Thus, women have been trained to be incapable, to generate only the behaviors that permit their survival as oppressed victims.

Individuals subordinated to others do what they must to survive in a world they do not control. Oppression distorts their skills and self-perception. In such a context, their bonds with others lack equality, and they turn to manipulating others. Dominated individuals adjust to the dominating power. This in turn produces a dependency, which allows stronger personalities to make decisions for them. Public or private institutions, communal leaders, and leaders of social organizations often display this pattern.

Nonstructured organizational environments offer women flexibility to develop organizational models adapted to their interests and needs and to their social experience as women. The lack of structure creates a participatory environment in which women can learn problem solving without being threatened by masculine power, in which what they do is valued, and in which they control the product of their labors.

But just as an unstructured environment can favor humanization, it can also hurt women—through leadership problems, inefficiency, political ineffectiveness, and loss of control of the movement or organization. From a feminist point of view, a leader's authority must come from the quality of the relationships she establishes with group members. The leader must train all the others, not only a few. Group leaders must develop the skills of passing on power without avoiding their responsibilities.

Yet, even if an organization fosters participatory democracy and an informal flexible structure, this does not guarantee that its members will function accordingly. Sally Yudelman (1987) contends that women often give the impression of being incapable of maintaining participatory organizations free of conflict and in good working order. This difficulty may be the result of an intense emotional commitment of the members to charismatic leaders. For Ferguson (1985), the problem lies in women's experience and the attitudes they developed being responsible for others and being subordinate. Yudelman and Ferguson suggest an ideal alternative: The rotation of female leadership, in which authority and responsibility are not based on domination and subordination.

Conclusion

As I indicated initially, this discussion is incomplete. The questions I have raised here show that we women must redefine concepts and models that have dominated organizational analysis up to now. The notion of gender must be incorporated as an essential component if we are to capture reality and interpret it. This will have implications for the development of policies and actions to strengthen organizations.

We must strive toward rigorously quantifying women's participation in all groups and organizations, not only in those to which patriarchal society assigns prestige. This effort must be directed toward identifying qualitative aspects that define women's organizational capacity and differentiate it from men's capacity.

Women must take primary responsibility for this revision of organizational analysis, though men concerned with gender relations may join us. We must understand that if we do not begin to discover and value who we are—without false modesty and with full awareness of our weaknesses—we will never achieve the goal of having others recognize our presence in all areas of society and our contributions to organizations.

Biodata

Laura Guzmán Stein, a Costa Rican, has a licenciatura in social work from the Universidad de Costa Rica and a Ph.D. in social work from Arizona State University in Tempe, Arizona. A professor with the Escuela de Trabajo Social (School of Social Work) and the Programa Interdisciplinario de Estudios de Género (PRIEG) (Interdisciplinary Gender Studies Program) at the Universidad de Costa Rica, she also coordinates the Programa de Derechos Humanos (Women and Human Rights Program), Instituto Interamericano de Derechos Humanos (Inter-American Institute of Human Rights). She is a lecturer in cross-cultural women's issues and social work practice at Arizona State University and a consultant in curriculum development for schools of social work in Panama, Ecuador, and Guatemala. Her research has focused on women in the *maquila* industry, women in organizations, gender policy, and planning. With Alda Facio of ILANUD and Rhonda Copelon of the City University of New York, she taught a graduate extension seminar Mujer, Género y la Ley (Women, Gender, and Law), at the Universidad de Costa Rica. Since 1993 she has been teaching in the new joint Maestría Conjunta en Estudios de la Mujer, Universidad de Costa Rica-Universidad Nacional.

References

Carro, Carmen, and Marta Picado. 1980. *La mujer en Costa Rica: aspectos laborales, educativos y organizacionales.* San José, Costa Rica: Dirección Nacional de Mujer y Familia.

Escalante, Ana Cecilia, Macarena Barahona, and Laura Guzmán. 1989. "Balance sobre la situación de la mujer en la política en Costa Rica." In *Memoria del seminario sobre estudios de la mujer*, pp. 73–86). San José, Costa Rica: Universidad de Costa Rica, State University of New York at Albany, and Centro Nacional para el Desarrollo de la Mujer y la Familia.

Everett, Janet, and Mary Savara. 1987. "Organizations and Informal Sector Women: Social Control or Empowerment." Paper presented at the meeting of the Association for Women in Development (AWID), Washington, D.C., April 15–17, 1987.

Ferguson, Kay. 1985. *The Feminist Case Against Bureaucracy*. Philadelphia: Temple University Press.

González, Mirta. 1977. "La mujer en Costa Rica, división de trabajo, salarios y distribución de puestos directivos." *Revista de Ciencias Sociales* 14 (October): 31–42.

Guzmán, Laura, Lorena Vargas, and Carmen Blanco. 1985. *Situación de la mujer en Costa Rica*. San José, Costa Rica: Alianza de Mujeres Costarricenses.

Jiménez, Mireya. 1988. *Diagnóstico preliminar de la participación de la mujer en el Movimiento Cooperativo costarricense*. San José: National Institute of Cooperative Development.

Lomnitz, Larissa. n.d. "The Role of Women in an Informal Economy." Mimeo. Mexico: IIMAS/UNAM.

Moritz, Nancy. 1988. *Diagnóstico situacional de los grupos productivos femeninos en Costa Rica*. No. 5. San José: Centro Nacional para el Desarrollo de la Mujer y la Familia.

Nash, June. 1980. "A Critique of Social Science Roles in Latin America." In June Nash and Helen Icken Safa, eds., *Sex and Class in Latin America*, pp. 1–21. New York: Praeger Publishers.

Osorio, Rodolfo, Lidia Torrico, Francisco Guido, and Luis David. 1986. *Las mujeres integrantes de los grupos asociativos femeninos en Costa Rica: características socioeconómicas, demográficas y culturales*. San José, Costa Rica: Centro de Orientación Familiar (COF).

Peña, Devon. 1982. "Emerging Organizational Strategies of Maquila Workers in Mexico-U.S. Border Industries." Paper presented at the tenth annual meeting of the National Chicano Studies Association, Arizona State University, Tempe, Ariz.

Romero, Carmen María. 1989. "Educación popular y problemática femenina." In *Memoria del seminario sobre estudios de la mujer*, pp. 87–96. San José, Costa Rica: Universidad de Costa Rica, State University of New York at Albany, and Centro Nacional para el Desarrollo de la Mujer y la Familia.

Sojo, Ana. 1985. *Mujer y política: Ensayo sobre el feminismo y el sujeto popular*. San José, Costa Rica: Editorial Departamento Ecuménico de Investigación.

Weber, Max. 1944. *Economía y sociedad*. Mexico: Fondo de Cultura Económica.

Yudelman, Sally W. 1987. *Hopeful Openings: A Study of Five Women's Development Organizations in Latin America and the Caribbean*. Hartford, Conn.: Kumarian Press.

VI ✳ THE WOMEN'S MOVEMENT
AND FEMINISM IN THE ARTS

Yadira Calvo Fajardo with her two daughters, Coralia and Talía Chamorro C.

COSTA RICAN WOMEN have contributed to the arts in many ways. They serve not only as models, providing themes for artistic expression, but also as creative artists in the visual arts of painting and sculpture, in music, literature, theater, dance, and film making. The arts are a medium for portraying women's traditional roles as mothers, housekeepers, caretakers, lovers, or idols of beauty, but they also permit artists to raise questions about these stereotypical roles and to offer a critical assessment of women's treatment by society.

The three selections in this section represent examples of this questioning of women's roles by women painters; of the perpetuation of stereotypes about women's roles in popular music; and of the effort to see the treatment of women by society in perspective, through feminist literary analysis and women's biography.

Feminist Visions: Four Women Artists in Costa Rica, by Sally R. Felton

Sally Felton introduces four women artists whose work questions the role of women and reflects their feminist viewpoints. Their art portrays women's doubts and criticism about their traditional identity and roles and their awareness of their exploitation and isolation. The study outlines the active participation of women in Costa Rican art since the 1930s. It traces the changes in women as subjects or themes in art, from visions of women as saints or mothers to more critical perceptions of maternity and of women as participants in society.

Women and Love: Myths and Stereotypes in Popular Songs Broadcast in Costa Rica, by Sandra Castro Paniagua and Luisa Gonçalves

In their analysis of popular music, Sandra Castro and Luisa Gonçalves stress the continuing power that traditional female stereotypes exert on contemporary women. Operating from the premise that media represent the worldview of a given culture, the authors present a content analysis of six popular songs played over Radio Sensación in San José in late 1987. Their aim was to identify myths and stereotypes reinforcing patterns of domination, subordination, and submission in male-female relationships in Costa Rican society. The songs are assessed in terms of their message—for example, whether they present myths that justify the man-woman relationship and the meaning of love or reinforce stereotypes that specify appropriate male and female role behavior.

Yadira Calvo: Costa Rican Feminist Writer par Excellence, by Sonia de la Cruz Malavassi

Sonia de la Cruz offers a short commentary on the three books that have earned Yadira Calvo the status of Costa Rica's "feminist writer par excellence": *La mujer, víctima y cómplice* (Women, Victims and Accomplices, 1981, now in its second edition), *Literatura, mujer y sexismo* (Literature, Women, and Sexism, 1984), and *Angela Acuña, forjadora de estrellas* (Angela Acuña: Forging Stars, 1989). The first book documents the rise and the philosophical underpinnings of patriarchy, with its patterns of male domination and female subjugation. The second work examines twenty-seven centuries of famous writings in world literature that represent sexist ideology and thus perpetuate the model of the subordinate woman. The third book is the biography of Angela Acuña, the first woman lawyer in Costa Rica, who led the struggle for women's right to vote, represented Costa Rica at the Organization of American States, and is considered the first "self-conscious" Costa Rican feminist. Acuña combined— *à la Tica* (in true Tico style)—the characteristic of "not making waves" with a persistent struggle for women's empowerment.

25 ❊ Feminist Visions

Four Women Artists in Costa Rica

Sally R. Felton

A considerable number of women are currently recognized as fine artists in Costa Rica. Their works demonstrate technical expertise as well as thematic exploration, abstract or figurative, and gain acceptance for their artistic merits, without bias toward the creator's gender. In this essay, after a short historical overview of women as artists and their themes in Costa Rica, I sketch the contribution four women artists are making to feminist visions in contemporary Costa Rican art.

Historical Overview of Women in Contemporary Costa Rican Art

Throughout colonial history and in the nineteenth century, Costa Rican art closely followed European trends. Local artists copied European art styles—for instance, effusive, highly expressive Baroque forms—without cultural affinity to them. Moreover, Costa Rican men were discouraged from being artists—art was seen as an "effeminate" profession—while women did art as a pastime.

At the end of the nineteenth century, the increasing prosperity from coffee exports fostered an interest in the fine arts on a small scale, limited primarily to oil or water color painting and stone or wood sculpture, as the technology for other media remained unavailable.

Then, in the 1930s, local artists developed an interest in Costa Rican culture and identity. Costa Rican landscapes, buildings, and lifestyles became preferred subjects. This constituted a "rebellion" in Costa Rican fine arts against the traditional academic realism that Western culture inherited, through the Renaissance, from Greece and Rome. Costa Rican artists instead portrayed a sense of national identity and individuality. They also rediscovered pre-Columbian indigenous motifs.

The change brought an upsurge of interest in the fine arts, which went hand in hand with expanding technologies and options for artistic expression. The number of people who chose to be artists grew. That growth also brought an increase in the proportion of women painters, graphic artists, and photographers. Moreover, women became part of the vanguard in such related fields as restoration, theater direction, dance performance and choreography, film making, prose, and poetry. The extent of women's talents and participation is evident in the positions of eminence they have achieved as curators and museum directors, editors, and holders of office in the Ministry of Culture. Some arts or crafts, such as textiles and ceramics, are predominantly feminine. These media now enjoy a status comparable to the traditional fine arts, and this recognition has allowed many more women to be incorporated into the circle of creative artists in Costa Rica.

Two Recent Generations of Artists

Within this setting, over the last fifty years, roughly two active generations can be distinguished in the pictorial arts. The first generation includes eminent women such as Margarita Bertheau, Dinora Bolandi, Lola Fernández, Sonia Romero, and others who for several decades were influential artists working in various media. Fiercely independent in her personal life, Margarita experimented with water colors and frescoes. Dinora's work ranges through geometric landscapes, still lifes, and loving portraits. Lola is exploring innovative stenciled textures, bas-reliefs, and figures. And Sonia pursues ever-evolving styles of figures in her drawings. As professors at the Universidad de Costa Rica's Fine Arts Faculty, these artists have greatly contributed to the formation of the second generation of artists, who are the focus of this article.

Changing Themes of Woman as Subject in Costa Rican Art

The view of woman as a subject matter in Costa Rican art has evolved through a number of different stages. Since the Spanish conquest and throughout the colonial period in Latin America, Costa Rica included, the image of woman as a virgin martyr has reigned; it is still revered by many as the prototype of female propriety. Colonial statuary—*imaginería,* an instrument of conversion and maintaining the faith—retained the characteristic European "Baroque gesture" of highly expressive movement, even though Aztec, Mayan, or Incan artisans manufactured the works in the three great centers of Mexico, Guatemala, and Peru. During this period, women's creative participation was limited to dressing the figures or to the great honor of donating their own hair to crown the statuary. In nineteenth-century Costa Rica, itinerant portrait painters did occasionally paint some women's portraits, but the view of woman remained unchanged.

Only in the 1930s did another idealized woman, the mother figure, appear. Again, this theme was portrayed primarily in sculpture. However, as part of the rebellion mentioned earlier, the female figure was redrafted. No longer a Greco-Renaissance goddess, woman became representative of the burgeoning middle class.

Two curious tendencies prevailed at that time. First, the woman's figure becomes distorted and stylized; the cranium shrinks while the pelvis is exaggerated, so that a rather pyramidlike figure emerges, tapering from a broad base to a diminished intellect. Second, maternity becomes the theme of numerous sculptures. These works characterize mothers as contented, expressionless, reproductive vessels on the pedestal of maternal fulfillment. Some of the works that include maternity in their titles portray animals with their offspring; in others, women's depiction is inlayed with a moral animalism, portraying such instincts as the fierce protection of the child. Curiously, this theme of woman as mother coincided with the epoch when Costa Rica's fertility rate was among the world's highest. Even forty years later, in the early 1980s, with 121.3 births for 1,000 females of reproductive age, the Costa Rican fertility rate was twice that of the United States, and three times that of West Germany (U.N., 1984). And even in the 1980s, maternity remained a theme favored by many men sculptors, frequently in their designs for public monuments.

Today, a few male sculptors make their own statement in favor of a liberated view of women. One exceptional piece is Crisanto Badilla's *Mujer que Avanza* (Woman Advancing), a stone carving of a woman on her knees yet moving forward. Another is Mario Parra's *Mujer Sandinista* (Sandinista Woman), a suspended wood carving of a female guerrilla fighter with a semiautomatic rifle, executed as a martyr.

Four Feminist Costa Rican Women Artists

Works that interpret women's circumstances in Costa Rica from a feminist viewpoint are relatively few. Although the theme is popular in other countries, it is still only nascent in Costa Rica because the tides of change arrive here several years later than in the northern hemisphere. The theme also confronts a special challenge in Latin American society, with its cultural pattern of *machismo* (male domination of women). Nevertheless, some Costa Rican artists, particularly women, are portraying a new image of women in their work.

Four women artists—Paola Pignani-Boncinelli, Ana Griselda Hine, Grace Blanco, and Joan Martha—have repeatedly explored aspects of the traditional machista-dominated situation. In so doing, they have dared to confront the status quo and to hold up a mirror to this society. I have chosen them not only for the content of their works but also for their technical excellence and the fact that their works can be appreciated in black-and-white reproduction.

Though the works of these four artists ably transmit their own messages, a brief text accompanies the reproductions to clarify their intent. In some cases, the artists comment on their own work; in others, I comment on the social and artistic context.

Paola Pignani-Boncinelli

Paola Pignani-Boncinelli has pursued controversial themes portraying woman's enforced obligations, stereotypes, and inane diversions. Speaking about her pastel *Maternity* (see exhibit 25.1), Paola said "TV and books give an image of motherhood as an idyll instead of what I have observed as a responsibility, so very intense" (pers. comm., October 10, 1989). Her *Maternity* stands in sharp contrast with the earlier sculptures portraying woman as virgin, martyr, or contented mother. It also conflicts with men's outsider perspective on this "natural fulfillment," which to many sensitive women means a total transformation of their former life. Paola's *Maternity* illustrates a taboo subject and has therefore provoked considerable controversy. Its sincerity is courageous.

In her 1983 *Self-Portrait* (exhibit 25.2), Paola has rendered herself in subtle tones, encircled by a dark vortex of scenes. From the lower left, clockwise, men are gathered around a table, drinking in segregated bonhomie at the cantina. Above them, the good wife and homemaker is incarcerated by jagged black lines, an emphatic arrow pointing to her continuing engagement in domestic tasks, which she carries out alone. Reclining above the head, a nude woman lies ready to comply with the amorous obligations of matrimony, while to the right she stands, according to Paola, "making a very specific Italian gesture . . . that means 'I don't want anything like this situation in my life!'" Finally, in the lower right corner, "the roses are the end of the story-drawing," the token offered to the bride in lieu of the real commitment she deserves (pers. comm., January 30, 1990).

Paola is an intuitive feminist who responds in a voice resonating with outrage over the social wounds that demand expression in her visual language.

1. Paola Pignani-Boncinelli, *Maternity*, 1982. Pastel on paper, 102 × 79 cm.; 40″ × 31″. Collection of the artist.

2. Paola Pignani-Boncinelli, *Self-Portrait,* 1983. Mixed media on paper, 67.5 × 51 cm.; 26½″ × 20″. Collection of the artist.

Ana Griselda Hine

The next artist, Ana Griselda Hine, is here represented by etchings from a series she executed in 1983 at the University of Cincinnati while on a Fulbright scholarship. Exhibit 25.3 reproduces an etching she originally titled *Pacer;* she translated it as *Mujer en la Sala* (Woman in the drawing room) which does not, however, transmit the same clue to her intentions. But the image itself strongly implies the direction she was then exploring. Ana Griselda expressed that intent as "Loneliness, confinement, a woman who is looking for her inner self, confronting in some way . . . obstacles." Her works of this period are dark interiors with "furniture in the way" (pers. comm., January 20, 1990). These are claustrophobic seraglios in which the figures are trapped—not even a window permits contact with the outside world. *Pacer,* like a caged tigress, is stalking, striding to and fro in this reduced world—a slender woman, her expression distressed.

Gemelas (Twins) is a title that supplements the scene in Exhibit 25.4 of a "woman confronting herself," her reflection in the mirror implying a dual yet

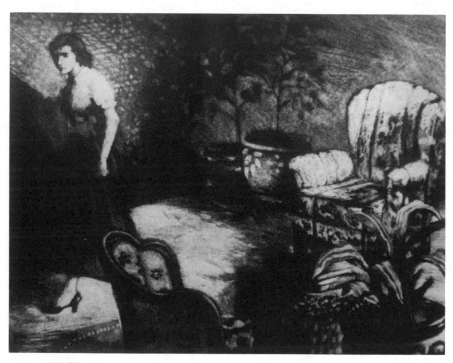

3. Ana Griselda Hine, *Pacer,* 1983. Etching, 44.5 × 60 cm.; 17½″ × 23½″. Collection of El Banco Central.

4. Ana Griselda Hine, *Twins*, 1983. Etching, 44.5 × 60 cm.; 17½″ × 23½″. Collection of the artist.

monotonous identity. The implication is "anguish, not vanity," as she examines herself in the mirror. The placement of the furniture plus the angle of perspective give a vertiginous sensation, as if "everything wants to overcome her" (pers. comm., January 20, 1990).

Ana Griselda's etchings reflect her experience of the woman's role in Costa Rica. She says "more than anything, in Latin America, the mothers themselves educate their male children differently from their daughters," thereby encouraging and perpetuating *machismo* alongside female subservience (pers. comm., January 20, 1990).

Grace Blanco

Grace Blanco, the third artist, wrote of the feminist movement in Costa Rica: "The process is slow because it implies laying the foundation of new codes beginning in infancy; in the home, the school, the society. The hope is that future generations will settle into a human relationship that is more just and agreeable" (pers. comm., February 6, 1990).

Grace is renowned for her figure drawings; precise yet fond drafting reveals her devotion to her subject. "Now the center of my work is woman as a

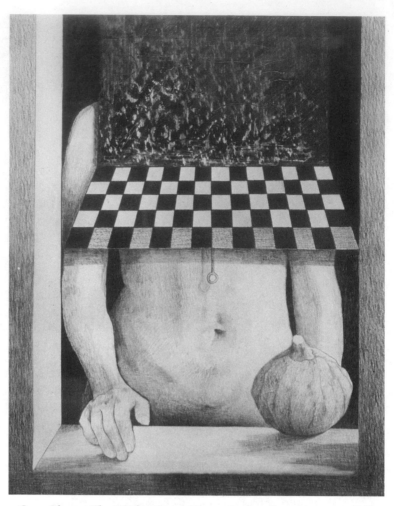

5. Grace Blanco, *The Window Series, No. 2*, 1982. Pencil, 40 × 32 cm.; 15¾″ × 12½″. Colección Corporación L & S.

universal symbol of the energy that shelters life, fecund, constant, serene." She works in series of related variations on a theme. *The Window Series* (*Serie La Ventana*) strikes a different note from her other series, a "surrealistic symbolizing art" (Echeverría, 1983; *La Nación, Ancora*, p. 4). The elements comprise a view of a window seen from the outside; curtains or blinds are drawn in such a way that the female nudes are headless, exposed torsos. This decapitation, with its absence of intellect, is striking; we see just flesh without a face to portray personality or identity. These women are objects, converted by "the daily routine" into "furniture, window, fruit" (pers. comm., February 6, 1990).

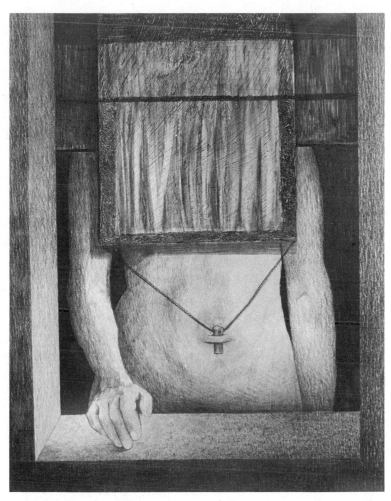

6. Grace Blanco, *The Window Series, No. 3*, 1982. Pencil, 40 × 32 cm.; 15¾" × 12½". Colección Corporación L & S.

In each of the two reproductions (nos. 2 and 3) from that series, the figure is incorporated into the overall arrangement. The vegetable on the window sill in *The Window Series, No. 2*, is a complete orb; the checkerboard projecting from the blind is so dynamic that the figure retreats and is of less importance than in traditional figure painting. In *The Window Series, No. 3*, the curtain and frame are attached to the woman through her navel; the woman becomes an accessory, acting as anchor for the furnishings. If one sees *The Window Series* as structured as a stage, with the curtain descending from the proscenium frame, the female figures become scenery flats, a backdrop for the curtain itself.

Joan Martha

Joan Martha, the final artist presented here, is well known in Costa Rica for her abstract paintings in color harmonies. She has created many collages but recently has shifted from framed, wall-mounted pieces to what she calls "wearable art"—pendants and earrings. Her work was included in the 1988 Amulets of Power Exhibit at the Centro Cultural Costarricense Norteamericano (U.S. Cultural Center) (pers. comm., February 2, 1990). She is presently painting a series of portraits of women.

The works reproduced here represent one phase of Joan's artistic explorations. The pen and ink drawings (see exhibits 25.7 and 25.8), done in 1983 during a period of difficult transition, are from a journal of spontaneous images—"strokes which poured forth onto the paper . . . uncensored." Collectively they are facets of a self-portrait "composed of internal imagery" and created in an unconventional and personal procedure: a "daily ritual, much like meditation, and vital to my well-being, . . . a therapeutic outlet during a period of intimate redefinition" (pers. comm., February 2, 1990).

"To these stream-of-consciousness drawings words appeared in the same manner, clarifying the images and reflecting my feelings at the time." An expression of Joan's inner voice, these drawings are not calculated symbols; the juxtaposition of image and word are revelations. After completing one drawing she wrote, "The energy is up and buzzing"; after another, "Taking care of

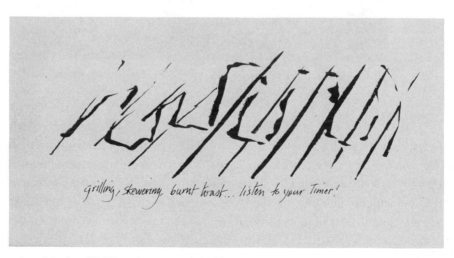

7. Joan Martha, "Grilling, skewering. Burnt Toast . . . Listen to your Timer!" 1983. Pen and ink, 14 × 19 cm.; 5½" × 7½". Collection of the artist.

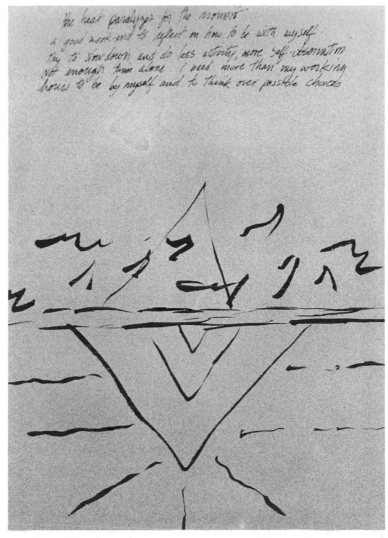

8. Joan Martha, *"The heat paralyzes for the moment. A good weekend to reflect on how to be with myself. Try to slow down and do less activity,"* 1983. Pen and ink, 22 × 15 cm.; 8¾" × 6". Collection of Joan Martha.

business without ever leaving the house. Surprisingly, unhasseled. A day of accomplishments and feeling good."

Joan dedicates much energy to exploring the spiritual side of her art; she is active as a lesbian feminist, both in Costa Rica and the United States. Her artistic work is the product of her progress.

Feminist Women Artists in the Mother Role

I asked all of the artists I interviewed whether they had encountered any discrimination in the "artists' guild" because they were women; all responded with a firm no. This has also been my observation. All four artists have children. When we artists become mothers, our own artistic participation necessarily changes. Our artistic careers, which in most cases demand full-time attention, assume a lower priority while we are raising infants. Most mother-artists feel the same: at this stage, until the child is older and more independent, their child is their "work of art." Grace Blanco described her dual commitment to "two projects that require space, time, physical force, intellect, and feelings. Personally, I'd say *two creations,* so human and vital, each meriting full time" (pers. comm., February 6, 1990). Male colleagues may not be able to comprehend the mother-artist's diminished production under these circumstances. Maternity, not as the subject of a piece of art but as an issue in the woman's own life, is a current all working mothers navigate, whatever their profession. The women artists' double commitment evokes for us Costa Rican filmmaker Patricia Howell's film of the late 1970s, *Dos Veces Mujer* (Twice a Woman), which exposed the plight of mothers who were also factory or field workers and the demanding responsibility of the Doble Jornada—the double workday consisting of a full day of housework and a full day of work outside the home.

Yet, an artist-mother has the advantage of flexible hours worked at home. Paola Pignani-Boncinelli, for example, prepared an exhibition of drawings that she executed while watching her crawling daughter—on duty, so to speak. Of course, she had to modify her methods and materials, abandoning her easel for the more portable format of work in pencil.

Reaching Beyond Costa Rica

The works of these four Costa Rican women artists—born of their own intimate experience or of situations they observed—transcend the specifically Costa Rican. Their images are significant beyond national or regional Central American or even Latin American frontiers, because the essential woman emerges, in protest or self-examination, to establish her new identity above the morass of machismo. Worldwide today, all can share these Costa Rican women artists' images, their searching reevaluation of woman's role, which they portray through their art.

Biodata

A painter, Sally R. Felton was born in Manhattan and studied in Philadelphia, Boston, Florence, and San José. She completed a *licenciatura* in art at the Universidad de Costa Rica. Since 1973, she has been lecturing about Costa Rican art history.

References

Bibliographic material on Costa Rican art history is quite limited. Besides a motley collection of exhibition catalogs, personal interviews, and careful recordkeeping, I relied on my more than twenty years of experience in Costa Rica. During those years I have studied under, gone to school with, or otherwise befriended most contemporary women artists.

Department of International Economic and Social Affairs. 1984. *Demographic Yearbook 1982*. New York: United Nations.

Echeverría, Carlos Francisco. 1983. "Una expresión contenida." *La Nación, Ancora*. December 18, p. 4.

Acknowledgments

The author thanks the four artists for their time and permission to display their work; Don Carlos Lachner Guier, collector and owner of La Colección Corporación L & S, for permission to reproduce Grace Blanco's works; to Sally Campos, former curator of that collection; to Joan Martha and Luis Howell for photographing the works reproduced here; and to Emilia Díaz André of the Centro Latinoamericano de Demografía (CELADE) (Latin American Center of Demography) for help with research.

26 ✵ Women and Love

Myths and Stereotypes in Popular Songs Broadcast in Costa Rica

Sandra Castro Paniagua and Luisa Gonçalves

Introduction

This study, a feminist content analysis of six popular songs, has two objectives. The first is to share with other women our analysis of an element of daily life, popular music, which quite innocuously contributes to the perpetuation of the social inequality of women and men. The second is to demonstrate that these songs, which members of the lower and middle working classes listen to and sing, perpetuate myths about women as inferior beings of little value, thereby strengthening the stereotypical domination-submission pattern of behavior through which women and men relate.

Myths and Stereotypes: A Worldview

Communication media are important agents in the transmission of ideology in all societies. Radio, television, books, movies, and other media transmit the worldview of the culture and are responsible for the diffusion of many myths and stereotypes.

The present study focuses on the worldview of male domination and female subordination; men and women conform to this worldview by applying mental categories through which they interpret their experiences (Afanasiev, 1983; Goldmann, 1975). These categories lead them to construct or perceive their social reality. The major elements that contribute to the formation of this worldview are myths, beliefs about how social life ought to be organized, and stereotypes, schematic, inflexible expectations about characteristics and behavior of people which produce certain behaviors in individuals (Mattelart, Puccini, and Mattelart, 1976; Sawvy, 1962). Through socialization, women internalize the myths, obey the stereotypes, behave submissively in their daily lives, and thus accept their inferiority in relation to men.

However, it must be acknowledged that myths always contain a bit of truth. It is impossible "that a myth be based on pure lies," as Alfred Sawvy observed (1962: 49). He went on to point out that myths give relevance to facts humans (in this case, males) want to stress, while they hide what to them is irrelevant. Myths are perpetuated, as a rule, through pleasant messages that conform to the ideology of the masses, such as our popular songs.

Stereotypes are fully as comprehensive as myths (Gaetano Cersósimo, as cited in Camacho, 1974, p. 150). A stereotype almost always arises from a pragmatic way in which people face reality. It is directly related to the extent of conformism or criticism that society requires of or permits an individual (Mattelart et al., 1976).

When these observations are applied to male-female relationships in Costa Rica, it becomes clear that what society presents as the idea of femininity is linked to myths about women's intuition and qualities like fragility, self-denial, obedience, passivity, and resignation. These are the very characteristics that affirm stereotypical domination-subordination-submission behavior, which is clearly conceptualized in *machista* (male-dominant) society and is used to justify the social discrimination experienced by women.

This stereotypical vision of women's behavior is based on the dialectic of master and slave. It produces the double conscience of the slave who on the one hand must struggle to survive and on the other must find ways to do what the master wants. This game of double conscience clearly describes the situation of the dominated person which, for women, is the negation of their own being and their identity.

Content Analysis of the Songs

We used content analysis to study six selected songs. This technique requires a qualitative analysis of the text of each song, followed by a summary and assessment of the information. Content analysis allowed us to focus not only on the domination-submission characteristics in the man-woman relationship but also on the myths and stereotypes relating to women. We formulated the questions with the intention of inquiring about an innocent topic such as "love" as an indicator of Costa Rican perceptions about women's role. Table 26.1 displays the elements of the content analysis.

Table 26.1. Elements of the Content Analysis

1. Who speaks?	a woman, a man
2. Of whom does the person speak?	of self, others, animals, a relationship
3. Of what topics does the person speak, or in which categories do the topics fit?	of work, religion, love life, social relations, adventures, fantastic beings
4. To whom does the person speak?	to self, a special person, a group, an animal
5. Characteristics of the language	type of use, reiteration of myths or stereotypes

The Myths and Stereotypes Contained in the Songs

The six songs were part of the Costa Rican "Hit Parade" of Radio Sensación, in October–November 1987. We selected six of the ten songs most often requested during that period. The songs also appeared in popular song books at that time.

Table 26.2 summarizes our analysis. In five of the six songs, the woman speaks; the man is the speaker in only one. All six speakers talk about themselves and their partners; two address the audience, the other four the partner. All six speakers refer to their affection for the partner, whereas only two of the six touch on other subjects, such as religion, nature, time (i.e., past and future), and social life. The language is repetitive, emotionally charged, and points to the myths and stereotypes the songs portray.

Given the small size of our sample, we cannot generalize. But we can point out the ideological messages that strengthen the myths and stereotypes about love and about women's role. Doing so, we will refer to some of the theoretical elements we presented earlier.

We assessed the messages of the songs in terms of four analytical categories: Two categories represent myths about the man-woman relationship and the meaning of love; the other two represent stereotypes of the male role and personality and of the female role and personality.

The Man-Woman Relationship

In Latin America, the man-woman relationship is one of permanent inequality. The man, the dominant partner, imposes his worldview. Marriage becomes

Table 26.2. Content Analysis of Six Popular Songs

Title Song	Who Speaks	Of Whom	To Whom	Topics	Characteristics of the Language
"Ella" (She)	a man	a woman, himself	radio listeners	affection, home	repetitive; destructive relationship with himself and with her
"El Pecado" (The Sin)	a woman	a man, herself	a man	affection, religion, social life	self-reproach, guilt, remorse, self-punishment; woman as victim; religious feelings of sin; destructive attitude toward life
"De Mí Enamórate" (Fall in Love With Me)	a woman	herself, a man	a man	affection, religion, social life	monologue; woman's dependence; relationship; loss of identity; passivity; woman exalts man; belief in destiny
"El Hombre de Mi Vida" (The Man of My Life)	a woman	a man, herself	a man	affection, nature, destiny	reiterates: women and pain, submission, dependence; idealizes man; love = destiny
"Será, Será" (It Will Be)	a woman	a man, herself, others	a man	affection, nature, time	imperative language; image of stereotypical traditional woman; passivity, submission
"Por Culpa de El" (It Is His Fault)	a woman	herself, others, a man	radio listeners	affection, love, past, future	repetitive; destructive relationship; present destroyed by past; guilt personified by other; dependence in love

a career or profession for women. It legitimizes the domination-subordination relationship, the ideal man-woman relationship in which she is occupied with domestic life, husband, and children. As the woman in "El Hombre de Mi Vida" (The Man of My Life) says, "*Tu eres mi sueño desde niña*"—You have been my dream since I was a girl.

The Meaning of Love

Love is the central theme of the songs. In Latin American culture, the idea of love is intimately linked with women. Love occupies a priority position in their lives, becomes a female practice, and, in many cases, leads to a cancellation of the woman's role in politics and culture. The woman-love relationship stems from the patriarchal nature of Costa Rican society. In the songs, love becomes relevant for women in relation to a man. In the unequal relationship that results from this love, the woman loses her identity. "When I saw you, I lost myself," from "De Mí Enamórate" (Love Me); "In my head, you are the only one, nobody else," from "De Mí Enamórate"; "He destroyed my soul, my being, and then he left," from "Por Culpa de Él" (It Is His Fault). The woman realizes herself through loving and serving a man; matrimony represents economic, social, and "emotional" stability. The following fragments illustrate: "With my pure love I will protect you. It will be an honor for me to devote myself to you," from "De Mí Enamórate".

The Male Role and Personality

In the five songs in which the woman speaks, the man appears as the central theme in relation to love. He is the idol, and from that position he passes to being the central focus of all female suffering and dreams. "You are the essence of severity and strictness," from "El Pecado" (The Sin).

The Female Role and Personality

In patriarchal society the mass media transmit a series of beliefs about what a woman must be. One of these beliefs is that women are less intelligent than men: "I am coquettish, timid, deceitful, and a woman," from "Será, Será" (It Will Be), and "I am no longer going to be the stupid one," from "El Pecado".

All songs uphold the myths about the womanly personality—dependent, self-sacrificing, sentimental, and submissive—and about the loss of female identity.

The Message of Social Inequality

In the end, we agree with Costa Rican writer Carmen Naranjo (1989), who calls uncovering myths "a step toward getting to know the situation of women who are not yet free from the weight of cultural tradition." One of the objectives of this analysis was to decipher the messages transmitted by certain popular songs that conceptualize women as sensual, soft, and loving objects. This message supports a continued domination-submission relationship that has existed for centuries. We hope to stimulate reflection and debate about the occurrence of this message in the apparently innocent situations described in popular love songs. We also confirm that the message transmitted by those songs portrays women according to the traditional stereotype of what it means to be a woman, and what a woman's relation to love is. The female prototype that these songs reaffirm is that of a woman who is totally submissive to the man of her dreams, who has no will of her own, and who lacks the capacity to live without the love she has waited for. Conversely, the songs reinforce the stereotype of the strong man, strict and severe, who is able to protect "weak" women.

Love in the six songs in our study is something marvelous, and rose colored. These songs represent women as constantly searching for love. With their emphasis on repetition of the same text, the messages tend to envelop and soothe the listener.

In sum, the norms and beliefs expressed in these songs differ for the two genders; they stress the preeminence of men and the inferiority of women. Similarly, the idea of love they express also means something different for each gender. For men, love is just one more activity in life, and in it a woman becomes the man's property. For women, love means denial, sacrifice, and submission. It entails a woman's full surrender to the other being and her forgetting about her own self-interests.

The songs reinforce our understanding that masculine domination and the popular conception of love translate into men's power and control over women. Any struggle women undertake must consider the distribution of power in Costa Rican society.

Biodata

Sandra Castro Paniagua is a Costa Rican and holds a *licenciatura* in sociology from the Universidad de Costa Rica. She did graduate work in Women's Studies at the Centro

Interdisciplinario de Estudios de la Mujer (CIEM) (Center for Interdisciplinary Women's Studies), now the Instituto de Estudios de la Mujer (IEM) (Institute for Women's Studies), at the Universidad Nacional. Castro now teaches Methods of Investigation at UNA and works as a consultant with APROMUJER. Earlier, she participated in the research project "Women and Community Health" at the Universidad de Costa Rica.

Luisa Gonçalves is a Brazilian living in Costa Rica. She holds a *licenciatura* in pedagogy from the Universidade Federal do Rio Grande do Norte (Federal University of Rio Grande do Norte) in Brazil and graduated with a degree in sociology from UNA, Heredia. She did graduate work in women's studies at CIEM, now IEM. She is currently working on a master's degree in agricultural extension at the Universidad Estatal a Distancia (UNED) (State University for Extension Studies) in San José, with a focus on women's issues.

References

Afanasiev, Victor. 1983. *Manual de filosofía,* 2nd ed. México: Editorial Cartago de México.

Cersósimo, Gaetano. 1974. "El estereotipo de comunista como instrumento de política." In Daniel Camacho, *La dominación cultural en el subdesarrollo.* San José, Costa Rica: Editorial Costa Rica.

Goldmann, Lucien. 1975. *Para una sociología de la novela,* 2nd ed. Madrid: Editorial Ayuso.

Mattelart, Armand, Mabel Puccini, and Michel Mattelart. 1976. *Los medios de comunicación de masas. La ideología de la prensa liberal,* 3rd ed. Argentina: El Cid Editor.

Naranjo, Carmen. 1989. *Mujer y cultura.* San José, Costa Rica: EDUCA.

Sawvy, Alfred. 1962. "Mythes et mirages économiques." *Cahiers internationaux de sociologie* 32 (July–December): 49–65.

27 ❀ Yadira Calvo

Costa Rican Feminist Writer par Excellence

Sonia de la Cruz Malavassi

Yadira Calvo's writings are an integral part of Costa Rican feminism. The following reviews comment on the progression of ideas in Yadira Calvo's work to show that, while inspired by Western tradition and thought, this feminism is beginning to focus on its own essence and history.

La mujer, víctima y cómplice (1981)

In her earliest book, *La mujer, víctima y cómplice* (Women: Victims and Accomplices), Yadira Calvo presents a well-reasoned argument about the rise of patriarchy, showing how it permeated social institutions to form a culture of masculine omnipotence and feminine subjugation. She illustrates how patriarchy perpetuated this unjust system with the help of mythologies, religions, and "scientific" concepts based on deceit. She goes on to explain that, even today, many women believe in the truth of those fallacies and "in all sincerity convert themselves into accomplices of their oppressors" (1981: 8). The author then delineates the ways that prejudices and beliefs throughout history converted themselves into "truths" or, worse yet, dogmas that have persisted into the twentieth century.

Blaming the Victim

Calvo pursues the theme that for millennia, androcentric thought has blamed women for all evil and has attributed to itself all that was positive. Males assigned to women the forces of irrationality and created Pandora and Eve, the causes of evil in the world, as archetypes that have served as an excuse for men's domination of women throughout history.

This intricate ideological net has been woven with many strands, among them the stereotype of women's submission. From it arose, as a logical consequence, the archetype of maternity and the dogma of purity, which allows the male to legitimize his descendants. Corollaries of the dogma of purity are the sin of adultery and the promotion of prostitution, both of which ensure "social morality" at the same time that they provide for the sexual satisfaction of the male.

The writer gives a comprehensive overview not only of the punishments meted out to adulterous women over time but also of the religious and cultural justifications on which they were based. "All of the societies we know that lived under a patriarchal regimen established far more cruel punishments for adulterous women than for criminals, while polygamy was acceptable for husbands," Calvo asserts (1981: 116).

The Origin

From this patriarchal origin rose the traditional conception of the family as a fertile ground in which the seeds of sexual segregation thrived. It encouraged hostility among the sexes and resulted in the typical master-slave relationship. The author argues that the concept of family "must be modified so that it stops rooting humanity in a slavery that induces the male to maintain a false idea of his own high value and status, and the woman to accept the misleading idea of her dependence and inferiority" (1981: 9).

It is not surprising, Calvo says, that after millennia of patriarchal ideology focusing on women's anatomical qualities, the value of women has become so distorted that they are willing to accept an arrangement in which their security and happiness depend on sexual attractiveness. She adds that it is remarkable that biological differences, which are not inherently disadvantageous to either sex, have been used as the basis for the creation of social factors that create more powerful effects than the biological differences themselves.

Political Rights and Social Conditioning

If women have not enjoyed minimal human rights inside the family, they have enjoyed even fewer outside of it. The author analyzes feminist struggles for political equality—specifically for the right to vote—over the last two centuries. She adduces reasons why few women are in positions of power in societies where women have such rights. "We can easily see how a woman who dedicates her life to procreation and housework will have no chance to participate in other spheres of life, which signifies an unbelievable segregation" (1981: 98).

Subjugated Intelligence

Given the configuration described earlier, it does not appear at all strange that this ideology would be based in part on the suppression of female intelligence.

"The most efficient way to dominate others is to deny them the opportunity of cultivating their spirit. Just as women were obliged to be artificially beautiful, so they had to conform by being artificially dumb," Calvo states, adding that such widespread convictions tend to maintain sexual segregation, the most persistent form of discrimination today (1981: 125).

Calvo's reasoning shakes hallowed conceptions and beliefs and challenges us to reflect, to take a stand on a phenomenon that is intimately linked with our culture.

Literatura, mujer y sexismo (1984)

Three years after the publication of *La mujer, víctima y cómplice*, Calvo considered diverse manifestations of sexist ideology in an exhaustive analysis of famous writings in world literature in her *Literatura, mujer y sexismo* (Literature, Women, and Sexism). "The reality we have faced from Homer until today reflects a society in which the feminine is subordinated to the masculine, identified respectively by deficiency and excellence," she asserts (1984: 13).

The individuals she analyzes belong to literary creations spanning twenty-seven centuries. Their authors hail from the Greek, Latin, Nordic, English, Spanish, and French cultures, all of them part of Western civilization. "Literature," states Calvo, "has transmitted a model of femininity that abides by the rules of the sexist ideology from which it emerges, and whose permanence is assured by great authors and their works, through the educational power of art" (1984: 13).

The Feminine in the Genesis of Western Culture

A reinterpretation focusing on four women of antiquity, Penelope, Medea, Deyanira, and Clytemnestra, heroines of works by Homer, Euripides, Sophocles, and Aeschylus, constitutes the first chapters of this book. These characters appear in works written before the Christian era, in the culture that brought forth Western civilization.

From a gender perspective, Calvo analyzes the personalities in whom ancient writers of twenty-seven centuries ago embodied an archetype of the feminine that is still alive in contemporary culture. "Penelope, undistinguished, without profile, prototype of womanly virtue, together with Medea and Deyanira, symbolize a marginalized, passive, ahistoric, subhuman, suffering femininity, which Christianity sanctified" (1984: 14).

Clytemnestra also provides a moral example, but a negative one—her rebellion and opposition to the system are fruitless. She must pay for having gone beyond her role as wife and self-denying mother, for her independence of character, her courage in facing her own actions, and her capacity to make decisions. Clytemnestra assumes complete responsibility for her deeds and is castigated, a lasting lesson for humanity.

Centuries Thereafter in the Graeco-Latin Perspective

From Homer and the tragic Greeks, Calvo moves to the second century of the Christian era and Graeco-Latin culture. There she examines the story of Psyche and Cupid, which is included in *The Golden Ass,* a picaresque novel by Apulius. Psyche is characterized by a faintheartedness harmful to her own will; whenever she obtains something against her husband's wishes, it turns bad. She is an antiheroic heroine. When she wants to know reality, she loses the well-being she enjoyed in ignorance, and she wins only when she learns how to obey.

Again, in another time and space, curiosity and initiative on the part of women are punished and ignorance and submission are rewarded. Many centuries have passed in vain as far as sexism goes, Calvo notes, because the figure of Psyche is a twin of the feminine symbols transmitted by the Greek epics and tragedies.

From Spain, Centuries Later

History goes on. More than thirteen hundred years later, in Spain, Fernando de Rojas writes his tragicomedy *Calixto and Melibea.* Calvo analyzes Melibea, the young girl seduced by Calixto, and the other woman, capable, shrewd Celestina.

Like Greek tragedies, this work portrays the double face of femininity within the masculine system of values—honorableness, personified by the girl, and shamelessness, embodied by the procuress. For a woman to be honorable, she must be ignorant and live removed from the world that surrounds her, above all the world of sexuality. From the writer's perspective, Melibea is a faithful, true representative of the honorable woman in search of the best offer she can find in the marriage market. She has been educated for the subjugation of which she will become victim as a "natural" consequence of her sex. On her count, Celestina is the shameless one, the prostitute, the independent, the wise one—and, therefore, the sinner who, of course, does not represent the feminine ideal.

In Calvo's reinterpretation, Melibea matures as she faces society. Suicide is for her a supreme act of liberation; she is meeting her lover and with her death she is overcoming the prejudices of her era. What Fernando de Rojas intends as an instructive message to the female sex is for Calvo an example of female self-determination.

An Individual Meets Herself After Three Centuries

Two female figures follow each other, as if they were parts of one and the same person, though they belong to two different epochs and societies: Catherine, of Shakespeare's *Taming of the Shrew*, in sixteenth-century England, and Nora, of Ibsen's *Dollhouse*, in Norway during the last century.

The two embody the history of women in inverse processes of submission and liberation. Catherine, autonomous and self-assured, is transformed by her husband into a model of docility and submission, whereas Nora begins to acquire power as she becomes aware that she too is a human being, as Calvo says, "defined by the same terms, and . . . she recognizes herself as a parasite, living off the dance she performs to flatter her companion" (1984: 104).

An Obligatory Interlude

Between Shakespeare's England and Ibsen's Norway falls Molière in seventeenth-century France, who begins and ends his dramatic production with *Les Précieuses Ridicules* (*The Affected Young Ladies*) and *Les Femmes Savantes* (*The Blue-Stockings*). In these works, Molière ridicules educated, learned women and denigrates them by presenting them as hateful, vain, and petulant. This, of course, is meant to keep the female gender from the error of preferring knowledge to ignorance. Molière mocks intellectual women because for him intellectualism and pedantry are the same when women are involved. Thus, Bélise, Armande, and Philaminte remained forever immobilized in caricature, a warning to women who do not conform, as Henriette does, to living in happy ignorance in limbo.

A Fitting Digression

To close, no character is more appropriate than the figure of Don Juan Tenorio, by Tirso de Molina, Spaniard of the seventeenth century. Calvo notes, "Tirso invented one of the great literary symbols of virility, defined by arrogance and aggressiveness on the one hand, and by amorous infidelity and domination of women on the other" (1984: 122).

In Calvo's view, Don Juan lacks national definition. He is nothing but the product of a social organization that equates *human* values with virile *male* values, a victim of a milieu that deems masculine violence an attribute of natural selection and that cannot see relations between men and women in terms other than that of hunter and prey.

Ostracism

Calvo's gender perspective allows her reader to see Western culture corrupted by patriarchy. Without fanaticism, in clear, direct style, and with a certain mischievousness, she leads the reader on a pilgrimage to literary sources of Western civilization to demonstrate how concepts of masculinity and femininity became charged with sexist ideology.

Literatura, mujer y sexismo invites reflection and debate about twenty-seven centuries of myths and stereotypes that are based on an unjust social orthodoxy, in which women have been mutilated by culture and the true nature of the feminine has been ostracized.

Angela Acuña, forjadora de estrellas (1989)

In 1989, Calvo's *Angela Acuña, forjadora de estrellas* (Angela Acuña: Forging Stars) was published. It is the life story of the woman who personifies the beginning of feminism in Costa Rica. Calvo is moved by the desire to reconstruct from the inside the will of a woman who never gave up; if she seemed to, it was only to begin anew at another place.

To construct an excellent biography, a writer must accumulate all the facts, scrutinize them, examine their relevance, and reintegrate them into their living context. Calvo achieves this. One must appreciate her talent for managing the language and her capacity as an investigator.

Angela Acuña, an indefatigable pioneer, graduated from a secondary school for boys which she had to attend in order to qualify for admission to law school. In 1913, she began to study law and was the first woman to opt for that career in Costa Rica. Graduating with honors, she became Costa Rica's first woman lawyer. Her fight enabled future generations of women to study law and to become lawyers as well as to hold other important posts in the Costa Rican legal system.

Acuña, however, made her real mark leading the fight of Costa Rican women for the right to vote, a goal she did not achieve until June 20, 1949, when she was sixty-two years old. She was a tireless woman. As ambassador of Costa Rica, she was the first woman to occupy a seat in the Organization of American States (OAS), where she was also a member of the Human Rights Commission. She was selected as Woman of the Americas by the Union of

American Women, an organization that recognized her as "feminist, educator, true leader, and great Pan-American" (1989: 213).

With this work Calvo proposes to reestablish the name of a woman who earned an honorable place among the founding fathers and mothers of Costa Rica. Acknowledging Angela Acuña's deeds will stimulate Costa Ricans to revise national history and include the other half of our people who were always present but always ignored. Calvo's work should be required reading for those who wish to know Costa Rican culture and the women within this culture.

Biodata

Sonia de la Cruz Malavassi, a Costa Rican, has an M.S. in television production from Syracuse University in New York, which she completed under a Fulbright fellowship. She is a journalist and a television producer, and she was a professor and deputy director at the Escuela de Ciencias de la Communicación Colectiva (School of Mass Communications) of the Universidad de Costa Rica. She is now chief of the División de Comunicación (Communications Division) of the Instituto Interamericano de Cooperación para la Agricultura (IICA) (Inter-American Institute for Cooperation in Agriculture).

References

Calvo, Yadira. 1981. *La mujer, víctima y cómplice*. San José, Costa Rica: Editorial Costa Rica.
——. 1984. *Literatura, mujer y sexismo*. San José, Costa Rica: Editorial Costa Rica.
——. 1989. *Angela Acuña, forjadora de estrellas*. San José, Costa Rica: Editorial Costa Rica.

VII ✻ THE CONSTANTLY EVOLVING STATUS OF WOMEN'S STUDIES

Costa Rican publications in women's studies

THIS SECTION FOCUSES on the development of women's studies programs in Costa Rica and then presents a few research analyses from this complex field. The process of legitimizing and institutionalizing women's studies in Costa Rica's academic world has been slow and sometimes difficult. After an informal beginning, the process consolidated itself over time until, in the early 1990s, after arduous battles with the academic bureaucracy, women's studies acquired legitimacy and finally became formally institutionalized.

If one considers legitimate women's studies to be only those academic programs that give credit and confer degrees, then Costa Rica reached that stage in the fall of 1993, with the inauguration of a joint master's program in women's studies—Maestría Conjunta en Estudios de la Mujer—at the Universidad de Costa Rica and Universidad Nacional. However, if activities such as open courses, lecture series, workshops, and research into diverse women's issues on the basis of a gender perspective are also acknowledged as legitimate practice of women's studies, then Costa Rican universities have been involved in such an academic endeavor since the early 1980s.

The process is continuing with great vigor. The first four articles in this section reflect the situation in 1992. Since then, important modifications of programs, procedures, and personnel have occurred, but they have been building on the initial philosophy and infrastructure and often even on the initial financing. In some cases, anticipated financing did not materialize and well-developed research agendas ground to a halt. But the momentum, the drive toward women's studies and gender-focused research continues strongly vibrant.

From CIEM to IEM: The Consolidation of Women's Studies at the Universidad Nacional, by Cora Ferro Calabrese

Cora Ferro details the growing acceptance of women's studies at Costa Rica's Universidad Nacional where initial advisory services and workshops changed to free courses, including graduate courses, under the auspices of the Centro Interdisciplinario de Estudios de la Mujer (CIEM) (Center for Interdisciplinary Women's Studies). A full-fledged academic graduate program for a master's degree in women's studies began operation in the fall of 1993. It is carried out jointly by the two largest universities of the state university system, the Universidad de Costa Rica and the Universidad Nacional. Ferro reports the change from CIEM to Instituto de Estudios de la Mujer (IEM) (Institute of Women's Studies), a change much more than just in name. The word *Instituto* in local academic usage denotes an interdisciplinary program, here of women's studies, that is integrated into the permanent organizational structure of the university.

The underlying philosophy of IEM is that social transformation can take place only if IEM's teaching, research, and extension work go on in partnership with the women who experience the hardships of the Central American economic recession and if this academic work employs a gender-based theoretical and methodological approach. The article also illustrates the mission of state universities—beyond teaching, research, and publications into action-oriented extension work—through the Casa de la Mujer (Women's House). The Casa de la Mujer offers counseling, consulting, and training services to women's grassroots organizations and to individual women.

Gender Studies at the Universidad de Costa Rica, by Laura Guzmán Stein

Laura Guzmán's chapter reminds me of a discussion I had at a meeting of Costa Rican social scientists in 1984. When I used the word *gender*, nobody understood the term's intended new social science meaning, whereupon I suggested that my Costa Rican colleagues might want to familiarize themselves with the important new definition of this term. Only four years later, in 1988, an informal gender studies program, Programa Interdisciplinario de Estudios de Género (PRIEG) (Interdisciplinary Gender Studies Program) was established at the Universidad de Costa Rica, and the term *gender* was everywhere.

Laura Guzmán describes PRIEG's many informal activities in teaching, research, publications, and extension work. She also discusses the planning at that time for the recently inaugurated joint UCR/UNA master's program in women's studies. She further notes that PRIEG hosted the Quinto Congreso Internacional Interdisciplinario de la Mujer (Fifth International Interdisciplinary Congress on Women) on the UCR campus in February 1993. This is just one example of the wide international networks of cooperation and information exchanges that indicate the growing interest in women's studies and gender studies in Costa Rica and the integration of new conceptualizations and insights from women's studies into general university teaching, research, publications, regional and international meetings, and scientific cooperation as well as outreach into social action, planning, and policy making.

CSUCA's Approach to Women's Studies and Its Projected Program in Central America, by Helga Jiménez

Documenting a similar international connectedness in women's studies, with a focus on a program serving all of Central America, Helga Jiménez describes the activities of the Consejo Superior Universitario Centroamericano (CSUCA), which was instrumental after the mid-1980s in promoting women's studies at seven state universities in six Central American countries. After a severe cut-back in the operations of CSUCA in early 1992 because of administrative and financial problems, CSUCA was forced to pull out of women's studies for the foreseeable future. New academic enterprises are, however, stepping in. One, for example, is the recently established Instituto Latinoamericano de Investigación Feminista (ILIFEM) in San José.

Timely, Relevant, Trustworthy, Precise, Ongoing: Toward a Gender-in-Development Information Network, by Mafalda Sibille Martina

Mafalda Sibille reports on the development of an information network that will give researchers and policy makers access to truly appropriate information on women. She favors "gender-in-development" data, arguing that differentiating customary statistics by gender is insufficient; it is imperative to collect information of particular relevance to women. Central Americans must coordinate and integrate this information according to appropriate categories, developed through a gender perspective.

Sibille describes the four phases in the creation of the Red Nacional de Información sobre Mujer y Desarrollo (National Information Network on Women and Development) at the IEM at Costa Rica's Universidad Nacional. She details the network's initial determination of cooperating organizations and the nature of the desired information, the elaboration of a gender-based theoretical framework for the collection of appropriate information on women in development, the creation and national distribution of information, and the future regional extension to other Central American countries. The report is based on the author's several years of experience with the creation of the national network.

Women's Presence in the University: The Case of the Universidad Nacional in Heredia, by Matilde López Núñez

Part VII closes with three examples of women-focused research. In the first of these, Matilde López examines the position of women in the hierarchy of the Universidad Nacional for the period 1982 to 1987. During that time period, women constitute a substantial proportion of students and professors at the university, but they are most heavily represented in the lowest echelons of the university's bureaucratic structure and do not regularly ascend into power positions. Women represent about two-fifths of all administrators, for example, but they are heavily overrepresented among secretarial and office workers and librarians and are underrepresented in upper-level positions. Interestingly enough, however, the president of the Universidad Nacional from 1989 to 1995 was a woman, Rose Marie Ruíz Bravo.

The study, which differentiates among academics, administrators, and students, is part of a larger quantitative investigation that eventually will be included in a regionwide analysis of all Central American state universities.

Problems of Joint Interdisciplinary Research in Women's Studies: An Effort to Integrate Disciplines for More Fruitful Analysis, by Margarita Brenes Fonseca, May Brenes Marín, and Sandra Castro Paniagua

Outlined in this reading are problems Margarita Brenes, May Brenes, and Sandra Castro encountered in their interdisciplinary feminist research on the occurrence of depression in Costa Rican women. Each participant in the joint project represented a different discipline (anthropology, psychology, and sociology). Their interaction convinced them that research partners in interdisciplinary work must make deliberate efforts to accept different disciplinary preparations and perspectives to avoid friction that might undermine valuable projects. The authors also caution against territorialism when areas of expertise overlap, citing examples from their own experience of setting parameters for their respective expertise, and learning to understand one another's technical vocabulary. They conclude that "our challenge is to manage our differences," so as to "develop an integrating science." Their findings raise serious questions about the appropriateness of current medical diagnoses and treatment of depression in Costa Rican women.

The Predictability of Cesarean-Section Births: A Case Study of Students in Costa Rican Childbirth Classes, by Jennifer Kozlow-Rodríguez

Drawing on her experience with 375 students in her childbirth education classes, Jennifer Kozlow-Rodríguez discusses the excessive incidence of cesarean-section births in private maternity clinics in San José. Based on her research, she developed a prediction process that identifies the relative effects of nonmedical factors predisposing women to cesarean versus natural births. The author found that five main factors affect pregnant women's desire for a nonmedicated or a medicated birth and influence the women's susceptibility to cesarean-section births.

The study is an outgrowth of an earlier study, in which the author explored cultural differences that seemed to produce a disparity between the birth outcomes of foreign women and local women in her classes. From data in that study, she concluded that the same tendencies in local women's experiences that made them more susceptible to medicated births also caused them to experience a higher rate of cesarean-section births.

28 ❈ From CIEM to IEM

The Consolidation of Women's Studies at the Universidad Nacional

Cora Ferro Calabrese

In 1976, members of the faculty of the Humanities Division of the Universidad Nacional began an advisory service for women's organizations and groups of women about to form organizations. Through this service we learned about women's needs and aspirations in their daily lives. In 1986 we organized UNA's first course about women's problems for professionals who were working with women's programs. The response was excellent. We became known and developed expertise. When we created the Centro Interdisciplinario de Estudios de la Mujer (CIEM) in 1987, we already had gained a national reputation. On June 21, 1991, CIEM celebrated the inauguration of the Instituto de Estudios de la Mujer (IEM), which converted the temporary CIEM into a permanent institutional structure within UNA, and the first such institution within the Costa Rican state university system (Universidad Nacional, 1991). The event signified UNA's recognition of the legitimacy of and permanent need for women's studies.

Today, IEM operates with a multidisciplinary team of seven professionals, who deal with women's studies through the academic disciplines of communications, history, informatics, philology, psychology, sociology, and theology.

As a creative nucleus, IEM coordinates academic programs and research on women and their problems. It bases its work and its principles of operation on experiences with organized women who provided crucial insights into women's true concerns. Three basic principles guide IEM's work:

1. The determination to join forces with other institutions to make rational use both of human and financial resources and of within-country experiences;
2. The decision to ensure that women—especially those women who suffer most from the sudden effects of economic recession—are always active partners in IEM's efforts and principal beneficiaries of those efforts;

3. The conviction that IEM does not start its work from ground zero but can build on the accumulated experiences of national, Latin American, and universal historic processes.

These three principles require IEM to assess its successes and difficulties, to open new paths, and to struggle to obtain space in the public domain for the academic discussion of problems women face. This means that IEM must make a concentrated effort to demystify ancient prejudices that have isolated women.

Economic Recession from a Women's Perspective

Thematic Priorities

Implementing the principle that IEM does not start from ground zero, IEM accepts four thematic priorities set by researchers of the Network MUDAR/ DAWN, Red de Mujeres por un Desarrollo Alternativo (Development Alternatives with Women for a New Era), a Peruvian organization of hemispheric importance and influence, whose theoretical posture local academics and practitioners accept. These thematic priorities, which guide the analysis of the impact of the economic crisis on women's lives are (a) the comparative impact of alternating periods of economic growth and recession on patterns of female and male employment (including unemployment, area of work, number of working hours, labor status, and income); (b) the effect of the economic crisis on household units and families; (c) public policies regarding women; and (d) the relationship between the economic crisis and women's movements.

The Overall Goal and Ways of Reaching It

IEM will participate creatively and systematically in the development of an interdisciplinary archive of information for the study of women's problems in all spheres of our national life (Alvarado, Ferro, and Durán, 1991). IEM's participation will take the form of specialized teaching, integrated research, participatory extension services, and, finally, the development of information services for women (see Sibille, chap. 31 below).

SPECIALIZED TEACHING

Women's need to assert their presence as active participants in the history and society of Costa Rica must be recognized and must constitute the basis of scientific knowledge about women, for the acceptance of this knowledge, and for its integration into the scientific process. From this perspective, IEM proposes to offer courses based on the concept of gender. These courses will focus in particular on Costa Rican women's reality but will also consider the reality of Central American and Latin American women in general.

Since the creation of CIEM in 1987, the consolidation of women's studies according to these guidelines has progressed in response to the demand for graduate courses and the prestige CIEM/IEM acquired through its scientific work. This progression has culminated in a master's-degree program in women's studies jointly undertaken by IEM and the Universidad de Costa Rica's Programa Interdisciplinario de Estudios de Género (PRIEG) (see Guzmán, chap. 29 below).

Graduate courses offered by CIEM/IEM in the years 1986 through 1992 have included Psychotherapy of Women, Women's Problems, Violence Against Women, Psychotherapy of the Family, Women and the Family, Women and Power, Women and Development: A Comparative View, Women in History: From Invisibility to Visibility, Women and Self-Esteem, Women and Their Relationships, Women and Natural Medicines, and Women and Communication. Courses at the undergraduate level were Women and Economics, Women in Decision-Making Positions: Managerial Communications, Women and Religious Communication, and Women in Society.

IEM has also offered workshops on relevant topics in national and Central American development, such as Women Facing Life and Law, Women and Social Communication: In Search of a New Discourse, and In Search of Our Identity: Contributions of Psychoanalysis, Theater and Bodily Expression, and Popular Narrative.

INTEGRATED RESEARCH

In view of the traditional androcentric slant of science that has treated women as tangential objects of study, IEM supports an alternative option that defines women as a central analytical theme. This option regards women as a legitimate subject of scientific inquiry and underscores the theoretical-methodological requirements of carrying out such studies.

To respond to the challenge required by this option, IEM has initiated a series of concrete steps in short-, medium-, and long-term research, which will permit researchers to accumulate experience and evaluate results, with the intention of confirming the proposed alternative option. Projects in process as of this writing include the following:

1. Research to identify the political dimension of the psychosocial realm and of inter-personal relations, both considered social and public dimensions within which women are active. Some projects now under way are Women in Costa Rican History—From Invisibility to Visibility: A Contribution to the 500th Anniversary of the Discovery of America; Costa Rica: Women in Positions of Power, 1948–1989; A Qualitative Analysis of Women's Presence in the State Universities of Central America; Women in Positions of Power at the Universities; Women in Positions of Power at Banks; and Women in Positions of Power in the Executive Branch of the Government.

2. Research to reveal women's ongoing participation in people's struggles, such as movements of workers, pacifists, religious groups, ecological groups, and all those who claim a right to live and participate. Topics of some current research include Women, Housing, and Production; Biological Gardens—Women to the Rescue of the Ecological Equilibrium; and Women, Religious Reality and Communication.

3. Research that offers conceptual and operational support for criteria to redefine national policies on women in health, education, employment, income generation, and others. Relevant projects are Women in Household Units; Discrimination in Access to Institutional Resources; and Evaluation of Policies in Support of Women.

PARTICIPATORY EXTENSION SERVICES

This is a sphere in which social transformation occurs. The transformation process depends on a reciprocal relationship between IEM and the women in the community. In this relationship the real needs of women's daily lives inspire IEM's academic work, and IEM reciprocates by carefully administered extension services. Through these IEM guides women to become agents of collective transformation or social change.

To achieve this transformation, IEM has established the Casa de la Mujer, which is located on the Omar Dengo Campus of UNA in Heredia and is espe-cially receptive to women of the Costa Rican national community. At the Casa, they can obtain information, education, and support on everything that relates to their daily lives and their participation in the national development process.

Moreover, IEM has to date generated the following periodical publications: the quarterly bulletin *UNA-MUJER,* several anthologies, and the journal *Casa de la Mujer.*

Conclusion

The relevance of a project is directly related to the importance of the problem it addresses and the creativity of the responses it proposes. Through its teaching, research, and extension activities, IEM is addressing the theme of women with professionalism and is efficiently generating answers to the questions arising from Costa Rican women's complex reality.

Biodata

Cora Ferro Calabrese is also a co-author of "Women in Colonial Costa Rica," which appears earlier in this *Reader* (see chap. 6) and carries with it her biodata.

References

Alvarado Boza, María Luisa, Cora Ferro Calabrese, and Vilma Durán Jiménez. 1991. "Seminario de evaluación y programación." Mimeo. Heredia: Universidad Nacional, CIEM.

Universidad Nacional. 1991. "Hoy fue constituído el Instituto de Estudios de la Mujer." Press release, June 21. Mimeo. Heredia: Universidad Nacional.

29 ❀ Gender Studies at the Universidad de Costa Rica

Laura Guzmán Stein

The Women's Decade, declared by the United Nations in 1975, called attention of international organizations, national governments, and society in general to the problem of discrimination and oppression against women. In 1979, the U.N. General Assembly approved the *Convention on the Elimination of All Forms of Discrimination Against Women,* which Costa Rica ratified on March 4, 1984.

The Universidad de Costa Rica (UCR) participated in the process this convention initiated. Like its Latin American, North American, and European counterparts, UCR sponsored during the Women's Decade a large number of courses, research projects, conferences, seminars, extension projects, theses, and lectures about women and gender problems. Slowly, an academic nucleus evolved as a basis for developing women's studies as a discipline, for challenging the androcentric prejudices characteristic of the sciences in general, and for reconceptualizing from a women's perspective dominant theories, methods, and interpretations.

As this process continued throughout the late 1970s, the need arose to integrate the diverse activities in research, teaching, and social action at the university. This finally culminated in 1987 in the creation of the Programa Interdisciplinario de Estudios de Género (PRIEG) (Interdisciplinary Gender Studies Program) within the UCR Division of Social Sciences. In 1988, PRIEG was confirmed as a permanent priority program and attached to the office of the vice rectory of academic affairs.

The push for women's studies at UCR is not accidental. As an autonomous institution of higher education, comprising a teaching, administrative, and student community, UCR is dedicated to contributing to the achievement of social justice, the nation's overall development, and the complete freedom and total independence of the Costa Rican people, as expressed in Article 3 of the UCR Statutes (UCR, 1989). This mission obligates the university to bring about in Costa Rican society changes that eliminate existing inequalities between men and women.

The Mission of PRIEG/UCR

As a university institution, PRIEG is charged with producing and disseminating qualitative and quantitative information about women and gender problems; with improving university services to university women (teachers, administrators, and students) as well as to women outside the university through extension programs (through courses and community service); and with providing professional practice and the obligatory social service required of graduating students. This requirement consists of three hundred hours of community service performed in a variety of governmental and nongovernmental institutions and is usually performed during the three-month summer vacation from December through February.

PRIEG contributes to analyzing the subordination of women, and to identifying more egalitarian alternatives and a more acceptable social structuring of relations between women and men. This orientation obligates PRIEG to the following:

1. Contributing to consciousness raising about the situation of women in Costa Rica and promoting egalitarian gender relations;
2. Promoting policies at UCR to eliminate discrimination against women;
3. Supporting academic projects that address the essential social and ideological dimensions of discrimination against women;
4. Fostering the creation and application of feminist theory and methodology in instruction, research, social action, and student life, in order to generate projects that analyze the status of women in Costa Rica and promote women's full development;
5. Promoting the publication of studies containing findings that are compatible with PRIEG's objectives;
6. Collaborating with national and international universities, institutions, organizations, and feminist groups that agree with PRIEG's objectives.

In keeping with its interdisciplinary nature, PRIEG is directed by a faculty commission representing diverse fields (social sciences, humanities, engineering, mathematics, law, and health sciences). It includes teaching and administrative staff and students from academic departments interested in joining the program and strengthening women's studies; the staff also includes visiting professors from institutions with which the UCR maintains agreements of exchange.

Components of PRIEG's Program

PRIEG is involved in teaching, research, publications, regional and international cooperation, and outreach programs.

Teaching

PRIEG's teaching has taken various forms. First among its teaching programs, beginning in the spring of 1989, was the Women's Forum lecture series for the academic analysis of women's problems. Since then, PRIEG has sponsored specialized courses on various topics related to gender studies for teaching personnel and professionals. Taught by Costa Rican or foreign specialists, the courses have attracted teachers, researchers, leaders of women's organizations, and graduate students.

Regular UCR teaching programs also focus attention on women's problems. Among these programs are the required introductory seminars on "The National Reality," and the seminars of the lower level General Studies Program in a variety of academic disciplines, such as anthropology, sociology, social work, psychology, communications, political science, law, education, nursing, medicine, economics, architecture, and nutrition. As a result, many students have chosen topics relating to women for their required research in undergraduate or graduate courses. However, the greatest challenge for PRIEG is the new master's program in women's studies, initiated in the fall of 1993, which brings together PRIEG and UNA-IEM in a project of continuous academic cooperation.

Research

PRIEG supports research on women in UCR research centers, divisions, or departments. Thus PRIEG is cooperating with various UCR institutions in research sponsored by the vice rectory of research on such topics as "Women Transmitting Ideology and Popular Culture in Poor Urban Neighborhoods" and "The Impact of Participation in Women's Income-Generating Groups on the Status of Women." In cooperation with Arizona State University's Department of Women's and Family Studies, PRIEG is involved in a comparative study, "The Impact of the Family on the Quality of Life of Elderly Women," for which the two universities signed a cooperative agreement in August 1989. At the UCR regional center in Guanacaste, in the northwestern Pacific coast region, PRIEG acts as consultant for the creation of a field research pilot program, which later will be extended to other regional centers.

Research on women's problems has grown in quantity and quality as a result of renewed interest of research institutes and faculty. Since 1981, the Instituto de Investigaciones Sociales (Institute of Social Research) has conducted the Women and Society program. The Instituto de Investigaciones Psicológicas (IIP) (Institute of Psychological Research), the Instituto de Ciencias en Nutrición y Salud (Institute for Nutrition and Health Sciences), the Centro de Investigación de Tecnología en Alimentos and the Instituto de Investigaciones en Ciencias Económicas (Institute of Economic Research) are pursuing various research projects, either directly or indirectly related to women's problems.

In fact, many academic units have carried out research on women or are in the process of doing so. For example, during the academic year 1992–93, forty-five research projects on women received funds from UCR. PRIEG is producing an inventory of research completed and in progress, which will be made public through the Red Nacional de Información sobre Mujer y Desarrollo (National Information Network on Women and Development) (see Sibille, chap. 31 below). An assessment by the university's vice rectory of research indicates that from 1982 to 1989 research on women grew by 13 percent.

The last few years have also seen an increasing number of graduation projects or theses on the topic of women. PRIEG has advised students and thesis advisers and is hoping to systematize this activity for major impact.

Publications

Two UCR journals have dedicated issues to women. *Kañina,* a humanities journal, dedicated one issue (1985, 9, no. 2); *Revista de Ciencias Sociales* (Journal of Social Science), a social science journal, devoted three issues to this topic (1977, October, no. 14; 1983, October, no. 25; 1988, March, no. 39). A fourth issue is to come out in late 1994, and a fifth one in late 1995. PRIEG supports such initiatives for sharing research on gender and women nationally and internationally.

Regional Central American and International Activities

PRIEG has participated in various courses offered by the Consejo Superior Universitario Centroamericano (CSUCA) (Council of Central American Universities) at the regional level (see Jiménez, H., chap. 30 below). With CSUCA, PRIEG coordinated further training for teaching and research. The studies "Quantitative and Qualitative Analysis on Women's Presence in Central American Universities" (see López, chap. 32 below) and "Women in Community Health," as well as a workshop with Central American participants on women and violence, resulted from the joint effort.

Internationally, PRIEG is taking advantage of women's studies expertise of various U.S. universities with which UCR has agreements. With these institutions PRIEG has organized seminars and workshops addressing women's issues. In 1990, for example, the following workshops were held: Women and AIDS, The Medicalization of Women's Health, and Grant Writing and Funding. In 1991, the list included Women in History, Women in Politics, and a teleconference on Women and AIDS, with the participation of the women's studies programs of Arizona State University of Tempe, Arizona, and the Central American universities affiliated with CSUCA. With some cooperating institutions, such as the State University of New York at Albany and Arizona State, existing programs are being expanded. This is particularly true with regard to the effort that went into developing the master's program, in which UCR and UNA began to cooperate in the fall of 1993 (see Ferro, chap. 28 above, and Jiménez, H.).

Outreach Programs

In social programs, UCR has developed initiatives with projects such as the obligatory social service of graduating students, training programs for leaders working with women in governmental and nongovernmental organizations, and extension courses to train UCR personnel who work with women. PRIEG has tried to organize these efforts in such a way that women become active, completely integrated participants. Projects for training instructors in this respect, as part of PRIEG's social action program, meant a significant change in the approach to work with women.

PRIEG has promoted several training projects for personnel who offer services to university women; the goal of these projects is to improve all university employees' understanding of women's needs and interests. One project provides training for the staff of student counseling offices on issues of sexual harassment, rape, and domestic violence. Another assists academic departments in formulating policies on sexual harassment. In addition, through its Women and Culture project, PRIEG offers activities that raise participants' consciousness that women transmit culture in many ways—offering extension courses to nonuniversity women about women as cultural subjects, seeking to spread the theoretical and methodological advances on gender, and promoting artistic, scientific, and popular activities that portray women as active producers.

In February 1993, PRIEG hosted the Quinto Congreso Internacional Interdiciplinario de la Mujer (Fifth International Interdisciplinary Congress on

Women) on the UCR campus. Two thousand women attended the Fourth Conference, at Hunter College in the United States in 1990, and a similar number of women from more than seventy countries attended the Fifth Congress at UCR in 1993. PRIEG/UCR brought out the proceedings, "Memoria del Quinto Congreso Internacional e Interdisciplinario de la Mujer," in late 1995.

Biodata

Laura Guzmán Stein is also the author of "Reconceptualizing the Theory of Women in Organizations," which appears earlier in this *Reader* (see chap. 24) and carries with it her biodata.

References

Congreso Universidad de Costa Rica. 1990. *Comisión: La mujer universitaria*. San José, Costa Rica: Universidad de Costa Rica, Oficina de Publicaciones.
Universidad de Costa Rica. 1989. *Estatuto orgánico de la Universidad de Costa Rica*. San José, Costa Rica: Oficina de Publicaciones.

30 ❈ CSUCA's Approach to Women's Studies and Its Projected Program in Central America

Helga Jiménez

From 1948 to 1992, the Consejo Superior Universitario Centroamericano (CSUCA) (Council of Central American Universities) worked to achieve regional integration for the activities of the state universities of the six member countries: Costa Rica, El Salvador, Guatemala, Honduras, Nicaragua, and Panama. Believing that culture has a liberating effect, the organization coordinated studies of regional problems and furthered academic cooperation between member institutions in teaching, research, extension work, and publications. During its operation, CSUCA's base was in San José, Costa Rica, but its programs took place in all member countries, which together served approximately 200,000 students as of the early 1990s.

Women's Studies Program

In 1988, as a result of a pilot project aimed at developing women's studies at all Central American universities, CSUCA created a Regional Women's Studies Program. Through additional instruction, practical training, and research projects, CSUCA worked to enhance and consolidate recently established programs, such as the Programa Interdisciplinario de Estudios de Género (PRIEG) (Interdisciplinary Gender Studies Program) (see Guzmán, chap. 24 above) at the Universidad de Costa Rica, the Centro Interdisciplinario de Estudios de la Mujer (CIEM) (Center for Interdisciplinary Women's Studies) now the Instituto de Estudios de la Mujer (IEM) (Institute of Women's Studies) (see Ferro, chap. 28 above) at Costa Rica's Universidad Nacional, and others that grew directly out of the CSUCA pilot project, such as the women's studies commissions at the universities of El Salvador, Honduras, Nicaragua, and Panama and at the University of San Carlos in Guatemala.

The overall goal of CSUCA's program was to improve the situation of women and to increase gender equality through social change. CSUCA's work contributed to undoing the social construction of gender inequality and the pattern of subordination and domination of women. CSUCA supported efforts to rethink gender relations, to establish and advance feminist theories and methods of analysis, and to introduce gender into the analysis of social and political problems (Benería, 1989).

Women's Studies Program Activities

CSUCA's Women's Studies Program sponsored projects and activities in instruction, research, extension work, and publications. Through this sponsorship, CSUCA honored the traditional mission of Latin American universities, which—beyond higher education, research, and publications—are committed to serving the population at large—in this case, the female population (Jiménez, 1990; 1991).

Instruction

Given that teaching is a university's principal educational function, CSUCA began its work with a pilot project of instruction. The goal was to train more than 250 teachers and researchers so as to enable them to create and spread an awareness of women's problems, together with specific knowledge and adequate theoretical and methodological skills, to further develop and consolidate women's studies in Central America. Over the years 1988 through 1990, the project included six courses, which were taught at the graduate level in various member countries. The courses were Theory and Methodology of Women's Studies; Rural Women; Women and Habitat; Women in the Informal Urban Sector; Violence Against Women; and Research on Women with a Gender-Focused Methodology. Participants were university teaching personnel and other professionals.

The courses aroused great interest not only in academic circles but also in governmental and nongovernmental agencies, institutions, and organizations working with women. Participants recognized women's studies as a scientific discipline that enables them to develop the critical analysis they needed for their work with women. Moreover, the courses created a multiplier effect as university administrations became supportive of women's studies at their institutions. The courses consolidated the theoretical approach for work at the member universities and with the base communities that the universities serve.

With the development of a critical mass and the increase of specific research on women in the Central American region, CSUCA hoped to support the establishment of a regional, interdisciplinary program for a master's degree in gender studies, based on the experiences of the program being developed jointly by the Universidad de Costa Rica and the Universidad Nacional, which in fact began operating in the fall of 1993 (Ferro, and Guzmán).

Research

CSUCA carried out several research projects focusing on gender analysis at the regional level. One such project—in three stages—was "A Quantitative and Qualitative Analysis of Women's Participation in Central American Universities." The first stage was identifying the proportion of women among (a) all students, by fields of study, and all graduates and those who failed to complete their studies; (b) administrators; (c) teaching personnel; and (d) the university hierarchy. The study's second stage was analyzing the role and issues of gender in these groups. The third stage was describing sexism in the university structures. The overall goal of this study was to further the participation of women in all phases of university careers and activities through the promotion of changes in the academic policies.

CSUCA also sponsored sixteen research fellowships on the topics of women and health, women and work, women and power, and women and social organization. In addition, it conducted a regional investigation of women's participation in community health programs to explore the effect of gender on health policies and health programs.

Extension Activities

Other efforts by CSUCA focused on integrating women into activities they avoided in the past. CSUCA, together with the ministries of science and technology and of education, sponsored a course, Mathematics for the Family, in Costa Rica. CSUCA's plans also called for the creation of a Central American Information Network on Women in Health, in cooperation with the Organización Panamericana de Salud (OPS) (Pan-American Health Organization) and the Centro Latinamericano de Demografía (CELADE) (Latin American Center of Demography). For the project, CSUCA trained technicians in gender-focused analysis.

A further project was consolidating women's studies documentation and information at Central American universities, on the basis of the pioneering work of the envisioned future Red Centroamericana de Información sobre

Género y Desarrollo (Central American Gender-in-Development Information Network) at the Universidad Nacional's CIEM, now IEM (see Sibille, chap. 31 below). Beginning in September 1990, CSUCA offered a series of teleconference courses, with interaction by speakers and participants from Central America (Guatemala, El Salvador, Honduras, Nicaragua, and Costa Rica) and Panama.

Publications

CSUCA also produced various publications, primarily anthologies, course bibliographies, a book on women in Panama, and a special issue on women of the journal *Estudios sociales centroamericanos* (1989). In collaboration with the Universidad de la Paz (University of Peace) outside San José and the Facultad Latinoamericana de Ciencias Sociales (FLACSO) (Latin American School of Social Sciences), CSUCA also published *Mujeres centroamericanas, vol. 1, Tendencias estructurales;* and *vol. 2, Efectos del conflicto* (Women in Central America, Vol. 1., Structural Tendencies, and Vol. 2, Impact of the Conflict; 1989).

Future Projections

In early 1992, because of serious administrative and financial problems, the forty-four-year-old educational institution of CSUCA was reduced to a skeleton operation. However, all women's studies activities under way at the time of the reduction were completed in 1992. CSUCA will not head the program in the future. However, the Council of Central American Universities at its meeting in March 1992 declared women's studies as a priority for future academic activities.

CSUCA's experience with women's studies has shown the serious need both for an institutional and operational platform for scholars and other interested individuals and for a feminist approach to the knowledge of social problems. In response, scholars and concerned women created the Instituto Latinoamericano de Investigación Feminista (ILIFEM) (Latin American Institute for Feminist Research) not only to guarantee the continuity of the work in women's studies begun by CSUCA but also to expand the scope of that work. By 1993, ILIFEM had become operational on a small scale. Its activities are slowly expanding in response to demands by institutions and individuals interested in continuing the work CSUCA began.

Throughout the activities for expanding women's studies in the region, we who participated were aware that we were witnessing the rise of a new Central American feminism. Beyond our excitement over the emergence of this movement, we see two challenges: First, this new feminism must respond to the needs of all the people in the region through cooperation among all member countries, integration of program ideas and mechanisms, and the free sharing of know-how and resources. Second, and more important, the new Central American feminism must respect and nurture the diversity among the member countries' historical, cultural, ethnic, and even economic and political characteristics. Through such respect and nurturance, the rich uniqueness of each Central American society will remain healthy and alive.

Biodata

Helga Jiménez has studied philology and letters in England, Costa Rica, the Philippines, and Germany. She completed a Ph.D. in literature and linguistics at the University of Santo Tomás in Manila, the Philippines. A professor of Latin American Studies at the Free University in Berlin from 1975 to 1984, she was sent by the German government to CSUCA in 1984 to work as an expert in assessing research and training programs. The lack of formal women's studies at the Central American member universities led her to develop a multifaceted women's studies program at CSUCA, the first regionwide women's studies program in Central America that involved academic institutions in all countries of the region. The goal was to train staff and raise consciousness on women's issues throughout the Central American region. She is now executive director of ILIFEM.

References

Benería, Lourdes. 1989. Evaluación del proyecto CSUCA-UNIFEM "Estudios de la Mujer en Centroamérica." Mexico: Naciones Unidas, PNUD/UNIFEM.

Jiménez, Helga. 1990. Final report, Reunión Tripartita de Evaluación Naciones Unidas (PNUD/UNIFEM), Gobierno de Costa Rica, CSUCA. Proyecto de estudios de la mujer en las universidades centroamericanas. San José, Costa Rica: Subprograma de Estudios de la Mujer, PNUD/NU, CSUCA.

———. 1991. "Los estudios de la mujer y su inserción en la educación superior de Centroamérica." *Estudios sociales centroamericanos/ESCA* 55 (January–April): 15–24.

Acknowledgments

The members of the women's studies commissions in the participating universities of the Central American region with their personal engagement and support were instrumental for our carrying out CSUCA's Women's Studies Program. Special thanks go to Ligia Delgadillo of CSUCA, without whose competent assistance the program would not have become a reality.

31 ❀ Timely, Relevant, Trustworthy, Precise, Ongoing

Toward a Gender-in-Development
Information Network

Mafalda Sibille Martina

The creation of policies to advance the well-being of Central American women is frequently hindered by a lack of appropriate information about them. In addition to often being inaccessible because of technological or resource limits, the available information is partial, inconsistent, nonspecific, and inappropriately conceptualized. It is not categorized by gender, urban versus rural residence, or age, and it persists in labeling women who carry the load of household labor and child rearing as "not working." Moreover, the available information frequently represents a duplication of effort. Appropriate information, however, constitutes a vital resource for planning and for policy making and its execution.

This analysis provides an overview of the author's effort over several years to create an information service that offers appropriate, women-focused information in Costa Rica and, eventually, in the Central American region, through the Programa de Información de la Mujer (PIM) (Women's Information Program) at Costa Rica's Universidad Nacional (Crowther, Cubero, and Sibille, 1990; Sibille et al., 1989). The project is ongoing. As of this writing, two stages, start-up and conceptualization, are complete and an operationalization phase is now under way. A fourth stage, the long-term application of service to Costa Rica and the Central American region, lies in the foreseeable future.

Start-Up: Creation of the Red Nacional de Información sobre Mujer y Desarrollo

In 1985, under the sponsorship of the Fundación Acción Ya (Action Now Foundation) and with the financial backing of what later became UNIFEM,

Costa Rican professionals developed the PIM. Two years later, PIM became associated with the Instituto de Estudios de la Mujer (IEM) (Institute of Women's Studies) at the Universidad Nacional in Heredia, Costa Rica. Since that time, the program has been funded by the Canadian International Development Research Center in Ottawa, Canada. PIM became part of the university's diverse program of activities in research, teaching, and extension service; PIM participates in fulfilling UNA's special mission of serving primarily the poor—in this case, poor women—and those who are working with them.

PIM has established a two-pronged approach for generating and disseminating information on women. It created the Centro de Documentación Especializado en el Tema Mujer y Desarrollo (Documentation Center Specializing in Women and Development), which houses a variety of print materials, and the Red Nacional de Información sobre Mujer y Desarrollo (National Information Network on Women and Development), which offers its users access to information on problems and policies. From the beginning, the PIM staff has planned the eventual extension of this network across the Central American region.

The network staff has not had any precedent on which to build. They devised their procedures in a hands-on, learning-by-doing manner, identifying tasks, formulating theoretical perspectives and methodology, and devising steps to institutionalize both methodology and its application.

In an attempt to determine which organizations in Costa Rica could become providers of or customers for information, the network staff identified 213 organizations, of which 145 were linked to women's issues—124 directly and 21 indirectly. Of these organizations, 58 percent were nongovernmental organizations, 22 percent were voluntary women's organizations, 14 percent were governmental organizations, and 6 percent were international organizations. From these 145 organizations, the staff selected those which were most interested in active cooperation, 34 in all; those organizations became the group that would begin working with data.

During their collection effort, PIM staff members created three databases, offering bibliographic, institutional, and statistical information. In this effort they cooperated with the institutional documentation centers of the 34 organizations, which represented 15 government organizations, 8 universities, 6 private institutions, and 5 international organizations. In the process the staff trained 38 technicians and published nine manuals on data processing.

Reconceptualization: A Gender-Based Theoretical Framework

During the start-up phase, staff members learned that the demand for information on women is not matched by a corresponding supply of data. The reason for this disparity lies in the inappropriate theoretical conceptualization of information on women, rather than in improper information technology. Consequently, the staff stipulated that an appropriate theoretical framework would need to be developed, which would specify the precise character of information the users would need and would provide the basis for a proper methodology to present it in ways relevant to women's needs.

The key criterion for such a framework is that it must promote analysis on the basis of gender. It must focus on specific problems that affect women differently from men; examples of such problems include the status of poor women in development processes, employment policies affecting women, income generation for women, land tenure, health, and education. Given this gender orientation, the information will be appropriate for use in planning medium-term and long-term policies, as well as in coordinating current efforts. This criterion ensures that data will be significant and the database will be an important resource. Thus the staff will be able to provide data that show that poor women are economically and socially underprivileged and that they suffer from gender-based hierarchies and patterns that encourage subordination. The staff will be able to demonstrate that women's work is not socially recognized and that it remains undervalued, even though it is vital for human survival and reproduction.

In fact, recent investigations have shown that information on women and development is scarce, deficient, not generalizable, and not up to date. As a result, policy making, the definition of priorities, the formulation of projects, and the allocation of resources for women are all based on estimates, and the reliability of those estimates is questionable. As long as data are not reliable, policy-making decisions are merely an expression of wishful thinking; they may help, hurt, or simply overlook precisely those women who most need support. For example, according to a recent statement of the Organización Panamericana de Salud (OPS) (Panamerican Health Organization), most countries cannot count on appropriately categorized health information. Even though information is continually gathered, the information is not available to users because of logistical problems.

Few information systems expressly serve women particularly in Central America. Even fewer are run by women. The author knows only of the Costa

Rican national network, the information system of the Instituto Nicaragüense de Investigación sobre la Mujer (INIM) (Nicaraguan Institute of Research on Women), and a few still limited attempts in other countries.

Moreover, the Red Nacional de Información sobre Mujer y Desarrollo is much more than an information network promoting gender-based analysis regarding women and development. As an institution, it contributes to the advancement of gender-related theory, offers considerable methodological and technical expertise in data processing and management, and—most important—promotes a strong commitment to sharing its information resources equally with all who are interested in gender in development, above all with the women who live the development process and struggle with it. The network staff sees its task not only as working with Costa Rican women, women's organizations, and institutions, but also as working with international bodies, such as UNIFEM or the Organización Panamericana de Salud, and as extending the work of the network across Central America.

To the gender-in-development framework, the network is adding a reconceptualization of gender-sensitive communications, practices that it hopes other countries will make their own as they establish their respective networks. Early in the design of the services that a networked information system will provide, planners must understand who will use the network, and what the users want to know. Three components of a successful network are the following:

1. Assessing the demand for information according to the users' needs;
2. Developing the supply of information in response to that demand;
3. Providing service to help institutions develop their own data management capacities so that they will fulfill requirements 1 and 2 above.

Such a gender-sensitive communications system requires the rethinking of such terms as *user, client,* or *beneficiary* to make sure that the system includes meaningful information and makes it available to all participants—above all, to the women themselves.

Operationalization: Serving Its Costa Rican Customers

As noted earlier, the Red Nacional de Información sobre Mujer y Desarrollo is—at the time of this writing—in its third stage, the phase of operationalization. It has determined its theoretical position and specified the information on women it needs, as the title of this essay describes, and is accessible for use by essential institutions. In Costa Rica, these institutions include the

Radio Nacional (National Radio), the Comité Nacional de la Mujer Cooperativista (National Committee of Women's Cooperativists) (see Jiménez, M.,
chap. 21 above), Ministerio de Planificación Nacional y Política Económica
(MIDEPLAN) (Ministry of National Planning and Economics), the Defensoría de la Mujer (Office of the Women's Defender) (now part of the Defensoría de los Habitantes), the IEM, various institutions involved in media
programs, income-generation programs, government planning offices, legal
defense groups, educational facilities, and outreach programs. These information users will in turn help the network staff reach a better understanding of
the demand for information on women; the result will be an elaboration of
appropriate types of information to satisfy all demands.

Long-Term Application: Regional Extension

The fourth phase, long-term application, is planned to begin in the mid-1990s.
Since this analysis was written, the author has left the Costa Rican program
and is now working on the Central American application (Sibille, 1992). The
fourth phase of the project should bring a much-needed extension of the
network throughout the Central American region. This regional extension will
help women by providing the information necessary for sound planning and
policy making, and it will do so while avoiding a duplication of effort.

With its work, the Red Nacional de Información sobre Mujer y Desarrollo
has been making a consciously feminist contribution. It determined the inap-
propriateness of previously available information. It established characteristics
of newly needed, gender-related information on women in the development
process. And it is developing procedures for providing this information to its
users—be they planners, administrators, officials of political or academic institutions, community leaders, project supervisors, or the women who are the
active participants in the development process.

Biodata

Mafalda Sibille Martina is a Peruvian living in Costa Rica. She has a licenciatura in
sociology from the Universidad Xaveriana (Xaveriana University) in Bogotá, Colombia, and she has done graduate studies at the Centro Regional de Educación Funcional
para América Latina (CREFAL) (Regional Center for Functional Education in Latin
America), a joint program of UNESCO and the Mexican government, located in
Pátzcuaro, Michoacán, and at the University of Louvain in Belgium. In 1977 she designed the Sistema de Información Indigenista de América Latina (Information System
on Latin American Indigenous Peoples) at the Instituto Indigenista Interamericano

(Inter-American Institute of Indigenous People), a Peruvian institution, and in 1983 she began to develop the information system for women. She created the Programa de Información de la Mujer (PIM), of which the Red Nacional de Información sobre Mujer y Desarrollo is part. Currently she is an independent consultant to international agencies on information regarding women in development. In that capacity, she has recently done research, with funding by Norwegian and Swedish government agencies, to evaluate Central American information centers of gender and development and the use of that information in forty-eight development projects.

References

Crowther, Warren, Flor Cubero, and Mafalda Sibille Martina. 1990. *Estrategias de información*. San José, Costa Rica: Instituto Centroamericano de Administración Pública.

Sibille, Mafalda. 1992. "Diseño de la investigación centroamericana: Información y género en el desarrollo." Mimeo. San José, Costa Rica: Autoridad Sueca para el Desarrollo Internacional and Autoridad Noruega para el Desarrollo Internacional.

Sibille, Mafalda, Yadira Calvo, Laura Guzmán, and Elizabeth Aguilar. 1989. *Diagnóstico y propuesta de organización de un sistema de información sobre mujer y desarrollo en Costa Rica*. Heredia: Programa de Información de la Mujer, Universidad Nacional.

Acknowledgments

Thanks to Warren Crowther and Flor Cubero for their contribution in our elaborating the methodology for designing information strategies for public policy in *Estrategias de información* (Information Strategies) (1990), at the Instituto Centroamericano de Administración Pública (ICAP) (Central American Institute of Public Administration), in which we formalized our approach to gender-in-development information.

32 ✸ Women's Presence in the University

The Case of the Universidad Nacional in Heredia

Matilde López Núñez

This essay presents a brief analysis of women's presence among the Universidad Nacional's academic and administrative personnel, as well as among its students from 1982 to 1987. The Universidad Nacional (UNA) is one of four state universities, the other three being the Universidad de Costa Rica, the Universidad Estatal a Distancia (UNED) (State University for Extension Studies), and the Instituto Tecnológico (Institute of Technology). UNA was founded in 1973, as the successor to the Teachers' College, and in recent years it has had approximately 7,000 to 9,000 students. This study focuses on the years 1982 and 1987 and examines trends and major characteristics of the three groups.

Women Academics

Gender and Age

As table 32.1 indicates, women account for roughly one-third of UNA's academic staff (33% in 1982; 37% in 1987). The teaching staff is surprisingly young. In 1982, more than half of the faculty (55% of the women and 51% of the men) were in the age group of 28 to 38 years. An additional 21 percent of women and 26 percent of men fell in the 39-to-40 age group in 1982. For the year 1987, the percentage of women aged 28 to 38 shrinks to 49 percent, and of men, to 45 percent. The next older group, of 39 to 49 years, increases notably in 1987 to 27 percent and 35 percent, respectively.

Salary

In 1982, two-thirds of both women and men (66% and 64%) were in the low-salary range (<4,000–10,000 colones); one-third (34% and 36%) were in the middle range (10,000–18,000 colones); and negligible numbers (up to 1%) were in the high-salary range (18,000–26,000 colones). By 1987, slightly over two-fifths (43% and 43%) were in the low range (<4,000–18,000); not quite one-third (31%, 27%) fell in the middle (18,000–36,000); and not quite one-

Table 32.1. Universidad Nacional (UNA) Academic Staff, Comparison by Gender

| | 1982 | | | | | 1987 | | | | |
| | Male | | Female | | % F of | Male | | Female | | % F of |
Category	No.	%	No.	%	Total	No.	%	No.	%	Total
Age										
18–28	106	14	62	17	37	83	10	90	18	52
28–38	387	51	204	55	35	375	45	241	49	39
39–49	195	26	77	21	28	293	35	131	27	31
50+	67	9	26	7	28	79	10	29	6	27
TOTAL	755	100	369	100	33	830	100	491	100	37
Salary										
Low	481	64	242	66	33	353	43	209	43	37
Middle	269	36	126	34	32	227	27	150	31	40
High	5	1	1	—	17	250	30	132	27	35
Academic Preparation										
<B.A./B.S.	54	7	18	5	25	58	7	15	3	21
B.A./B.S.	165	22	119	32	42	200	24	168	35	46
Licenciatura	407	54	205	56	33	401	49	244	51	38
M.A./M.S.	58	8	19	5	25	97	12	39	8	29
Ph.D.	71	9	8	2	10	64	8	8	2	11
Teaching Appointment										
Full Time	203	27	119	32	37	199	24	142	30	42
Part Time	552	73	250	68	31	621	76	332	70	35

Notes: Totals are not the same in all categories of data; percentages do not add up to 100 because of rounding.
% F of total = percentage of females in category.
Salaries in colones compared to account for inflation:

    Low: (1982) 4,000 to 10,000   (1987) 10,000 to 18,000
    Middle: (1982) 10,000 to 18,000   (1987) 18,000 to 36,000
    High: (1982) 18,000 to 26,000   (1987) 36,000 to 70,000

At any time, the high salary range is probably equivalent to $500–$1,000 U.S. per month.
Licenciatura: Academic Degree between B.A./B.S. and M.A./M.S.
Academic personnel comprise teaching, research, and extension staff. Data on research staff, extension staff, and teaching staff are not comparable, so the table shows only teaching staff. However, women in both years account for about one-third of all personnel, and most hold only part-time positions.

third (27%, 30%) were in the high-salary range (36,000–70,000+). The different salary ranges for the two years illustrate that, over time, the salaries were adjusted for inflation. A crude comparison of exchange rates for each year suggests that the high-salary range, both in 1982 and 1987, is approximately equal to $500 to $1,000 U.S. a month.

Academic Preparation

Two facts emerge on academic preparation. First, at UNA about one-third of all faculty hold a bachelor's or lesser degree. In 1982, this was true of 37 percent of the women and 29 percent of the men; in 1987, comparable figures were 38 percent and 31 percent respectively. Another half of the faculty (1982, 56% and 54%; 1987, 51% and 49%) hold a *licenciatura*, a degree that is more than the bachelor's but less than the U.S. master's degree. In rounded numbers, the percentage of UNA faculty with a master's degree or a Ph.D. was 14 percent in 1982 (7% of the women, 17% of the men). In 1987, 16 percent of the faculty held such degrees (10% and 19% respectively). In many fields, advanced degrees require study abroad, which is not easily available to most academics.

Even though the data suggest a basic ratio of distribution between women and men of roughly 1:2, at lower levels of academic preparation this ratio approaches 1:1, whereas at the Ph.D. level it tends toward 1:10. In other words, women cluster at the lower levels of academic preparation, and only a few of them are found among Ph.D.'s.

Time Commitment

Teaching is increasingly done by part-time faculty at UNA. In 1982, 68 percent of women and 73 percent of men held part-time teaching positions. Comparable figures for 1987 were 70 percent for women and 76 percent for men. The existing records do not indicate the proportion of graduate-student teaching assistants. The proportion of full-time women is higher (42%) than their overall proportion (37%) among academic staff. This suggests a perpetuation of the stereotype that teaching is a feminine activity. Also, more men than women seem to use a part-time affiliation with the university for status, pursuing other activities outside of academia—often justifiably so, because university salaries are not generous.

Schools

Some schools within UNA attract an unusually high proportion of women. These schools offer "typically feminine" professional training. Thus the humanities faculty is 46 percent women. Women also comprise 44 percent of the faculty of the Centro de Investigación y Docencia en Educación (CIDE) (Center for Research and Teaching in Education), which was formerly the School of Education. The Facultad de Ciencias Sociales (School of Social Sciences) lists 33 percent of its faculty as women. That division includes such fields as professional secretarial studies, social planning and community organization, history, and sociology, and the interdisciplinary Instituto de Estudios de Trabajo (IESTRA) (Institute of Labor Studies).

Positions of Power

An important aspect of women's presence at UNA is their increasing participation in policy and decision making, i.e., in power positions. In 1982, women held only 2 of 12 positions (17%) in the president's office, the university council, the general secretariat, and the various head offices for the major university functions (such as administration, academic affairs, research, extension, and student life). Women improved their position in 1986, reaching 23 percent with 7 of 31 positions, but this proportion is not stable. Nonetheless, in 1989 UNA elected a woman to its highest post, president of the university. This is the first time any woman has held this post in Central America.

Administrative Staff

Gender and Age

Regarding university administration, the study demonstrates a sustained increase of women at UNA between 1982 and 1987. The number of female personnel increased by 27 percent, and male personnel by 6 percent. In 1987, of 1,042 administrators, 498 were women, for a female participation of 48 percent. Among older employees, though, men still predominate. In 1987, in the age group 44 years and older, the female to male ratio was 1:3, whereas in the age group 24 to 28 years, the ratio was 2:1.

Job Function and Power

The ratio of women to men in university administration does not give a complete view of women administrators' status at UNA. Most women are secretaries and office workers; in the higher ranks, such as in the planning office and computer direction, men predominate, holding an average of 80 percent of administrative positions. Fields that record relatively large numbers of women administrators—for example, general studies, philosophy, the liberal arts/humanities, and social sciences—repeat the pattern found earlier among the academic staff. In general, women do less valued jobs and thin out in the upper ranks. In the university's top echelons, the ratio is one woman to four men; of 43 top positions in 1987, eight (19%) were held by women, 35 by men. In the next-lower echelon, directors of offices, comprising 27 positions in 1982, women held only 6 positions (22%). In 1987, of a total of 31 such slots, 7 were occupied by women (26%). The same 1:4 ratio holds for positions that need high academic or technical qualifications, such as planners, officials in the treasurer's office, programmers, analysts, technicians in the graphic arts, and lab assistants. Women are also in the minority among support staff. They are in the majority as secretaries, office workers, or librarians.

Student Population

Available figures for women students are not strictly comparable to those for faculty and staff, and they allow only general observations. The proportion of women among UNA students seems high, at 44 percent for 1982 and 51 percent for 1987. Most students—women and men—are single, but in the categories of common-law marriage and divorced persons, women predominate. In 1982, 71 percent of the women students and 63 percent of the male students did not work in the formal labor market; for 1987, the figures rose to 79 percent for women and 67 percent for men. In 1982, 42 percent of all women students received total scholarship support, 37 percent received partial support, and only 21 percent paid for their education with no aid. The percentage for total support remained nearly the same in 1987 (41%), but the proportion of women paying for their education rose to 44 percent. In both years, smaller proportions of male students received total support (36% in 1982 and 37% in 1987).

Fields of Study

Some fields retained their popularity and attracted the greatest number of women students in both 1982 and 1987. These fields were literature and linguistics, education, professional secretarial studies, labor studies, and librarianship. History, biological sciences, and planning and community organization, which were popular in 1982, were losing out in 1987 to international studies, mathematics, and economics. Women do have a reputation—not yet statistically confirmed—of registering for more diverse class work and of studying harder than men.

Conclusion

The foregoing study invites several observations: Women's presence at UNA in terms of numbers is, although not equal, at least respectable; women account for approximately one-third of the academic faculty, 40 percent of the administrative staff, and a majority of the students. Moreover, all categories displayed a fairly consistent trend toward an increase in women's participation. Women and men share some problems, such as low salaries, which result in the overwhelming majority of academics working part-time at the university and pursuing other careers outside.

However, women's presence is nowhere a presence on equal terms. Men hold most power positions on both the academic faculty and the administrative staff, and they predominate in prestigious fields of study. Women, both as faculty and as students, predominate only in "typically feminine," less prestigious, and less remunerated fields of study.

Biodata

Matilde López Núñez, a Costa Rican, holds an A.B.D. in sociology of literature from the Ecôle des Hautes Etudes en Sciences Sociales (School of Advanced Studies in the Social Sciences) in Paris and an M.A. in Hispanic American literature from the Sorbonne Nouvelle (New Sorbonne) in Paris. Before her retirement from the Instituto de Estudios de la Mujer (IEM) (Institute of Women's Studies) at UNA, she was a researcher and editor of the information bulletin *UNA-Mujer* and the review *Casa de la Mujer* (Women's House). From late 1992 until early 1994 she participated in a regional research project sponsored by the Women's Program of the Instituto Interamericano de Derechos Humanos (Inter-American Institute of Human Rights) to investigate women's perception of their rights in various Central American countries. She is currently completing research on women's career choices in a project sponsored by the Consejo Superior Universitario Centroamericano (CSUCA) (Council of Central American Universities), which has seen delays because of recent changes in the CSUCA program (see Jiménez, H., chap. 30 above).

References

López N., Matilde. 1989. "Análisis cuantitativo y cualitativo de la participación de la mujer en las universidades estatales centroamericanas." Mimeo. Primera parte: Universidad Nacional, Costa Rica. n.p.: Centro Interdisciplinario de Estudios de la Mujer.

Acknowledgments

This is a selective summary of an investigation the author carried out in 1989 for CIEM, now IEM, as part of a study sponsored by the Women's Studies Program of CSUCA to determine the presence of women in the region's universities.

33 ❀ Problems of Joint Interdisciplinary Research in Women's Studies

An Effort to Integrate Disciplines for More Fruitful Analysis

Margarita Brenes Fonseca, May Brenes Marín, and Sandra Castro Paniagua

One of the goals of current scientific work is producing scientific knowledge by integrating the approaches of various disciplines. As scholars and feminists, we carried out a joint interdisciplinary research project on depression among Costa Rican women. This report identifies and summarizes some of the most important difficulties we faced in employing an interdisciplinary methodology for a scientific investigation, difficulties we encountered despite the feminist values we three investigators shared. We hope that by sharing our experiences we can facilitate the work of other women who might select a similar methodology. We believe the goals of this methodology are attainable if feminist scholars base their cooperation on the universality of a feminist view of the social and psychological sciences. We conclude this report with a summary of our most important insights into depression among the Costa Rican women we investigated.

From our shared feminist perspective, we began the task of assessing the problem of mental health among Costa Rican women; we combined the approaches of three scientific disciplines: anthropology, psychology, and sociology. The specific problem we set out to study was depression in Costa Rica (Brenes, Castro, and Pinto, 1990); depression has been identified specifically as a women's problem around the world, in both developed and developing countries (Weissman and Klerman, 1977).

An important component of a feminist approach to science is considering the personal and environmental aspects of scientific phenomena. This led us to base our investigation upon the analysis of the life histories of a group of fifteen hospitalized women patients who had been diagnosed as depressive.

The resulting analysis integrates the perspectives of our three disciplines. Before arriving at these results, however, we had to learn to manage our own differences.

Analyzing Our Difficulties

We began our project in a spirit of cooperation based on a shared set of values. We were surprised to find that our first problem was understanding and trusting each other. We will briefly describe the problems we encountered, discuss their possible causes, and, finally, present the solution we found for overcoming them.

"We Must Contribute Equally."

Differences in our individual academic training produced not only different bodies of specialized information but also differences in our conception of the world and our work and differences in our specific skills. The training of professionals in Costa Rica is based on fairly inflexible study programs. Students have few alternatives for choosing courses. This is quite appropriate for a country such as Costa Rica in which economic resources are scarce and university budgets are necessarily limited.

Consequently, we members of the investigating team were women with different capacities, skills, and conceptions. As we developed our study we found it difficult to accept these differences. This manifested itself in various ways. Each of us doubted her partners' commitment to the project and their willingness to put forth an equal amount of effort in various areas—the number of bibliographic sources they would contribute, their application and understanding of theory, or the division of practical chores during fieldwork. Our psychologist, for example, had more bibliographic sources than the other two professionals because our topic was one that psychologists had traditionally studied. And the anthropologist and sociologist had more experience with fieldwork, which is a standard part of those disciplines. These and other issues produced feelings of competitiveness among us.

The attitude of cooperation we three investigators shared contrasted repeatedly with the distrust, competition, and lack of support that characterized our initial management of differences. Thus we disagreed, for example, on assessments of theory or practice and on the value of a technical or spontaneous approach, to mention only two areas of conflict. At various moments, such issues threatened the continuation of the project. In the end, however, the discussion and evaluation of our differences precluded such a result. Our group effort to convert into reality the values of sisterhood and cooperation—which we as feminist investigators consider fundamental for achieving a comprehensive appreciation of reality—permitted us not only to continue and achieve our goals but also to find out how to learn from our differences.

"This Is My Area of Expertise."

During our study we faced another problem that characterizes all interdisciplinary work: We had to recognize the differences between, and the limits of, our disciplines.

Our psychologist colleague frequently commented on the work of the sociologist and anthropologist, saying, "What you wrote is psychology, not sociology (or anthropology)." On other occasions, the protest was directed with equal force at her. These protests caused us to evaluate the traditional attitudes and conditions that have established the parameters for social science research. Generally, these traditions had led us to compartmentalize our sciences, considering ourselves experts on one or another topic and, in many cases, disregarding the contribution of the other disciplines.

To behave in this fashion means ascribing each science to one branch of knowledge. Our practice taught us that we cannot distinguish precise limits between different branches of knowledge. We overcame this problem by understanding our disciplines in their broadest meaning, taking into consideration interaction, knowledge, scientific theory, and socioeconomic development of the society—without ignoring, of course, the peculiarities of each investigator, her previous experience, and her interpretation of the world.

To approach science from this broadest point of view caused us to accept the fact that our knowledge was not absolute and, most important, it allowed us to be aware that we needed to learn more. This awareness gave us a clearer vision of our investigative activity. In the end, we confirmed the value and necessity of interdisciplinary investigation, specifically for the study of women's problems. Having done so, we were able to achieve a more comprehensive study, which was more committed to women and to the well-being of humanity.

"What Does It Mean? What Are You Saying?"

Any scientific discipline, especially those of the social sciences, contains appropriate theories, practices, and methodologies that it employs in the analysis of the phenomena it wishes to investigate. Each discipline also tailors its vocabulary to its theories, practices, and methodologies. Although many terms overlap and have identical meanings, others carry an entirely different definition.

The difficulty we had to resolve in our study was defining the meaning of the technical vocabulary for each discipline. In the case of our three social sciences, for instance, we had to check and define such terms as *socialization process* and *roles*. Equally perplexing was whether we equate what psychologists call a "case study" with what the anthropologist knows as a "life history." Did the terms describe the same phenomenon? In this particular example, we asked ourselves whether the two terms were similar, complementary, or mutually exclusive; then we discussed the limits and emphases that each discipline puts on details or certain aspects of the two definitions. We decided that in our investigation, we would combine the life history approach with case study techniques. Since our research took place in a hospital with patients who had been diagnosed for depression, we resorted initially to the case study method. We taped our interviews at the hospital. Together, we then analyzed the tapes, to explore specific details, so that we could confirm or explain certain points when we visited the patients' families at their homes—an aspect much more akin to the anthropological life history method.

We learned from this experience that it is of the utmost importance for the participants in an interdisciplinary study to gain an understanding, if only a very general understanding, of what the theories of the different disciplines and their techniques and methods contribute to the investigative process.

Discussion: An Integrating Science

We can summarize the various difficulties we encountered under the overall problem of learning to manage our differences. Accepting the differences among ourselves—without letting those differences lead us to compete with each other or to give up the project—constituted a basic step in the process of learning to produce less atomized knowledge, knowledge that can integrate diverse aspects of reality, the private and the public, the psychological and the socio-anthropological. These categories reflect, above all, the development of sciences that divide the world and foster a hierarchical, compartmentalized world vision.

To develop an integrating science that unites different spheres and dimensions is a goal and a challenge for us as human beings. The feminist perspective of science helps us to overcome the difficulties of a new construction, not only of the scientific paradigms but also of the methodologies we must employ if we are to reach these new goals.

Our Insight into Depression in Costa Rican Women

The heterogeneity of the social, cultural, and psychological factors we found responsible for the occurrence of depression in the fifteen women in our study caused us to doubt the diagnoses in the medical records for many of the participating women. These diagnoses tended to relate the women's depression to specific causes in their immediate past. We suggested instead that the depression was more likely to be related to profound long-term problems in the women's lives. Those problems arise from the violence women experience daily—physical or mental aggression, incest, and rape.

In our study, even disregarding violence in the form of beatings in childhood or as adults, 60 percent of the women had suffered sexual aggression, and 33 percent had experienced incest (Brenes et al, 1990: 137–38). One respondent, for example, had been battered by her husband, who then also violated the respondent's daughter (his stepdaughter). The daughter was herself then hospitalized with depression in another institution (Brenes et al., 1990: 124). In another case, a woman had refused sexual relations with her husband, who had acted irresponsibly in money matters. He responded with such a brutal sexual attack that she needed to be hospitalized (Brenes et al., 1990: 125).

In our study of these fifteen women, we found that the patriarchal norms that regulate the women's conformity behavior—and thus enforce the subordination of the feminine by the masculine gender—are part of their daily lives, together with the values that establish and reinforce those norms. In their need to respond to their situation, some of these women sought help and support in religion or looked for an explanation in supernatural forces.

We concluded the following:

1. The treatment of depressed women during their hospital stay must be more holistic; the course of treatment should be designed not only to guide the women out of depression but also to offer them group therapy with the relevant members of their social group.
2. We should promote support groups for those women so that not only will the phenomenon of depression be treated in the individual patient but the women will also be enabled to share and analyze their experiences.

3. In each diagnosis and treatment, professionals from various disciplines should participate, which will allow a holistic analysis of the problem of depression from an interdisciplinary perspective.

Biodata

Margarita Brenes Fonseca is a Costa Rican. She holds an M.S. in psychology from Arizona State University in Tempe, Arizona. She is a professor at the Universidad de Costa Rica and a member of the Programa Interdisciplinario de Estudios de Género (PRIEG) (Interdisciplinary Gender Studies Program). Her major research interests are gender and socialization. In early 1993 she went on leave from UCR and is working in the United States as a psychotherapist with Latina women in the bilingual program of the Family Service Association in Lawrence, Massachusetts.

May Brenes Marín, a Costa Rican, has a licenciatura in anthropology from the Universidad de Costa Rica. She has worked as a consultant for UCR's Training Project for Rural Women and, since 1993 has been the editor of the review *Casa de la Mujer* (Women's House) at the Instituto de Estudios de la Mujer (IEM) (Institute for Women's Studies) at UNA. In 1992 she published *Matinino, por los mismos caminos de la historia con otros ojos* (Matinino, watching the course of history with other eyes). With Mayra Zapparoli Zecca she published *¡De que vuelan, vuelan...! Un análisis de la magia y la brujería en Costa Rica* (They say they don't fly—but they do! An analysis of magic and witchcraft in Costa Rica; 1991).

Sandra Castro Paniagua is also an author of "Women and Love," which appears earlier in this *Reader* and contains her biodata (see chap. 26 above).

References

Brenes Marín, May, Sandra Castro Paniagua, and Roxana Pinto López. 1990. *Mujer y depresión*. San José, Costa Rica: APROMUJER.

Weissman, M. N., and G. L. Klerman. 1977. "Sex Differences and the Epidemiology of Depression." *Archives of General Psychiatry* 34 (January).

Acknowledgments

This analysis is based on the experience of writing an interdisciplinary *licenciatura* thesis, for which May Brenes Marín and Sandra Castro Paniagua worked with Roxana Pinto López, who did not participate in the elaboration of the present report. Margarita Brenes Fonseca was the thesis director.

34 ❀ The Predictability
of Cesarean-Section Births

A Case Study of Students in Costa Rican Childbirth Classes

Jennifer Kozlow-Rodríguez

Something is causing an ever-accelerating increase of cesarean births in Costa Rica and, thus, an abuse of normal obstetrical ethics because any cesarean section that can be predicted for nonmedical reasons is theoretically unethical. This analysis is an attempt to begin a process of predicting the likelihood that a particular pregnancy will result in a cesarean-section birth because of factors other than medical ones. If such predictions can be made, it will be possible to recognize women with a strong preference for a medicated birth. Such an attitude might ultimately put some of these women at risk for a cesarean section.

Acceptable and Excessive Occurrences of Cesareans

The Organización Mundial de la Salud (World Health Organization) has stated that no region in the world, regardless of how poor or privileged, can justify a rate of cesarean-section births higher than 15 percent of all births in the population (International Childbirth Education Association, 1989). This criterion is met in few developed countries; in Costa Rica, a country in the process of development, the rate of cesarean births seems excessively high.

The hospitals of the government-supported Caja Costarricense de Seguro Social (CCSS) (Costa Rican Social Security Service) are not the source of the problem. These hospitals perform cesarean sections only in cases of absolute medical necessity and they maintain a 15 to 18 percent rate, which nearly corresponds to the WHO recommended range. In contrast, the rate of cesarean births in private maternity clinics far exceeds the level WHO considers justifiable. Determining the actual rate in such institutions is difficult because cesarean birth rates are considered an indication of a hospital's standards of efficiency—the lower the rate, the better. Institutions that have high rates of such births are therefore reluctant to reveal their figures and to justify their methods.

Some estimates do circulate informally, however. One doctor confided to me that he believed the rate of cesarean sections in a particular San José clinic was about 80 percent. Another estimate is possible by extrapolating the experience of 375 students who attended my childbirth classes over a five-year period. Among these women, 33 percent of the deliveries were by cesarean section. Even within this group of students, however, statistics vary greatly from hospital to hospital and from one doctor to another. Whatever the estimate used, the rate of cesarean-section births in Costa Rica is too high.

Why should such a high rate exist? Is there some peculiar set of circumstances in Costa Rican living conditions—some aspect of diet, climate, or national genetic make-up—that produces this high rate? This is not a likely answer. Many factors determine whether a woman will have a natural vaginal birth, a medicated (epidural) normal birth, or a cesarean-section birth. Some of these factors are cultural, determined by the country or society in which the woman lives or was brought up. Culture-related factors such as religion, values, or the nature of human relationships are important. Other relevant factors are individual and are determined by the woman's personality, her particular doctor, her attitude toward pain and birth, her socioeconomic status, and her physical condition. In the context of cesarean births, individual factors acquire increased importance when the medical reasons for surgery are not convincing—in other words, when the cesarean section appears to have been performed for emotional reasons relating to the woman or because the doctor personally preferred surgical deliveries.

To determine which of these variables might be producing the high rate of cesarean births among Costa Rican women, I compiled data based on my observations of 375 pregnant women who attended twenty-five childbirth preparation courses I taught in a five-year period between 1987 and 1992. Although these women are not representative of Costa Rican women as a whole—the upper-middle and upper classes are overrepresented in the sample—their experiences nevertheless provide insight into the high incidence of cesarean-section births in Costa Rica. The results follow.

Predicting Cesarean-Section Births Among
Childbirth-Class Participants

Background

As a certified childbirth educator, I have taught classes in Costa Rica on child-birth preparation since 1986. During that time, I have become increasingly concerned about the high incidence of cesarean-section births. Although many cesareans are necessary, many others are not. I have come to believe that cesareans are sometimes performed for nonmedical reasons because two atti-tudes coincide: Some doctors believe women do not need the chance to deliver their children normally, and some women feel incapable of handling the birth experience. Together, they become accomplices in an excessive cesarean birth rate. Consider the following two hypothetical situations:

> Marcela squeals with delight when the woman to her right at a baby shower says her labor began well but ended in a cesarean section. Marcela blurts out, "Isn't it fantastic? They put you out, no pain, so nice and tidy, and there's your baby. Don't you think so?" Marcela is expecting her second, and with childlike eyes she says mischievously she wouldn't change having a baby abdominally "for anything in the world."

> Dr. González sits patiently, and without fixing his gaze on María del Carmen, he comforts her, telling her that everything she is feeling is normal. He assures her that when the time comes, he will handle things and now he looks over to her husband and says "Well, she *is* rather narrow and since her mother *did* deliver *her* by ce-sarean, of course, there *is* the possibility. . . . But," he adds, "one cannot interfere with God's wishes, and at least it is a simple procedure with no risk to the baby and"—he winks—"no stretching out of place for the mother." As he shows them out he says, "Now be a good girl and don't you worry."

Marcela gives herself away. All Costa Rican women are not like Marcela but neither is she unusual. Because Marcela is not the type to take a childbirth education course, she is not part of my study, but residuals of her attitude are. And are all doctors like Dr. González? No, but many will become patronizing if their patients don't resist it. Dr. González could go either way, depending on how forthright his patient is. This common doctor's office scene shows the doctor's testing ground—he suggests the idea of a cesarean, and without inter-ference, the patient's acceptance will grow with each visit.

Why are there so many cesarean-section births among private clinic pa-tients? Apart from the specific training of a given obstetrician—as a rule, Costa

Rican physicians receive their medical training at home and go abroad, mostly to the United States, for specialties such as obstetrics—and the technological "temptations" available to them, both doctor and patient may offer each other the opportunity to establish a new norm for birthing, almost as if it were a status symbol of their unique social attitudes. In such cases, the outcome of the birth as a cesarean section will be based on the patient's attitudes or the doctor's preference for surgical deliveries. I hypothesize that at least half the cesareans of students in my classes are of this nonmedical nature.

The Variables

Table 34.1 is based on twenty-five childbirth preparation courses I taught between 1987 and 1992 and the birth experiences of the students in those classes. The observations cover 375 couples. My reasons for developing this table were two: to identify women at risk for a medicated and/or a cesarean birth and to help women understand what will enable them to achieve their childbirth goals. The table ultimately also highlights factors affecting cesarean-section abuse and therefore helps clarify the true ratio of necessary cesareans among the students.

In the analysis of my observations, I assigned values ranging from 0 (lowest) to 3 (highest) for each of five variables: personality, doctor's rate of cesarean sections, woman's attitude about pain and birth, woman's socioeconomic status, and woman's physical condition. The scores represent degrees of risk of cesarean birth. When scores for the five individual categories are totaled, they give a combined score representing a woman's total risk of cesarean-section birth. The lower the total score for the individual, the better the chance of a natural birth. The higher the score, the more likely the risk of cesarean section. Deliveries with an epidural anesthesia fall within the middle scores. A score of 3 in any one category is enough reason to consider the woman a high-risk case. If a woman with a low score for nonmedical risks has a cesarean, this only adds credibility that the surgery was medically necessary. Of course, a natural birth is not necessarily everyone's first choice. Some women feel they could give birth naturally but do not see the point of attempting it.

I based the point scores on my assessment of the students during the nine class sessions of each course. The students also answered questions about fear, change, how they viewed themselves as mothers, what mattered to them, and so on. On two occasions they completed written questionnaires. I relied on my intuition and experience in the category of the woman's personality.

Table 34.1. Factors Predicting Cesarean Birth

	Active Participant		Passive Observer	
Factor Score	*0*	*1*	*2*	*3*
Pregnant Woman's Personality	assertive, out-spoken, knows what she wants; reads about birth; often Anglo-European	neither extreme; often from other Latin-American countries	submissive; husband does all the talking in class; soft-spoken; mostly Costa Rican women	nervous; jittery; clingy; immature
Doctor[a]	Social Security hospitals; more open to alternatives, liberal; usually younger; 15–25% cesarean rate	26–36% cesarean rate	medically conservative; 37–75% cesarean rate; patronizing	76–100% cesarean rate
Pregnant Woman's Attitude About Pain and Birth	anti-interventionist; sees birth as personal challenge	normal anxiety level; realistic about birth	no intention of trying for non-medicated birth; complains a lot about pregnancy; doting husband	open verbal indifference to having cesarean
Pregnant Woman's Socioeconomic Status	middle	middle	upper, or well-known family; known to have money; possibly Jewish; single woman	constrained by family connection to doctor, who is friend of family or relative
Pregnant Woman's Physical Condition	excellent; feels great, is active; strong ability to handle stress; athletic, at times competitive, experience; has experienced yoga, relaxation exercises prior to pregnancy	normal	bed rest prescribed; overweight before pregnancy; gains over 45 lbs.; teenager; has had problems getting pregnant; older than societal norms dictate or accept for giving birth (37 or older)	multiple births; low-lying placenta over cervix; verified *total* CPD[b]; malpresentation; maternal conditions going 12–14 days past due date; medical conditions that make a normal birth less likely, depending on doctor's style

a. The assessment underlying the classification of doctors in the three categories is based on their cesarean rates *with my students only.*

b. Cephalo-Pelvic-Disproportion

The two main personality types in the classes were what I call *passive observer* or *active participant*. I viewed this as a continuum. At one extreme is the assertive woman who has definite ideas about what she wants and is outspoken and informed about her options. At the other extreme is the submissive, almost fragile woman who lets her husband do most of the talking. As she interacts with her husband, so also does she interact with her doctor. She feels it is not her place to disagree. Moreover, passive observers rarely add to their learning outside of class. This variable is not a judgment of strong versus weak character; rather it is an assessment of the outward portrayal of the woman's own self-image, self-confidence, and inner will. These create an impression by which others will judge her.

Interestingly, this category easily identifies women who are foreigners, either from another Latin American country or from North America or Europe. Foreign women have a better chance than local women of reaching their goals, possibly because their life in another country speaks for their having had to acquire a greater independence in handling new situations. Many come from large cities that have challenged their capacity to survive and succeed. Foreign women of either group also have a better chance of reaching their goals because they usually are not affected by judgments imposed by San José's elite; they can birth anonymously. Yet there are differences among the foreign women. Upper-class Latin American women are usually diplomatic and not very forceful about their needs. This leaves most North American and European (Anglo-European) foreigners as prototypical examples of active-participant personality types. In fact, in my sample, all the diverse foreign women reached their goal of achieving a natural birth twice as often as did Costa Rican students. They constitute 15 percent of my students (see Table 34.2).

In part, additional factors help Anglo-European women reach their goals of natural childbirth more consistently: one is their culture's advocacy of natural childbirth methods and of women as leaders and as individuals who control their own destiny and have rights to self-determination and legal protection. Another is that they usually are not overly self-conscious about the way they appear to their doctor or nurse during labor, so they are more likely to ask questions (such as, "What are you putting in my intravenous drip?") and to make more demands (for example, "I'd rather continue walking than lie down"). They also seem more willing to sacrifice their own comfort for the sake of the baby and will opt for a natural birth because it decreases the

Table 34.2. Types of Birth Experience, by Patient Group[a]

	Anglo-European Women	Latin-American Women
Nonmedicated birth, by hospital category		
Social Security hospitals	0%	10%
Private clinics	69	18
TOTAL	69	28
Medicated birth, exclusively in private clinics		
Intended	5	18
Not intended	7	24
TOTAL	12	42
Cesarean section, exclusively in private clinics		
Intended	0	0
Not intended	19	30
TOTAL	19	30
TOTAL WOMEN	100	100

a. According to hospital category for nonmedicated births; according to patients' preference for medicated births or cesarean sections.

incidence of complications. Some of my local students seemed more concerned about their own welfare and, like Marcela, willing to undergo the less safe experience of abdominal surgery rather than suffer needlessly. In the event of a difficult delivery, a cesarean section may be the safest option. But when done irresponsibly, merely for the convenience of the mother or physician, it carries far more risk of prematurity, infection, lower respiratory effort of the newborn, and infant and maternal morbidity and mortality.

Of course, abdominal surgery means a difficult and often painful recovery, but this is not part of a woman's thought process when her fear of vaginal birth is paramount. Foreign women seem to automatically rate lower scores in the other categories like attitudes about pain and birth, which represent more of a personal challenge and mature acceptance that pain is a necessary part of the whole. They usually put greater emphasis on maintaining a healthy physical and mental condition throughout pregnancy. Therefore, being a woman of Anglo-American or European background is enough to greatly lower the risk of a medicated or cesarean birth.

On the opposite end of the scale for this variable, the 3 score for personality represents an abnormally nervous woman who is uncomfortable with childbirth classes, cannot watch birth videos, is almost visibly jittery, and is un-usually clingy and dependent on her husband.

THE DOCTOR

The most important decision a woman will make when planning her birth experience is her choice of doctor. This decision alone will greatly affect the outcome. When her cervix is dilating from 5 to 10 centimeters, almost any woman—no matter how assertive or self-confident, and no matter what her prior ideas about labor—will consider anesthesia. Of paramount importance for the woman in this difficult period is her husband's reaction to her, but even more influential is her doctor's reaction. Some doctors don't like the helpless-ness or loss of omnipotence they feel when a woman is acting irrationally and obviously struggling with her self-control. How does the doctor react as the ultimate authority in the presence of her panicky self-doubt? The woman in labor wonders if everyone else is doubting her as well. Since the doctor is the expert, if he or she—roughly 10 percent of Costa Rican obstetricians are women—thinks the expectant mother should use anesthesia, it must be the case that she can't make it otherwise. The strongest women are vulnerable and scared during this phase of labor and need added assurance and support to reach their goal. With a doctor who works with the woman in a hands-on, "you-*can*-make-it-through-this" stance, the woman soon reaches her goal and lives with an incredible sense of accomplishment for having done so. But unfortunately for those women who truly desire a nonmedicated birth, most doctors routinely suggest anesthesia because they see no contraindications that cannot be resolved medically. Rarely do they consider the psychological conse-quences of their actions for a woman's self-image. Obstetricians also may prefer a medicated birth because it becomes more manageable, predictable, and, possibly, lucrative. (Some doctors are their own anesthesiologists.)

Pregnant women may experience a delicate emotional balance that affects how they choose their doctors. Authors on preparation for birth have sug-gested that women who feel powerless before authority figures will in all likelihood select physicians who will take care of things (see, for example, Rahima Baldwin and Terra Palmarin, 1986). During her monthly prenatal visits, the woman is sending a message to her doctor about how active a role she plans to take during delivery. How important is the birth experience for her and her husband? Does she always come with her husband or mother and let one or the other of them do most of the talking? How firm is her tone of voice? What is her style of dressing? What does her body language say about how important she thinks her feelings are? Does she phone the doctor often about mild discomforts rather than deal with them herself? The obstetrician is naturally going to respond to each patient individually according to an assessment of these and other factors during the prenatal visits.

But not every doctor will take advantage of an insecure patient. Doctors differ in their judgments about the point at which they intervene and how drastically they deal with anomalies. Liberal doctors wait longer, try other options, consider the couple's feelings on the matter, avoid unnecessary interventions, and get a second opinion. Medically conservative doctors take any variation from "textbook" labor as reason for a cesarean; they do not take labor dynamics into consideration in addition to the other factors they weigh before beginning a medical intervention. Instead, they intervene when women go five to seven days beyond the due date, operate three to six hours after membranes have ruptured, and refuse to allow the woman to attempt a vaginal birth after a cesarean, to name a few examples. The delivery comes down to an enactment of the doctor's own personal beliefs about the nature of childbirth.

Many of the high-cesarean-rate doctors truly believe they are doing the woman a favor by not putting her through labor. And plenty of women are happy to oblige them rather than confront their tremendous fears about pain and birth. Many women would like to change doctors but feel obligated to stay because their conservative doctor is a friend of the family and it "wouldn't look right." This personal relationship can at times be a liability. The doctor almost takes advantage of the confidence and, knowing no doubts will be expressed, performs a cesarean, claiming that the woman was too small-boned (an excuse that almost flatters the figure-conscious woman), was presumably deficient of amniotic fluid, had an aged or calcified placenta, or a baby in a less than optimal position (4% of all fetal positions). Mortimer Rosen and Lillian Thomas have suggested that women have a better chance of avoiding unnecessary cesareans if they form a strong relationship with their obstetricians (1989).

In sum, a woman may have a low score in all areas of Table 34.1 except that of her doctor, but this will still be enough to put her at risk for a cesarean section.

CCSS hospitals offer whichever obstetrician, resident, or nurse-midwife is on duty. They do not provide epidural anesthesia and, because of the cost to themselves, they perform far fewer cesarean sections than privately owned clinics. The 10 percent of the students in this study who went to the Social Security Services hospitals could therefore be more confident than private clinic patients that their cesarean was necessary.

Doctors receiving a score of 1 in Table 34.1 do not always use epidurals and do recommend childbirth classes. Doctors who received a score of 2 do not usually recommend classes and always use medication, thereby putting the women at a higher risk for a cesarean. The score of 3 was reserved for one doctor in San José. During the four years with the students I am reporting on, I had only twelve of his patients, but *all* had cesarean-section births. Of course, the assessment underlying the classification of doctors in the three categories is based on their cesarean rates with my students only. Considering that these students are almost entirely nulliparas (giving birth for the first time), these are very high rates since they do not include high repeat cesareans after the initial one.

ATTITUDE ABOUT PAIN IN BIRTH

In one class of the course we talk about personal experiences with pain—physical or emotional. Some women cannot recall even having had a bad headache. Interestingly enough, people who have never experienced pain tend to show more fear of it. Obviously those who have experienced pain have also learned they can live through it. An experience like birthing can be the most character- and self-esteem-building milestone in a woman's life. Yet, if she is unsuccessful in achieving the birth she thinks she is capable of, she may revert more deeply to feelings of passivity, as do the many cesarean-section mothers who subsequently never attempt a vaginal birth.

The Costa Rican women in my classes exhibit a genteel quality; they are unusually polite and rarely outspoken. They almost never criticize their husbands or doctors in public or speak excitedly; an outburst of emotion would be in bad taste. Their controlled self-portrayal creates obstacles for dealing with realities of child bearing. The more natural the birth image, the more contradictory their feelings. One of my videos of a home birth consistently produces feelings of awkwardness in class and questions about why the woman took off *all* her clothes. Having the baby she could not help, they say, but did she have to do it naked? They cannot imagine doing that. The media image of birth has so alienated these women from the birth process that they feel more like aristocratic mannequins than women with bodies capable of having babies.

The lowest risk in the pain category, score 0, is for women who see the path toward birth as a natural one with its own rhythm and speed, where interventions "in case of a problem" are unwarranted. These women may be a bit idealistic about the pain involved but they truly see themselves as capable of handling labor. A score of 1 on this variable represents a more balanced expectation; scores of 2 and 3 represent irrational phobias about not being able to withstand the pain. Women who fall into the 2 and 3 range have no intention of avoiding medication—they don't think they could. They therefore downplay the importance of avoiding complications, experiencing birth in full awareness, or suffering pain because it is safer than surgery. They subtly insinuate (score of 2) or openly state (score of 3) that a cesarean would be better. Sixty percent of those who imply or state this preference end up with a cesarean. The importance of determining which women will use epidurals is that they can become more susceptible to having a cesarean because of such attitudes. Often, the husbands are doting and overly protective of their wives.

SOCIOECONOMIC STATUS

The women in my classes are not representative of Costa Rican women as a whole. Many are members of the upper-middle to upper class, and many were raised in a protected world. Most appear to be passive observers despite the sense that they command great attention. Partly as a result of Catholicism, the national religion, and of the patriarchal system, these women simply accept what God has decided for them—after all, God has done pretty well by them so far. Their own mothers felt it was not their place to interfere with decisions made by the men in their lives, and they did have influence although they enforced it indirectly by manipulation. The goal set for many of these women in their childhood was to be dependent on a "good" husband rather than to weather the hard world out there independently. Many had no experience handling changes or crises—like going away to college, traveling, or living on their own in big cities—and this puts them at a disadvantage. Without having learned that they *can* handle difficult moments and become stronger people, these women maintain traditional ways of dealing with problems, which keeps them from taking the responsibility for becoming active participants.

These students feel obliged to behave as is expected of them according to their social standing in society, and thereby to maintain their socioeconomic status. Only certain stylish maternity clothes, certain imported strollers and car seats, and certain obstetricians are acceptable. Being exposed to society's judgment of their behavior increases their anxiety. Such students fear appearing foolish, and that fear is greater for them than it is for other women who, because of their social class, birth anonymously. The self-inflicted expectations of the passive-observer students play on their doubts about being able to pull off this birth "performance" with any integrity. They usually give in to an epidural anesthesia in order to "play it safe," for image's sake. Cesarean sections are almost proof that they had the means to buy their way out of an unpleasant situation (i.e., labor). The local women who do reach their birth objectives are women who tend to gain their self-worth independently of what others believe.

The scores 0 and 1 are self-explanatory. The score of 2 for this variable contains interesting possibilities other than just being wealthy. A couple could carry a well-known family name without actually having a lot of money. Their parents may be recognized as running a successful business or owning a local company. Simply being Jewish is included in this category because there is a high correlation in San José between being Jewish and working in traditional high-income occupations—business, the sciences, and the professions. A mix of upper-class social relations, specific class standing, personal preferences, and related nonmedical factors may account for this phenomenon. Being a single expectant mother also puts a woman into the high-risk category, because such women often have little motivation to "prove" themselves.

THE WOMAN'S PHYSICAL CONDITION

The low-risk scores of 0 and 1 go to expectant women who eat health-conscious diets and allow themselves to gain only what is appropriate prior to the onset of labor. These women enjoy their pregnancies, continuing to work, exercise, and relax. They handle stress well, and they rarely need to call the doctor. A score of 2 represents women for whom bed rest has been prescribed (20% of my students have been told at some time to rest and not to work or drive. I attribute this high rate to the doctor's perception of the woman as sickly, an impression the women themselves may have conveyed.) They may be overweight to begin with or may have gained over 45 pounds. Teenagers are at a higher risk as well, as are women who had problems getting pregnant. What matters here is the woman's perception of how healthy she is.

A score of 3 represents valid medical reasons that merit cesarean sections. The score is limited to medical conditions recognized prior to the onset of labor, since the table is designed to predict high-risk women during their pregnancies, not to reflect all reasons for all cesarean sections.

The Role of Costa Rican Husbands in the Childbirth Classes

Husbands play an important role in childbirth classes and seem to affect a woman's risk of delivery by cesarean section. Of the women who attended classes alone, 62 percent had cesarean-section births. Having a nonattending mate apparently puts these students at high risk, possibly because they were more vulnerable to doctors wanting to take the "caretaker" or "patronizer" role.

An interesting observation was that Costa Rican husbands at this socioeconomic level do not necessarily fit the image of the nonparticipatory, dominating and stereotypical Latin macho. Yet the husband's participation may have various explanations. On the one hand, it seems that the higher the socioeconomic status is, the less stereotypically macho the man will be. The exposure to other cultures may play a role, or the true sense of sharing with his wife in a team effort. I saw more men taking the initiative in Costa Rica than I did while teaching in the United States. During the first class, some men made nervous wisecracks or displayed a stony indifference, but this phase dissipated as they came to understand the seriousness of their role. Once they learned the extent to which coaching can enhance the birth experience, their sense of responsibility overcame their feelings of inadequacy so that the husband participated often more than his wife. In fact, the more passive observer the wife was, the more involved was the husband. Thus, the strong-man notion may have led the husband to think, "If I do not take the initiative in coaching my wife, who will?" In some cases, the man's participation may even have created fear in his wife about being able to live up to *his* expectations, and the result was that she talked a lot about using anesthesia.

This scenario seems to fortify the woman's dependence on her husband as the provider. The husband fulfills the cultural expectation of caring for his wife, even during labor. This dependence is particularly strong in women who want medicated births because they feel incapable of handling the birth experience. Some show great anxiety over the possibility of being separated from their husbands during labor since they have openly handed over to their husbands the responsibility for relaxation, breathing, and maintaining control. Though the husband enjoys the wife's confidence, he may also be overwhelmed.

In some cases, women seemed to underestimate their husbands and prevented them from participating in birthing because of their own fear of failing. If a woman believes in her strength to survive independently, she knows that having the baby's father present as an equal, and not as her authority, will add respect and beauty to their union. By wanting him to share in the birth, she takes a big step toward believing in herself.

Initially, most men in my classes were skeptical about the importance of their participation. They felt at a disadvantage, their mothers-in-law being their biggest competition. Often, especially with passive observers, the pregnant woman's mother is still dominant in her life, and the woman has yet to identify herself as a soon-to-be mother in her own right. About 30 percent of all the women spent part of their postpartum period in their parents' home, often with a nurse. This arrangement implies that the new mother is incapable of coping alone, a message these women had heard throughout their lives. I generally recommend that the mother not arrive until the laboring woman is about to go into delivery. Her husband is perfectly capable of caring for her, and he needs to believe this as much as she does.

Conclusion

The findings in this analysis raise ethical concerns: any cesarean that can be predicted for reasons other than medical ones is theoretically unethical. As stated earlier, doctors and women can be accomplices in an excessive cesarean rate. Table 34.1 is a predicting tool that lends credibility to the cesareans that are necessary. An analysis of it can, for example, indicate that if a woman with a score of less than 5 has a cesarean delivery, she has had it for sound medical reasons. But there is no margin of error given for this table because the results can never be tested. All the scores can do is evoke caution and suspicion for women at high risk or credibility and confidence for women at low risk.

Consider two scenarios. Scenario A features an outspoken, self-confident foreign woman, who is an excellent student, misses no childbirth classes, practices diligently, swims and walks daily, and anticipates with enthusiasm the experience of giving birth.

She chooses a doctor whom a neighbor recommended. (This doctor would, because of his history, receive a score of 2 in Table 34.1.) Labor starts slowly. She is admitted to the clinic with a one-centimeter dilation. Progress is slow, and medical personnel decide to augment the contractions with medication. Then they break the sac containing the amniotic fluid. This creates a strong labor dynamic, but progress is still slow. The doctor, calling the condition "failure to progress," decides to do a cesarean at 4-centimeter dilation, eight hours after labor started. He claims the "failure to progress" was due to "cephalopelvic disproportion" (CPD). And maybe it was. Another doctor (with a score of zero) would probably not have admitted her so early, would not have augmented the labor, and would not have intervened at that point. A cesarean may have resulted nonetheless, but the credibility of the decision would have been stronger.

In scenario B, a second student, a Costa Rican, thinks only about how painful labor will be, and she fails to take seriously her breathing and relaxation exercises. This student has a combined score of eight. Labor begins and from the beginning she is in pain. Progress is slow. Ill at ease, she tenses up with each contraction. By the time she reaches a dilation of 3 centimeters, she is crying and asking the doctor how long she needs "to suffer before he does something." This labor ends in a cesarean for an angry mother who feels her doctor should have intervened even earlier. Her "failure to progress" was probably due to her uncooperative, fear-ridden state rather than to any physical handicap.

Although these two scenarios are hypothetical, they reflect the experiences of many students in my classes. Of the 375 women in this analysis, 124 had cesarean sections. Breaking these 124 cases down by total scores for all categories in Table 34.1, 75 (60%) of them had scores of 7 or higher; 18 (15%) scored 6 points; and 31 (25%) scored 5 or lower.

Estimating how many cesareans were truly due to medical reasons in each group, I would calculate that only 15 of the 75 women with relatively high-risk scores of 7 and above—that is 20 percent—were medically justified cesareans, compared with 9 (50%) of the 18 women with scores of 6; and 25 (80%) of the 31 women with scores of 5 and lower. Thus, of the 375 couples, 49 women, or 13 percent, had valid cesareans that were influenced only by medical factors.

Jessica Lipnack (1989) says about childbirth that "both parents and professionals in the birthing field are realizing the importance of a positive birth experience. As a result, the balance of power . . . is . . . shifting . . . from the doctor to the parent(s) and child. . . . A woman must decide whether she wants to define her own desires or put herself into the hands of the medical establishment."

Costa Rica follows the birth patterns of the United States. As women feel more independent of traditional authority figures, they expect more for themselves and take care to provide choices for their most important life changes. Childbirth classes bring enablement. Not all couples take a preparation course, but those who do are asking for a sense of empowerment. They begin the process of feeling more like active participants. The cesarean rate among nonstudents at private clinics is bound to be high since they don't have the skills that give them every possible advantage. Taking classes, then, is a first step, and a commitment.

Table 34.1 is a tool based on five years of observations of the factors that differentiate women in my classes. It will undergo years of being tested as a predictor of high-risk situations. As each couple graduates from my courses, I will include their scores and await verification when their baby is born. The new data will help me adjust the table until its efficiency is optimal. I contend that the elaboration of Table 34.1 is accurate in general terms. It will be fine tuned as further experiences warrant.

Postscript

In the eighteen months since completing this study, I have witnessed a consistent private-clinic cesarean-section rate of 48 to 58 percent. This may reflect a rise in the apparent acceptance of or lack of objection to this new norm in birthing procedures. Pregnant women say,

"It is not my place to question my doctor."

"I'm afraid of making a fool of myself."

"I definitely want anesthesia, and if it's got to be a cesarean, so be it."

"I don't consider myself very strong, physically or mentally."

"I'm not accustomed to defending my rights."

Moreover, the ever-present advantage to the doctor—it takes less time, is performed at a conveniently scheduled hour, brings in more money, covers all possibilities of apparent negligence in a legal suit—together with the persistence of family members' ignorant belief that it is safer for the baby to avoid the mother's birth canal, may account for this perturbing tendency.

Childbirth education still has a long way to go before Costa Rican women fully realize their right and privilege to make choices about the way they give birth; to see the harmonious, the beautiful, and the healthful in the natural way to give birth; and to fight the various notions that move women to accept cesareans.

Biodata

Jenny Kozlow-Rodríguez is a certified childbirth educator. Born in Detroit, she has taught in the United States and, since 1986, in Costa Rica, where she resides with her husband and three children. As founder of the organization Previda—a multidisciplinary, adult-education company that specializes in addressing parenting skills beginning with childbirth education—she teaches prenatal courses, but also parenting, first aid for children, sibling preparation, and sex education courses. She also publishes and edits *Padres de Hoy* (Today's Parents)—an annual social-service magazine supported by advertisers—which serves as a free supplement to prenatal courses throughout Costa Rica, as well as a pregnancy calendar that will eventually be available throughout Latin America.

References

Baldwin, Rahima, and Terra Palmarin. 1986. *Pregnant Feelings*. Berkeley, Calif.: Celestial Arts.

International Childbirth Education Association. 1989. *Childbirth Fact Sheet*. Minneapolis, Minn.: ICEA.

Lipnack, Jessica. 1989. "A New Attitude Toward Birth." *New Age Journal* (September–October): 69.

Rosen, Mortimer, and Lillian Thomas. 1989. *The Cesarean Myth*. New York: Viking Penguin/Penguin Books.

Conclusion for an Action-Oriented Research Agenda,

by Ilse Abshagen Leitinger

Women's support group at annual Women's March Against Violence,
November 24, 1995

THE CONCLUSION TO THIS READER highlights the contrasts and contradictions in current Costa Rican society, the continuing diversity of the women's movement and feminism, and the contribution to overall Costa Rican development that this diversity will enable women to make. It also offers suggestions for future research in the field.

The insiders' contributions in this collection allow the reader to explore the distinct character of Costa Rican women's experiences. They confirm that while in some ways these experiences are similar to those of women elsewhere on the continent, in others they differ significantly from what is happening in the women's movement and feminism in Latin American societies in general (Miller, 1992).

Thus the articles present truly a "context of contrasts and contradictions," as I suggested in the introduction to this *Reader*. On the one hand, they illustrate the often perplexing mix of features that are unique to Costa Rica, among them Costa Ricans' historic isolation and poverty as well as their proverbial human warmth and kindness; a strong, at times inconsiderate individualism, frequently hidden behind a front of nonconfrontational behavior; and a traditional commitment to the family rather than to the larger community. On the other hand, they describe the effect upon Costa Rica of worldwide, twentieth-century phenomena of change, such as growing ethnic and cultural diversity, growing socioeconomic inequality increasingly accompanied by violence, and expanding linkages with and dependence upon the outside world.

Throughout this complexity appears—in the society as a whole but particularly among women—a great desire to uncover women's active participation in history and demand compliance with and respect for the legal equality and human rights of women, a growing readiness to identify women's problems and an impressive willingness to debate formerly taboo issues, a felt need to redefine the role of women in society and in politics, and to act upon new insights. Guiding this process is a sophistication that has brought a deeper understanding to all women about the diverse roots—synthesized here as the political, the theoretical-philosophical, the grassroots, and the individual-efficacy roots—of the women's movement and feminism in Costa Rica today.

Diversity in Women's Situation and Actions

As for women's efforts to face and resolve their problems, both the women's movement and feminism are getting stronger, even though they are still far from including or even reaching out to every woman in the country. The authors do not suggest a likelihood of fusion between the two almost parallel tendencies, even though some organizations within the women's movement are moving slowly in the direction of feminism. In Costa Rica as elsewhere, disagreements among organizations and institutions exist, but the parallelism and the multiplicity within both tendencies are an asset not a liability. Women of diverse convictions or ideological persuasions can locate some place in which they will find empathy and an invitation to participate. Overall, though, the authors clearly detect a rise in women's awareness, and, yes, in feminist consciousness.

At the same time, more important than differences between the women's movement and feminism are their similarities because they allow women to come together. United by their common urgent needs, women are looking beyond their philosophical disagreements. Feminists as well as members of the women's movement share an orientation toward action—academics call it *investigación-acción,* or action-oriented research—and a readiness to engage in dialogue. Moreover, in both tendencies women face the necessity that they must learn how to gain power and manage it. They must learn organizational and management skills, whether they hope to accomplish projects among themselves, as do the women in CASEM, the crafts cooperative (see Leitinger, chap. 23 above), or to participate within society as a whole—be it demonstrating for men's democratic rights (see Calvo, chap. 1 above) or working for women's right to vote (see Sharratt, chap. 8 above) or running as a candidate for president (see Jiménez, M., chap. 21 above).

Costa Rican women's orientation toward action and their willingness to take risks has produced a tendency among women professionals to dare to cross disciplinary boundaries and to work interdisciplinarily more easily than elsewhere. If they believe it is necessary, they will attack problems, even in areas in which they are not specialists; in some cases, they may be the only individuals around with some training or with enough concern and energy to address a problem (see Escamilla and Vargas, chap. 10 above).

As they continue their fight for equality, Costa Rican women can build on the relative openness of their society and its people's willingness to engage in dialogue. They can also count on a noticeable rise in institutionalization of processes of analysis, treatment, justice, job training, consciousness raising, and development of self-respect and efficacy.

This specific societal context gives women a chance to make their own unique contribution toward changing the traditionally patriarchal top-down management into a new and more appropriate way of bottom-up decision making. They can also set an example to the men in their society regarding the persistence, discipline, and organization for community action that Costa Rican commentators who are not feminists have found so sadly lacking in Costa Rican society (Cersósimo, 1986; Rodríguez, 1979). Will women be able to change societal patterns in that respect?

Further Questions and Actions

As every Costa Rican woman knows, further analyses are needed to describe and assess women's situation and their contribution to the survival of their society. Costa Rican women must document the historic evidence as completely as possible to make women's social and historical roles more visible. They must build on the many examples of women who, even though they did not know that term, were feminists—like Pancha Carrasco, the nineteenth-century heroine (see Calvo, chap. 1 above) or the women demonstrating for the female vote (see Sharratt, chap. 8 above). They must continue to push for a gendered analysis of the diverse experiences and problem-solving practices of women in the many ethnic groups, nationalities, and different religions in this diverse nation, including an evaluation of the impact of various foreign influences, the type of agencies represented, and any possible contradictions arising from these influences. This is where the search for and use of data of specific relevance to women is essential (see Sibille, chap. 31 above).

In addition, Costa Rican women must explore not only the successes of individual women, women's groups, women's organizations, women in organizations, and women in politics, but they must also seriously analyze the reversals of women's progress in order to learn what caused them and how to avoid them in the next round of the fight for women's true equality.

They must encourage problem solving through management training, flexible institutionalization, and persistence, and they must build on women's great resource, their creative orientation toward other people.

Problems and Successes

In sum, the *Reader* offers a picture of problems and successes. Costa Rican women have come a long way and still have a long way to go. But they are not alone; women all over the world are waging similar struggles. In some ways, Costa Rican women in the early 1990s are far behind women elsewhere in the world, but in other ways they are far ahead of those other women—at times, remarkably farther ahead.

However, although Costa Rican women receive information and inspiration from their international sisterhood, they will arrive at successful solutions only "à la Tica" (in true Tico style), respecting their local traditions and culture even as they set out to transform them.

References

Cersósimo Guzmán, Gaetano. 1986. *Los estereotipos del Costarricense*. San José, Costa Rica: Editorial de la Universidad de Costa Rica.

Miller, Francesca. 1992. "The Literature of Conscientización: Women in Latin America." *Latin American Research Review* 27, no. 2: 180–01.

Rodríguez Vega, Eugenio. 1979. *Apuntes para una sociología costarricense*. San José, Costa Rica: Editorial Universidad Estatal a Distancia.

GLOSSARY

INDEX

Glossary

Academia Costarricense de la Lengua—Costa Rican Academy of the Language. Local organization of the Real Academia Española, which determines what constitutes correct Spanish vocabulary or usage.

Academia de Geografía e Historia de Costa Rica—Costa Rican Academy of Geography and History. Belongs to the National Archives, which are part of the Costa Rican Ministry of Culture.

Afro-Caribeño—Afro-Caribbean. Term Costa Rican social scientists use to identify black population in Costa Rica along the Caribbean coast.

à la Tica—In true Tico style. (The person referred to is a woman; for a man, it would be *à lo Tico*.)

Albergue Belén—Shelter Bethlehem. A women's shelter in San José which existed only (under precarious conditions) from 1984–1985.

algodón—Cotton.

algodonera—Cotton mill. Women's prison (where they must work with cotton).

Alianza—See Asociación Alianza de Mujeres Costarricenses.

Alianza de Cooperativas Internacional—International Alliance of Cooperatives. NGO, to give support to cooperatives.

Alianza de Mujeres Costarricenses (AMC)—See Asociación Alianza de Mujeres Costarricenses.

AMC—See Asociación Alianza de Mujeres Costarricenses.

APROMUJER—See Asociación Programa Nacional de Asesoría y Capacitación para la Mujer.

Archivo Nacional—National Archives. Collection of public records and documents, part of Costa Rican Ministry of Culture.

Asociación Alianza de Mujeres Costarricenses (AMC or Alianza)—Alliance of Costa Rican Women. Oldest organization of the Costa Rican Women's Movement, dating from 1952. NGO, nonprofit; national scope; mission consulting on problem solving, women's self-esteem, legal advice.

Asociación Centro de Orientación Integral—Center for Comprehensive Counseling. A group of San José professionals that opened, in 1984, the Shelter Bethlehem (see Albergue Belén).

Asociación Conservacionista Monteverde (popularly **Liga Conservacionista**)—Monteverde Conservation League (the League). NGO, nonprofit conservation organization in Monteverde.

Asociación de Desarrollo Integral de (comunidad)—Integrated Development Association of (community name). Common name for communal development associations, followed by name of community.

Asociación de Trabajadoras Domésticas—Association of Domestic Workers. Costa Rican NGO, cooperating with Alianza.

Asociación Programa Nacional de Asesoría y Capacitación para la Mujer (APROMUJER)—National Advisory and Training Program for Women Cooperativists. Costa Rican NGO; nonprofit; founded 1987; national scope; mission is to prepare women for participation and leadership in the cooperative movement.

Association for Women in Development (AWID)—International organization, joins academics and professionals interested in women.

Avispa, La—The Wasp. Bar and long-time meeting place of lesbians in San José.

AWID—See Association for Women in Development.

Benemeritazgo de la Patria—Award for Distinguished Citizenship. Highest honor in Costa Rica, bestowed by Costa Rican Legislative Assembly, usually posthumously.

Benemérito(a) de la Patria—Distinguished Citizen (m/f) of the Nation. Recipient of Benemeritazgo.

Biblioteca Nacional—National Library. Part of the Costa Rican Ministry of Culture.

Caja Costarricense de Seguridad Social (CCSS)—Costa Rican Social Security Service. Costa Rican public health service, supported and regulated, but not run, by government; responsible for all hospitals that are not private; offers services to all Costa Ricans.

Cámara de Turismo (Monteverde)—(Monteverde) Chamber of Tourism.

canasta básica—Market basket, that is, subsistence cost for a family of four.

Candidatas, Las—*The Women Candidates*. Play (1942) directed against suffragists' efforts to obtain the vote.

capellanías de misas—Chaplaincies for saying mass in colonial Costa Rica.

capital social—Social capital, obligatory contribution of CASEM cooperative members for expense/investment account of CoopeSE, from which they can withdraw only if they cease to be members.

Capitanía General—Regional colonial government unit during time of Spanish-American empire, part of Spanish colonial viceroyalty.

Casa de Enseñanza de Santo Tomás, La—Santo Tomás High School. First secondary school in Costa Rica.

Casa de la Mujer—*Women's House*. Journal of the Casa de la Mujer, published by the Institute for Women's Studies (IEM), at UNA.

Casa de la Mujer, La—Women's House. Programs and support services for women at Universidad Nacional (UNA).

Casa de la Mujer de los Barrios del Sur, La—Women's House in the Southern Suburbs (of San José).

CASEM—See Comisión de Artesanos Santa Elena-Monteverde.

caserío(s)—Small rural community(ies), hamlet(s).

Cátedra Libre Eugenio Fonseca (UCR)—Eugenio Fonseca Lecture Series. Open lecture series at the Universidad de Costa Rica (UCR), scheduled intermittently, devoted to changing topics.

CCCA—See Conferencia de Cooperativas del Caribe y Centroamérica.

CCSS—See Caja Costarricense de Seguro Social.

CEFEMINA—See Centro Feminista de Información y Acción.

CELADE—See Centro Latinoamericano de Demografía.

CENECOOP—See Centro Nacional de Educación Cooperativa.

Centro Científico Tropical—Tropical Science Center, San José. NGO, nonprofit, contracts out research services, administrates Monteverde Cloud Forest Reserve.

Centro Creativo—See Centro de Educación Creativa.

Centro Cultural Costarricense Norteamericano—U.S. Cultural Center. U.S. Information Center in San José.

Centro de Cooperación Internacional para el Desarrollo Agrícola—Center of International Cooperation for Agricultural Development (CINADCO). GO of the Israeli Ministry of Agriculture.

Centro de Documentación Especializado en el Tema Mujer y Desarrollo—Documentation Center Specializing in Women and Development. Part of Instituto de Estudios de la Mujer (IEM), Universidad Nacional (UNA), together with the information network Red Nacional de Información sobre Mujer y Desarrollo.

Centro de Educación Creativa (popularly **Centro Creativo**)—Creative Learning Center, Cerro Plano, Monteverde Region. Bilingual private school in Cerro Plano, Monteverde region; curriculum based on sustainable development, environmental protection. Awards partial scholarships to low-income families.

Centro de Estudios para la Acción Social (CEPAS)—Research Center for Social Action. Former nongovernmental research organization, investigating development problems, working with Costa Rican community organizations, producing training workshops, publications. Ceased to exist in 1994.

Centro de Investigación de Tecnología en Alimentos (CITA)—Center for Research in Food Technology. Research institution at the Universidad de Costa Rica (UCR).

Centro de Investigación y Docencia en Educación (CIDE)—Center for Research and Teaching in Education. Formerly School of Education at the Universidad Nacional (UNA); that is, part of the national system of higher education.

Centro Feminista de Información y Acción (CEFEMINA)—Feminist Center for Information and Action. Early, explicitly and consciously feminist organization in San José; NGO, nonprofit; founded in 1975 as Movimiento para la Liberación de la Mujer; became CEFEMINA in 1981; national focus, primarily urban; support to women on many issues and daily problems through workshops, publications, conferences, and political action.

Centro de Filantropía—Center for Philanthropy. Program of the Arias Foundation.

Centro Interdisciplinario de Estudios de la Mujer (CIEM)—Center for Interdisciplinary Women's Studies. First Women's Studies Institute at the Universidad Nacional (UNA), 1989–1992; replaced in 1992–1993 by the permanent Instituto de Estudios de la Mujer (IEM).

Centro Latinoamericano de Demografía (CELADE)—Latin American Center of Demography.

Centro Nacional de Educación Cooperativa (CENECOOP)—National Center for Cooperativist Education. Fulfills special functions as support organism for CONACOOP.

Centro Nacional para el Desarrollo de la Mujer y la Familia (CMF; Mujer y Familia for short)—National Center for the Development of Women and the Family. Ministerio de Cultura, Juventud y Deportes (MCJD). GO, part of Costa Rican Ministry of Culture, dates from 1985; national focus; mission is support of women's needs and interests; training workshops, library, lectures, publications, official acts, and celebrations.

Centro para el Progreso Humano—Center for Human Progress. Program of the Arias Foundation for women in Central America (see Fundación Arias).

Centro Regional de Educación Funcional para América Latina (CREFAL)—Regional Center for Functional Education in Latin America. Part of UNESCO, in Mexico.

CEPAS—See Centro de Estudios para la Acción Social.

CIEM—See Centro Interdisciplinario de Estudios de la Mujer.

CIM—See Comisión Interamericana de Mujeres.

CINADCO—See Centro de Cooperación Internacional para el Desarrollo Agrícola.

CIDE—See Centro de Investigación y Docencia en Educación.

CITA—See Centro de Investigación de Tecnología en Alimentos.

CLADEM—See Comité Latinoamericano por la Defensa de los Derechos de la Mujer.

CMF—See Centro Nacional para el Desarrollo de la Mujer y la Familia.

cofradías—Brotherhoods, religious associations.

Colectivo Pancha Carrasco—Pancha Carrasco Collective. San José women's support organization, NGO.

Colegio Agro-Pecuario, Santa Elena—Technical high school with emphasis on agriculture.

Colegio de Abogados—National Lawyers Association. Costa Rican national professional organization, a public institution regulated, but not run, by the government, to which practicing legal professionals must belong.

Colegio de Médicos—Professional organization of medical doctors. Costa Rican national professional organization, a public institution regulated, but not run, by the government to which medical doctors must belong.

Colegio de Nuestra Señora de Sión, El—Girls' High School of Our Lady of Sión.

Colegio Superior de Señoritas, El—Girls' High School and Normal School-Teachers' College.

Comisión (originally Comité) de Artesanos Santa Elena-Monteverde (CASEM)—Artisans' Commission (originally Committee) of Santa Elena-Monteverde. Women's crafts cooperative, one of four parts of the Cooperativa de Servicios Múltiples Santa Elena, R.L.; highly successful commercial operation led by local women artisans.

Comisión de Honores—Honors Commission. Institution of the Costa Rican Legislative Assembly.

Comisión Interamericana de Mujeres (CIM)—Inter American Commission of Women. Part of the Organization of American States (OAS).

Comisión Nacional de Esperanza Solidaria—National Commission of Solidary Hope. Interdenominational organization of the Latin American Council of Churches.

Comité del Niño Agredido—Committee for Battered Children. Part of the Children's Hospital of the public health service.

Comité Latinoamericano por la Defensa de los Derechos de la Mujer (CLADEM) — Latin American Committee for the Defense of Women's Rights. NGO, Latin American women's network connected to the Institute of Human Rights, working to protect women's rights. Produces publications, books, and so on.

Comité Nacional de la Mujer Cooperativista—National Comittee of Women Cooperativists. Established 1987; support organization for CONACOOP.

Comité Nacional por la No Violencia Contra la Mujer—National Committee for the Prevention of Violence Against Women. In cooperation with CEFEMINA, the Comité created Mujer No Estás Sola (Woman, You Are Not Alone), a national NGO; nonprofit; founded 1988; focus on women's self-help groups; mission is to find an alternative for shelters.

Comité Patriótico Nacional (COPAN)—National Patriotic Committee. Successor organization to Organización Socialista de Trabajadores (OST), a leftist party of the 1970s.

Comité por la Igualdad de la Mujer en el Deporte—Committee for Women's Equality in Sports. One of the programs of CEFEMINA.

Comité Regional de la Mujer Cooperativista de Centroamérica y del Caribe—Regional Committee of Central American and Caribbean Women Cooperativists. Support organism of the Conferencia de Cooperativas del Caribe y Centroamérica (CCCA), an international organization.

compañero—Common-law husband, partner.

CONACOOP—See Consejo Nacional de Cooperativas.

Conferencia de Cooperativas del Caribe y Centroamérica (CCCA)—Caribbean and Central-American Conference of Cooperatives.

"¿Con la Coope? ¿O sin ella?"—With the Coop? Or without it? Memo circulated during the discussion about whether or not CASEM should formally join the CoopeSE R.L.

Consejo Latinoamericano de Iglesias—Latin American Council of Churches.

Consejo Nacional de Cooperativas (CONACOOP)—National Council of Cooperatives. Costa Rican public service institution, regulated but not run by the government.

Consejo Nacional de Rehabilitación—National Council for Rehabilitation. Costa Rican public service institution, regulated but not run by the government.

Consejo Superior Universitario Centroamericano (CSUCA)—Council of Central American Universities. Central American institution, created in 1948 by the presidents of the Central American Universities for cooperation in research. The Subprograma de Estudios de la Mujer operated from 1988 to 1992 with the mission of advancing women's studies and of training women professionals.

Cooperativa de Servicios Múltiples Santa Elena R.L. (CoopeSE)—Multiple-Service Cooperative, Santa Elena. Cooperative in Santa Elena-Monteverde region, dating from the 1970s. Four parts, Technical Sales/Supermarket, Savings, Coffee, and CASEM, the women's crafts cooperative.

CoopeSE—See Cooperativa de Servicios Múltiples Santa Elena R.L.

Coordinadora Nacional por Vivienda Digna—National Coordinating Committee for Dignified Housing. Costa Rican umbrella organization for all local housing committees, founded in 1980.

COPAN—See Comité Patriótico Nacional.

CREFAL—See Centro Regional de Educación Funcional para América Latina.

CSUCA—See Consejo Superior Universitario Centroamericano.

CUM—See Primer Congreso Universitario de la Mujer.

Curia Metropolitana—Metropolitan Curia. The archbishop's house/office.

Defensora de los Derechos Humanos de las Internas del Sistema Penitenciario Nacional—Defender of the Human Rights of Women Prisoners in the National Prison System. Former office of the ministry of justice whose task has been taken over by the Defensoría de los Habitantes in their section of the Defender of Women.

Defensoría de la Mujer—Office of the Women's Defender, later Defensoría de los Derechos Humanos de la Mujer, originally in the Ministerio de Justicia y Gracia, now part of the autonomous Defensoría de los Habitantes. GO, an office for the defense of women's rights, focus national, mission urban and rural. First created by decree as a temporary institution by President Arias in 1989.

Defensoría de los Habitantes—Office of the Defender of the Inhabitants. See Defensoría de la Mujer.

Delegación de la Mujer, Ministerio de Gobernación y Policía—Women's Delegation, Ministry of the Interior and Public Safety. Government office to accept women's complaints and accusations about domestic violence.

Deportistas, Las—The Athletes. One of several groups of lesbians in San José, affiliated informally with Las Entendidas.

Día Internacional de la No Violencia Contra la Mujer—International Day for the Prevention of Violence Against Women. Celebrated in Costa Rica since 1988.

Doble (Triple) Jornada, La—The Double (Triple) (Work) Day.

doctrina—Mission.

doctrinero—Missionary.

Ecôle des Hautes Etudes en Sciences Sociales—School of Advanced Studies in the Social Sciences in Paris, France.

Editorial Universitaria Centroamericana (EDUCA)—Central American University Press.

EDUCA—See Editorial Universitaria Centroamericana.

Enclosetadas, Las—The Hidden Ones. One of several groups of lesbians in San José, informally associated with Las Entendidas.

Encuentro Centroamericano Feminista—Meeting of Central American Feminists. Celebrated March 1992 in Nicaragua.

Entendidas, Las—Those in the Know. Informal Costa Rican organization; nonprofit; founded in 1986; focus San José; mission: mutual support among lesbians.

Entendidas, Las—Quarterly bulletin of lesbian group in San José.

Escuela de Ciencias de la Comunicación Colectiva—School of Mass Communications. School within the Universidad de Costa Rica (UCR).

Escuela de Pedagogía—School of Education, UCR. See Escuela Normal de Heredia.

Escuela de Planificación y Promoción Social—School of Planning and Social Development. Part of the Universidad Nacional (UNA).

Escuela de Trabajo Social—School of Social Work. School within the Universidad de Costa Rica (UCR).

Escuela Laboratorio—Laboratory school. Founded by Emma Gamboa.

Escuela Normal de Heredia—Heredia Normal School. Teachers' College, later Departamento, now Escuela de Pedagogía, at the UCR.

escuelas mixtas—Coeducational (primary) schools.

Estilo Monteverde—Monteverde style.

Estrategias de Información—*Information Strategies.* Special methodology for designing information strategies.

Facultad de Ciencias Sociales—School of Social Sciences. Universidad Nacional (UNA).

Facultad de Derecho—Law School, Universidad de Costa Rica.

Facultad de Filosofía y Letras—School of Philosophy and Arts, Universidad Nacional (UNA).

Facultad Latinoamericana de Ciencias Sociales (FLACSO)—Latin American School (faculty in European usage) of Social Sciences. International, intergovernmental, regional, autonomous organization, constituted in 1957; women's program constituted in 1989. Publisher of diverse social-science studies.

filibusteros—Freebooters, filibusters. Fighting with William Walker in Central America.

FLACSO—See Facultad Latinoamericana de Ciencias Sociales.

fonda-hoteles—Inns.

Fondo de las Naciones Unidas para Actividades de Población—United Nations Population Fund.

Frente Popular—Popular Front. Costa Rican leftist party, 1970s.

FUNCRESER—See Fundación Ser y Crecer.

Fundación Acción Ya—Action Now Foundation. Costa Rican NGO, nonprofit; helps low-income women; works with micro-enterprises and people with disabilities largely in San José.

Fundación Arias para la Paz y el Progreso Humano—Arias Foundation for Peace and Human Progress. Founded by Oscar Arias in 1988 with Nobel Peace Prize money; NGO; focus on Central America, urban/rural.

Fundación de Solidaridad (FUNDESO)—Solidarity Foundation. NGO, provides support for women who have had surgery for breast cancer.

Fundación PANIAMOR—Foundation for Bread and Love. Nongovernmental, nonprofit, without any political affiliation. Founded in 1987, funded locally (donations) and internationally (UNICEF, foreign embassies), and through selling its training program services. Its mission is the protection of children's rights.

Fundación para el Desarrollo de la Mujer Cooperativista (FUNDACOOP)—Foundation for the Development of Women Cooperativists. Support organism of Conferencia de Cooperativas del Caribe y Centroamérica.

Fundación Promoción, Capacitación y Acción Alternativa (PROCAL)—Foundation for Advancement, Training, and Alternative Action. Nongovernmental organization, financed by donations, working in support of adolescent mothers.

Fundación Ser y Crecer (FUNCRESER)—Foundation for Life and Growth. Costa Rican NGO, nonprofit; founded in 1990; focus metropolitan area; mission: treatment of victims of incest.

FUNDACOOP—See Fundación para el Desarrollo de la Mujer Cooperativista.

FUNDESO—See Fundación de Solidaridad.

Género y Envejecimiento—Gender and Aging. A social service program.

gynophobia—Cross-cultural male fear and hatred of women.

handicappism—Prejudice against individuals with disabilities, judging them as "handicapped" or "disabled," instead of as normal people who happen to have a disability or a handicap.

heterofeminist—A feminist who is heterosexual.

homophobia—Fear of feelings of love for the same sex (from *homo*, Greek, meaning the same); for example, aversion between lesbian and heterosexual women or gay and heterosexual men.

Hospital de Niños Dr. Carlos Sáenz Herrera—Children's Hospital. One of the Costa Rican Social Security Services hospitals.

ICAP—See Instituto Centroamericano de Administración Pública.

IDA—See Instituto de Desarrollo Agrario.

IEM—See Instituto de Estudios de la Mujer.

IESTRA—See Instituto de Estudios del Trabajo.

igualdad real—True equality.

IICA—See Instituto Interamericano de Cooperación para la Agricultura.

IICE—See Instituto de Investigaciones en Ciencias Económicas.

IIP—See Instituto de Investigaciones Psicológicas.

ILANUD—See Instituto Latinoamericano de Naciones Unidas para la Prevención del Delito y Tratamiento del Delincuente.

ILIFEM—See Instituto Latinoamericano de Investigación Feminista.

ILPES—See Instituto Latinoamericano de Planificación Económica y Social.

imaginería—Colonial statuary, sacred images that serve as instruments of conversion and for maintaining the faith.

INA—See Instituto Nacional de Aprendizaje.

INCIENSA—See Instituto de Ciencias en Nutrición y Salud.

INCOFER—See Instituto Costarricense de Ferrocarriles.

INFOCOOP—See Instituto Nacional de Fomento Cooperativo.

INIM—See Instituto Nicaragüense de Investigación sobre la Mujer.

Instituto Centroamericano de Administración Pública (ICAP)—Central American Institute of Public Administration.

Instituto Costarricense de Ferrocarriles (INCOFER)—Costa Rican Railway Institute.

Instituto de Ciencias en Nutrición y Salud (INCIENSA)—Institute for Nutrition and Health Sciences, Universidad de Costa Rica (UCR).

Instituto de Desarrollo Agrario (IDA)—Agricultural Development Institute. Has existed under different names since 1960, a section with focus on women since 1970.

As an autonomous institution—that is, a public corporation charged with a limited task—it is free from control of the central government but government supported. Focus on rural areas, the farm family.

Instituto de Estudios de la Mujer (IEM)—Institute for Women's Studies. Since 1992–1993, a permanent part of the Universidad Nacional (UNA), within Facultad de Filosofía y Letras (Humanities); see Centro Interdisciplinario de Estudios de la Mujer.

Instituto de Estudios del Trabajo (IESTRA)—Institute of Labor Studies. Part of the Universidad Nacional (UNA).

Instituto de Investigaciones en Ciencias Económicas (IICE)—Institute of Economic Research. Institute at the Universidad de Costa Rica (UCR).

Instituto de Investigaciones Psicológicas (IIP)—Institute of Psychological Research, Universidad de Costa Rica (UCR).

Instituto de Investigaciones Sociales—Institute of Social Research. Institute at the Universidad de Costa Rica (UCR).

Instituto del Niño, Centro de Investigación y Docencia en Educación (CIDE)—Children's Institute, Center for Research and Training in Education. Part of the Universidad Nacional (UNA).

Instituto Indigenista Interamericano—Inter-American Institute of Indigenous People. Peruvian institution.

Instituto Interamericano de Cooperación para la Agricultura (IICA)—Inter-American Institute for Cooperation in Agriculture. International organization, part of the system of the Organization of American States (OAS); founded in 1942, women's program in 1989; focus is rural; mission is to help women agriculturists with production of food crops and with providing equal opportunities for women in income generation and loans.

Instituto Interamericano de Derechos Humanos—Inter-American Institute of Human Rights. Located in San José, affiliated with the Inter-American Court of Human Rights, financed by donations.

Instituto Latinoamericano de Investigación Feminista (ILIFEM)—Latin American Institute for Feminist Research. Nongovernmental, nonprofit research institution, founded in 1992; seat in Costa Rica, focus on gender in Latin America.

Instituto Latinoamericano de Naciones Unidas para la Prevención del Delito y Tratamiento del Delincuente (ILANUD)—United Nations Latin American Institute for the Prevention of Crime and Treatment of Offenders. GO, part of the United Nations.

Instituto Latinoamericano de Planificación Económica y Social (ILPES)—Latin American Institute for Economic and Social Planning. Chilean institution.

Instituto Monteverde—Monteverde Institute. A Costa Rican institution for education in conservation and environmental protection in Monteverde.

Instituto Nacional de Aprendizaje (INA)—National Institute for Occupational Training. A Costa Rican autonomous institution—that is, a public corporation charged with a limited task, free from control of the central government, but government supported.

Instituto Nacional de Fomento Cooperativo (INFOCOOP)—National Institute for the Development of Cooperatives. Organism of the state, to advance, support, and develop financing and control of coops, autonomous institution similar to IDA, INA, and so on.

Instituto Nacional de Vivienda y Urbanización (INVU)—National Housing and Urbanization Institute. A Costa Rican autonomous institution—that is, a public corporation charged with a limited task, free from control of the central government, but government supported.

Instituto Nicaragüense de Investigación sobre la Mujer (INIM)—Nicaraguan Institute of Research on Women. A Nicaraguan institution.

Instituto Tecnológico de Costa Rica—Costa Rican Institute of Technology. One of four universities in the Costa Rican state education system, located in Cartago.

Intelectuales, Las—The Intellectuals. One of several groups of lesbians in San José, informally affiliated with Las Entendidas.

investigación-acción—Action-oriented research.

INVU—See Instituto Nacional de Vivienda y Urbanización.

Junta de Administración Portuaria y de Desarrollo Económico de la Vertiente Atlántica (JAPDEVA)—Board of Port Administration and Economic Development of the Atlantic Coast. A Costa Rican institution.

LA—See Libro(s) de Actas.

Ladinos—Spanish-indigenous mixed population.

lechería—Cheese plant. In Monteverde, owned by Productores de Monteverde.

lesbophobia—Anti-lesbian attitudes and feelings.

Ley de Promoción de la Igualdad Social de la Mujer—Law for the Promotion of Women's Social Equality. Law, originally introduced as Bill for Women's True Equality into the Costa Rican Legislative Assembly in 1988. Passed, somewhat changed, under the above name in 1990.

Liberación Nacional—See Partido Liberación Nacional.

Libro(s) de Actas (LA)—Book(s) of Records. Business records of CASEM, women's crafts cooperative, Santa Elena-Monteverde region.

licenciatura—Academic degree more than B.A. or B.S., less than M.A. or M.S.

Liceo de Niñas—First Girls' High School in Costa Rica.

Liga Feminista—Early feminist organization to help women, particularly in obtaining the vote. Founded by Angela Acuña in 1923.

Liga Conservacionista, La—See Asociación Conservacionista Monteverde.

Liga Internacional de Mujeres Ibéricas e Hispanoamericanas—Iberian and Hispano-American Women's International League.

machismo—Male domination of women.

machista—Male dominant (adj.), or a domineering male (n.).

Maestría Conjunta en Estudios de la Mujer (UCR/UNA)—Joint Master's Program in Women's Studies.

maquila—Relating to assembly industries.

maquiladora **operations**—Assembly line operations or plant.

MCJD—See Ministerio de Cultura, Juventud y Deportes.

MEP—See Ministerio de Educación Pública.

MIDEPLAN—See Ministerio de Planificación Nacional y Política Económica.

Ministerio de Ciencia y Tecnología—Ministry of Science and Technology. Costa Rican government ministry.

Ministerio de Cultura, Juventud y Deportes (MCJD)—Ministry of Culture, Youth and Sports. Costa Rican government ministry.

Ministerio de Educación Pública (MEP)—Ministry of Education. Costa Rican government ministry.

Ministerio de Gobernación y Policía—Ministry of the Interior and Public Safety. Costa Rican government ministry.

Ministerio de Planificación Nacional y Política Económica (MIDEPLAN)—Ministry of National Planning and Economics. Costa Rican government ministry.

MLM—See Movimiento para la Liberación de la Mujer.

Monteverde 2020—See Plan de Desarrollo Integral Monteverde 2020.

Movimiento para la Liberación de la Mujer (MLM)—Women's Liberation Movement. Forerunner of CEFEMINA.

Movimiento Revolucionario del Pueblo—People's Revolutionary Movement. Leftist Costa Rican party of the 1970s.

MUDAR/DAWN—See Red de Mujeres por un Desarrollo Alternativo.

Mujer, Género y Derecho, Universidad de Costa Rica—Women, Gender, and Law, University of Costa Rica. Course at the university.

Mujer—Women. Journal published by CEFEMINA.

Mujeres—Women's trade union, one of CEFEMINA's programs.

Mujer/Fempress—Feminist monthly magazine, published in Santiago, Chile.

Mujer No Estás Sola—Woman, You Are Not Alone. One of CEFEMINA's programs to serve battered women, against domestic violence.

Mujer No Estás Sola—Woman, You Are Not Alone. Pamphlet published for women who suffer from violence.

Mujer y Administración de Justicia—Women and the Administration of Justice. One of CEFEMINA's programs.

Mujer y cultura—Women and Culture. Book by Carmen Naranjo.

Mujer y Familia—See Centro Nacional para el Desarrollo de la Mujer y la Familia.

Museo de Arte Costarricense—Museum of Costa Rican Art. Public institution, part of Ministry of Culture.

Museo Nacional de Costa Rica—National Museum of Costa Rica. Public institution, part of Ministry of Culture.

nos estamos dando el gusto—We do it for fun, we enjoy it, we allow ourselves the pleasure.

OEA—See Organización de Estados Americanos.

Oficina Nacional de la Mujer—National Women's Office. Original office for women's affairs in the Ministry of Culture, Youth and Sports. See Centro Nacional para el Desarrollo de la Mujer y la Familia (CMF).

OIT—See Organización Internacional del Trabajo.

OMS—See Organización Mundial de la Salud.

OPS—See Organización Panamericana de Salud.

Organización Católica de Participación en la Financiación de Programas de Desarrollo—Catholic Organization for Participation in the Financing of Development Programs. Dutch, nongovernmental, internationally connected agency.

Organización de Estados Americanos (OEA)—Organization of American States (OAS).

Organización Internacional del Trabajo (OIT)—International Labor Organization (ILO).

Organización Mundial de la Salud (OMS)—World Health Organization (WHO).

Organización Panamericana de Salud (OPS)—Pan-American Health Organization.

Organización Socialista de los Trabajadores (OST)—Socialist Workers' Organization. Leftist Costa Rican political party in the 1970s.

OST—See Organización Socialista de los Trabajadores.

Pacto Social Interino del Estado de Costa Rica—Interim Pact of the State of Costa Rica (1821).

Padres de Hoy—*Today's Parents*. Social service magazine supplementing prenatal courses, supported by advertisers.

PANI—See Patronato Nacional de la Infancia.

Partido Liberación Nacional (PLN)—National Liberation Party. A political party of social democratic ideology, corresponding somewhat to the Democratic Party in the United States. One of the two most powerful Costa Rican parties at the national level, and the one that most often is in power.

Partido Socialista—Socialist Party. Leftist Costa Rican political party in the 1970s.

patria potestad—Right of parental authority over minor children.

Patronato Nacional de la Infancia (PANI)—National Agency for Child Protection. An autonomous institution—that is, a public corporation charged with a limited task, free from control of the central government, but government supported.

picarona zamba—Despicable, roguish, mischievous black-Indian woman.

PIM—See Programa de Información de la Mujer.

Plan de Desarrollo Integral Monteverde 2020 (popularly, Monteverde 2020)—Plan for Integrated Development of the Monteverde Region by the Year 2020. Community organization founded in 1989 to support sustainable development by coordinating the activities of diverse community organizations in the Santa Elena-Monteverde region.

Plásticas, Las—The Plastic Ones. One of several groups of lesbians in San José, informally associated with Las Entendidas.

PLN—See Partido Liberación Nacional.

prestaciones—Severance pay.

Previda—Multidisciplinary, adult education organization addressing parenting skills.

PRIEG—See Programa Interdisciplinario de Estudios de Género.

Primera Consulta Nacional para Elaborar Propuestas de Políticas Públicas en Relación a la Violencia Contra la Mujer—First National Conference for the Elaboration of Public Policy Proposals on Violence Against Women.

Primer Congreso Universitario de la Mujer (CUM)—First University Congress on Women. Celebrated 1984.

Primer Encuentro Centroamericano y del Caribe Sobre Violencia Contra la Mujer—First Central American and Caribbean Meeting on Violence Against Women. Celebrated 1991.

PROCAL—See Fundación Promoción, Capacitación y Acción Alternativa.

Productores de Monteverde—Monteverde producers. See *lechería*.

Programa de Información de la Mujer (PIM)—Women's Information Program. At IEM/UNA, consists of (1) a library Centro de Documentación Especializado en el Tema de Mujer y Desarrollo, and (2) a databank Red Nacional de Información sobre Mujer y Desarrollo.

Programa Interdisciplinario de Estudios de Género (PRIEG)—Interdisciplinary Gender Studies Program begun informally in 1987 at the Universidad de Costa Rica.

Programa Mujer, Género y Justicia, Instituto Latinoamericano de Naciones Unidas para la Prevención del Delito y Tratamiento del Delincuente (ILANUD)—Women, Gender and Justice Program, United Nations Latin American Institute for the Prevention of Crime and Treatment of Offenders. One of the programs of ILANUD.

Programa Mujer y Derechos Humanos, Instituto Interamericano de Derechos Humanos—Women and Human Rights Program, Inter-American Institute of Human Rights. Does research, provides information for the legislature.

Proyecto de Ley de Igualdad Esencial de la Mujer—Bill for the Basic Equality of Women.

Proyecto de Ley sobre la Igualdad Real de la Mujer—Bill for Women's True Equality. Bill introduced into the Costa Rican legislature in 1988. Passed as Ley de Promoción de la Igualdad Social de la Mujer in 1990.

Proyecto de Ley sobre la Igualdad de Derechos entre Hombres y Mujeres—Bill for the Equality of Rights Among Men and Women.

Proyecto EduMujer—Women's Education Project. Jointly sponsored by the Costa Rican Ministerio de Educación Pública and the Organización Internacional de Trabajo (OIT).

quedar bien—To get along, make a good impression, appear amiable.

Quinto Congreso Internacional Interdisciplinario de la Mujer—Fifth International Interdisciplinary Congress on Women. Celebrated in San José at UCR, spring 1993.

Radio Nacional—National Radio, a radio network.

Red Centroamericana de Información sobre Género y Desarrollo—Central American Gender-in-Development Information Network. Projected for the future.

Red de Mujeres por un Desarrollo Alternativo (MUDAR)—Development Alternatives with Women for a New Era (DAWN). A Peruvian-based women's organization.

Red Latinoamericana de Mujeres—Latin American Women's Network.

Red Nacional de Información sobre Mujer y Desarrollo—National Information Network on Women and Development. Future computer network consisting of three databases on bibliographic, institutional, and statistical information. In 1992, this was part of the Programa de Información de la Mujer (PIM) at UNA Red de Información sobre Género en el Desarrollo.

Registro Nacional de Minusválidos—National Register of the Handicapped. Part of the Centro Nacional de Rehabilitación.

República Federal de Centro América—Federal Republic of Central America. One of the attempts, 1824–1838, to achieve Central-American political unity.

Reserva del Bosque Nuboso Monteverde—Monteverde Cloud Forest Reserve.

Revista de Ciencias Sociales—*Journal of Social Sciences*. Journal of the Instituto de Investigaciones Sociales, UCR.

¡Salado!—Too bad! Tough luck! Comes from "something salty, spicy."

Salud Vivencial—Healthful Living. CEFEMINA program.

Segundo Congreso Universitario de la Mujer (CUM)—Second University Congress on Women. Celebrated in 1988.

Segundo Encuentro de Lesbianas Feministas de América Latina y el Caribe—Second Encounter of Feminist Lesbians of Latin America and the Caribbean. Celebrated in San José in 1990.

sin hacer olas—Without making waves.

Sistema de Información Indigenista de América Latina—Information System on Latin American Indigenous Peoples. See Indigenista Interamericano.

Sociedad Federal de Trabajadores—Federated Worker's Union. First labor union, founded in 1912.

Sorbonne Nouvelle—New Sorbonne. Paris, France.

tercerillas—Thirds. Vouchers or notes, worth one-third of nominal value of teachers' salary, paid under Tinoco's dictatorship, 1917.

Tractoras, Las—The Braves. One of several groups of lesbians in San José, informally associated with Las Entendidas.

Tribunal Supremo de Elecciones (TSE)—Supreme Electoral Tribunal. Costa Rican governmental body to supervise and assure fair elections.

TSE—See Tribunal Supremo de Elecciones.

tugurio(s)—Squatter settlement(s).

tutela—Guardianship. During colonial times, putting women under guardianship deprived them of their decision-making power and allowed men to control them.

UACA—See Universidad Autónoma de Centro América.

UCR—See Universidad de Costa Rica.

UNA—See Universidad Nacional.

UNAM—See Universidad Nacional Autónoma de México.

UNA-Mujer—*Women at UNA*. Quarterly bulletin of IEM/UNA.

UNA-Palabra—Words at UNA. Annual literary competition at the Universidad Nacional (UNA).

UNED—See Universidad Estatal a Distancia.

UNICEF—United Nations Children's Emergency Fund.

UNIFEM—United Nations Development Fund for Women.

Unión de Mujeres Americanas—Union of American Women.

Unión Panamericana—Pan-American Union.

Universidad Autónoma de Centro América (UACA)—Autonomous University of

Central America. One of fifteen or more private universities in Costa Rica, located in San José.

Universidad de Costa Rica (UCR)—University of Costa Rica. One of the four universities of the Costa Rican state system, corresponds to the U.S. "University of (name of state)." Largest university in Costa Rica, located in San José.

Universidad de la Paz—University of Peace. Private university, located near Ciudad Colón, southwest of San José.

Universidad de Santo Tomás—Santo Tomás University. First university in Costa Rica, 1843–88.

Universidade Católica do Minas Gerais—Catholic University of Minas Gerais, Brazil.

Universidade Federal do Rio Grande do Norte—Federal University of Rio Grande do Norte, Brazil.

Universidad Estatal a Distancia (UNED)—State University for Extension Studies. One of the four universities of the Costa Rican state system, located in San José.

Universidad Nacional (UNA)—One of the four universities of the Costa Rican state system. UNA corresponds to the U.S. "State University of (name of state)," located in Heredia.

Universidad Nacional Autónoma de México (UNAM)—Autonomous National University of Mexico.

Universidad Xaveriana—Xaveriana University.

Valle Central—Central Valley. Highland area between Caribbean and Pacific lowlands, containing more than half of Costa Rican population, and most Costa Rican cities.

Ventana—Window. A former informal women's consciousness-raising organization.

Ventana—_Window_. Journal formerly published intermittently by Ventana.

Vice Rectoría de Docencia—Vice Rectory of Academic Affairs.

Vice Rectoría de Investigación—Vice Rectory of Research. Both this and the Vice Rectoría de Docencia are part of the UCR administration.

Walker, William—U.S. adventurer who invaded Costa Rica, 1856–1857.

Walker's Filibusters—Freebooters.

Woman of the Americas—Title bestowed by the Union of American Women.

Index

Academia de Geografía e Historia de Costa Rica, 59
Academia Costarricense de la Lengua, 33
Acosta García, Julio, 8, 9, 73
action-oriented feminism, xi, 3, 24, 27, 279, 335
action-oriented research. *See investigación-acción*
Acuña Braun, Angela, 8–9, 35, 38, 65–66, 70–81, 85–87, 247, 274–75; and Mujer de las Américas, 9, 80–81, 87, 274–75. *See also* Benemeritazgo
Afro-Caribbean, 18, 142–45
Afro-Caribbean women, 138, 141–46; of Limón, 18, 142; as female heads of household, 142–44; prostitution, 144; survival strategies, 144–45
Albergue Belén. *See* Mujer No Estás Sola
algodonera, 46
Alianza. *See* Asociación Alianza de Mujeres Costarricenses
Alianza de Cooperativas Internacional, 193. *See also* women in the cooperative movement
androcentrism, 38, 69, 102, 128, 132–35, 269, 284, 287
androgynism, 15
APROMUJER. *See* Asociación Programa Nacional de Asesoría y Capacitación para la Mujer
Archivo Nacional, 52, 171
Arias, Oscar. *See* Arias Sánchez, Oscar
Arias Sánchez, Oscar, xiii, 11, 66, 106, 114–15, 158, 193, 203
Army, Costa Rican, xiii, 66, 211
Asociación Alianza de Mujeres Costarricenses (AMC or Alianza), v, 3–4, 24–28
Asociación Centro de Orientación Integral, 162
Asociación Conservacionista de Monteverde (La Liga). *See* Comisión de Artesanos Santa Elena-Monteverde

Asociación de Trabajadoras Domésticas, 27
Asociación Programa Nacional de Asesoría y Capacitación para la Mujer (APRO-MUJER), 182, 193–97. *See also* women in the cooperative movement
Avispa, La, 148–51

bananas. *See* exports
Benemeritazgo de la Patria, vi, 37–38, 84–88; and Acuña Braun, Angela, 35, 86–87; and Gamboa Alvarado, Emma, 79, 85–86; and Solórzano Alfaro, María Emilia, 85
Benemérito de la Patria, vi, 84–88
Biblioteca Nacional de Costa Rica, 59
Bill for Women's True Equality. *See* Proyecto de Ley sobre la Igualdad Real de la Mujer
Blanco, Grace, 255–57

Caja Costarricense de Seguro Social (CCSS), 316
Calderón Fournier, Rafael Angel, 11, 193
Calderón Guardia, Rafael Angel, 77–78
Cámara de Turismo. *See* Comisión de Artesanos Santa Elena-Monteverde
Canadian Development Agency. *See* Comisión de Artesanos Santa Elena-Monteverde
Canadian International Development Research Center, Ottawa, 299
canasta básica, 141
capellanías de misas, 42–43
Capitanía General (de Guatemala), 40, 46
Carillo, Braulio, 56
Carrasco, Francisca (Pancha), 2, 6–7, 87, 336
Carvajal, María Isabel (Carmen Lyra), 72–77, 87. *See also* suffragism
Casa de Enseñanza de Santo Tomás, La (1814), 56, 66
Casa de la Mujer. *See* Universidad Nacional
Casa de la Mujer (magazine). *See* Universidad Nacional
Casa de la Mujer de los Barrios del Sur, 109

357

Castro Madríz, José María, 56

Cátedra Libre Eugenio Fonseca. *See* Universidad de Costa Rica

Catholic Church. *See* women and religion

CEFEMINA. *See* Centro Feminista de Información y Acción

Central American Information Network on Women in Health. *See* Consejo Superior Universitario Centroamericano

Central Valley. *See* Valle Central

Centro Científico Tropical. *See* Comisión de Artesanos Santa Elena-Monteverde

Centro de Cooperación Internacional en Desarrollo Agrícola (CINADCO) (Israel), 196

Centro de Educación Creativa. *See* Comisión de Artesanos Santa Elena-Monteverde

Centro de Estudios para la Acción Social (CEPAS), 17

Centro de Filantropía. *See* Fundación Arias

Centro de Investigación de Tecnología en Alimentos. *See* Universidad de Costa Rica

Centro Feminista de Información y Acción (CEFEMINA), v, 3, 19–23, 118, 139, 160–69; and Comité Nacional por la No Violencia Contra la Mujer, 22, 109, 165–66; and Comité por la Igualdad de la Mujer en el Deporte, 22; and *Mujer*, 21, 23, 160; and Mujer, No Estás Sola (program), 22, 125, 139, 160–69; and Mujeres (trade union), 22; and Mujer y Administración de Justicia program, 22; and Salud Vivencial program, 21; small loan fund of, 21. *See also* housing movement

Centro Interdisciplinario de Estudios de la Mujer (CIEM). *See* Instituto de Estudios de la Mujer

Centro Latinoamericano de Demografía (CELADE). *See* Consejo Superior Universitario Centroamericano

Centro Nacional de Educación Cooperativa (CENECOOP), 195, 226. *See also* women in the cooperative movement

Centro Nacional para el Desarrollo de la Mujer y la Familia (CMF), 4, 106, 125, 166; as Oficina Nacional de la Mujer, 33

Centro para el Progreso Humano. *See* Fundación Arias

Centro Regional de Educación Funcional para América Latina (CREFAL), 302

cesarean-section births: doctor's attitude toward, 319, 323–25; incidence of, 281; and

Padres de Hoy, 331; predictability of, viii, 281, 316–32; and Previda, 331; and role of husband, 327–29; and socioeconomic status, 319, 326–27; and woman's attitude about pain, 319, 325–26; and woman's personality, 319, 321–23; and woman's physical condition, 319, 327

CIEM. *See* Centro Interdisciplinario de Estudios de la Mujer

CIM. *See* Comisión Interamericana de Mujeres

Clarence Thomas-Anita Hill hearings, 101, 107

Clayton-Bulwer Treaty (1850), 54

CMF. *See* Centro Nacional para el Desarrollo de la Mujer y la Familia

coffee. *See* exports

cofradías, 42–50

Colegio de Abogados, 120

Colegio de Médicos, 179

Colegio de Nuestra Señora de Sión, 57, 68, 85. *See also* Solórzano Alfaro, María Emilia; schools for girls

Colegio Superior de Señoritas, 57, 67, 75. *See also* schools for girls

Comisión de Artesanos Santa Elena-Monteverde (CASEM), vii, 183, 210–33, 335; and Asociación Conservacionista de Monteverde, 213, 227; and Cámara de Turismo, 213, 227; and Canadian Development Agency, 213, 215; and *caseríos*, 214; and Centro Científico Tropical, 213; CENECOOP, 226; as community force, 226–30; conservation movement and, 212, 220; and Cooperativa Múltiple Santa Elena, 210–19; five-year plan of, 227–30; growth of, 214, 215; and Instituto Monteverde, 213; and IAF, 213, 214; organizational structure of, 217–19; and Plan de Desarrollo Integral Monteverde 2020, 213, 227; and Productores de Monteverde (lechería), 211–12; and Quakers, 211; quality control of, 219–22; and Reserva del Bosque Nuboso Monteverde, 212–13, 227; and tourism, 212; trouble shooting of, 222–24; and women's empowerment, 210, 217, 224–26; and World Wildlife Fund, 213

Comisión de Honores, 84–88

Comisión Interamericana de Mujeres (CIM), 9, 87

Comisión Nacional de Esperanza Solidaria, Consejo Latinoamericano de Iglesias, 50

Comité del Niño Agredido, Hospital de Niños. *See* Mujer No Estás Sola

Comité Latinoamericano para la Defensa de los Derechos de la Mujer (CLADEM), 104. *See also* women's legal status; women and violence

Comité Nacional de la Mujer Cooperativista, 193, 302. *See also* women in the cooperative movement; Programa de Información de la Mujer

Comité Nacional por la No Violencia Contra la Mujer. *See* Centro Feminista de Información y Accion

Comité Patriótico Nacional. *See* housing movement

Comité por la Igualdad de la Mujer en el Deporte. *See* Centro Feminista de Información y Accion

Comité Regional de la Mujer Cooperativista de Centroamérica y del Caribe, 183, 196. *See also* women in the cooperative movement

Consejo Latinoamericano de Iglesias, 50

Consejo Nacional de Cooperativas (CONA-COOP), 194. *See also* women in the cooperative movement

Consejo Nacional de Rehabilitación, 155

Consejo Superior Universitario Centroamericano (CSUCA), viii, 18, 33, 179, 279–80, 290–91; 293–97, 309; and CELADE, 295; and Central American Information Network on Women in Health, 295; and FLACSO, 296; and ILIFEM, 296 mission of, 293–97; and Red Centroamericana de Información sobre Género y Desarrollo, 295–96; and Universidad de la Paz, 296

Constitutions, Costa Rican, 62–66, 80, 120, 130–35

Convention on the Elimination of All Forms of Discrimination Against Women. *See* United Nations Convention on the Elimination of all Forms of Discrimination Against Women

Cooperativa Múltiple Santa Elena, R.L. *See* Comisión de Artesanos Santa Elena-Monteverde

cooperative movement. *See* women in the cooperative movement

Coordinadora Nacional por Vivienda Digna. *See* housing movement

Cortés Castro, León, 10, 77–78

Costa Rican feminism, roots of, v, 2, 5–12

Cruz, Ramona, 80

CSUCA. *See* Consejo Superior Universitario Centroamericano

Curia Metropolitana, 36, 39–50

Day care, 116, 123–24

Defensoría de la Mujer, Ministerio de Justicia, 18, 106, 107, 115, 122–23. *See also* Defensoría de los Derechos Humanos de la Mujer; Defensoría de los Habitantes

Defensoría de los Derechos Humanos de las Internas del Sistema Penitenciario Nacional, 109

Defensoría de los Derechos Humanos de la Mujer, 100, 109, 115, 167

Defensoría de los Habitantes, 18, 100, 106, 167, 302

Delegación de la Mujer, Ministerio de Gobernación y Policía, 106, 167

Día Internacional de la No Violencia Contra la Mujer, 166

disability, vii, 139, 153–59; and asexuality, 155; compounded by gender, 156; women with, 153. *See also* discrimination

discrimination, 137–79; and disability, 138, 139, 153–59; domestic violence, 138, 139–40, 160–69, 170–79; in organizations, 182; for race/gender, 120, 138, 141–45; for sexual preference, 138, 147–52; through sexual segregation, 271; UN definition of, 122

Distinguished Citizen of the Nation. *See* Benemérito de la Patria; Benemeritazgo

divorce. *See* women and family life

doble/triple jornada, la, 32, 96, 236. 260

doctrina, 48

doctrinero, 41–50

double day, double (triple) workday, 15, 32, 124, 193. *See also doble/triple jornada*

Ecôle des Hautes Etudes en Sciences Sociales, Paris, 309

Editorial Universitaria Centroamericana (EDUCA), 33

empowerment. *See* women and empowerment

Encuentro Centroamericano Feminista (1992), 139, 151

Entendidas, Las, vi, 138–39, 147–52

equality. *See* Igualdad; political equality

Escalante, Manuela, 2, 5–7

heterofeminists, 147–52
heterosexuality, 134, 147–52
Hine, Ana Griselda, 254–55
homophobia, 147–51. *See also* gynophobia, lesbophobia
housing movement, vii, 21, 183, 198–209
Howell, Patricia, 260
Humanities Division. *See* Facultad de Filosofía y Letras

IEM. *See* Instituto de Estudios de la Mujer
Igualdad, 99–136. *See also* Ley de Promoción de la Igualdad Social de la Mujer
ILANUD. *See* Instituto Latinoamericano de las Naciones Unidas para la Prevención del Delito y Tratamiento del Delincuente
Immediate Action Plan for Equality. *See* Ley de Promoción de la Igualdad Social de la Mujer
incest. *See* women and violence
INCOFER. *See* Instituto Costarricense de Ferrocarriles.
individual-efficacy. *See* Latin American women's movements, roots of
Instituto Centroamericano de Administración Pública (ICAP), 303
Instituto Costarricense de Ferrocarriles (INCOFER), 188. *See also* Peace Corps
Instituto de Desarrollo Agrario (IDA), 106. *See also* women and work
Instituto de Estudios de la Mujer (IEM). *See* Universidad Nacional
Instituto de Investigaciones en Ciencias Económicas (IICE). *See* Universidad de Costa Rica
Instituto de Investigaciones Psicológicas (IIP). *See* Universidad de Costa Rica
Instituto de Investigaciones Sociales. *See* Universidad de Costa Rica
Instituto del Niño del Centro de Investigación y Docencia en Educación (CIDE). *See* Universidad Nacional
Instituto Indigenista Interamericano (Peru), 302; and Sistema de Información Indigenista de América Latina, 302
Instituto Interamericano de Cooperación para la Agricultura (IICA), 18, 275
Instituto Interamericano de Derechos Humanos, 17, 243, 309; and Programa Mujer y Derechos Humanos, 243
Instituto Latinoamericano de Investigación Feminista (ILIFEM), 231, 280, 296

Instituto Latinoamericano de Naciones Unidas para la Prevención del Delito y Tratamiento del Delincuente (ILANUD), 17, 179, 243
Instituto Latinoamericano de Planificación Económica y Social (ILPES) (Chile), 196
Instituto Monteverde. *See* Comisión de Artesanos Santa Elena-Monteverde
Instituto Nacional de Aprendizaje (INA), 106, 156. *See also* women and work
Instituto Nacional de Fomento Cooperativo (INFOCOOP), 196. *See also* women in the cooperative movement
Instituto Nacional de Vivienda y Urbanización (INVU), 201, 205. *See also* housing movement
Instituto Nicaragüense de Investigación sobre la Mujer (INIM), 301
Instituto Tecnológico, 304
Inter-American Foundation. *See* Comisión de Artesanos Santa Elena-Monteverde
Interdisciplinary Research in Women's Studies, viii, 281, 310–15; and differences between disciplines, 311; and holistic knowledge, 313–15; and overlap of disciplines, 312; and technical terms and concepts, 312–13
International Women's Day, 15, 114
investigación-acción, xii, xviii, 334–35. *See also* action-oriented feminism

JAPDEVA. *See* Junta de Administración Portuaria y de Desarrollo Económico de la Vertiente Atlántica
Jaquette, Jane, xv.
Jiménez Zamora, Jesús, 56
Joint Master's Program in Women's Studies. *See* Maestría Conjunta en Estudios de la Mujer
Junta de Administración Portuaria y de Desarrollo Económico de la Vertiente Atlántica (JAPDEVA), 188–89. *See also* Peace Corps volunteers

labor code. *See* legal system
Ladinos, 41
Latin American women's movements:
grassroots of, xv–xviii, 2, 3, 20–23, 24–28, 71, 183, 202, 334; individual-efficacy roots of, xv–xvii, 2, 5–12, 36–38, 137–79, 182, 334; political roots of, xv–xvi, 2, 37, 334;

Nature Conservancy. *See* Comisión de Artesanos Santa Elena-Monteverde

obstacles to women's rights. *See* legal equality
Odio, Elisabeth, 193
Office of the Defender of the Inhabitants. *See* Defensoría de los Habitantes
Office of the Ombudsman. *See* Defensoría de los Habitantes
Office of the Women's Defender or of the Defender of Women's Human Rights (1989). *See* Defensoría de la Mujer
Oficina Nacional de la Mujer. *See* Centro Nacional para el Desarrollo de la Mujer y la Familia
oligarchy, male, 63–64. *See also* machismo
Organización Católica de Participación en la Financiación de Programas de Desarrollo, 26
Organización de Estados Americanos (OEA), 9, 18, 35, 81, 87, 247, 274
Organización Internacional de Trabajo (OIT), 51
Organización Mundial de la Salud (OMS), 155, 316
Organización Panamericana de Salud (OPS), 295, 300, 301
Organización Socialista de los Trabajadores (OST), 201, 202. *See also* housing movement
Organization of American States (OAS). *See* Organización de Estados Americanos

Pacto Social Interino del Estado de Costa Rica (1821), 53
Padres de Hoy (annual), 331. *See also* cesarean-section births
PANI. *See* Patronato Nacional de la Infancia
Partido Liberación Nacional (PLN), 203
Partido Socialista, 201. *See also* housing movement
patria potestad. See legal system
patriarchy, 2, 24, 29–33, 36–38, 39, 47, 61–81, 103–35, 138, 147, 151–52, 170–72, 176–77, 236, 241, 243, 266, 326; triple, 36, 49; and women's subordination, 29–33, 314
Patronato Nacional de la Infancia (PANI), 104–08, 166
Peace Corps volunteers, 182, 185–90
Penal Code. *See* legal system
Penón Góngora de Arias, Doña Margarita, 114, 125, 193, 335

Picado, Teodoro, 77–79
Pignani-Boncinelli, Paola, 251–53
PIM. *See* Programa de Información de la Mujer
Plan de Desarrollo Integral Monteverde 2020. *See* Comisión de Artesanos Santa Elena-Monteverde
political equality: and citizenship, 129–30; and *human being*, 127–28; of men and women, 130–31; redefinition of, 127–35
political roots. *See* Latin American women's movements
poverty, feminization of, xiv, 25, 155
Previda. *See* cesarean-section births
Primera Consulta Nacional Para Elaborar Propuestas de Políticas Públicas en Relación a la Violencia Contra la Mujer (1991), 168. *See also* Mujer No Estás Sola
Primer Congreso Universitario de la Mujer (CUM), 161
Primer Encuentro Centroamericano y del Caribe Sobre Violencia Contra la Mujer, 22, 168
productores de Monteverde. *See* Comisión de Artesanos Santa Elena-Monteverde
Programa de Información de la Mujer (PIM), viii, 280, 290, 298–303
Programa Interdisciplinario de Estudios de Género (PRIEG). *See* Universidad de Costa Rica
Programa Mujer, Género y Justicia. *See* Instituto Latinoamericano de Naciones Unidas para la Prevención del Delito y Tratamiento del Delincuente
Programa Mujer y Derechos Humanos. *See* Instituto Interamericano de Derechos Humanos
Proyecto de Ley de Igualdad Esencial de la Mujer. *See* Ley de Promoción de la Igualdad Social de la Mujer
Proyecto de Ley sobre la Igualdad de Derechos entre Hombres y Mujeres. *See* Ley de Promoción de la Igualdad Social de la Mujer
Proyecto de Ley sobre la Igualdad Real de la Mujer. *See* Ley de Promoción de la Igualdad Social de la Mujer
Proyecto EduMujer, 50

Quakers, 211–33
Quinto Congreso Internacional Interdisciplinario de Estudios de la Mujer, xv, 279, 291–92

women in the cooperative movement (*cont.*) 210–33. *See also* Comisión de Artesanos Santa Elena-Monteverde

Women's Delegation, Ministry of the Interior. *See* Delegación de la Mujer, Ministerio de Gobernación y Policía

women's legal status, vi, 54–55, 99–136

women's liberation, 31

women's liberation movement. *See* Centro Feminista de Información y Accion; Movimiento para la Liberación de la Mujer

Women's Studies, Joint master's program, Maestría Conjunta en Estudios de la Mujer.

See Universidad de Costa Rica; Universidad Nacional

women with disabilities, vii, 139, 153–59; in education, 156; and freedom of movement, 158; health care experiences of, 157–58; poverty of, 158; social acceptance of, 158; in workforce, 156

working-class women, vii, 182, 185–91

world literature, feminist reinterpretation of, viii, 247, 269–75. *See also* feminism in the arts

World Wildlife Fund. *See* Comisión de Artesanos Santa Elena-Monteverde